Accountability across Borders

Accountability across Borders

Migrant Rights in North America

EDITED BY XÓCHITL BADA AND SHANNON GLEESON

University of Texas Press   *Austin*

Requests for permission to reproduce material from this work should be sent to:
 Permissions
 University of Texas Press
 P.O. Box 7819
 Austin, TX 78713-7819
 utpress.utexas.edu/rp-form
♾ The paper used in this book meets the minimum requirements of ANSI/NISO
Z39.48-1992 (R1997) (Permanence of Paper).

Library of Congress Cataloging-in-Publication Data
Names: Bada, Xóchitl, editor. | Gleeson, Shannon, 1980– editor.
Title: Accountability across borders : migrant rights in North America /
edited by Xóchitl Bada and Shannon Gleeson.
Description: First edition. | Austin : University of Texas Press, 2019. |
Includes bibliographical references and index.
Identifiers: LCCN 2018044845 | ISBN 978-1-4773-1835-5 (cloth : alk. paper) |
ISBN 978-1-4773-1836-2 (pbk. : alk. paper) | ISBN 978-1-4773-1837-9
(library e-book) | ISBN 978-1-4773-1838-6 (nonlibrary e-book)
Subjects: LCSH: Foreign workers—Government policy—North America. |
Foreign workers—Civil rights—North America. | Aliens—Civil rights—
North America. | Aliens—Government policy—North America. | North
America—Emigration and immigration.
Classification: LCC HD8045 .A33 2019 | DDC 331.6/2097—dc23
LC record available at https://lccn.loc.gov/2018044845

doi:10.7560/318355

Contents

Acknowledgments

This edited volume is the result of many colleagues who provided support and feedback throughout the process.

Our ongoing work on transnational advocacy has benefited from support and feedback over the years from our colleagues at the University of Illinois–Chicago (UIC), the University of California–Santa Cruz (UCSC), and Cornell University. Grant funding from UIC's College of Liberal Arts and Sciences (LAS), the UIC Institute for Research on Race and Public Policy, UIC's Chancellor´s Undergraduate Research Award and LAS Undergraduate Research Initiative, the UCSC Committee on Research, UC MEXUS-CONACTY, and the Cornell Institute for the Social Sciences made this research possible.

In December 2016, with generous support from the Cornell University ILR School Pierce Memorial Fund, we hosted a workshop on the Cornell campus with the authors in this volume. The chapters benefited enormously from the feedback of discussants and participants, including Lance Compa, Maria Lorena Cook, Angela Cornell, Mary Jo Dudley, Maria Figueroa, Sergio Garcia-Rios, Kate Griffith, Pilar Parra, Mario Rios Perez, Ken Roberts, Patricia Rodriguez, Alexis Silver, and Sofia Villenas. Simultaneous interpretation assistance was provided by María de Lourdes Ramírez-Flores and Amui Chong, and Odalis Flores and Albaro Tutasig also provided logistical support.

Late in May 2017, we were fortunate to receive funding from a National Science Foundation–backed grant to the Law and Society Association International Research Collaboratives. This supported a roundtable of academicians and advocates at the LSA meetings in Mexico City who informed the framing of this volume. Participants included Emily Norman and Jillian Wagman (Instituto para las Mujeres en la Migración), María Dolores París Pombo (Colegio de la Frontera Norte), Jaime Rivas Castillo (Universidad Don Bosco), Fabienne Venet (Instituto de Estudios y Divulgación sobre Migración), Alejandra Ancheita (Proyecto de Derechos Económicos, Sociales y Culturales), and Rachel Micah Jones and Adelina Vasquez Cedillo (Centro de los Dechos del Migrante).

We would like especially tto thank Maria Lorena Cook and Andreas Feldmann for substantial feedback on the framing of our introductory chapter. Cathleen Caron, Lance Compa, Margit Fauser, Kate Griffith, Rachel Micah-Jones, and Kevin Middlebrook also provided valuable suggestions to chapter 3. Support from a Cornell University Mario Einaudi Center for International Studies funded additional data collection and analysis for chapter 3.

Cornell ILR Worker Institute Undergraduate Research Fellows Hannah Cho, Clady Corona, Amy Saz, Albaro Tutasig, Zakiya and Williams Wells, along with UIC students Michaela Byrd, Jackie Estrada, Nick Ghezavat, Vanessa Guridy, Debbie Patiño, and Ashwini Reddy, have all helped with critical data analysis over the years. Manlio Correa, Ruben Espinoza, Patricia Nicolás Flores, Claudia Lopez, Gloria Marvic, David Rocha Romero, Tania Cruz Salazar, Heidy Sarabia, and Guillermo Yrizar-Barbosa also provided invaluable research support throughout various phases of the project.

Claire Concepción at Cornell and Bruce Tyler at UIC provided much of the hidden labor that takes place behind the scenes of faculty research, and we are indebted to them for their ongoing support.

Special thanks to the University of Texas Press, including Kerry Webb and the art department staff for their commitment to the project. Editing support from Matt Seidel was superb, and Lisa Rivero provided excellent indexing services. We also recognize the accurate translation provided by Matt Ginsberg-Jaeckle for chapters 4 and 5. We are grateful also to photographer José Hernández-Claire for generously giving us permission to use work from his *Migration Series* (*Serie migración*) for the book cover, on very short notice no less.

Finally, we thank our authors and colleagues in this volume, for their patience and commitment to the project, and for their solidarity with the communities whose story they tell here. Their work is more important now than ever.

Accountability across Borders

Introduction: Enforcing Rights across Borders

SHANNON GLEESON AND XÓCHITL BADA

Both origin and destination countries have become increasingly proactive in responding to the needs of growing immigrant diasporas. This phenomenon has emerged not out of state benevolence but rather, we contend, in response to pressure from migrant advocates on both sides of the border. Migrant civil society has demanded accountability for the well-being of migrant populations who collectively remit on the order of $582 billion of their earnings to their home countries, according to World Bank projections (Migration Policy Institute 2018). These organizations and the migrants they represent have lobbied for rights and services in arenas such as employment, health, and education, pushing rights bureaucracies in origin and destination countries to be accountable to the needs of these new (and old) populations. In this volume we adopt a transnational lens to examine the dual roles of migrant civil society and state migration governance in realizing these rights. We employ the term "transnational" in line with existing analyses, referring not only to those cross-border activities by migrant individuals but also to the organized spaces that represent their interests and the governments purporting to act on their behalf (Basch, Glick Schiller, and Szanton Blanc 1994; Faist, Fauser, and Reisenauer 2013; Pries 2008). We conceive of "rights" in the formal sense (as provided by national and supranational legislation and tied to judicial and administrative bureaucracies that enforce them) as well as in the normative sense (so as to include the aspirational rights that migrants are currently demanding without an existing legal basis to their claims) (Benhabib 2004; Bosniak 2006; Fraser 2009; Somers 2008).

With a geographical focus on North America, we examine three main actors involved in enforcing rights across borders. To begin, we discuss the importance of migrant civil society in creating and maintaining transnational advocacy networks, as scholars have amply highlighted (Armbruster-Sandoval 2003; Bada 2014; Keck and Sikkink 1998). Many studies have already demonstrated the importance of an organizational lens in understanding the civic and political lives of migrant communities (e.g., Bada 2014; de Graauw 2016; Ramakrishnan and Bloemraad 2008). We argue that civic spaces are important for advocating for migrant rights in destination countries but also for holding the governments of origin countries accountable to their conationals living abroad. We examine the role of Mexico as the major sending country to Canada and the United States, but also consider the less discussed role that Mexico has played as a destination for Central American migrants who transit through and often settle in the country. We also consider Mexico's role as a reluctant destination country for returnees and their children in an era of increased US immigration enforcement during the Obama administration. This trend further intensified under the Trump administration.

Multisited and Multiscalar Approaches to Evaluating Transnational Advocacy

Pedroza, Palop, and Hoffmann (2016) have provided one of the most comprehensive systematic reviews of emigrant policies, focusing on twenty-two Latin American and Caribbean countries. They conclude that what is distinctive about the recent forms of transnational and translocal activity is that origin states today "get deeply involved in setting the framework for these engagements," and as a result, emigration no longer entails an "abrupt disconnection" with the state of origin (7). Distinguishing the external administrative apparatus, including the consular network, from the home administration, Pedroza, Palop, and Hoffmann (2016) operationalize twelve sociocultural, political, and economic policy dimensions in which origin states engage their emigrant populations. In this volume we do not attempt to evaluate as broad a range of policies or geographies but instead target the way Mexico, Canada, and the United States engage their migrant populations in the North American region.

In this inquiry we consider the roles of origin and destination states and how they engage with nonstate actors. In her comparison of five origin countries in Latin America (Ecuador, Uruguay, Mexico, Argentina, and Brazil), Margheritis (2015:189) likens efforts to reach out to emigrant populations to "courting practices" that over time have delineated "a new constituency and a new area of state interventionism across borders." Such developing relationships can sometimes evolve into cooperative initiatives carried out by state and nonstate actors that can be productive as well as problematic. The case studies presented in this volume confirm the benefits and pitfalls of diaspora policies, emphasizing the important role that migrant civil society has played in prompting and facilitating the Mexican state's engagement. Building especially on work by Alexandra Délano (2011), the studies home in on Mexico's outreach to migrant populations in the United States, where 98 percent of its migrants end up, and Canada, which relies on Mexican migrants for more than half of its seasonal agricultural labor. They also acknowledge the hemispheric mobilities of Central Americans moving north and the role of the Mexican government in surveilling its southern border.

Other volumes have focused on cases outside the North American context (Fitzgerald and Cook-Martín 2014; Freeman 1995), relied on large-N data (Givens and Luedtke 2005; Wright and Bloemraad 2012), surveyed public attitudes toward immigration (Mayda 2006), and evaluated individual migrant outcomes (McKay, Markova, and Paraskevopoulou 2012). In contrast, we rely on institutional analyses of North and Central America based on qualitative case studies. We seek a thick understanding of the genesis of bilateral and regional cooperation around migrant rights, of the actors who drive the implementation of the agreements, and of the mechanisms that make it all happen. We examine public documents, interviews with government officials and civic actors, and federal, state, and local institutions at work.

We focus on migration governance activity in three main arenas: education, labor, and health, highlighting civil society's contributions in Mexico, Canada, and the United States. We have gathered an array of interdisciplinary approaches from migrant rights practitioners and scholars across the region. The work of international relations and legal scholars José María Serna de la Garza and Adriana Sletza Ortega Ramírez lays the groundwork for understanding the mechanisms of global governance, bilateral cooperation, and the different roles played by federal and subnational state governments. The ethnographic work of anthropologists Patricia Baquedano-López and Castañeda et al. in their extended observations help us grasp how institutions function on the ground level. Institutional analyses by sociologists Luin Goldring, Patricia Landolt, and Gaspar Rivera-Salgado and political scientists Alexandra Délano Alonso, Jonathan Fox, and Mónica Jacobo-Suárez provide a nuanced examination of state and civic/political participation through documentary analyses and in-depth interviews with organizational leaders and individual migrants.

The case studies in this volume highlight the roles of origin-state actors such as the Institute for Mexicans Abroad and subnational migrant affairs offices and destination-state actors such as the US Department of Labor, county hospitals and clinics, and public schools, as well as voices of migrant advocates themselves, including formalized hometown associations and ad hoc worker rights alliances. We consider various forms of individual and collective migrants' rights mobilizations; among them are elite actors pursuing formal litigation in state and national arenas, such as the Mexican Forensic Commission and Migrant Unit of the Mexican Ministry of Justice; regional and international cases, such as public petitions filed against the North American Agreement on Labor Cooperation; major campaigns launched on behalf of migrant-led organizations or other groups whose membership is comprised largely of migrants, such as the United Food and Commercial Workers labor union representing seasonal farmworkers; and individual migrants themselves, such as deported parents who, after returning to Mexico, struggle to integrate their US-born children into the Mexican educational system.

The devolution and privatization of immigration enforcement across the Global North (Coleman 2009; Lahav 1998) necessitates a multilevel scalar analysis. From this multisited and multiscalar approach emerges a taxonomy of relevant actors in the genesis and operation of rights enforcement arenas. Our approach considers the extent to which national actors or subfederal government systems like criminal justice, education, and health care control policy negotiations over resource allocation and how best to determine at what point the privileging of federal, binational coordination becomes a hindrance to formalizing cooperation with state and local governments, which may in fact be better equipped to serve communities of migrant workers. Another important scale to observe involves the varying national responses to migrant integration and consular coordination and how outreach strategies in large, central cities differ from those in outlying areas. Finally, it is important to analyze the different levels of power and legitimacy that states of origin enjoy in traditional destination communities where immigration has a long history compared to new destinations and/or anti-immigrant contexts. As these key themes indicate, a cross-border frame is vital for understanding the unique dynamics behind various migrant-related issues. For example, it is important to note that collective bargaining is an overwhelmingly federal matter in the United States but a provincial one in Canada.

Governing Migrant Rights in North America

When it comes to migrant rights, state power is a double-edged sword. At times repressive and at times emancipatory, state actors can protect and advance the rights of various groups or curtail them. In these analyses we examine to what extent national political dynamics affect outreach efforts to migrants and the efficacy of formal enforcement mechanisms. For origin and destination countries, domestic politics shape priorities and allegiances.

States also act dialectically, as the actions of one state affect the strategies of another. For example, in the United States, ramped-up immigration enforcement has spurred the Mexican government to recalibrate its behavior and revamp its own migration legislation, a largely symbolic gesture enacted in an attempt to gain moral standing in relation to its northern neighbor. Moreover, supranational enforcement regimes such as the North American Agreement on Labor Cooperation are implemented and enforced differently depending on the particular regime in power.

Migration scholars over the years have stressed the importance of examining the destination country's social and political context (Reitz 1998). Cross-national comparisons of immigration have examined how issues including labor market integration (McKay, Markova, and Paraskevopoulou 2012), access to the welfare state (Zuberi 2006), refugee resettlement (Hamlin 2012), and civic and political incorporation (Bloemraad 2006) have affected migrant outcomes. The roles of state and local governments have become a central inquiry as well, especially in the United States, where there has been an explosion of pro- and anti-immigrant policies (de Graauw 2016; Gulasekaram and Ramakrishnan 2015; Varsanyi et al. 2012). In an important shift, however, migration scholars have moved beyond the constraints of methodological nationalism and interrogated the role of the origin countries in affecting migrant experiences. Their studies have concentrated on Mexico, where the state has primarily focused on granting migrants voting rights as a way to keep them interested in subsidizing infrastructure with remittance matching funds programs (Fitzgerald 2008), and on the Philippines, which has supported its worldwide emigrant population by acting as an important temporary labor-agreement broker for nurses and domestic workers in the United States and several other countries (Guevarra 2009).

State responses to migrant rights are determined by social and political context, emerging as they do against a backdrop of heightened militarization and rampant insecurity. In Mexico, violence against women in industrial border zones and elsewhere across the country has become commonplace and a cause around which women's and human rights groups can rally (Fregoso and Bejarano 2009). The post-9/11 militarization of the US-Mexico border has also had profound effects on the northern and southern border crossings and across the hemisphere and played into criminal stereotypes of migrant communities (Andreas and Biersteker 2003; Rosas 2012). Indeed, the elevation of US security priorities above all others has shaped Mexico's relations with its diaspora and its treatment of Central American migrants. Despite a 2011 Mexican migration law that recognizes the rights of migrants in transit, apprehensions and deportations of Central American migrants at Mexico's southern border have increased significantly. This scrutiny responds in part to political pressure from the United States, such as when concerns over the "surge" of Central American unaccompanied minors in the summer of 2014 pushed Mexico to crack down even further. By viewing Central American migrants primarily as a "threat to be controlled," Mexico has become complicit in a pattern of human rights violations—if not perpetrating injustices, then granting them tacit approval (Isacson, Meyer, and Morales 2014, 20). Taken together, the case studies in this volume illuminate the factors determining the government's ability to protect or restrict rights in often unstable and violent environments.

In this volume we examine the role of migrant organizations in determining the policies and practices of origin and destination states. To begin, we review the policy context for governing migrant rights in each country.

Mexico

Mexican foreign policy toward emigrants shifted in the 1990s from a model of state introversion to one of state extension, with the explicit goal of engaging migrant communities abroad (Bada 2014; Bada and Gleeson 2015; Sherman 1999). This was a decidedly political move, as President Carlos Salinas de Gortari (1988–1994) of the ruling Partido Revolucionario Institucional (PRI) realized that migrants living in the United States overwhelmingly supported Cuauhtémoc Cárdenas Solórzano in the general election on July 6, 1988, and again in his race against PRI candidate Ernesto Zedillo in 1994. The credible opposition presidential candidate Cárdenas had campaigned in the United States among Mexicans; despite having seemingly obtained the most votes, he was not recognized as the winner in 1988 (Bruhn 1997; García y Griego 1988).[1] In a politically calculated response, Salinas de Gortari´s successor, Zedillo (1994–2000), the last PRI-backed presidential administration prior to a democratic transition, crafted a series of new programs and policies supported by civic organizations on both sides of the border. First among them was a constitutional amendment to the Nationality Law to allow Mexican migrants who had adopted a foreign nationality and the first generation born to Mexican nationals abroad to claim Mexican nationality (Becerra Ramírez 2000). The reforms included municipal and state funds to match migrant remittances earmarked for community infrastructure. The programs were facilitated by associations operating transnationally in traditional migrant regions of origin and in major immigrant metropolises in the United States in the late 1990s. These programs were scaled up in 2002 at the federal level by President Vicente Fox, who in 2000 overturned seven decades of PRI presidential succession (Iskander 2010).

Remittance-matching policies laid the groundwork for Mexico's more proactive involvement in managing its diaspora. Délano (2011) argues that this stance represents a fundamental change in the bilateral relationship between the United States and Mexico; now the prevailing view is that managing the 30 million Mexican migrants and their children in the United States is a shared responsibility. In this book we recount the governance structures that have facilitated the shift and then address the specific dynamics for migrant worker rights, educational access, health care access, social accountability, and civic integration on both sides of the border. In addition, we carefully attend to the particular experiences of indigenous migrants, whose analysis is often subsumed within broader nation-state politics and whose migration north is often the result of forced displacement off their lands. We extend the analysis of Mexico's expanding immigration-related policies through case studies in the United States, Mexico, and Canada. Each study focuses on the challenges across various levels of governance and stresses the importance of migrant civil society in holding government actors accountable.

The building block of the Mexican state's outreach apparatus has been its consular network, with more than fifty offices in the United States and Canada. The offices often must deal with a range of issues pertaining to Mexican foreign nationals such as child support and foster care for children with parents detained in the United States, support payments to children still living in Mexico, representation for Mexican nationals on death row in the world's largest penal system, expatriate voting, access to documentation necessary to apply for deportation relief, and even repatriation of bodies postmortem (Félix 2011; Gambetta 2012; Mummert 2014). The increasing migration of indigenous populations adds other vital dimensions to consular work such as translation for the linguistically diverse indigenous migrant communities seeking access to social institutions.

The challenges and pitfalls of providing consular assistance are well documented. Consular offices are run by diplomatic appointees who cycle in and out every few years as well as by a smaller number of permanent domestic staff. Staff members have been accused of replicating the elitist, classist, and racist attitudes that embody migrants' stereotypical anxieties about their home-country bureaucracies. Functionally, consular institutions suffer from enormous turnover, uneven resource allocation in which larger offices have far greater bureaucratic capacity for outreach and engagement, and often fickle leadership that dictates office priorities. Consular offices nonetheless possess relative legitimacy among the migrant community and enjoy diplomatic access that bureaucracies in the destination country simply do not have, particularly in an era of stepped-up immigration enforcement (Bada and Gleeson 2015; Gleeson 2012).

Beyond the federal apparatus, an array of bilateral, trilateral, and regional institutions has laid the groundwork for Mexico's more robust engagement with its diaspora, as José María Serna de la Garza discusses in chapter 2. Some of the institutions emerged in response to pressures from international migration governance agreements; regional free trade policy, such as the NAFTA labor accords we, Xóchitl Bada and Shannon Gleeson, discuss in chapter 3; and a shared interest of origin and destination states in improving population health such as the Binational Health Week discussed by Liliana Osorio, Hilda Dávila, and Xóchitl Castañeda in chapter 10. Various subnational offices complement the services offered by the consular network, and some of them have established a presence in the United States as well, as Ortega Ramírez describes in chapter 4).

Moreover, Mexico's relations with the United States are influenced by concerns over US treatment of Mexican migrants, especially the more than 5 million unauthorized ones (Krogstad, Passel, and Cohn 2016), but also by Mexico's own efforts to stem the tide of other migrants en route to the United States (Domínguez and Iñiguez Ramos 2016; Vogt 2013). Mexico is a major destination and transit country for Central Americans and other migrants headed north. The migrants raise a key humanitarian concern, especially as Mexico has become implicated in US efforts to check migration from and increase deportations to Central American countries. Border crackdowns in southern Mexico, in response to pressure from the United States, have led activists to call for greater transparency in operations that have trampled the rights of the detained and often been implicated in the disappearance of Central American migrants (Martínez 2014). Since the turn of the twenty-first century, insecurity and violence have flared in Central America's Northern Triangle region due to entrenched social inequalities, neoliberal privatizations, climate change, state corruption, and the rising power of criminal organizations as well as repressive measures implemented by states to curb them (Bada and Feldmann 2017; Rubio Díaz Leal and Pérez Vázquez 2016). Across large areas of El Salvador, Honduras, Guatemala, and Mexico, the respective governments have been unable to guarantee minimal levels of security as criminal groups operate with impunity. Faced with the threat of extortion, kidnapping, and reprisals for denouncing the groups, many people have fled to large urban centers or abroad to seek shelter and protection with relatives and friends (Cantor 2014; Rios Contreras 2014). In 2014 an increase of unaccompanied minors occurred in the southwestern United States, and 68,541 of them were apprehended that year by border enforcement officials (CPB 2015). Many of the young migrants identified an indigenous language as their first language and reported experiencing language barriers in detention and deportation proceedings (Wang 2014). Their cases illustrate the complexity of migrants' rights. Given the dire situations facing migrants in transit, Mexico's efforts to ensure the rights of its emigrants living abroad are being closely watched by groups advocating on behalf of migrants. Advocates likewise are watching the Mexican government's promises and investments abroad as they seek justice for Mexican citizens and Central Americans fighting for their rights in Mexico itself.

Canada

Compared to the United States, Canada boasts a more proactive federal regime of immigrant integration and invests more resources to promote naturalization and nurture immigrants' civic capacity (Bloemraad 2006). Home to a much larger population of refugees than that in the United States and a major destination for asylum-seekers from Mexico and elsewhere, Canada has an administrative system to determine refugee status that is relatively insulated from political and legal tinkering and as a result, more stable and generous to claimants (Hamlin 2012). Although Canada has often been assumed to be a friendlier and more welcoming partner in the region and has a smaller population of undocumented migrants, major barriers do exist for temporary migrants, in particular, who are not eligible for the same educational opportunities as refugees (Goldring, Berinstein, and Bernhard 2009; Vosko 2006). Mexican migrants make up more than half the participants in the Seasonal Agricultural Workers Program (Budworth, Rose, and Mann 2017) and face enormously exploitive labor conditions (Goldring 2017; Vosko 2016) that unions struggle to remedy (Vosko and Thomas 2014). To combat the shortcomings, networks of nongovernmental organization activists have crafted a forceful human rights narrative to demand labor and social rights and improve migrant life in Canada (Basok 2009).

The work of Patricia Landolt and Luin Goldring (2010) underscores contradictions in Canada's immigration and citizenship policies. In the late 1970s an entry system based on racially biased criteria was replaced with a point system to select permanent residents based on education and language criteria. At the same time, Canadian civil society and a cadre of civil servant allies pushed to balance post–cold war priorities with wider humanitarian concerns in order to institutionalize and expand access to refugee status (Landolt and Goldring 2010; Simalchik 1993). The Canadian government funded services promoting the settlement and integration of immigrants and refugees (Bloemraad 2006).

And even though it has constructed an integrative and increasingly progressive framework, Canada also has built up a robust population of temporary entrants such as asylum seekers, international students, and temporary foreign workers, all of whom remain ineligible for settlement services

(Goldring and Landolt 2013; Hennebry 2014; Sharma 2006). There has been an increase in the numbers of unauthorized migrants—some who enter undetected, stay beyond their study and employment visas, have refugee claims denied, and so forth—as well as of precarious noncitizen migrants (Landolt and Goldring 2016; Wouk et al. 2006). Concerns over the viability of exceptions granted under the Safe Third Country Agreement (Macklin 2005) along with anti-immigrant policies under the Trump administration have triggered an increase in unauthorized border crossers claiming asylum and often denied their rights to due process (Markusoff et al. 2017; Maynard 2018). Anti-immigrant political shifts have been accompanied by more restrictive humanitarian policies, an ongoing concern over the legitimacy of refugee claims including thousands of petitions by Mexicans asking protection from violence, a large backlog in the refugee determination process, limited access to publicly supported legal aid, and inequities in acceptance rates (Bada and Feldmann 2018; Rehaag 2016, 2017; Villegas 2015).

All these factors have given rise to a diverse population of noncitizens whose precarious legal status creates barriers, with some enjoying more certain access to permanent status than others do. They often have only limited access to employment and social rights and are at the center of tense public debates over access to services such as public education and health care (Goldring and Landolt 2012). Temporary foreign workers often face strict employment conditions such as working for a single employer, and they may endure low wages and dangerous work environments (Faraday 2012). In sum, the presumed pro-immigrant Canadian utopia is more complicated than it appears.

United States

In the United States, Mexican migrants make up nearly a third of all immigrants and more than half of the undocumented population (Hoefer, Rytina, and Baker 2009), estimated at 11 million (Krogstad, Passel, and Cohn 2017). The estimated number of Mexican migrants living in the United States without authorization declined from 6.9 million in 2007 to 5.8 million in 2014 (Krogstad, Passel, and Cohn 2017). Declining Mexican migration to the United States stems from long-studied factors such as changes in Mexican demographics and decreasing fertility rates, improved conditions in Mexico's labor market, higher levels of education, dramatic increases in the costs of crossing the border, the recession of 2007, and decreasing family remittances that could finance new migrant trips (Cave 2011; Durand and Arias 2014). As a result, in what used to be the most important migration corridor in the world, the net balance of Mexican nationals departing to and returning from the United States has gone to zero (Gonzalez-Barrera and Krogstad 2015).

Nevertheless, Mexican migrants have been a major target for immigration enforcement actions under Clinton, Bush, Obama, and even more systematically and brazenly under the Trump administration.[2] More migrants from Mexico were deported in fiscal year 2017 than from any other country: 128,765 of 220,649 removals not including voluntary returns (ICE 2017). The United States has for decades increased border militarization in an attempt to stem the northward flow that began before US borders were even drawn (Dunn 1996; Nevins 2002). Restrictive immigration policies have been accompanied by ill-informed public perceptions about what contributions migrants make; Mexican migrants embody a narrative about Latino migrants in the United States that is at once complex and reductive. They are frequently held up to be hard-working people (Baker-Cristales 2009; Gleeson 2015), a criminal threat (Chavez 2008; Santa Ana 2002), a cultural stain on democracy and mainstream assimilation (Huntington 2004), or in part owing to biased perceptions of their high fertility rates (Parrado 2011), a drain on the welfare state (Romero 2008). Exacerbating the anti-immigrant dynamics is the racist rhetoric under the Trump administration, which has instituted a series of repressive measures that include a vast expansion of the groups prioritized for deportation (Law 2017), arrests of subjects at places previously considered safe (Hanson 2017), a plan to hire 15,000 more immigration agents (Rein 2017), a broad ban on refugees and even on basic travel by migrants from several majority-Muslim countries (*Al Jazeera* 2017), and the creation of a Victims of Immigrant Crime Enforcement Office (Beinart 2017; Gleeson and Sampat 2018).

Despite composing more than half the estimated unauthorized migrant population (Krogstad, Passel, and Cohn 2017), "lawfully present" Mexican immigrants outnumber them (Cohn 2017). Still, compared to the 74 percent naturalization rate of eligible non-Mexican immigrants, Mexican migrants have a low rate of naturalization, at 42 percent, due in large part to language and cost barriers (Cohn 2017; Gonzalez-Barrera 2017). Unlike Canada, the United States has taken a laissez-faire approach to immigrant integration, which partly explains disparities between the two countries in naturalization rates (Bloemraad 2006) and accounts for the fact that in the United States formal citizenship is not always accompanied by a sense of belonging (Chen 2018). While the federal government is more hands-off, state and local governments take up the slack, playing a substantial role in developing immigrant policies in the United States on issues ranging from enforcement to benefits and services (Gulasekaram and Ramakrishnan 2015; Varsanyi et al. 2012). In 2017, according to the National Center for State Legislators, states enacted 206 laws on issues ranging from so-called sanctuary policies to refugee resettlement, education/civics, and in-state tuition (NCSL 2018).

Yet US immigrant policies are as contradictory as Canada's. While the

US Supreme Court has guaranteed children's right to a free public education regardless of immigration status, undocumented high school students face blocked pathways to college and the workplace (Gonzales 2016). Even for citizen children, persistent disparities reflect racialized inequities that migration scholars have pointed to as evidence of downward assimilation (Telles and Ortiz 2008). The situation of unauthorized migrants reveals the same contradictions. Unable to legally work due to employer sanction policies, they nonetheless have high levels of labor-force participation and are critical to low-wage industries such as construction, hospitality and food service, and agriculture. Similar incongruities are found in the workplace, where migrants are subject to frequent violations. Most federal and state laws formally protect workers regardless of their immigration status, though in practice the ability to make claims and access those remedies is limited at best (Griffith 2012; Gleeson 2016).

In sum, migrant rights in the United States are subject to major changes as presidential administrations shift, best demonstrated by recent buildups in immigration enforcement and the rescission of the Deferred Action for Childhood Arrivals program, whose beneficiaries are nearly 80 percent Mexican migrants (López and Krogstad 2017). Meanwhile, congressional change comes slowly in the United States, where the last major legalization program was enacted more than three decades ago. In this context, immigrant civil society plays a significant role in advocating for and ensuring the implementation of local pro-immigrant policies (de Graauw 2016).

Migrant Rights, Civil Society, and Transnational Accountability

Case studies in this volume examine migrant rights from several perspectives: the formal definitions laid out by international institutions such as the International Labor Organization (ILO), those rights broadly defined by domestic governments, and those outlined within specific institutional arenas such as education, labor, and health. We distinguish between the "soft law" of the international arena, which has little influence on the actions of the US government, and "hard law," those rights that may be represented in national or state courts and defended by specific models of administrative enforcement.

The chapters illuminate how differences in national and state laws affect success in legal arenas. Variations across legal and political arenas can improve migrant rights in certain cases, as with public education access under *Pyler v. Doe*; restrict rights in others, as with health care in the United States, which still bars undocumented migrants from the Affordable Health

Care Act; and give rise to contradictory rights in labor and employment law whereby, thanks to the 2002 *Hoffman Plastic* case, undocumented workers enjoy significant rights but are left without remedies should those rights be violated. Because of the variation, migrants may face blocked access along one avenue but, by taking another route, may initiate a productive search for alternative allies and venues in which to air their grievances. Several chapters in this volume adopt a cross-border and multiscalar lens to fully represent the complex systems that migrants must navigate, in domestic cases concerning migrant health care access, for labor rights enforcement, and for equal access to justice and education, among others.

The case studies examine various ways that migrant civil society is holding origin and destination governments accountable through a range of legal and institutional tools. Examples across each country demonstrate the importance of local context and history for migrant organizers in determining these strategies: What political opportunity structures emerge for civic actors in some places but not others? How do certain geographic and institutional contexts influence the ways civic groups frame issues? As previous literature on legal mobilization has amply shown, legal rights are meaningless if not enforced, and the ability of immigrant civil society to access resources and carry out its work can vary greatly across destination regions (de Graauw, Gleeson, and Bloemraad 2013). As we demonstrate, though, regions of origin can differ in their abilities to advocate for their compatriots abroad (Bada 2014; Fox and Bada 2008).

An organizational lens is thus imperative for understanding processes of immigrant integration writ large (Ramakrishnan and Bloemraad 2008). Civic organizations—grassroots and grasstops—are central actors in the analyses. This volume provides examples of highly institutionalized transnational struggles such as the United Food and Commercial Workers campaigns to organize workers across the continent. Similar to the pioneering works of Dale Hathaway (2000) and Brooks and Fox (2002), our analyses highlight the power imbalances and challenges that emerge through top-down and bottom-up attempts to build solidarity and coalitions across borders. In texts written by practitioners in civic organizations, we present unmediated, first-person accounts of struggles to improve institutional capacities for making migrant rights real. These chapters also examine the importance of cross-sectorial links in building a migrant rights movement and institutionalizing migrant protections; they follow the bottom-up analytical tradition of studies on destination contexts such as García Agustín and Jørgensen (2016). Rather than focus solely on elite actors, in our volume we examine migrants as political actors in their own right. We study the resulting solidarity and tensions that arise across a variety of institutional contexts.

Overview of the Chapters

We begin with a theoretical framework for understanding the role of civil society in advocating for migrant rights. In chapter 1, Fox and Rivera-Salgado offer ten propositions for migrant civil society based on lessons learned from diverse migrant rights defense initiatives including human rights, labor rights, and cross-border efforts to support development in communities of origin. In their theoretical synthesis the authors revise the concept of migrant civil society by addressing migrants' diverse collective identities, relations with other social and political actors, connections to societies of origin and reception, forms of organization, advocacy strategies, coalition dynamics, and the persistent disconnect between migration and development agendas.

The two chapters in part I provide an overview of regional governance structures in North America. In chapter 2, Serna de la Garza introduces a theoretical framework for protecting migrant worker rights in North and Central America through global governance instruments. He highlights the enormous legal challenges of home, transit, and host countries in protecting migrant workers, especially with normative solutions based on soft law. He details the mechanisms of the North American Free Trade Agreement (NAFTA) put in place to protect migrant workers, and in so doing he elucidates the limitations of state-centered strategies and the importance of supranational norms and institutional structures. Next, in chapter 3, Bada and Gleeson examine the functioning of the North American Agreement on Labor Cooperation. We document the efforts leading up to the 2014 joint declaration of the US Department of Labor and Mexico's Secretariat of Labor and Social Welfare in which the parties committed to improving the quality and clarity of information available to Mexican migrants in the United States with H-2A and H-2B temporary work visas.[3] Transnational civil society organizations were crucial to those efforts, which culminated in three public petitions submitted to Mexico's National Administrative Office of the North American Agreement on Labor Cooperation on behalf of H-2 workers. While the petitions were largely unsuccessful and the core accountability mechanisms proved deficient, we emphasize the transformative role the petition efforts had in building solidarity among civic groups and gaining a legitimate voice for migrant organizers in the international arena. Next we examine state-society relations in each country, starting with Mexico, the largest migrant-sending country in the region, a major transit country for Central Americans, and the destination for many Mexican American children who return with their deported parents.

Part II, on Mexico, begins with shifting to the subnational scale in chapter 4, where Ortega Ramírez focuses on the role of subfederal governance there, describing how migrant affairs offices in state governments complement the work of Mexican consulates abroad. The offices' programs provide direct assistance, process remittances, interface with migrant civic organizations, promote temporary visa programs for work in the United States and Canada, and serve as institutional liaisons for transnational migrant rights advocacy. Their work makes apparent the difficulties and legal challenges of sorting through and enforcing migrant protections across federal and state laws in origin and destination countries. Ortega Ramírez examines the advocacy strategies of migrant-led organizations on both sides of the border. In chapter 5 the human rights practitioners Ana Lorena Delgadillo, Alma García, and Rodolfo Córdova Alcaraz consider the experience of Central American migrants in Mexico. They relate how human rights organizations in Central America and Mexico have held the Mexican state accountable for the murder of hundreds of migrants; in 2013 the organizations created the Forensic Commission and Migrant Unit of the Attorney General's Office, the first forensic commission specializing in crimes against migrants. The authors describe the strategies pursued by the transnational coalition of families of disappeared migrants as well as the key support offered by the Argentine Forensic Anthropology Team (Equipo Argentino de Antropología Forense). The authors evaluate the strategies and effectiveness of the historic Special Migration Program in terms of delivering justice, truth, and reparations to the victims of violence against migrants. In chapter 6 Jacobo-Suárez sheds light on the experiences of 600,000 Mexican American children who returned to Mexico because of their parents' deportations and face obstacles to integrating into Mexican society. In many cases the children had spent most if not all of their lives up to that point in the United States, attended American schools, and adopted English as their preferred language. Jacobo-Suárez analyzes the legal and other barriers that Mexican American children encounter in exercising their educational rights in Mexico. She highlights the important advocacy work performed by civic organizations, academia, and deported young people in advancing the rights of their peers.

Part III turns to Canada, a major though often overlooked destination for migrants ranging from temporary foreign workers employed in seasonal agriculture to asylum seekers and other migrants in urban centers such as Toronto. In chapter 7, Andrea Galvez, Pablo Godoy, and Paul Meinema focus on an arm of migrant advocacy in Canada—the labor movement. The three authors, union officials from the United Food and Commercial Workers, provide a firsthand account of the union's reliance on transnational solidarity in advocating for seasonal workers in Canada. The Seasonal Agricultural Workers Program between Mexico and Canada is still considered a model of binational, legal, and orderly migration despite its deep flaws. This popular program, some argue, provides an opportunity to escape rural poverty and unemployment, though it does create a class of highly exploitable workers, even if they are relatively privileged. Meanwhile, aggrieved workers themselves have adopted strategies to resist exploitive practices. They are supported in their efforts by the United Food and Commercial Workers, which mounts legal challenges to protect worker freedoms, funds legal aid programs, and stages organizing drives as the law permits in order to have greater impact in an arena previously dominated by employers and governments. In chapter 8, Landolt and Goldring examine the politics of public school administrators in Toronto, Canada's largest city. They examine the uneven and contradictory implementation of the school district's 2006 Don't Ask, Don't Tell policy and the city council's 2014 sanctuary city policy. The authors draw on the notion of noncitizenship as an assemblage of experiences and rights, all restricted to varying degrees, to analyze the patchwork nature of access to public education for migrants of precarious legal status. They highlight how school administrators support broader multicultural, liberal narratives of inclusion that minimize the prominence of status while spatially displacing—or outsourcing to other bureaucratic actors—the practices of documentation and academic assessment that put up barriers to those students. After the students' enrollment, administrators continue to obfuscate their status by conflating equality with equity, claiming that they treat everyone the same.

The chapters in part IV present examples of transnational migrant rights advocacy in the United States. In chapter 9 Baquedano-López describes how local school policies in San Francisco evolved to meet the needs of the growing community of transnational indigenous Yucatec Maya students in the city's Mission District. She examines how students and their families in the diaspora contend with discourses and practices of indigeneity, Latinization, and Americanization. The author highlights the tensions that emerge as indigenous migrants from Mexico strive to maintain their linguistic and cultural heritage by reappropriating and resignifying the liberal multiculturalism prevalent in California's urban education sector. Next, in chapter 10 Osorio, Dávila, and Castañeda document the binational effort to connect Mexican migrants with health services in the United States through the annual Binational Health Week, a joint initiative between the Mexican consular network and a variety of nonprofit health providers in the United States. Inspired by the Semana de Salud model widely used in Mexico and other Latin American countries, the binational public-private partnership increased access to culturally and linguistically sensitive health services by drawing on the resources of educational institutions to accomplish its objectives. Finally, in chapter 11 Délano Alonso considers the extent to which Mexico has addressed the rights of its citizens residing beyond its national territorial boundaries as well as its motivations for doing so. The author focuses on how the Mexican government aided undocumented youths in applying for the Deferred Action for Childhood Arrivals program and its push to facilitate access to US naturalization programs.

The volume concludes with our epilogue, in which we offer some lessons for understanding the scope and limitations of transnational advocacy strategies to enforce the human, social, political, and economic rights of vulnerable Mexican migrants. We summarize the main takeaways from each of the case studies and suggest new research agendas for the future.

Notes

The authors extend gratitude especially to Patricia Baquedano-López, Maria Lorena Cook, Patricia Landolt, and Luin Goldring for pointed feedback on this introduction.

1. Official evidence of the electoral fraud of 1988 was never found. Three years after the Mexican government declared a "system shutdown" as the only explanation for Salinas de Gortari's miraculous victory after losing in the preliminary vote count, the Mexican Congress ordered the election ballots burned, and the only hard evidence of the fraud committed that July night in 1988 went up in smoke (La Jornada 2004).

2. President Obama inherited a well-oiled deportation machine from the two previous administrations. However, as resources and strategies shifted, during the Obama administration "noncitizen removals increased significantly, while apprehensions and overall deportations both remained far lower than the numbers seen under the Bush and Clinton administrations." In fact, President Clinton "deported" more people altogether than Obama did, more than 12.2 million compared to more than 5.2 million under Obama, once forced removals and voluntary returns are included (Chishti, Pierce, and Bolter 2017).

3. Translations throughout the volume are those of the authors unless otherwise indicated.

References

Al Jazeera. 2017. "US Supreme Court Allows Trump's Broad Refugee Ban." September 13. http://www.aljazeera.com/news/2017/09/supreme-court-trump-broad-refugee-ban-170913002508258.html.

Andreas, Peter, and Thomas J. Biersteker. 2003. *The Rebordering of North America*. New York: Routledge.

Armbruster-Sandoval, Ralph. 2003. "Globalization and Transnational Labor Organizing: The Honduran Maquiladora Industry and the Kimi Campaign." *Social Science History* 27 (4): 551–575.

Bada, Xóchitl. 2014. *Mexican Hometown Associations in Chicagoacán: From Local to Transnational Civic Engagement*. New Brunswick, NJ: Rutgers University Press.

Bada, Xóchitl, and Andreas E. Feldmann. 2018. "How Insecurity Is Transforming Migration Patterns in the North American Corridor: Lessons from Michoacán." In *New Migration Patterns in the Americas: Challenges for the 21st Century*, edited by Andreas E. Feldmann, Xóchitl Bada, and Stephanie Schütze. New York: Palgrave Macmillan.

Bada, Xóchitl, and Andreas Feldmann. 2017. "Mexico's Michoacán State: Mixed Migration Flows and Transnational Links." *Forced Migration Review* 56:12–14.

Bada, Xóchitl, and Shannon Gleeson. 2015. "A New Approach to Migrant Labor Rights Enforcement: The Crisis of Undocumented Worker Abuse and Mexican Consular Advocacy in the United States." *Labor Studies Journal* 40 (1): 32–53.

Baker-Cristales, Beth. 2009. "Mediated Resistance: The Construction of Neoliberal Citizenship in the Immigrant Rights Movement." *Latino Studies* 7 (1): 60–82.

Basch, Linda G., Nina Glick Schiller, and Cristina Szanton Blanc. 1994. *Nations Unbound: Transnational Projects, Postcolonial Predicaments, and Deterritorialized Nation-States*. London: Gordon and Breach Amsterdam.

Basok, Tanya. 2009. "Counter-Hegemonic Human Rights Discourses and Migrant Rights Activism in the US and Canada." *International Journal of Comparative Sociology* 50 (2): 183–183.

Becerra Ramírez, Manuel. 2000. "Nationality in Mexico." In *From Migrants to Citizens: Membership in a Changing World*, edited by Alexander T. Aleinikoff and Douglas Klusmeyer, 312–341. Washington, DC: Carnegie Endowment for International Peace.

Beinart, Peter. 2017. "Trump Turns Unauthorized Immigrants into Scapegoats." *The Atlantic*, March 1. https://www.theatlantic.com/politics/archive/2017/03/trump-scapegoats-unauthorized-immigrants-for-crime/518238/.

Benhabib, Seyla. 2004. *The Rights of Others: Aliens, Residents, and Citizens*. Cambridge, England: Cambridge University Press.

Bloemraad, Irene. 2006. *Becoming a Citizen: Incorporating Immigrants and Refugees in the United States and Canada*. Berkeley: University of California Press.

Bosniak, Linda. 2006. *The Citizen and the Alien: Dilemmas of Contemporary Membership*. Princeton, NJ: Princeton University Press.

Brooks, David, and Jonathan Fox. 2002. *Cross-Border Dialogues: U.S.-Mexican Social Movement Networking*. San Diego: Center for U.S.-Mexican Studies, University of California, San Diego.

Bruhn, Kathleen. 1997. *Taking on Goliath: The Emergence of a New Left Party and the Struggle for Democracy in Mexico*. University Park, PA: Penn State University Press.

Budworth, Marie-Hélène, Andrew Rose, and Sara Mann. 2017. "Report on the Seasonal Agricultural Worker Program." San José, Costa Rica: Inter-American Institute for Cooperation on Agriculture Delegation in Canada. http://www.iica.int/sites/default/files/publications/files/2017/bve17038753i.pdf.

Cantor, David James. 2014. "The New Wave: Forced Displacement Caused by Organized Crime in Central America and Mexico." *Refugee Survey Quarterly* 33:34–68.

Cave, Damien. 2011. "Better Lives for Mexicans Cut Allure of Going North." *New York Times*, July 6. http://www.nytimes.com/interactive/2011/07/06/world/americas/immigration.html?_r=0#.

Chavez, Leo R. 2008. *The Latino Threat: Constructing Immigrants, Citizens, and the Nation*. Palo Alto, CA: Stanford University Press.

Chen, Ming Hsu. 2018. "Constructing Citizenship for Noncitizens." Colloquium presentation, Center for the Study of Law and Society, University of California, Berkeley, March.

Chishti, Muzaffar, Sarah Pierce, and Jessica Bolter. 2017. "The Obama Record on Deportations: Deporter in Chief or Not?" *Policy Beat*. Washington, DC: Migration Policy Institute. http://www.migrationpolicy.org/article/obama-record-deportations-de porter-chief-or-not.

Cohn, D'Vera. 2017. "5 Key Facts About U.S. Lawful Immigrants." *Pew Research Center* (blog). August 3, 2017. http://www.pewresearch.org/fact-tank/2017/08/03/5-key -facts-about-u-s-lawful-immigrants/.

Coleman, Mathew. 2009. "What Counts as the Politics and Practice of Security, and Where? Devolution and Immigrant Insecurity after 9/11." *Annals of the Association of American Geographers* 99 (5): 904–913.

CPB. *See* US Customs and Border Protection (CPB).

de Graauw, Els. 2016. *Making Immigrant Rights Real: Nonprofits and the Politics of Integration in San Francisco*. Ithaca, NY: Cornell University Press.

de Graauw, Els, Shannon Gleeson, and Irene Bloemraad. 2013. "Funding Immigrant Organizations: Suburban Free Riding and Local Civic Presence." *American Journal of Sociology* 119 (1): 75–130.

Délano, Alexandra. 2011. *Mexico and Its Diaspora: Policies of Emigration since 1848*. Cambridge, England: Cambridge University Press.

Domínguez, Roberto, and Martín Iñiguez Ramos. 2016. "The South/North Axis of Border Management in Mexico." In *Externalizing Migration Management: Europe, North America, and the Spread of Remote Control Practices*, edited by Ruben Zaiotti, 225–237. New York: Routledge.

Dunn, Timothy J. 1996. *The Militarization of the US-Mexico Border, 1978–1992: Low-Intensity Conflict Doctrine Comes Home*. Austin: University of Texas Press.

Durand, Jorge, and Patricia Arias. 2014. "Escenarios locales del colapso migratorio: Indicios desde los altos de Jalisco." *Papeles De Población* 20 (81): 9–23.

Faist, Thomas, Margit Fauser, and Eveline Reisenauer. 2013. *Transnational Migration*. Cambridge, England: Polity.

Faraday, Fay. 2012. "Made in Canada: How the Law Constructs Migrant Workers' Insecurity." Toronto: Metcalf Foundation. https://metcalffoundation.com/stories/pu blications/made-in-canada-how-the-law-constructs-migrant-workers-insecurity/.

Félix, Adrián. 2011. "Posthumous Transnationalism: Postmortem Repatriation from the U.S. to México." *Latin American Research Review* 46 (3): 157–179.

Fitzgerald, David. 2008. *A Nation of Emigrants: How Mexico Manages Its Migration*. Berkeley: University of California Press.

Fitzgerald, David, and David Cook-Martín. 2014. *Culling the Masses: The Democratic Origins of Racist Immigration Policy in the Americas*. Cambridge, MA: Harvard University Press.

Fox, Jonathan, and Xóchitl Bada. 2008. "Migrant Organization and Hometown Impacts in Rural Mexico." *Journal of Agrarian Change* 8 (2): 435–461.

Fraser, Nancy. 2009. *Scales of Justice: Reimagining Political Space in a Globalizing World*. New York: Columbia University Press.

Freeman, Gary P. 1995. "Modes of Immigration Politics in Liberal Democratic States." *International Migration Review* 29 (4): 881–902.

Fregoso, Rosa-Linda, and Cynthia Bejarano. 2009. *Terrorizing Women: Feminicide in the Americas*. Durham, NC: Duke University Press.

Gambetta, Ricardo. 2012. "Positive Crossroads: Mexican Consular Assistance and Immigrant Integration." Washington, DC.

García Agustín, Óscar, and Martin Bak Jørgensen. 2016. *Solidarity without Borders: Gramscian Perspectives on Migration and Civil Society Alliances*. London: Pluto Press.

García y Griego, Manuel. 1988. "The Bracero Policy Experiment: U.S.-Mexican Responses to Mexican Labor Migration, 1942–1955." PhD diss., University of California, Los Angeles.

Givens, Terri, and Adam Luedtke. 2005. "European Immigration Policies in Comparative Perspective: Issue Salience, Partisanship, and Immigrant Rights." *Comparative European Politics* 3 (1): 1–22.

Gleeson, Shannon. 2012. *Conflicting Commitments: The Politics of Enforcing Immigrant Worker Rights in San Jose and Houston.* Ithaca, NY: Cornell University Press.

———. 2015. "'They Come Here to Work': An Evaluation of the Economic Argument in Favor of Immigrant Rights." *Citizenship Studies* 19 (3–4): 400–420.

———. 2016. *Precarious Claims: The Promise and Failure of Workplace Protections in the United States.* Oakland, CA: University of California Press.

Gleeson, Shannon, and Prerna Sampat. 2018. "Immigrant Resistance in the Age of Trump." *New Labor Forum* 27 (1): 86–95.

Goldring, Luin. 2017. "Resituating Temporariness as the Precarity and Conditionality of Non-Citizenship." In *Liberating Temporariness? Migration, Work, and Citizenship in an Age of Insecurity,* edited by Leah F. Vosko, Valerie Preston, and Robert Latham, 218–254. Montreal: McGill-Queen's University Press.

Goldring, Luin, Carolina Berinstein, and Judith K. Bernhard. 2009. "Institutionalizing Precarious Migratory Status in Canada." *Citizenship Studies* 13 (3): 239–265.

Goldring, Luin, and Patricia Landolt. 2012. *The Impact of Precarious Legal Status on Immigrants' Economic Outcomes.* IRPP Study 35. Montreal: Institute for Research on Public Policy. October 23. http://irpp.org/research-studies/study-no35/.

———. 2013. *Producing and Negotiating Non-Citizenship: Precarious Legal Status in Canada.* Toronto: University of Toronto Press.

Gonzales, Roberto G. 2016. *Lives in Limbo.* Oakland: University of California Press. http://www.ucpress.edu/book.php?isbn=9780520287259.

Gonzalez-Barrera, Ana. 2017. "Mexican Lawful Immigrants among the Least Likely to Become U.S. Citizens." Hispanic Trends, June 29. Washington, DC: Pew Research Center. http://www.pewhispanic.org/2017/06/29/mexican-lawful-immigrants-among-least-likely-to-become-u-s-citizens/.

Gonzalez-Barrera, Ana, and Jens Manuel Krogstad. 2015. "What We Know About Illegal Immigration from Mexico." *FactTank,* March 2. Washington, DC: Pew Research Center. http://www.pewresearch.org/fact-tank/2015/11/20/what-we-know-about-illegal-immigration-from-mexico/.

Griffith, Kati L. 2012. "Undocumented Workers: Crossing the Borders of Immigration and Workplace Law." *Cornell Journal of Law and Public Policy* 21:611–697.

Guevarra, Anna Romina. 2009. *Marketing Dreams, Manufacturing Heroes: The Transnational Labor Brokering of Filipino Workers.* New Brunswick, NJ: Rutgers University Press.

Gulasekaram, Pratheepan, and S. Karthick Ramakrishnan. 2015. *The New Immigration Federalism.* Cambridge, England: Cambridge University Press.

Hamlin, Rebecca. 2012. "International Law and Administrative Insulation: A Comparison of Refugee Status Determination Regimes in the United States, Canada, and Australia." *Law and Social Inquiry* 37 (4): 933–968.

Hanson, Jessica. 2017. "School Settings Are Sensitive Locations That Should Be Off-Limits to Immigration Enforcement." May 4. Los Angeles: National Immigration Law Center. https://www.nilc.org/news/the-torch/5-4-17/.

Hathaway, Dale A. 2000. *Allies across the Border: Mexico's "Authentic Labor Front" and Global Solidarity*. New York: South End.

Hennebry, Jenna. 2014. "Falling through the Cracks? Migrant Workers and the Global Social Protection Floor." *Global Social Policy* 14 (3): 369–388.

Hoefer, Michael, Nancy Rytina, and Bryan C Baker. 2009. "Estimates of the Unauthorized Immigrant Population Residing in the United States: January 2008." Policy Directorate, Population Estimates series, February. Washington, DC: Office of Immigration Statistics, US Department of Homeland Security. http://www.dhs.gov /xlibrary/assets/statistics/publications/ois_ill_pe_2008.pdf.

Huntington, Samuel. 2004. "The Hispanic Challenge," *Foreign Policy* (March–April): 35–40.

ICE. *See* US Immigrations and Customs Enforcement (ICE).

Isacson, Adam, Maureen Meyer, and Gabriela Morales. 2014. *Mexico's Other Border: Security, Migration, and the Humanitarian Crisis at the Line with Central America.* Washington, DC: Washington Office on Latin America. https://www.wola.org/files /mxgt/report/.

Iskandar, Natasha. 2010. *Creative State: Forty Years of Migration and Development Policy in Morocco and Mexico*. Ithaca, NY: Cornell University Press.

Keck, Margaret E., and Kathryn Sikkink. 1998. *Activists Beyond Borders: Advocacy Networks in International Politics*. Ithaca, NY: Cornell University Press.

Krogstad, Jens Manuel, Jeffrey S. Passel, and D'Vera Cohn. 2016. "5 Facts about Illegal Immigration in the U.S." *FactTank*, November 3. Washington, DC: Pew Research Center. http://www.pewresearch.org/fact-tank/2016/11/03/5-facts-about -illegal-immigration-in-the-u-s/.

———. 2017. "5 Facts About Illegal Immigration in the U.S." *FactTank*, April 27. Washington, DC: Pew Research Center. http://www.pewresearch.org/fact-tank/2017/04 /27/5-facts-about-illegal-immigration-in-the-u-s/.

La Jornada. 2004. "1988: Fraude sin castigo." Editorial, *La Jornada*, March 16. http:// www.jornada.com.mx/2004/03/16/edito.php?fly=2.

Lahav, Gallya. 1998. "Immigration and the State: The Devolution and Privatisation of Immigration Control in the EU." *Journal of Ethnic and Migration Studies* 24 (4): 674–694.

Landolt, Patricia, and Luin Goldring. 2010. "Political Cultures and Transnational Social Fields: Chileans, Colombians and Canadian Activists in Toronto." *Global Networks* 10 (4): 443–466. http://doi.org/10.1111/j.1471-0374.2010.00290.x.

———. 2016. "Inequality and Assemblages of Noncitizenship in an Age of Migration." *Discover Society* 31 (April). https://discoversociety.org/2016/04/05/inequa lity-and-assemblages-of-noncitizenship-in-an-age-of-migration/.

Law, Anna O. 2017. "This Is How Trump's Deportations Differ from Obama's." *Washington Post*, May 3. https://www.washingtonpost.com/news/monkey-cage/wp/2017 /05/03/this-is-how-trumps-deportations-differ-from-obamas/?utm_term=.48 d0470fdd82.

López, Gustavo, and Jens Manuel Krogstad. 2017. "Key Facts About Unauthorized Immigrants Enrolled in DACA." *Fact Tank*, September 25. Washington, DC: Pew Research Center. http://www.pewresearch.org/fact-tank/2017/09/25/key-facts -about-unauthorized-immigrants-enrolled-in-daca/.

Macklin, Audrey. 2005. "Disappearing Refugees: Reflections on the Canada-U.S. Safe Third Country Agreement." *Columbia Human Rights Law Review* 36 (2): 365–426.

Margheritis, Ana. 2015. *Migration Governance across Regions: State-Diaspora Relations in the Latin America-Southern Europe Corridor*. New York: Routledge.

Markusoff, Jason, Nancy Macdonald, Aaron Hutchins, and Meagan Campbell. 2017. "How Canada's Border Towns Are Dealing with a Growing Stream of Refugees." *Macleans*, July 11. http://www.macleans.ca/down-on-the-border/.

Martínez, Oscar. 2014. *The Beast: Riding the Rails and Dodging Narcos on the Migrant Trail*. London: Verso.

Mayda, Anna Maria. 2006. "Who Is against Immigration? A Cross-Country Investigation of Individual Attitudes toward Immigrants." *Review of Economics and Statistics* 88 (3): 510–530.

Maynard, Robyn. 2018. "Do Black Migrants Lives Matter at the U.S.-Canada Border?" Opinion, *The Star* (Toronto), January 23. https://www.thestar.com/opinion/contributors/2018/01/23/do-black-migrants-lives-matter-at-the-us-canada-border.html.

McKay, Sonia, Eugenia Markova, and Anna Paraskevopoulou. 2012. *Undocumented Workers' Transitions: Legal Status, Migration, and Work in Europe*. New York: Routledge.

Migration Policy Institute. 2018. *Global Remittances Guide*. Washington, DC: Migration Policy Institute. https://www.migrationpolicy.org/programs/data-hub/global-remittances-guide.

Mummert, Gail. 2014. "Tout reste en famille (transnationale): Des alternatives pour élever les enfants des migra." In *Adoptions, dons et abandons au Mexique et en Colombie: Des parents vulnérables*, edited by Françoise Lestage and María Eugenia Olavarria, 107–140. Paris: L'Harmattan.

National Conference of State Legislatures (NCSL). 2018. "Immigration and State Immigration Laws Information and Summaries." State Immigration Laws. Denver: NCSL. http://www.ncsl.org/research/immigration.aspx.

Nevins, Joseph. 2002. *Operation Gatekeeper: The Rise of the "Illegal Alien" and the Making of the US-Mexico Boundary*. New York: Routledge.

Parrado, Emilio A. 2011. "How High Is Hispanic/Mexican Fertility in the United States? Immigration and Tempo Considerations." *Demography* 48 (3): 1059–1080.

Pedroza, Luicy, Pau Palop, and Bert Hoffmann. 2016. *Emigrant Policies in Latin America and the Caribbean*. Santiago, Chile: FLACSO Chile. https://www.giga-hamburg.de/en/publication/emigrant-policies-in-latin-america-and-the-caribbean.

Pries, Ludger, ed. 2008. *Rethinking Transnationalism: The Meso-Link of Organisations*. London: Routledge.

Ramakrishnan, S. Karthick, and Irene Bloemraad. 2008. "Making Organizations Count: Immigrant Civic Engagement in California Cities." In *Civic Hopes and Political Realities: Immigrants, Community Organizations, and Political Engagement*, edited by S. Karthick Ramakrishnan and Irene Bloemraad, 45–76. New York: Russell Sage Foundation.

Rehaag, Sean. 2016. "2016 Refugee Claim Data and IRB Member Recognition Rates." Montreal: Canadian Council for Refugees. http://ccrweb.ca/en/2016-refugee-claim-data.

———. 2017. "Holding Refugees Hostage at Legal Aid Ontario." *Slaw: Canada's Online Legal Magazine*, June 19. http://www.slaw.ca/2017/06/19/holding-refugees-hostage-at-legal-aid-ontario/.

Rein, Lisa. 2017. "Trump Plan to Hire 15,000 Border and Immigration Personnel Isn't

Justified, Federal Watchdog Says." *Washington Post*, July 2. https://www.washing
tonpost.com.

Reitz, Jeffrey G. 1998. *Warmth of the Welcome: The Social Causes of Economic Success for Immigrants in Different Nations and Cities*. Boulder, CO: Westview.

Rios Contreras, Viridiana. 2014. "The Role of Drug-Related Violence and Extortion in Promoting Mexican Migration: Unexpected Consequences of a Drug War." *Latin American Research Review* 49 (3): 199–217.

Romero, Mary. 2008. "Go after the Women: Mothers against Illegal Aliens' Campaign against Mexican Immigrant Women and Their Children." *Indiana Law Journal* 83: 1355–1389.

Rosas, Gilberto. 2012. *Barrio Libre: Criminalizing States and Delinquent Refusals of the New Frontier*. Durham, NC: Duke University Press.

Rubio Díaz Leal, Laura, and Brenda Pérez Vázquez. 2016. "Desplazados por violencia. La tragedia invisible." *Nexos*, January 1. http://www.nexos.com.mx/?p=27278.

Santa Ana, Otto. 2002. *Brown Tide Rising: Metaphors of Latinos in Contemporary American Public Discourse*. Austin: University of Texas Press.

Sharma, Nandita Rani. 2006. *Home Economics: Nationalism and the Making of "Migrant Workers" in Canada*. Toronto: University of Toronto Press.

Sherman, Rachel. 1999. "From State Introversion to State Extension in Mexico: Modes of Emigrant Incorporation, 1900–1997." *Theory and Society* 28 (6): 835–878.

Simalchik, Joan. 1993. "Part of the Awakening: Canadian Churches and Chilean Refugees, 1970–1979." Thesis, University of Toronto.

Somers, Margaret R. 2008. *Genealogies of Citizenship: Markets, Statelessness and the Right to Have Rights*. Cambridge, England: Cambridge University Press.

Telles, Edward E., and Vilma Ortiz. 2008. *Generations of Exclusion: Mexican Americans, Assimilation, and Race*. New York: Russell Sage Foundation.

US Customs and Border Protection (CPB). 2015. "Southwest Border Unaccompanied Alien Children Statistics FY 2015." Washington, DC: CPB. https://www.cbp.gov/newsroom/stats/southwest-border-unaccompanied-children/fy-2015.

US Immigrations and Customs Enforcement (ICE). 2017. "Fiscal Year 2017 ICE Enforcement and Removal Operations Report." Washington, DC: ICE. https://www.ice.gov/removal-statistics/2017.

Varsanyi, Monica W., Paul G. Lewis, Doris Marie Provine, and Scott Decker. 2012. "A Multilayered Jurisdictional Patchwork: Immigration Federalism in the United States." *Law and Policy* 34 (2): 138–158.

Villegas, Paloma E. 2015. "Fishing for Precarious Status Migrants: Surveillant Assemblages of Migrant Illegalization in Toronto, Canada." *Journal of Law and Society* 42 (2): 230–252.

Vogt, Wendy A. 2013. "Crossing Mexico: Structural Violence and the Commodification of Undocumented Central American Migrants." *American Ethnologist* 40 (4): 764–780.

Vosko, Leah F. 2006. *Precarious Employment: Understanding Labour Market Insecurity in Canada*. Montreal: McGill-Queen's Press.

———. 2016. "Blacklisting as a Modality of Deportability: Mexico's Response to Circular Migrant Agricultural Workers' Pursuit of Collective Bargaining Rights in British Columbia, Canada." *Journal of Ethnic and Migration Studies* 42 (8): 1371–1387.

Vosko, Leah F., and Mark Thomas. 2014. "Confronting the Employment Standards Enforcement Gap: Exploring the Potential for Union Engagement with Employment Law in Ontario, Canada." *Journal of Industrial Relations* 56 (5): 631–652.

Wang, Hansi Lo. 2014. "Language Barriers Pose Challenges for Mayan Migrant Children." *Code Switch: Race and Identity Remixed*, July 1. NPR. https://www.npr.org/sections/codeswitch/2014/07/01/326426927/language-barriers-pose-challenges-for-mayan-migrant-children.

Wouk, Judith, Soojin Yu, Lisa Roach, Jessie Thomson, and Anmarie Harris. 2006. "Unaccompanied/Separated Minors and Refugee Protection in Canada: Filling Information Gaps." *Refuge: Canada's Journal on Refugees* 23 (2): 125–138. https://refuge.journals.yorku.ca/index.php/refuge/article/view/21360/20030.

Wright, Matthew, and Irene Bloemraad. 2012. "Is There a Trade-Off between Multiculturalism and Socio-Political Integration? Policy Regimes and Immigrant Incorporation in Comparative Perspective." *Perspectives on Politics* 10 (1): 77–95.

Zuberi, Dan. 2006. *Differences That Matter: Social Policy and the Working Poor in the United States and Canada*. Ithaca, NY: ILR Press.

CHAPTER 1

Mexican Migrant Civil Society: Propositions for Discussion

JONATHAN FOX AND GASPAR RIVERA-SALGADO

Migrant collective action is often grounded in transnational communities and shared collective identities. These social foundations constitute the basis of migrant civil society, which emerges in locally grounded public spaces that extend across national borders and expresses migrants' capacity for self-representation in the public sphere. Simply put, "migrant civil society" refers to migrant-led membership organizations and public institutions. Specifically, it includes four arenas of collective actors and actions: migrant-led membership organizations, migrant-led nongovernmental organizations (NGOs), autonomous public spaces such as large-scale cultural or political gatherings, and migrant-led media.[1]

To spell out what the four arenas look like, *membership organizations* are composed primarily of migrants and can range from hometown associations to worker organizations, religious associations, and indigenous rights groups. They tend to come together around four broad collective identities — territory of origin, shared faith, work, and ethnicity. Sometimes these multiple identities overlap, as in the cases of Oaxacan Catholics in Los Angeles or religious farmworkers in the US Midwest, where union leaders have been known to preside over weddings and baptisms. The second arena involves *migrant-led NGOs*. Because of the emphasis here on repertoires of self-representation, this category does not include those many nongovernmental organizations or nonprofits that serve migrant communities but are not directed by migrants themselves. One must keep in mind the distinction between NGOs and membership organizations, a distinction elided in the fuzzy US term "community-based organization." The key difference is who governs them; NGOs report to self-appointed boards of directors, while the leaders of membership organizations are ostensibly accountable to the members themselves.[2] *Public spaces* are gatherings where migrants set the agenda and can interact and express themselves with relative freedom

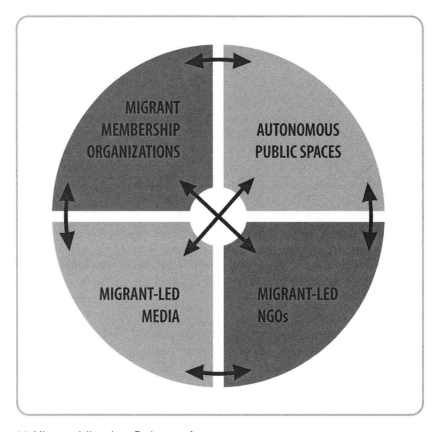

1.1. Migrant civil society: Pathways of synergy

and autonomy. Culture, religion, sports, and recreation encourage collective identity and a sense of belonging. *Migrant-led media* also bolster collective identity and voice. Migrant-led media include nonprofit initiatives but also extend beyond the traditional boundaries of civil society to encompass individuals and institutions in commercial media. In practice, the boundaries between these four arenas are blurred, and each can reinforce the others, as illustrated in figure 1.1.

This approach emphasizes the analytical importance of recognizing migrant-led organizations as a set of civic, social, and political actors that are qualitatively distinct from the advocacy organizations that most mass media, politicians, and scholars treat as the main interlocutors speaking on behalf of immigrants in the United States. In other words, the proposition here is that "pro-immigrant" and "immigrant-led" are not synonymous. The underlying question is one of who speaks on behalf of immigrants. While most observers and scholars elide that distinction, it matters to organized immigrants. The questions of representation and whose voice is heard become especially relevant when one is trying to understand the political discourse and advocacy positions of different actors regarding the ongoing immigration policy debate. For example, pro-immigrant political forces have been willing and able to take positions in the comprehensive immigration reform debate in the US Congress that may or may not have represented the interests of the undocumented population. During the brief window of political opportunity during the Obama administration, the leading pro-immigrant advocacy groups and their elected allies insisted on an eventual path to citizenship, a requirement that appears to have prevented winning over some Republicans to vote in favor of mass regularization. As designed in this insider compromise, the proposed pathway to citizenship was quite long and indirect, and it offered uncertain results. In this case, the positions of US civil rights–oriented organizations may not have taken into account the primary concerns of undocumented workers, which may have been regularization rather than a much more hypothetical pathway to citizenship. Yet immigrants' own organizations had little influence in the legislative agenda-setting process. The question is not whether political tradeoffs were made in the search for a viable comprehensive reform proposal; they clearly were, as in accepting a hardening of the border. The issue is whose views counted when the pros and cons of those policy tradeoffs were assessed and negotiating positions were staked out. Indeed, when the Dreamers movement—the undocumented youth movement that burst into the national political scene in the spring of 2010 with a flurry of occupations, hunger strikes, and demonstrations calling for support of the DREAM Act (Development, Relief, and Education for Alien Minors Act)—became a national political force, one of its main demands was to have a seat at the table when strategies and policies affecting them were discussed (Nicholls 2013). The Dreamers' capacity for self-representation, beginning in California and spreading across the country, transformed what had been a coalition of US immigration reform groups into a much more bottom-up, decentralized movement targeting multiple levels of government.

The rationale for focusing on the migrant-led dimension of civil society is to encourage migrant actors, observers, and potential allies to recognize the organizations through which migrants have strengthened their capacity for self-representation; such recognition would then serve as a basis for more balanced coalition building with other actors, notably US liberal elites. This is not to suggest that migrant-led and pro-immigration organizations are completely separate from each other, just that they are in some ways distinct. Migrant civil societies often emerge in dialogue with a broader civil society, though whether those relations are local, long-distance, or both varies widely.[3]

The "migrant civil society" umbrella category of collective actors and public spaces involves many different kinds of migrants. Migrants' varying degrees of rootedness in their countries of residence influence their capacity for building autonomous institutions and their capacity for self-representation. Meanwhile, within settled immigrant worker communities, legal status and the political environment also determine the capacity for collective action. Migrants also have differing interests and abilities to remain engaged with their homelands. States and societies of origin, in turn, differ in the degree to which they view their diasporas as remaining part of them. Often one of the central dilemmas for migrant individuals and their families is how to overcome the feeling of being from "neither here nor there" (Zavella 2011). Similarly, the challenge for migrant civil societies is overcoming exclusionary attitudes in sending and host societies to achieve recognition and inclusion both here and there.[4]

The concept of a migrant civil society is the point of departure for the following seven propositions, each of which is informed by a combination of research, coalition-building experience, and advocacy practice. The propositions address a series of related analytical questions involving migrant organizations, the struggle for migrant rights, and strategies to alleviate poverty and violence in sending communities and create viable alternatives to future migration. The propositions are illustrated by specific cases. While wide-ranging, the examples are not meant to represent the entire terrain of organizations, networks, and fields of activity covered by the concept of migrant civil society.

1. Forms of migrant organization are shaped by migrants themselves, by their political-institutional environments, and finally by nonmigrant allies in host countries.

As happens in collective action more generally, migrants do not organize in a vacuum. Their capacity to find the free spaces needed to come together in pursuit of common goals depends heavily on their social, civic, political, and spatial environments. Freedom of movement and of association are fundamental—yet those freedoms vary widely across countries, workplaces, and communities and depend heavily on individuals' immigration status. Similarly, access to the kinds of information needed to organize, including shared language, is highly uneven, yet such access is crucial for identifying potential allies and assessing opportunities for change.

Access to civil and social rights for migrants can be highly uneven within countries and across issue areas. An example is the disconnect between kinds of rights in the United States. On the one hand, undocumented workers are highly vulnerable to deportation and have limited rights to due process. On the other hand, migrants' children have a constitutional right to attend public school, migrants have the legal right at least on paper to receive care in hospital emergency rooms and be provided with interpreters, and their employers are nominally obliged to respect federal minimum wage and occupational safety laws (e.g., Gleeson 2010).

The local, national, social, and political forces of the host country—including its religious institutions, trade unions, legal defense groups, and political parties—also determine the availability of potential allies for migrant rights.[5] However, the density and disposition of potential allies within host countries can vary geographically as well as across languages, religions, issue areas, and ideologies. Migrants who share languages, religions, or ideologies within host-country civil societies are likely to have more opportunities to build strong social ties across borders.

The political-institutional environment that determines the possibilities for migrant action includes the government policies in countries of origin and transit. In the face of systemic, unpunished violations of the rights of transmigrants in Mexico, until very recently Central Americans in Mexico did not dare to come out publicly and protest their treatment. Conversely, the Mexican government has responded to the demands of its nationals in the United States and taken an active role in defending them and advocating for the undocumented in numerous ways. One of the most notable official Mexican responses has been to grant millions of consular IDs (*matrículas consulares*).[6] The Mexican government and immigrant defense organizations have persuaded many local government agencies, among them police and financial institutions, to accept the documents as official IDs. Despite these efforts, many Mexicans remain doubly undocumented in that they lack official recognition from the United States and their own country.[7]

One way to sum up this proposition is that "context matters" (Bada et al. 2010). That is, the local environment for organizing often varies widely within both the country of settlement and the country of origin. There are two major sources of this variation. First, the power of opponents of migrant rights is unevenly distributed. Second, the power of potential migrant allies is unevenly distributed within countries. In the United States the possibilities for forming powerful coalitions vary greatly because immigrant-friendly US institutions are much stronger in some cities than in others. Notably, supportive churches, labor unions, and Spanish-language broadcast media are dispersed unevenly across the US landscape. The core infrastructure for immigrant rights mobilization in the United States rests not so much on national organizations as on multisectoral, city-level coalitions that bring together migrant-led and US organizations. Importantly, the breadth and density of immigrants' most consistent coalition partners—the institutions of US Latino civil society—are vastly different across cities and states, as is US Latino citizens' capacity to organize politically (Bada et al. 2010).

Another way to illustrate how local political context matters is to examine how migrant-led organizations are shaped by migrants' own political backgrounds, the overall political situation, and the density of the civil society network where they live. Interaction between political capital and institutionalized local political structures gives rise to diverse political expressions in regions with high densities of both. This political diversity is reflected in the paths immigration reform campaigners have followed since 2001, when the DREAM Act to regularize child migrants was introduced in the US Senate, and especially after the December 2005 introduction of the Sensenbrenner bill in Congress to criminalize violations of federal immigration law, which triggered massive marches in the spring of 2006 (Bada, Fox, and Selee 2006; Voss and Bloemraad 2011).

The comprehensive immigration reform campaign was led by US civil rights–oriented advocacy organizations and their political allies from a center of gravity in Washington, DC. Though some analysts argue that the DC-based organizations that led the campaign, such as the National Immigration Law Center and the Center for Community Change, pursued a DC-insider strategy (Nicholls and Fiorito 2015), the groups also built a broad network of allies in Los Angeles, New York, Chicago, and many other cities. The Center for Community Change launched the Fair Immigration Reform Movement (FIRM) in 2000; FIRM's Immigrant Organizing Committee included some thirty groups including the Casa de Maryland, Gamaliel Foundation, Illinois Coalition for Immigrant and Refugee Rights, Massachusetts Immigrant and Refugee Advocacy Coalition, New York Immigration Coalition, and Coalition for Humane Immigrant Rights of Los Angeles (CHIRLA). Though the national conveners were US organizations, many of the citywide coalitions were migrant-led. That said, in contrast to those network members that were close politically to mainstream US organizations aligned with the Democratic Party, other migrant-led groups like the National Day Laborer Organizing Network, Central American Resource Center, and Dignity Campaign were more willing to openly criticize the Obama administration's immigration enforcement strategy and especially its Secure Communities program, which pushed local police forces to collaborate with immigration authorities.[8]

The national campaign revealed migrants' limited access to agenda setting. Such uneven terrain is especially relevant because while migrants have unquestionably demonstrated their capacity to build their own social and civic institutions, their capacity to take the next step and create one clear voice and secure political power in the policy process requires building coalitions with established institutions such as FIRM. Creating a shared space at the city or state level can, in turn, influence when and how migrants choose to engage in advocacy and collective action. This virtuous circle represents an important potential pathway for migrant empowerment but one that will become visible only if diverse patterns of civic engagement are unpacked at the local level. One must recognize the diversity of political practices and coalitions developed by different migrant-led organizations and networks to understand the opportunities and constraints they face.

2. The organizations that constitute migrant civil society are based on multiple, often overlapping collective identities.

Like collective action more generally, migrant organizations emerge from a combination of shared interests and identities. Some groups come together based primarily on their shared community or nationality of origin, perhaps encouraged by home-country governments or nongovernmental actors in either country.[9] Yet in terms of organizing, shared migrant identities are a double-edged sword; while they facilitate some organizing strategies, they can hinder others.

Other migrant rights groups, in contrast, bring together migrants from several countries, most notably to focus on the shared struggle for worker rights or legal status. In receiving societies, core issues concerning human rights and legal status can create shared interests among migrants who otherwise differ in terms of national origin, language, ethnicity, class, caste, or ideology. Despite such objectively shared interests, conscious political strategies are usually required to bring together migrant workers of different national origins. This is even the case where migrants from different countries share a language, as with Latino immigrant worker organizing initiatives in the United States, often led by immigrants who were politicized in their home countries.[10]

In migrant rights organizing, one of the most important distinctions is between groups that primarily relate to their home countries and those that primarily focus on their countries of residence. Over time, however, the distinction has eroded as an increasing number of migrant organizations pursue agendas that are both here and there. Migrants organize through multiple channels simultaneously, coming together as employees at their workplaces, for example, or as women or members of distinct ethnic groups—especially when their roles in the labor market or community are specifically gendered or racialized. At the same time, migrants may organize as members of the same villages of origin when supporting community development back home or as citizens of their home countries and/or supporters of homeland political parties when they call on their own governments to respond to their concerns. Yet while migrants often pursue different agendas simultaneously through different organizations, their full repertoire of actions may not be visible to migrants' potential allies.[11]

One such unnoticed example of migrant organizing involves the complex and lively debates about immigrant identities and political practices unfolding in migrant-led media. Antonieta Mercado (2011) argues that the proliferation of migrant-led media in the United States in recent decades has led to an accumulation of Mexican migrant communication practices particularly among indigenous migrants, an expression of what she and others call "cosmopolitan citizenship."[12] Mercado further asserts that "those practices offer a good example of how cosmopolitan engagement across nations is constructed from below, enriching instead of limiting the conception of citizenship" (2011:xxiv–xxv). The online station Radio TexMex FM-Identidad Migrante links migrant communities by bringing news from Mexico and the United States to a binational audience. The station has developed strategic partnerships with hometown associations, NGOs, advocacy organizations, and governmental offices on both sides of the border.[13]

In another of Mercado's case studies (2015) she demonstrates how migrant-led media within the Oaxacan community in the United States have played an important role in increasing the subgroup's public visibility. Its visibility is all the more impressive in a context in which ethnic difference within the Mexican migrant community is generally ignored (Fox and Rivera-Salgado 2004). Mercado (2015) analyzes issues of *El Tequio*, which was published by the Frente Indígena de Organizaciones Binacionales from 1991 through 2010, first as a monthly newsletter, then as a quarterly magazine beginning in 2006, and finally as a digital publication in 2015. Oaxacan-led migrant media also include the binational weekly radio show *La Hora Mixteca* transmitted by the Fresno-based Radio Bilingüe binational network; *El Oaxaqueño*, a weekly newspaper that circulated simultaneously in Los Angeles and Oaxaca City from 1999 to 2010; and the biweekly newspaper *Impulso de Oaxaca*, which appeared in Los Angeles in 2004. These migrant-led media initiatives fostered a powerful sense of community among their readers and listeners.

Commercial migrant-led media are also relevant for understanding how migrant collective identities are constructed and embedded in the community. Although commercial enterprises do not fit into the classic definition of civil society, an argument can be made that some new commercial media projects geared toward the Latino population, immigrant and US-born, overlap with the goals of nonprofit, migrant-led media initiatives. Both provide platforms on which to discuss political agendas and migrant-related issues.[14] For instance, commercial Spanish-language TV and radio obviously played a central role in mounting and guiding the unprecedented spring 2006 mass mobilizations in defense of immigrant rights (Bada, Fox, and Selee 2006).

The commercial Spanish-language media's civic leadership is especially evident in Noticias Univision (Univision News), which has publicly voiced concerns of the Latino community throughout the recent surge in strong anti-immigrant rhetoric.[15] Jorge Ramos, a leading Univision news anchor, has famously become a vocal advocate of the Latino community and a critic of Donald Trump (Calmes 2015). Ramos has declared, "Our position [at Noticias Univision] is clearly pro-Latino or pro-immigrant. . . . We are simply being the voice of those who don't have a voice" (in James 2013b). Based on their coverage of the 2016 presidential campaign, one can conclude that US Spanish mainstream commercial media—the two national TV networks, Univision and Telemundo, as well as radio and print media—are heavily pro-immigrant (Parkeraug 2015).

Another example of commercial migrant-focused media is the Fusion TV cable channel. This English-dominant, second-generation-oriented channel was launched in October 2013 in a partnership between Univision and ABC (James 2013a,b). Fusion relies on the star power of Univision's Jorge Ramos hosting the weekly program *Real America* and of Mexican-born León Krauze, news anchor at Univision's Los Angeles station KMEX-TV, Channel 34, and former host of Fusion's *Open Source* (Calmes 2015; Gabriel 2015; Johnson 2013). In 2018 Ramos had 3.3 million Twitter followers, more than all US Latino political leaders combined, demonstrating that commercial migrant-oriented media contribute to collective identity formation, a key component of civil society. Moreover, the institutions and individuals of commercial Spanish-language media have played an explicitly civic role, encouraging collective action and a defense of migrant rights, thereby blurring the conventional boundaries that define civil society.

3. Balancing the differences between service-oriented and defensive work on the one hand and more strategic policy advocacy work on the other requires sustained exchanges and deliberate strategies.

Supporting migrant workers takes many different forms. Migrants face hardships and traumas that affect them daily. Accordingly, it is important and necessary to have organizations that can aid them directly, whether by visiting them at detention centers, preparing them for return migrations, counseling them, or providing shelter for distressed workers. The list of potential issues is long. Service-oriented work in response to the problems will be forever needed if their roots are not addressed through focused policy advocacy. Without a deliberate strategy to initiate policy changes that protect the rights of migrants at each step in the migration process, there will be no end to the exploitation.

For organizations working on the US side, advocacy, politics, and service are part of their DNA despite the traditional view that nonprofit organizations do not engage in politics because of restrictions imposed on charity organizations in the United States.[16] An example of the mixture of advocacy, political activism, and service is seen in the work of the Coalition for Humane Immigrant Rights of Los Angeles (CHIRLA); its work includes legal services, policy advocacy, civic engagement, community organizing, and community education. CHIRLA has spun off a separate legal entity and incorporated it as a political action committee to allow the coalition to fully engage in the political process by lobbying openly for immigrant-friendly laws in California and by mobilizing members to support specific political fights and elections. Similar trends are visible among the largest immigrant advocacy organizations in other parts of the country, notably in Chicago, Los Angeles, New York, and the DC metro area.[17]

A new development in the consolidation of migrant civil society at the transnational level has been the emergence of Mexican actors defending immigrant rights in the United States as well as the rights of transmigrants within Mexico. The diverse mix of primarily Mexican organizations ranges from university research centers, both private and public, to legal advocacy organizations and shelters run by Catholic Charities. Several US-based organizations participate in the network. The advocacy network has taken shape as the Colectivo Migraciones para las Américas (COMPA).[18] It emerged in 2013 to advocate that Mexico's incoming government include a migration policy focusing on development, human rights, and gender in its 2013–2018 National Development Plan. The federal government ostensibly uses the plan to outline its priorities and asks the Mexican Congress to appropriate funds accordingly. The government eventually published a set of migration policy priorities, some of which responded to COMPA's suggestions, in the Special Migration Program, the Programa Especial de Migración 2014–2018.[19]

The adoption of the Special Migration Program, the first comprehensive Mexican government policy framework, as part of the National Development Plan was an important achievement for COMPA, which substantially influenced the process. The program was dropped in 2017, and the difficult task remains of sustaining the coordination among the many NGOs that came together to push for the policy.

COMPA set out to develop a public education campaign to promote inclusive and democratic participation in Mexican immigration policy issues, building on the work begun by several of its founding organizations. The network's original name was Colectivo Plan Nacional de Desarrollo-Migración (Colectivo PND-Migración). It sought to coordinate the efforts of several NGOs along with national and international networks to tackle issues surrounding migration from Mexico to the United States and the migration from Central American countries through Mexican territory. Its innovation was to network and advocate within Mexico on behalf of Central Americans and Mexican migrant communities of origin. At the time it was quite novel for Mexican civil society organizations to recognize their country not only as a sender but also as a receiver of immigrants. The network's stated objective was nothing short of building "a transnational strategic migration agenda, inclusive of the diverse expressions from the community itself and of the church's areas of work, with work aimed to support migrants and other emerging issues."[20]

Another migrant-led organization, the Frente Indígena de Organizaciones Binacionales (FIOB, Binational Front of Indigenous Organizations), has responded in similar ways across its three sites of activity—Oaxaca, Baja California, and California. Its strategy has been to separate the FIOB as a political membership organization from the service component, setting up sister organizations registered as nonprofits in states on both sides of the US-Mexico border. This arrangement is working relatively well in California, where FIOB-California maintains close relations with the Centro Binacional para el Desarrollo Indígena Oaxaqueño (Binational Center for Oaxacan Indigenous Development), a nonprofit service organization. FIOB-Oaxaca has been successful in working with its counterpart Desarrollo Binacional Integral Indígena, which itself has partnered with several national and international funding organizations to foster economic development and capacity-building opportunities for migrant-sending communities in Oaxaca. This arrangement has proven to be less fruitful in Baja California, where FIOB-Baja California has had limited success in developing its service-providing counterpart organization, Cuvandi Ichi (Haciendo Camino).

Tension exists between advocacy and service, but organizations have adopted strategies to respond to immigrant communities' increasing need for services and to engage in the political process while navigating different political and geographical contexts.

4. Migrant organizations often come together in networks, but only some networks can sustain coalitions.[21]

In practice, the term "coalition" is often used interchangeably with "network," "campaign," and "movement." The terms all refer to efforts in which distinct actors come together with the expectation that the whole will be greater than the sum of its parts. However, these everyday terms describe very different kinds of relations between partners, and it is useful to distinguish between them. While it may seem merely academic to differentiate a network from a coalition, a more nuanced approach could be useful insofar as partnerships are bolstered by agreed-upon expectations regarding their goals and capacities.

What, then, are the differences between networks, coalitions, and movements? There are many definitions of "network." Margaret Keck and Kathryn Sikkink's classic study offers a succinct formulation: "Networks are forms of organization characterized by voluntary, reciprocal, and horizontal patterns of communication and exchange" (1998:8). Coalitions, in contrast, are partnerships of distinct actors that coordinate action in pursuit of shared goals (Fox 2010).

The actual use of these terms can be confusing. Some dense coalitions refer to themselves as networks. Some thin networks refer to themselves as coalitions. While coalitions often begin as associations of organizations, the coalition leadership or staff can in effect become an organization, retaining the coalition label but not the practice of representing diverse constituent member groups. Coalitions that attempt to sustain representation of diverse constituencies face the challenges of seeking balance while crossing boundaries of class, gender, race, language, and national origins.

Some coalitions of disparate actors describe themselves as movements, overstating their degree of cohesion and shared collective identity (Fox 2010). Some movements, in turn, may identify themselves as coalitions of organizations. The global justice movement of the 1990s and 2000s was described as a "movement of movements." One way to frame the distinction between networks, coalitions, and movements is to consider each term as referring to a different point along a continuum of organizational density and social cohesion. Networks, coalitions, and movements can all engage in campaigns, which usually are joint actions with specific goals, targets, and time horizons. When networks do engage in actual campaigns, though, they pivot from communication and exchange to joint action and behave more like coalitions.

It is puzzling that while movements are always grounded in social networks, only some social networks generate movements. The idea of movements also implies a high degree of shared collective identity, yet neither networks nor coalitions *necessarily* involve significant horizontal exchange between participants. Indeed, many transnational networks and coalitions rely on a handful of interlocutors to manage relations between broad-based social organizations that may have relatively little awareness of the nature and actions of their counterparts. At the same time, some transnational movements achieve such a high degree of shared symbolism that active members can identify strongly with each other in spite of quite limited direct contact, as in the emblematic case of the anti-apartheid movement of the 1970s and 1980s.

The concept of transnational social movements suggests a much higher degree of density and much more cohesion than is involved in networks or coalitions. The more precise term "transnational movement organization" implies an organized membership base in more than one country, as in the Binational Front of Indigenous Organizations (FIOB) in the United States and Mexico. And yet many migrant organizations, though transnational in their worldviews and agendas, do not have organized social bases in their countries of origin.

Distinguishing between networks, coalitions, and movements also helps to avoid blurring political differences and power imbalances within what may appear from the outside to be homogeneous transnational movements. Keck and Sikkink point out that transnational networks face the challenge of developing a "common frame of meaning" in spite of cross-cultural differences (1998:7). In practice, such shared meanings are socially constructed through joint action and mutual understanding rather than merely through professed values and goals. Political differences within transnational networks are not to be underestimated, either, despite the apparently shared goals of their members.

One of the questions, then, is under what conditions networks become more goal-oriented coalitions capable of producing joint action. Coalitions are often a means to an end, but while the interest-based principle "The enemy of my enemy is my friend" may be enough to account for coalition formation among nation-states or political parties, it is rarely sufficient inspiration for civil society actors. Shared political ideologies certainly facilitate coalition formation, but they are not a precondition for it. Some basis for shared values is often crucial in bringing civil society organizations together in spite of their many differences. As a practical matter, shared targets are usually necessary to translate feelings of solidarity into joint action. Shared targets, simply put, help diverse groups to answer the ever-present question "What is to be done?"

Transnational exchanges between social organizations can produce networks, which can produce coalitions, which can in turn produce movements. Underscoring the distinctions does not imply any judgment that more cross-border cooperation is better. On the contrary, realistic expectations about what is possible are necessary to sustain collective action. Cross-border cooperation involves costs and risks that must be taken into account, and it depends heavily on finding appropriate counterparts with whom to ally.

These conceptual points draw from the Diálogos exchanges between social organizations in Mexico, the United States, and Canada in 1988–1998. The goal of this series of structured multisectoral conversations was to bring together counterparts to share perspectives on the social and political dimensions of North American integration. The concept of counterpart social organizations and public interest groups implies not similarity or agreement but rather analogous roles in their respective societies (Brooks 1992; Brooks and Fox 2002). In the US-Mexico-Canada Diálogos context, the strategy involved bringing together unions of auto workers, telephone workers, and teachers with family farm organizations, immigrant rights defenders, environmental activists, and human rights advocates to sit at the same table across from their respective cross-border counterparts in each sector or issue area. In contrast to solidarity gatherings, many of the counterparts did not share underlying political ideologies or even specific political stances on, say, NAFTA. Most were primarily domestically oriented groups that were addressing globalization for the first time. The structured conversations led to greater mutual understanding, and the terms of engagement included a willingness to agree to disagree as a basis for finding specific areas of common ground.

5. The construction of civil society coalitions that bring together organizations from host and sending countries requires a conscious strategy and sustained investment.

This proposition raises the question of what kind of social, civic, or political organization has the will and capacity to sustain strategic investments in immigrant organizing and coalition building. Conventional partisan political actors in the United States are primarily interested in citizens and, in particular, high-propensity voters in swing states. The social justice and internationalist elements within private philanthropic organizations can take a longer-term view, though they also can accede to the imperative to emphasize short-term results and adopt reactive strategies. Trade unions have certainly played a key role in immigrant gateway cities, and some have been revived by immigrant membership, but their rapidly shrinking presence in the private labor market limits their bargaining power. Outside of immigrant gateway cities, a substantial fraction of union members appears to be vulnerable to political messages that blame immigrants and international trade for the loss of high-paying manufacturing jobs, especially in the Rust Belt.

US citizen-led civil rights and immigrant defense organizations are on the front lines of immigrant organizing, supported by various foundations and unions, but outside of immigrant gateway cities, they often tend to be on the defensive. Meanwhile, the founding era of immigrant hometown organizing during the 1990s was driven in part by a different kind of external actor, the Mexican state itself, through its consular apparatus in the United States. Coalition building between the different kinds of organizations raises the question of who actually speaks for immigrants.

As immigrant organizing has tended to depend to varying degrees on external allies, how can migrant-led organizations build their own capacity for influencing organizing strategies? By the mid-2000s, some of them began to claim a larger role in representing their own perspectives. The National Alliance of Latin American and Caribbean Communities was formed in 2004 as a migrant-led organization to improve the quality of life for its member communities in the United States and their countries of origin. After its first decade, it was renamed Alianza Américas in 2015 to better reflect the increasing diversity of its member organizations. Alianza Américas seeks to build transnational leadership and has devoted a great deal of its work on reforming US immigration policies that address the root causes of migration as well as on challenges faced by migrants in the United States. Alianza Américas' cross-border advocacy engagement with home-country policies distinguishes it from other immigrant-led organizations. At the same time, its migrant-led character distinguishes it from established US Latino organizations that have close ties with elected officials.

The emergence of the Red Mexicana de Líderes y Organizaciones Migrantes (Mexican Network of Migrant Leaders and Organizations) exemplifies the complex process of consolidating specifically Mexican immigrant-led transnational coalitions that are developing their own long-term strategies. The network was incubated within the alliance now called Alianza Américas, which included some of the largest and most consolidated federations of Mexican hometown associations, especially in Chicago and (initially) in Los Angeles.[22] The Red Mexicana was first organized in the summer of 2012 as a kind of caucus within the larger alliance to bring together all the Mexican immigrant-led organizations in the United States to influence the immigration policies of the incoming administration of Mexican president Enrique Peña Nieto. The network's transnational political agenda included mobilizing an advocacy campaign across the United States and Mexico to enhance Mexican federal funding for programs aiding Mexican migrants living in the United States such as the Three-for-One program, which matched collective remittances for social investment projects, and to protect Central Americans crossing through Mexico on their way to the United States. The Red Mexicana collaborated closely with the Mexico-based COMPA network to secure funding for a specific set of programs contained in the massive National Development Plan.

In addition to the Mexican migrant campaign, the Red Mexicana launched public education campaigns aimed at its members in the United States. The Pro DAPA-DACA+ campaign informed the Mexican immigrant community about the opportunities for semiregularization offered through Obama's executive orders, providing information about the Deferred Action for Childhood Arrivals (DACA) application process and attempting to mobilize support for Deferred Action for Parents of Americans (DAPA). The Voto Digno 2016 campaign concentrated on mobilizing the immigrant vote leading up to the 2016 US presidential elections and No Más Deportaciones on stopping deportations. The Voto Digno 2016 campaign targeted young Latinos through public announcements featuring young voters addressing their peers about the importance of participating in the election. Lastly, keeping true to its transnational political platform, the Red Mexicana launched a simultaneous campaign it called Credencialízate y Vota, Es Tu Derecho for immigrants to obtain their Mexican voting IDs in time to vote in the July 2018 Mexican presidential and congressional elections.

The emergence of the Red Mexicana coincided with the consolidation of a certain type of civil society network in Mexico. These networks responded to the growing visibility of Mexico as not only a source of migration but also the primary cross-migration region for Central Americans and increasingly for migrants from other parts of the world. An example of migration advocacy networks in Mexico is the Red Regional de Organizaciones Civiles para las Migraciones (Regional Migrations Network of Civil Society Organizations). The Red Mexicana and the Alianza Américas have become important US-based counterparts to the regional networks based in Mexico that nevertheless have member organizations from the United States, Canada, Central America, and the Caribbean. Given the binational positionality of organizations like the Red Mexicana, they are valuable partners for other civil society organizations attempting to influence migration policies in sending countries.[23]

6. The "migration and development" agenda, which focuses on remittances, contrasts with the "development and migration" agenda, which addresses the promotion of alternatives to migration.

Migrant engagement with development projects at home can bolster local social infrastructure such as schools or water systems but does not readily lead to the sustainable jobs needed to curtail future migration. Up until now, the migration and development agenda has been largely confined to addressing the issue of remittances within families. While these transfers improve living standards and access to services including education, which should be considered an investment, only a small proportion of remittances generates enduring improvements to the public good, even in countries whose governments offer matching funds. These social infrastructure projects are the focus of many optimistic accounts of governmental migration and development initiatives.[24] However, as evidenced by Mexico's paradigm-case Three-for-One matching-funds programs, a small share of the resources go to sustainable job creation.[25] While the goal of "banking the unbanked" is certainly important to those migrant families who send remittances, the spillover effects on broader development challenges remain uncertain. Creative model projects seeking to channel remittances into productive investments have been few in number and tiny in scale. As a result, while the "migration and development" agenda addresses the quality of life of nonmigrants, primarily migrants' family members and their neighbors, thus far it has not addressed the systemic reasons for the lack of employment opportunities in communities of origin.

There are many reasons migrant-led community development projects have yet to focus on productive investment on a meaningful scale. Among the reasons is the dearth of investment opportunities in so many sending communities as well as the critical need for on-the-ground entrepreneurial and technical capacity. Such challenges of economic viability are compounded by the long-distance decision making involved. Credible oversight is crucial to the viability of collective remittance projects.[26] This raises the question, however, of the role of citizens in the communities of origin as well as of their public officials, who are sometimes democratically elected. Their degree of involvement in the selection and oversight of migrant-led projects varies widely. At one extreme, these actors can be largely bypassed by well-organized migrants and remain uninvolved in projects; at the other extreme, local officials can be highly proactive, traveling abroad to induce migrants to form hometown clubs to petition for funds in support of given project agendas. In Mexico's Three-for-One program, most hometown association-led projects lack counterparts from among local civic or social organizations with which to share decision-making duties and oversight. By 2007, the Mexican Social Development Ministry began establishing local project oversight committees, known as "mirror clubs," but it is not clear how many have survived. In the northern region of Guerrero, many hometown associations consolidated during this period. Their efforts to bolster oversight of the use of the public funds that matched their remittance contributions involved winning de facto veto power over project spending, including the right to cosign project-related checks with mayors (Méndez Lara 2013). However, more recent informal field reports indicate that the regionwide penetration of local government by organized crime has sharply curtailed civic oversight capacity of Three-for-One projects.

Important differences have emerged between public goods–type community development projects and economic development projects that involve investments in private enterprises including small-scale cooperatives. When organized migrants pool their hard-earned money for hometown development projects, they place a premium on investments that provide benefits to the community as a whole. Most job-creating investments, in contrast, directly affect only a small subset of the community, at least at first, before scaling up. The benefits of such projects may be perceived as vulnerable to being monopolized by local elites or well-connected kinfolk, demonstrating the difficulty inherent in long-distance accountability (Burgess 2016; Fox and Bada 2008).

The persistent disconnect between the remittance-oriented and development-oriented agendas stems from the predominant and narrow project framework. In the Mexican context, a project framework has not been accompanied by broader attention to crafting an alternative development policy agenda. Even states governed by political leaders who are ostensibly open to policy dialogue with organized migrants have yet to pursue alternative policy strategies that are more effective at generating substantial increases in employment.

If the causes of underemployment are systemic, then national-level policy shifts are required to create viable alternatives to migration, that is, more local jobs. In middle-income sending countries, the main constraint is not so much a lack of public resources as the priorities that guide the allocation of those resources. Mexican farm subsidy checks, for example, totaled more than $20 billion from 1994 to 2010 but were targeted primarily to medium and large commercial agribusiness rather than to small-scale family farmers (Fox and Haight 2010). Yet national-level pro-employment measures to re-direct substantial flow of public resources (such as farm subsidies)—in contrast to a project-level focus on local social infrastructure investments—may threaten vested interests.

Whether to focus migration and development advocacy agendas on (trans)local projects as opposed to broader development policies can easily be presented as though the first approach is pragmatic and the second more political. After all, a project-led approach has the advantage of achieving tangible results in the short term and doesn't risk butting heads with home-country governments. A project-led approach allows hometown associations to engage directly with local governments and communities in the sending countries. Advocacy for alternative development policies, in contrast, involves both a larger-scale approach and a longer time line as well as political uncertainty over how the potential reforms will affect clearly defined constituencies in specific places.

Pragmatic project initiatives, though, may be far from apolitical, as can be seen in the design of Mexico's Three-for-One matching-funds program. One of its strengths is that it draws on contributions from federal, state, and local governments, but that structure gives effective veto power to each level of government. The necessary consensus has led to a high concentration of projects in a small number of states where organized migrants have political leverage vis-à-vis state governments. Meanwhile, US-based migrant associations may well be excluded from access to governmental matching funds if they question the status quo by campaigning against human rights violations at home, call for broader development policy alternatives, or associate with the political opposition. Thus the choice to prioritize short-term, local projects is a distinctly political decision.[27]

Furthermore, when a home-country government comes to power that is willing to question a labor-exporting strategy and prioritize job creation at home, opportunities could arise for advocates of developmental policy alternatives. In that case, organized migrants may be able to move forward with translocal projects and contribute to national efforts to change economic development policy. More generally, the key to building alternative development agendas involves effective coalition building with civil society and political actors in the country of origin that are committed to policies designed to encourage large-scale job creation.

7. The coalitional dynamics involved in campaigning for migrant rights in the United States are different from those that address development issues and the causes of migration in Mexico.

There has been a persistent disconnect between campaigns for migrant rights in receiving countries and home-country campaigns for national alternative development policy agendas. The two change agendas may or may not fit neatly together. Given the structure of interests involved, the agendas of current migrants might have limited overlap with those of potential future migrants, who may have a bigger stake in encouraging their own governments to pursue job creation and development strategies at home.

Also worth considering is the debate over unauthorized workers in the United States. The current balance of US political forces suggests that in any scenario for immigration reform in the near future, there will be tradeoffs involving the treatment of current and future migrants. If Democrats regain legislative majorities in the future, possible legislative bargains may allow some current migrants to regularize their status, but only if the US government further tightens border controls and imposes harsher measures against those migrants unable to access what can be a very arduous, punitive, and possibly exclusionary regularization process. If that occurs, the resulting political-institutional situation could create tensions within migrant civil society between current and future migrants. Any opportunity for regularization is likely to be limited to some current migrants, whereas the further hardening of the border will affect future migrants. While regularization of status is the most pressing issue for current migrants, the national development agenda in a country of origin will have the most direct impact on potential future migrants. This structure of interests poses dilemmas for building and sustaining shared, cross-border migration and development agendas.

Meanwhile, from a sending-country perspective, there have been efforts to newly frame the relationship between migration and development. Mexican rural development strategist Armando Bartra (2003:33) bridges the migration, development, and rights agendas with the call to respect "the right to not migrate." Global Exchange (2008) and David Bacon (2013b) have called that prerogative "the right to stay home." After all, the Mexican Constitution still speaks of its citizens' right to "dignified and socially useful work." The right to not migrate is a useful bridging concept for promoting reflection and discussion between diverse actors who see the process differently. This principle recognizes that while migration is an option, it is a choice that stems from public policies that elevate some development strategies over others. In spite of this phrase's catchy emphasis on the underlying causes of migration, it did not catch on in the public discourse, judging from the low number of online searches for the term. Yet Mexico's incoming president, Andrés Manuel López Obrador, adopted the underlying idea in his campaign, with his emphasis on creating alternatives to migration.

Conclusion

When it comes to applying the concept of migrant civil society, there may be a tension between emphasizing processes (social networks, repertoires of collective action, organizations and coalitions) and emphasizing outcomes. How do civic actors and public spheres connect and empower their participants? But also, how do their actions influence the broader political and civic contexts?

For those who are primarily concerned with the challenges immigrants face in their daily lives, a focus on social, civic, and political processes — which might involve only a small proportion of the immigrant population at any one time — risks eliciting a "So what?" response, at least from some skeptical academics. We contend, however, that paying attention to the emergence and consolidation of migrants' ability to build their own social, civic, and political organizations is necessary but not sufficient to understand how they are treated by dominant public institutions in their societies of residence. Analysts interested in connecting the dots between the distinct public spheres within migrant civil society and the actions of sending and receiving states would do well to take three factors into account. First, considering the many obstacles to autonomous migrant collective action, the construction of migrant civil society has been an inherently uneven, long-term process. Second, migrants have, at best, relatively little influence over sending and receiving states, with the notable exceptions of migrant-sensitive institutional enclaves, such as municipal governments in immigrant gateway cities, and migrant support programs operated by the governments of sending states. Third, analysts need to be prepared for unexpected shifts that change migrants' terms of engagement with each other and with the state.

The 2016 US election results drove dramatic changes in the role of the federal government in immigrants' lives. Yet that threat may be pushing migrant-friendly enclaves and sending governments to take even more proactive, migrant-friendly stances. Whether and how mainstream nongovernmental institutions, notably churches, respond to a substantial hardening of anti-immigrant policies remains to be seen at this time. It is worth recalling a previous historical surprise that caught analysts completely off guard. This unprecedented 2006 wave of immigrant collective action in the United States was one of the largest mass civic protests of any kind in US history (Bada, Fox, and Selee, 2006; Fox and Bada 2011). This display of disciplined, self-organized activism convinced the US Senate to reject proposed hardline legislation that would have ratcheted up criminalization of undocumented immigration. In other words, there is a precedent for mass political action by immigrants to directly influence the US legislative process.

The 2016 presidential election results can be read through two lenses. Trump's victory revealed a resonance with a populist, nationalist discourse against immigrants and global trade. Yet Democratic contender Hillary Clinton's more immigrant-friendly, internationalist discourse probably contributed to her winning a majority of the US popular vote, especially in California.

One of the most salient long-term trends has been the increasing engagement of migrant civic, social, and political institutions with their counterparts in US society (Bada 2014; Bada et al. 2010). Over time, migrant civil society actors have transitioned from being outsiders to becoming "bothsiders." Despite the 2016 election's strong anti-immigrant message, an internationalist perspective retains solid political support in cities where most immigrants live and institutions of migrant civil society are most consolidated.[28]

Clearly, the post-2016 US political environment poses huge challenges to migrant networks and organizations. Experiences like the 2006 mass mobilization or the campaign begun during Barack Obama's presidency against city police turning undocumented immigrants over to federal authorities suggest that when it comes to federal policy, migrants may have more capacity to resist new threats than to promote actual regularization, with the notable exception of the DACA program, a proactive, inclusionary measure that was made possible by migrant-led protest and advocacy.

Whether and how the governments of states and cities where many immigrants live will be willing and able to fend off the likely hardening of anti-immigrant federal policies remain open questions. Moreover, the responses of migrant organizations and mainstream institutions of US civil society will reveal a great deal about the nature of their relations with each other. Under increased federal immigration enforcement pressure, will migrant and US civil society organizations close ranks or be pulled apart? How will cross-border networks respond? Webs of migrant organizations have gradually moved from the margins of civil society toward the US mainstream, promoting a discourse of rights for migrants on both sides of the border. Now, however, they are faced with a US government that rejects the very premise of migrant rights. The future will stretch those webs, putting their resilience to the ultimate test.

Notes

1. The definition encompassing four arenas follows the long tradition of defining civil society in contrast to both the state and the market and therefore does not include most private-sector actors, with the notable exception of migrant-oriented mass media. Our discussion of migrant civil society draws from Fox 2006, 2007 and Fox and Bada 2008.

2. The question of how civil society organizations are governed raises an issue that will not be resolved here, one of what counts as a "migrant-led NGO." Does the term refer to organizations with executive directors of migrant origin? Directors are hired and fired by NGOs' boards of directors. Therefore, a broad definition of "migrant-led NGO" would be based on the national origin of its executive director, and a more bounded definition would focus on the composition of a nonprofit's board of directors.

3. For discussion of the binational dimension of migrant civil society, see Fox 2007 and Fox and Bada 2008. When seen in a binational context, migrant organizations tend to emerge either through the newcomers' civic engagement with their destination societies or through links with their homelands. The public sphere can therefore refer either to the (e)migrant wing of a sending society or to (im)migrant communities within a receiving society. These distinct spaces sometimes overlap, and one major question is where, when, and under what conditions migrants engage both locally and transnationally. These cross-border and multilevel forms of active membership represent one dimension of the broader process of forming a transnational civil society.

4. Migrants in earlier historical periods faced similar issues. For a comprehensive review of the historical literature, see Moya 2005.

5. For a rare theoretically informed analysis of these coalitional dynamics in the European context, see García Agustín and Jørgenson 2016.

6. The total number of Mexicans with consular ID cards is not clear since official public data record the number issued each year without accounting for renewals or changes of address. The number is large; according to the 2010 *Informe de Gobierno*, Mexican consulates issued 9.4 million from 2000 to 2010. For further discussion of the politics of the ID cards, see Délano 2011, Varsanyi 2007, and Waldinger 2014.

7. In part to address the ID challenge, the Mexican public interest group Be Foundation led a small but influential campaign that produced a constitutional amendment in

Article 4 guaranteeing the "right to identity," specifically the right to birth certificates for the millions of Mexican citizens who lack such documentation. The constitutional reform eventually led Mexico's extensive network of consulates to begin helping nationals acquire birth certificates in spite of the long-standing reluctance of the Foreign Ministry to get involved (Asencio 2012).

8. See, for example, Bacon 2013a,b.

9. For a long-term strategic vision from the Mexican Foreign Ministry, see González Gutiérrez 2009.

10. On Latino immigrant worker organizing in the United States, see Bacon 2008, Fine 2006, and Milkman 2006.

11. For an ethnographic analysis of simultaneous multiple migrant identities, see Stephen 2007.

12. For a summary of the theoretical debate on this concept, see Dannreuther and Hutchings 1999. Will Kymlicka offers a variation on this theme in his acclaimed 1995 work, *Multicultural Citizenship: A Liberal Theory of Minority Rights*.

13. For a list of Radio TexMex's strategic partner organizations, see its webpage at http://radiotexmex.fm/category/alianzas-organizaciones/.

14. For different definitions of civil society, see Howell and Pearce 2001.

15. Headlines on the Univision News website at the end of January 2017, the weekend after Trump issued his immigration executive orders, were "Both Sides Lose in Falling Out between Mexico and United States"; "A List of Obama's Immigration Programs Now under Threat by President Trump"; "Trump to Preside Over an English-Only White House?" All were posted at Univision, http://www.univision.com/univision-news.

16. That said, many service-providing nonprofits are much more cautious about engaging in advocacy than the law actually requires, as spelled out in a public education initiative led by the flagship legal rights organization Alliance for Justice. See the alliance's website, http://www.bolderadvocacy.org.

17. For organizations in Los Angeles, see the websites of the Central American Resource Center, http://www.carecen-la.org/, and the National Day Laborer Organizing Network, http://www.ndlon.org. For Chicago, see Alianza Américas, http://www.alianzaamericas.org, and the Illinois Coalition for Immigrant and Refugee Rights, http://www.icirr.org. For New York, see the New York Immigrant Coalition, http://www.thenyic.org. For the DC area, see Casa Maryland, http://wearecasa.org.

18. For a list of member organizations of COMPA, see its webpage OSC Integrantes, http://migracionparalasamericas.org/osc-integrantes/. Many other prominent advocacy organizations are not included in the COMPA network. An example is Hermanos al Rescate, a shelter for Central American migrants in Oaxaca run by Father Solalinde; he is featured in the *New York Times* (Malkin 2012) about his work with Central American migrants crossing through Mexico.

19. COMPA's capacity to influence the implementation of the government's policy commitments was much more limited. See official details of the policy at its government webpage, http://www.politicamigratoria.gob.mx/es_mx/SEGOB/Programa_Especial_de_Migracion_2014-2018_PEM. For independent analysis of the government's migration-related spending, see Córdova Alcaraz 2013.

20. COMPA's objectives are described at its webpage, http://migracionparalasamericas.org/objetivos. Many of the Mexican institutions that support Central American transmigrants, notably through the network of safe houses, were quietly funded by religious orders and philanthropic organizations associated with the social teachings of the Catholic Church.

21. The discussion of this proposition draws on Fox 2001, 2002, and 2010.

22. For a full list of member organizations of the Red Mexicana, see its webpage, http://www.redmexicanamigrante.org/organizaciones_miembros.

23. In the case of Mexican migrants' impact on public policy in general, see Duquette 2011 and Rodríguez Ramírez 2012. The Three-for-One program has explicitly institutionalized the participation of hometown federations in its rules of implementation. The official rules of implementation for 2016 determined that in order to be eligible to participate in Three-for-One, the main requirement is "to be Mexican migrants residing abroad, organized into a migrant club or organization that has an up-to-date consular registration" (ser migrantes mexicanos radicados en el extranjero, organizados en un Club u Organización de Migrantes que cuente con Toma de Nota vigente) (SEDESOL 2015:4). Full participation in and evaluation of the federally funded coinvestment Three-for-One program were the main demands of the Zacatecan Federation, an immigrant-led organization representing dozens of hometown associations from Zacatecas, as the policy was developed (Rodríguez Ramírez 2012). Annual reviews and changes to the rules of the program require direct consultations with migrants.

24. In a comparison of migration and development initiatives in Mexico and Morocco, Natasha Iskander (2010) contrasts the failure of top-down efforts to channel migrant investments into poorly conceived business ventures with more successful, migrant-led social infrastructure initiatives.

25. For overviews of remittances and development issues in Mexico, see García Zamora 2009 and Fernández de Castro, García Zamora, and Vila Freyer 2009. For Latin America more generally, see García Zamora and Orozco 2009. In 2008, after several years' effort, the share of Mexico's Three-for-One projects considered "productive" reached 4 percent of the total number of projects (100) and 6.4 percent of federal program funding (only $2.6 million). Thanks go to Xóchitl Bada for these data.

26. See Bada 2014, Burgess 2016, Duquette-Rury 2014, and Duquette-Rury and Bada 2013. Participants have incentives to be politically cautious and avoid controversy that would cause one of the three levels of government involved to exercise their veto power. The Three-for-One program involves federal, state, and municipal government contributions—and therefore signoff power. Mexican states that have been slow to go through transitions to democracy have lagged noticeably behind in their inclusion of independently organized migrant citizens in Three-for-One projects, as in the case of Oaxaca.

27. David Ayón argues that the Mexican government's multifaceted strategy for engaging the diaspora successfully depoliticized the relationship: "Mexican authorities had outmaneuvered and ultimately overwhelmed opposition-minded migrant activists with the state's power to reach out and even reshape the organized diaspora. Over the course of three [presidential] administrations and a fundamental regime change, the underlying interest of the Mexican state in deflecting transnational migrant activism away from domestic politics had prevailed" (2010:245). See also Délano 2009, Iskander 2010, and Smith 2008.

28. In a detailed geographic analysis, Raul Hinojosa-Ojeda, Maksim Wynn, and Zhenxiang Chen (2016) have found that Trump's support was inversely correlated with the presence of Mexican immigrants.

References

Asencio, Karen Mercado. 2012. "The Under-Registration of Births in Mexico: Consequences for Children, Adults, and Migrants." *MPI Online Journal*, April 12. Washington, DC: Migration Policy Institute. https://www.migrationpolicy.org/article/un der-registration-births-mexico-consequences-children-adults-and-migrants/.

Ayón, David. 2010. "Taming the Diaspora: Migrants and the State, 1986–2006." In *Mexico's Democratic Challenges: Politics, Government and Society*, edited by Andrew Selee and Jacqueline Peschard, 231–250. Washington, DC: Woodrow Wilson Center Press; Palo Alto, CA: Stanford University Press.

Bacon, David. 2008. *Illegal People: How Globalization Creates Migration and Criminalizes Immigrants*. New York: Beacon.

———. 2013a. "The Dignity Campaign's Alternative Vision for Immigration Reform." *The Nation*, February 6.

———. 2013b. *The Right to Stay Home: How US Policy Drives Mexican Migration*. Boston: Beacon.

Bada, Xóchitl. 2014. *Mexican Hometown Associations in Chicagoacán: From Local to Transnational Civic Engagement*. New Brunswick, NJ: Rutgers University Press.

Bada, Xóchitl, Robert Donnelly, Jonathan Fox, and Andrew Selee. 2010. *Context Matters: Latino Immigrant Civic Engagement in Nine US Cities: National Report*. Washington, DC: Mexico Institute, Woodrow Wilson International Center for Scholars. http://www.wilsoncenter.org/migrantparticipation.

Bada, Xóchitl, Jonathan Fox, and Andrew Selee, eds. 2006. *Invisible No More: Mexican Migrant Civic Participation in the United States*. Washington, DC: Mexico Institute, Woodrow Wilson International Center for Scholars.

Bartra, Armando. 2003. *Cosechas de ira: Economía política de la contrareforma agraria*. Mexico City: Ithaca/Instituto Maya.

Brooks, David. 1992. "The Search for Counterparts." *Labor Research Review* 19 (Fall): 83–97.

Brooks, David, and Jonathan Fox, eds. 2002. *Cross-Border-Dialogues: US-Mexico Social Movement Networking*. La Jolla: Center for US-Mexican Studies, University of California, San Diego.

Burgess, Katrina. 2016. "Organized Migrants and Accountability from Afar." *Latin American Research Review* 51 (2): 150–173.

Calmes, Jackie. 2015. "Jorge Ramos, Voice of Latino Voters on Univision, Sends Shiver through G.O.P." *New York Times*, January 25.

Córdova Alcaraz, Rodolfo. 2013. *Una mirada al presupuesto del Instituto Nacional de Migración ¿Dónde estuvieron sus prioridades durante 2011?*. Report, May. Mexico City: Fundar.

Dannreuther, Roland, and Kimberly Hutchings, eds. 1999. *Cosmopolitan Citizenship*. London: Palgrave Macmillan.

Délano, Alexandra. 2009. "From Limited to Active Engagement: Mexico's Emigration Policies from a Foreign Policy Perspective (2000–2006)." *International Migration Review* 43 (4): 764–814.

———. 2011. *Mexico and Its Diaspora in the United States: Policies of Emigration since 1848*. New York: Cambridge University Press.

Duquette, Lauren. 2011. "Making Democracy Work from Abroad: Remittances, Hometown Associations, and Migrant-State Coproduction of Public Goods in Mexico." PhD diss., University of Chicago.

Duquette-Rury, Lauren. 2014. "Collective Remittances and Transnational Coproduction: The 3 × 1 Program for Migrants and Household Access to Public Goods in Mexico." *Studies in Comparative International Development* 49 (1): 11–139.

Duquette-Rury, Lauren, and Xóchitl Bada. 2013. "Continuity and Change in Mexican Migrant Hometown Associations: Evidence from New Survey Research." *Migraciones Internacionales* 7 (1): 65–99.

Fine, Janice. 2006. *Worker Centers: Organizing Communities at the Edge of the Dream.* Ithaca, NY: Cornell University Press.

Fernández de Castro, Rafael, Rodolfo García Zamora, and Ana Vila Freyer, eds. 2009. *El Programa 3x1 para migrantes ¿Primera política transnacional en México?.* Mexico City: Miguel Angel Porrúa/Instituto Tecnológico Autónomo de México/Universidad Autónoma de Zacatecas.

Fox, Jonathan. 2001. "Evaluación de las coaliciones binacionales de la sociedad civil a partir de la experiencia México-Estados Unidos." *Revista Mexicana de Sociología* 63 (3): 211–268.

———. 2002. "Lessons from Mexico-US Civil Society Coalitions." In *Cross-Border Dialogues: US-Mexico Social Movement Networking,* edited by David Brooks and Jonathan Fox, 231–418. La Jolla: Center for US-Mexican Studies, University of California, San Diego.

———. 2006. "Repensar lo rural ante la globalización: La sociedad civil migrante." *Migración y Desarrollo,* no. 5:35–58.

———. 2007. *Accountability Politics: Power and Voice in Rural Mexico.* Oxford: Oxford University Press.

———. 2010. "Coalitions and Networks." In *International Encyclopedia of Civil Society,* edited by Helmut Anheier and Stefan Toepler, 486–491. New York: Springer.

Fox, Jonathan, and Xóchitl Bada. 2008. "Migrant Organization and Hometown Impacts in Rural Mexico." *Journal of Agrarian Change* 8 (2–3): 435–461.

———. 2011. "Migrant Civic Engagement." In *Rallying for Immigrant Rights,* edited by Irene Bloemraad and Kim Voss, 142–160. Berkeley: University of California Press.

Fox, Jonathan, and William Gois. 2010. "La sociedad civil migrante: Diez tesis para el debate." *Migración y Desarrollo* 7 (15): 81–128.

Fox, Jonathan, and Libby Haight, eds. 2010. *Subsidizing Inequality: Mexican Corn Policy since NAFTA.* Mexico City: Wilson Center/Centro de Investigacion y Docencias Económicas/University of California, Santa Cruz.

Fox, Jonathan, and Gaspar Rivera-Salgado, eds. 2004. *Indigenous Mexican Migrants in the US.* La Jolla: Center for US-Mexican Studies, University of California, San Diego.

Gabriel, Trip. 2015. "At Donald Trump Event, Jorge Ramos of Univision Is Snubbed, Ejected, and Debated." *New York Times,* August 25. https://www.nytimes.com/.

García Agustín, Oscar, and Martin Bak Jørgenson, eds. 2016. *Civil Society without Borders: Gramscian Perspectives on Migration and Civil Society Alliances.* London: Pluto.

García Zamora, Rodolfo. 2009. *Desarrollo económico y migración internacional: Los desafíos de las políticas públicas en México.* Zacatecas, Mexico: Universidad Autónoma de Zacatecas.

García Zamora, and Manuel Orozco, eds. 2009. *Migración internacional, remesas y desarrollo local en América Latina y el Caribe.* Mexico City: Miguel Ángel Porrúa, Universidad Autónoma de Zacatecas, Inter-American Dialogue.

Gleeson, Shannon. 2010. "Labor Rights for All? The Role of Undocumented Immigrant Status for Worker Claims-Making." *Law and Social Inquiry* 35 (3): 561–602.

Global Exchange, ed. 2008. *The Right to Stay Home: Alternatives to Mass Displacement*

and Forced Migration in North America. San Francisco: Global Exchange. http://www
.globalexchange.org/.

González Gutiérrez, Carlos. 2009. "The Institute of Mexicans Abroad: An Effort to Empower the Diaspora." In Closing the Distance: How Governments Strengthen Ties with
Their Diasporas, edited by Dovelyn Rannveug Agunias, 87–98. Washington, DC: Migration Policy Institute.

Hinojosa-Ojeda, Raul, with Maksim Wynn and Zhenxiang Chen. 2016. "Donald Trump's
False Narrative on Mexican Migration and Trade: A Geopolitical Economic Analy-
sis." Paper, October 23. Los Angeles: North American Integration and Development
Center/Institute for Research on Labor and Employment, University of California.

Howell, Jude, and Jenny Pearce. 2001. Civil Society and Development. Boulder, CO:
Lynne Rienner.

Iskander, Natasha. 2010. Creative State: Forty Years of Migration and Development Policy
in Morocco and Mexico. Ithaca, NY: Cornell University Press.

James, Meg. 2013a. "Univision-ABC Channel Fusion Launching in a Bid for Young Latinos." Los Angeles Times, October 28. http://www.latimes.com/.

———. 2013b. "Univision's Jorge Ramos a powerful voice on immigration." Los Angeles
Times, June 3. http://www.latimes.com/.

Johnson, Reed. 2013. "León Krauze Aims for Millennial Set with News Show Open
Source." Los Angeles Times, November 9. http://www.latimes.com/.

Keck, Margaret, and Kathryn Sikkink. 1998. Activists beyond Borders. Ithaca, NY: Cornell University Press.

Kymlicka, Will. 1995. Multicultural Citizenship: A Liberal Theory of Minority Rights.
Oxford: Oxford University Press.

Malkin, Elizabeth. 2012. "A Priest Stands Up for the Migrants Who Run Mexico's Gauntlet." New York Times, July 13. http://www.nytimes.com/.

Méndez Lara, Marcos. 2013. "Transparencia y rendición de cuentas en el programa
3x1 para migrantes: Region norte del estado de Guerrero." Mexican Rural Development Research Reports, no. 25. Washington, DC: Mexico Institute, Woodrow Wilson
International Center for Scholars.

Mercado, Antonieta. 2011. "Grassroots Cosmopolitanism: Transnational Communication and Citizenship Practices among Indigenous Mexican Immigrants in the
United States." PhD diss., University of California, San Diego.

———. 2015. "El Tequio: Social Capital, Civic Advocacy Journalism, and the Construction of a Transnational Public Sphere by Mexican Indigenous Migrants in the U.S."
Journalism 16 (2): 238–256. http://escholarship.org/uc/item/5tg8z68n.

Milkman, Ruth. 2006. LA Story, Immigrant Workers, and the Future of the US Labor Movement. New York: Russell Sage.

Moya, Jose. 2005. "Immigrants and Associations: A Global and Historical Perspective."
Journal of Ethnic and Migration Studies 31 (5): 833–864.

Nicholls, Walter. 2013. The DREAMers: How the Undocumented Youth Movement Transformed the Immigrant Rights Debate. Palo Alto, CA: Stanford University Press.

Nicholls, Walter, and Tara Fiorito. 2015. "Dreamers Unbound: Immigrant Youth Mobilizing." New Labor Forum 24 (1): 86–92.

Parkeraug, Ashley. 2015. "Donald Trump Gets Earful in Spanish as Latino Outlets Air
Disdain." New York Times, August 26. http://www.nytimes.com/.

Rodríguez Ramírez, Héctor. 2012. "El papel de los migrantes mexicanos en la construcción de una agenda de políticas públicas: El caso del programa 3X1." Región y Sociedad 24 (53): 231–257.

SEDESOL (Mexico, Secretaría de Desarrollo Social). 2015. "Acuerdo por el que se emiten las reglas de operación del Programa 3X1 para Migrantes, para el ejercicio fiscal 2016." *Diario Oficial*, December 29. Mexico City: SEDESOL.

Smith, Robert Courtney. 2008. "Contradictions of Diasporic Institutionalization in Mexican Politics: The 2006 Migrant Vote and Other Forms of Inclusion and Control." *Ethnic and Racial Studies* 31 (4): 708–741.

Stephen, Lynn. 2007. *Crossborder Lives: Indigenous Oaxacans in Mexico, California, and Oregon*. Durham, NC: Duke University Press.

Varsanyi, Monica. 2007. "Documenting Undocumented Migrants: The *Matrículas Consulares* as Neoliberal Local Membership." *Geopolitics* 12 (2): 299–319.

Voss, Kim, and Irene Bloemraad, eds. 2011. *Rallying for Immigrant Rights: The Fight for Inclusion in 21st Century America*. Berkeley: University of California Press.

Waldinger, Roger. 2014. "The Politics of Cross-Border Engagement: Mexican Emigrants and the Mexican State." *Theory and Society* 43 (5): 483–511.

Zavella, Patricia. 2011. *I'm Neither Here nor There: Mexicans' Quotidian Struggles with Migration and Poverty*. Durham, NC: Duke University Press.

PART I

NORTH AMERICA

CHAPTER 2

Global Governance and the Protection of Migrant Workers' Rights in North America: In Search of a Theoretical Framework

JOSÉ MA. SERNA DE LA GARZA

Concept of "Global Governance"

Globalization is a multifaceted contemporary phenomenon that is having significant impacts on different spheres of society. Emerging alongside this complex phenomenon, the concept of global governance has been appearing increasingly in the social sciences.[1] However, the meaning of "global governance" is under dispute, and the term is used in diverse ways by different actors. For some, global governance refers to a set of rules and institutions that have been constructed over recent decades to organize collective action among state and nonstate actors and solve what are perceived as global problems.[2] For others, global governance is part of a hegemonic discourse accompanying the dominant transformations taking place at the international and national levels, a discourse that legitimizes market-oriented and private actors in areas that in the past were considered within the public sphere.[3]

For the purposes of this essay, I shall identify a series of phenomena and processes that are at the center of the conceptual debate on global governance. Doing so allows for better analysis of the options available for more effectively protecting migrant workers' rights in North America. The options form part of the political-institutional environment that determines the possibilities for collective action by what has been called a "migrant civil society" and the availability of potential allies for migrant rights.[4]

Looking at the current situation of global governance, one can make the following claims:

1. An unprecedented expansion is occurring in the formal and informal roles of multilateral international institutions.
2. A significant increase is taking place in the scope, density, and degree of

influence of rules created at the international level that in turn are increasingly influencing how national societies are organized.

3. Fundamental changes are happening in the political, legal, and ethical understanding of state sovereignty as well as in relations between the state, citizens, and the international community.

4. Complex transnational networks of state and nonstate actors have formed to generate rules governing global issues.

5. There is clear evidence that nation-states are allowing various international regimes to operate within their borders, and these regimes are playing a larger role in guiding behaviors and social relations at the domestic level.

6. Interpenetration in various fields is growing between international law and national law as well as between international institutions and national administrative apparatuses.

Indeed, public international law has a considerably expanded scope with respect to areas previously thought to be the exclusive jurisdiction of states. Its expansion suggests that the object of public international law is changing. International institutions of various kinds have been increasing their power and influence and begun exercising something like the state's public authority by directing and determining the behavior of states and individuals. Related to this phenomenon, a new generation of international treaties has emerged and, with them, monitoring and implementation mechanisms. Human rights treaties are a good example of the trend, changing the lives of many individuals in many different countries.[5]

The growing authority of international institutions has raised some concerns in academia and governments, including questions over the legitimacy of that authority. To wit: What is the foundation of these institutions' authority? Some authors have proposed that international institutions should be approached with a "constitutional sensibility," that is, as if they, like nation-states, imposed their own sets of laws. But is it appropriate to use that approach to analyze how international institutions manage global public affairs?[6]

Conversely, other scholars have pointed out that international law and international institutions have expanded beyond the reach of national representative bodies and mechanisms of democratic control. In this view, domestic law — expressions of domestic political commitments — seems to take a backseat to international or supranational law, usually as expressions of international commitments.[7]

Similar concerns over the growing power of undemocratic institutions have led some analysts to propose theories of participatory democracy, in which the legitimacy of international institutions rests on their use of democratic discourse and open decision-making procedures.[8] Other scholars have suggested that the procedures for appointing international public servants including international judges should be revised to make them more transparent and open.[9]

Another feature of global governance is the increasing extent to which nonstate actors are influencing the production of international legal norms. Margaret Keck and Kathryn Sikkink have argued that many nonstate actors interact with each other, with states, and with international organizations, forming transnational networks that are increasingly visible at the level of international politics. The authors explain that there are different types of networks, depending on the type of activity or interest of the participants. Keck and Sikkink focus on a particular type they call "transnational advocacy networks" (TANs), which have been expanding the scope and connectivity of the international advocacy system and challenging national sovereignty by making it possible for citizens to put pressure on states.[10]

TANs team up with relevant actors working internationally on an issue, united by shared values, a common discourse, and dense exchanges of information and services. The networks are novel in that nontraditional international actors are able to mobilize information strategically to help create new themes and categories and to persuade more powerful organizations and governments to adopt them. Exchanging information and promoting new standards are these networks' central tasks. They also monitor the implementation of and state compliance with international standards as well as exercise pressure on other actors to adopt new policies and standards.[11]

In a related line of inquiry, Ricardo Méndez Silva has outlined the important functions performed by another type of international actor, nongovernmental organizations (NGOs), as follows:[12] they contribute to establishing international standards; in many cases, negotiations related to treaty-making and international standards take into account or are circumscribed by the consensus of NGOs in a given field; NGOs actively participate in monitoring international standards and regularly draft compliance reports; they regularly attend meetings and work with specialized committees to review public international organizations and treaty compliance regimes; and they provide advice and support to people in the human rights field who, for example, appear before international courts, monitor the enforcement of judgments from international courts, and submit amicus curiae briefs.[13]

The notion of "soft law" also has been appearing in the global governance literature with greater frequency. Soft law refers to a number of normative standards and policy instruments characterized by their lack of mandatory or binding force as well as by the absence of sanctions and enforcement structures. The term covers various instruments that share at least one feature: while their normative content might have legal relevance and therefore produce practical effects, they are not legally binding.[14] Scholars have been studying this phenomenon since at least the 1980s, but no consensus has yet been reached as to what soft law concretely means — or even whether it really should be classified as law. Neither have they been able to draw a clear line between "hard law" and "soft law." The confusion surrounding this concept was discussed at the Eighty-Second Annual Meeting of the American Society of International Law, at which one panel identified the growing importance of soft law in the international legal field.[15]

Without fully wading into the debate, for the purposes of this work I accept Dinah Shelton's definition of soft law as constituting "normative provisions contained in non-binding texts."[16] It includes resolutions, recommendations, codes of conduct, and standards that result from the interaction between states and other actors at the international level in different fora. Soft law challenges the traditional positivist idea of international law by introducing legal instruments with different degrees of normative intensity. Importantly, emerging principles of soft law can undermine the legitimacy of existing national and/or international rules. States cannot simply ignore instruments of soft law because it provides a crucial normative framework in which future hard laws may emerge.[17]

What do international-level actors consider the pros and cons of using either hard or soft law? Antto Vihma has argued that the answer depends on whether one considers the question from a rationalist or constructivist perspective. Vihma finds that from a rationalist point of view, states and other international actors utilize hard law because it helps to reduce transaction costs, strengthen the credibility of their commitments, expand their range of political strategies, and resolve problems of incomplete contracting. However, using hard law has significant costs in terms of chipping away at state sovereignty, since it can effectively constrain state behavior.[18] From the rationalist perspective, soft law has the advantage of being less costly in terms of state sovereignty. However, Vihma also notes that soft law arguably represents a less credible commitment to the issue at hand than hard law does. States can use soft law cynically to take the heat off political leaders, allowing symbolic but empty promises to substitute for real action.[19]

The constructivist perspective, by contrast, focuses on "appropriate behavior," which refers to states developing or modifying their identities. Changes in state behavior can thus occur through processes of socialization and the expansion of norms, ideas, and principles. From this perspective, the soft-law approach is advantageous because it accommodates a wide spectrum of political actions and promotes shared norms and a sense of common purpose and identity. Constructivists analyze international law in terms of values and the formation of state identities, and thus from their perspective the world no longer needs to be thought of in terms of power and interest.[20]

This debate relates directly to migrant workers' rights, as Canada, Mexico, and the United States are currently immersed in a set of global and regional normative regimes that include hard- and soft-law instruments. The three countries interact with those regimes in different ways and with different levels of intensity. Three international regimes in particular influence how migrant workers' rights are protected in North America: the universal human rights system, the inter-American system for the protection of human rights, and the North American Free Trade Agreement (NAFTA) side agreement on labor cooperation. Some conclusions may be drawn from examining the regimes and their effects on the protection of migrant workers' rights in North America in the context of global governance.[21]

The Universal System for the Protection of Migrant Workers' Rights

Several universal instruments and institutions have established standards around migrant workers' rights. I examine six of them here.

Resolutions of the UN General Assembly and Reports of the UN Secretary-General

A fair number of UN General Assembly resolutions and UN secretary-general reports concern migrant workers' rights. UN resolutions may be considered soft law. The following resolutions and their corresponding reports serve as examples:

Resolution A/RES/69/167,[22] on the protection of migrants, and Report A/70/259;[23]

Resolution A/RES/64/139,[24] on violence against women migrant workers, and Report A/66/212;[25]

Resolution A/RES/66/128,[26] on violence against women migrant workers, and Report A/68/178;[27]

Resolution A/RES/68/179,[28] on the protection of migrants, and Report A/69/277;[29]

Resolutions A/RES/67/219,[30] A/RES/65/170,[31] on international migration and development, and Report A/68/190;[32]

Resolution A/RES/63/225,[33] on international migration and development, and Report A/65/203;[34]

and Resolution 67/172,[35] on the protection of migrants, and Report (A/68/292).[36]

General Assembly resolutions also can request reports from special rapporteurs. An example is Report A/69/302,[37] on the human rights of migrants, submitted in accordance with UN General Assembly Resolution A/RES/68/179, cited above, on the protection of migrants.

The UN General Assembly's Resolution A/RES/69/167 is relevant to the discussion because it refers not only to the rights of migrants in general but also to the rights of migrant workers in particular. The resolution asks all states

in conformity with national legislation and applicable international legal instruments to which they are party, to enforce labor law effectively, including by addressing violations of such law, with regard to migrant workers' labor relations and working conditions, *inter alia*, those related to their remuneration and conditions of health, safety at work and the right to freedom of association . . . [and to] remove unlawful obstacles, where they exist, that may prevent the safe, transparent, unrestricted and expeditious transfer of remittances, earnings, assets and pensions of migrants to their country of origin or to any other countries, in conformity with applicable legislation and agreements, and to consider, as appropriate, measures to solve other problems that may impede such transfers.[38]

Apart from resolutions related directly to migrant workers' rights, the UN General Assembly has issued others that benefit migrant workers, among them some that refer to health and education such as A/RES/34/58,[39] A/67/L.36,[40] and A/RES/56/116.[41]

The effectiveness of UN General Assembly resolutions varies according to several factors.[42] Regardless of their legal effects, many have symbolic and/or political impacts—symbolic because they represent the opinion of the community of states and therefore can shame those that do not comply and political because they provide legitimacy in international struggles for power.[43]

Finally, it is important to mention that in drafting the reports, the secretary-general receives written submissions from states, intergovernmental organizations, and NGOs. Migrant-led organizations that form part of migrant civil society should not lose sight of this ability to influence UN policies.

Universal Declaration on Human Rights and the UN Human Rights Council

There are three monitoring procedures of the UN Human Rights Council (UNHRC):[44] the universal periodic review, the special procedures, and the complaint procedure. I describe the first two, since the third has not yet addressed migrant workers' rights.

UNIVERSAL PERIODIC REVIEW

This process involves reviewing the human rights situation in every UN member state and is cooperative, as stated in the UN General Assembly Resolution 60/251 of March 15, 2006. Member states consent to open themselves up to the scrutiny of the international community under the auspices of the UNHRC.

Some of the conclusions of the universal periodic review procedure concerning Canada, Mexico, and the United States pertain to migrants in general and some to migrant workers in particular. The three reports cited here represent examples of soft law. The 2013 report on Canada recommended that the country ratify the International Convention on the Protection of the Rights of All Migrant Workers and Members of Their Families as well as further promote and protect migrants, particularly undocumented and irregular migrants.[45] As for Mexico, the 2009 report recommended that Mexico ensure the full realization of migrant rights in its territory by enacting legislation and providing training to concerned officials; it also suggested giving priority to the recommendations made by the special rapporteur on the human rights of migrants.[46] And as for the United States, the 2011 report recommended ratifying, without reservations, the International Convention on the Protection of the Rights of All Migrant Workers and Members of Their Families as well as refraining from enacting any repressive initiatives vis-à-vis the migrant community that violated migrants' rights by applying racial profiling or criminalizing undocumented immigration.[47]

SPECIAL PROCEDURES OF THE UNHRC

These procedures involve the UNHRC appointing an independent human rights expert who receives a mandate to report and advise on human rights from a country-specific or thematic perspective. In 1999 the Commission on Human Rights established the position of special rapporteur on the human rights of migrants, in Resolution E/CN.4/RES/1999/44; more recently, the UNHRC approved Resolution A/HRC/RES/26/19, which granted that special rapporteur on migrants additional responsibilities.

In her reports—which constitute another illustration of soft law—the special rapporteur on migrants treated cases such as the situation of women migrant workers and violence against them, unaccompanied minors and irregular migration (E/CN.4/2002/94), the deprivation of liberty in the context of migration management (E/CN.4/2003/85), the human rights of migrant domestic workers (E/CN.4/2004/76), and racism and discrimination against migrants (E/CN.4/2005/85). A report connected with migrant rights and the border between Mexico and the United States, E/CN.4/2003/85/Add.3,[48] addresses alleged violations of migrants' human rights and the use of physical or psychological violence against them, then makes a series of recommendations to alleviate the situation.[49]

Under the universal periodic review and the special procedures, NGOs can send a written submission on the human rights situation of any UN member state.[50] Again, migrant civil society could include this option as part of its repertoire of actions.

International Covenant on Civil and Political Rights and the Human Rights Committee

The International Covenant on Civil and Political Rights (ICCPR of December 16, 1966), an instrument that qualifies as hard law, is a key multilateral treaty that provides a range of protections for civil and political rights.[51] Its monitoring body is the Human Rights Committee, comprised of independent experts who verify state implementation of the ICCPR. The committee has the authority to issue "general comments," another example of soft law, relating to its interpretation of the human rights outlined in the ICCPR or the methods used to protect them.

While no general comment refers specifically to migrant workers, some refer to them indirectly, such as General Comment No. 15 on "The position of aliens under the Covenant," adopted at the twenty-seventh session of the Human Rights Committee, on April 11, 1986.

International Covenant on Social, Economic, and Cultural Rights and the Committee on Economic, Social, and Cultural Rights

The International Covenant on Social, Economic, and Cultural Rights (ICSECR) of December 16, 1966, is the leading multilateral treaty establishing recognition and protection for the wide range of rights outlined in its title. The monitoring body of the ICESCR is the Committee on Economic, Social, and Cultural Rights, which, like the Human Rights Committee, also issues general comments.

One document especially relevant to this discussion of migrant rights is General Comment No. 23 (2016), which deals with just and favorable work conditions and provides an interpretation of Article 7 of the ICESCR.[52] Other relevant general comments are General Comment No. 19 (2008) on the right to social security,[53] and General Comment No. 14 (2000) on the right to the highest attainable standard of health.[54]

International Convention on the Protection of the Rights
of All Migrant Workers and Members of Their Families

On July 1, 2003, the International Convention on the Protection of the Rights of All Migrant Workers and Members of Their Families (ICPRMW) entered into force. By January 10, 2017, forty-nine states had ratified it. ICPRMW is a comprehensive treaty concerning the protection of migrant workers' rights, and it emphasizes the link between migration and human rights.[55] Its purpose is to establish minimum standards for migrant workers and their family members, irrespective of their migratory status. The preamble reaffirms the rationale behind recognizing the rights of undocumented migrant workers, forcefully noting how irregular migrants are frequently exploited and face serious human rights violations. It also stresses that appropriate action should be taken to prevent and eliminate clandestine movements and trafficking in migrant workers while at the same time ensuring their human rights.[56]

The Committee on the Protection of the Rights of All Migrant Workers and Members of Their Families is the body of independent experts that monitors state implementation of the ICPRMW. State parties are required to submit regular reports to the committee on how the outlined rights are being implemented in their countries. For its part, the committee issues "concluding observations" with recommendations and concerns addressed to the corresponding state.

Canada and the United States are not party to this convention. Mexico, on the other hand, is, after ratifying the ICPRMW on March 8, 1999.[57] In the committee's report on Mexico, it highlighted the positive aspects of Mexico's policies toward migrant workers but also noted some problems in its section on "principal subjects of concern, suggestions and recommendations." Among the positive aspects, the report refers to "the amendment, in force since July 22, 2008, of the Population Act to abrogate the provision for prison terms of from 18 months to 10 years for undocumented migrant workers"; "the adoption of the Act to Prevent and Punish Trafficking in Persons and the General Act on Women's Access to a Life Free of Violence"; "the incorporation of the offence of human trafficking in the Federal Criminal Code, as recommended by the Committee"; "the establishment of the Office of the Special Prosecutor for Violent Crimes against Women and Trafficking in Persons"; "the promulgation of the National Program for the Prevention and Punishment of Trafficking in Persons"; and "the adoption by the National Institute for Migration of protocols for detecting, identifying and assisting foreign crime victims and for the possibility of issuing visas to crime victims and witnesses so that they may remain in the country legally."[58]

As for the negative aspects, the committee expressed deep concern at "the alarming number of cases of kidnapping and extortion of undocumented migrant workers coming up from the southern border."[59]

Normative Regime of the International Labor Organization

The International Labor Organization (ILO) is a tripartite, UN-specialized agency created in 1919 as part of the Treaty of Versailles. It brings together governments, employers, and worker representatives of 187 member states in order to define fundamental principles of workers' rights and international labor standards. These standards are expressed in dozens of international instruments framed within the ILO and ratified by many countries.[60] I focus here on two conventions that are particularly relevant for migrant workers: the Migration for Employment Convention (Revised), 1949 (No. 97), on equal treatment for nationals and regular migrant workers in labor-related areas; and the Migrant Workers (Supplementary Provisions) Convention, 1975 (No. 143),[61] on eliminating illegal migration and illegal employment, setting requirements for respecting the rights of migrants with an irregular status, establishing measures to end clandestine trafficking, and penalizing employers of irregular migrants.[62]

The ILO monitoring mechanisms operate on the basis of ratification; they are not binding for states that have not ratified the corresponding convention. However, on June 18, 1998, the ILO adopted the ILO Declaration on Fundamental Principles and Rights at Work and Its Follow-Up in Geneva.[63] The declaration made two important innovations. First, it recognized that the members of the ILO, even if they had not ratified the conventions in question, nonetheless had an obligation to respect, "in good faith and in accordance with the Constitution, the principles concerning the fundamental rights which are the subject of those Conventions."[64] Second, in pursuit of this aim, it implemented a procedure by which states that had not ratified the core conventions would be asked to submit reports on progress made in implementing the principles enshrined therein.

The ILO also produces soft law in the form of international nonbinding standards that provide direction to states for protecting migrant workers' rights. An example of these standards can be found in the ILO Multilateral Framework on Labor Migration.[65] After supplying guidelines on the means by which states, employers, and workers' organizations should engage in international cooperation to promote managed migration for employment purposes, the ILO outlines a range of ways to protect migrant workers' rights.

Another supervisory procedure exists within the framework of the ILO, the Committee on Freedom of Association (CFA), created in 1951 for the purpose of hearing complaints about violations in that arena regardless of whether the country concerned had ratified the relevant conventions.[66] The committee is particularly relevant to this discussion because in 2003 it issued a report on a case central to migrant workers' rights, that of *Hoffman Plastic Compounds v. National Labor Relations Board.*[67]

The complainants were the American Federation of Labor and the Congress of Industrial Organizations (AFL-CIO) and the Confederation of Mexican Workers;[68] they alleged that, following the Supreme Court decision in *Hoffman Plastic Compounds*, millions of workers lost their right to associate freely, including the right to organize and bargain collectively, on the basis of their immigration status. The court ruled that an undocumented worker did not have the right to back pay after being illegally dismissed for trying to exercise his rights as granted by the National Labor Relations Act. The complainants argued that the *Hoffman* decision and the continuing failure of the US administration and Congress to enact legislation to correct such discrimination put the United States in violation of its obligations under ILO Conventions Nos. 87 and 98,[69] as well as its obligations under the ILO's 1998 Declaration on Fundamental Principles and Rights at Work.[70]

In its communication dated May 9, 2003, the US government contended that it had not ratified ILO Conventions Nos. 87 and 98 and therefore had no obligation to abide by its provisions. Likewise, the government stated that the ILO declaration was a nonbinding statement of principles, not a treaty imposing legal obligations. For its part, the CFA accepted the United States' arguments, but it also noted that the committee itself had been given the task of examining complaints alleging violations of the freedom to associate, whether or not the country concerned had ratified the relevant ILO conventions. Its mandate stemmed directly from the fundamental aims set forth in the ILO Constitution, and therefore the committee declared its intention to pursue its examination of the complaint.

In the end, the CFA concluded that post-*Hoffman*, the remedial measures available to the National Labor Relations Board in cases of illegal dismissals of undocumented workers were inadequate to ensure effective protection against acts of anti-union discrimination. However, the CFA did not go so far as to state what precise remedy or sanction should be made available, merely writing that "this deficiency should be addressed by executive and congressional action so as to avoid any potential abuse and intimidation of such workers and any restrictions on their effective exercise of basic freedom of association rights." The committee invited the US government "to explore all possible solutions, including amending the legislation to bring it into conformity with freedom of association principles, in full consultation with the social partners concerned, with the aim of ensuring effective protection for all workers against acts of anti-union discrimination in the wake of the Hoffman decision." Finally, the US government was asked to keep the committee informed of measures taken in this regard.[71] The case shows how building coalitions with other actors capable of cross-border coordination and using political opportunity structures that exist at the transnational level can strengthen and consolidate a migrant civil society.

The Inter-American System for the Protection of Human Rights and Migrant Workers' Rights

The inter-American system for the protection of human rights is based on two international instruments: the American Declaration on Human Rights, which is broadly similar to the Universal Declaration on Human Rights, and the American Convention on Human Rights of 1969.[72] Also relevant to migrant workers' rights is the Additional Protocol to the American Convention on Human Rights in the Area of Economic, Social, and Cultural Rights, better known as the Protocol of San Salvador.

The monitoring bodies of these instruments are the Inter-American Commission on Human Rights (IACHR) and the Inter-American Court on Human Rights (IACrHR).

Inter-American Commission on Human Rights

The most important function of the IACHR is to promote the observance and protection of human rights in the Americas as established in Article 106 of the Organization of American States charter. To do so, it drafts a variety of annual reports, country reports, and thematic reports.[73]

In 1996 the IACHR created the Rapporteurship on the Rights of Migrants with a mandate to promote the rights of migrants and their families, asylum seekers, refugees, stateless persons, victims of human trafficking, internally displaced persons, and other vulnerable groups. The rapporteur monitors the human rights situations of migrants and their families in the Americas, consults with and makes recommendations on public policy to Organization of American States (OAS) member states as well as to political bodies of the OAS, and prepares reports and specialized studies.[74]

Inter-American Court on Human Rights

The IACrHR is an autonomous judicial institution tasked with applying and interpreting the American Convention on Human Rights.[75] It exercises adjudicatory and advisory jurisdiction. Correspondingly, it has the power to issue two kinds of decisions: judgments and advisory opinions. For the states that have accepted the jurisdiction of the Inter-American Court of Human Rights, both kinds of decisions represent hard law.

While some judgments have addressed issues connected to migrant rights,[76] as yet none has referred to migrant workers' rights in particular. In contrast, the IACrHR has issued a significant advisory opinion on the topic: Advisory Opinion OC-18/03 of September 17, 2003, requested by Mexico, on the rights of migrant workers irrespective of their migratory status.[77]

At times, such opinions can be requested by outside parties. On May 10, 2002, Mexico, based on Article 64(1) of the American Convention on Human Rights, submitted to the IACrHR a request for an advisory opinion on the "deprivation of the enjoyment and exercise of certain labor rights [of migrant workers], and its compatibility with the obligation of the American States to ensure the principles of legal equality, non-discrimination and the equal and effective protection of the law embodied in international instruments for the protection of human rights." The core question posed by Mexico's request was as follows: "Can an American state establish in its labor legislation a distinct treatment from that accorded legal residents or citizens that prejudices undocumented migrant workers in the enjoyment of their labor rights, so that the migratory status of the workers impedes *per se* the enjoyment of such rights?"

The IACrHR concluded "that the fundamental principle of equality and non-discrimination forms part of general international law, because it is applicable to all States, regardless of whether or not they are a party to a specific international treaty" and "that the migratory status of a person cannot constitute a justification to deprive him of the enjoyment and exercise of human rights, including those of a labor-related nature. When assuming an employment relationship, the migrant acquires rights that must be recognized and ensured because he is an employee, irrespective of his regular or irregular status in the State where he is employed. These rights are a result of the employment relationship."[78]

A more recent example of how the inter-American system touches on migrant workers' rights in North American can be found in Case 12.834, concerning the rights of undocumented workers in the United States.[79] In this case, petitioners claimed that a group of undocumented workers (Leopoldo Zumaya and Francisco Berumen Lizalde, among others) were excluded from employment rights and remedies available to their documented counterparts.[80] On behalf of the presumed victims, petitioners argued that the workers had been directly affected by the United States' denial of equal rights based on immigration status.[81] Petitioners further contended that the US

Supreme Court's *Hoffman* decision made the issue of immigration status relevant to workplace rights in that it encouraged employers to claim that undocumented immigrant workers lacked legal rights in contexts beyond those discussed in that case. For its part, the United States contended that it had the sovereign right to deny permission to work to those "illegally present" in the country or to those who had not obtained authorization to work. In addition, the United States claimed that the petitioners had "overstated" the impact of *Hoffman* and that undocumented workers still were entitled to protection under the National Labor Relations Act, including wage compensation and medical benefits.

In its report, the IACHR pushed back with a series of recommendations, concluding that

> the United States is responsible for violating Articles II and XVI of the American Declaration with respect to Leopoldo Zumaya and Francisco Berumen Lizalde and for additionally violating Mr. Lizalde's rights under Articles XVII and XVIII. As such, it recommends that the State: provide Mssrs. Zumaya and Lizalde with adequate monetary compensation to remedy the violations sustained in the present report; ensure all federal and state laws and policies, on their face and in practice, prohibit any and all distinctions in employment and labor rights based on immigration status and work authorization, once a person commences work as an employee; prohibit employer inquiries into the immigration status of a worker asserting his or her employment and labor rights in litigation or in administrative complaints; ensure that undocumented workers are granted the same rights and remedies for violations of their rights in the workplace as documented workers; establish a procedure whereby undocumented workers involved in workers' compensation proceedings, or their representatives, may request the suspension of their deportations until the resolution of the proceedings and the workers have received the appropriate medical treatment ordered by the presiding courts; and improve and enhance the detection of employers who violate labor rights and exploit undocumented workers and impose adequate sanctions against them.[82]

North American Agreement on Labor Cooperation

Shifting to international agreements related to migrant rights, I turn to one of NAFTA's side agreements: the North American Agreement on Labor Cooperation (NAALC).[83] Essentially, NAALC puts forth a series of labor-protection principles that the signing states agree to promote though their existing domestic labor law regimes. It also creates a set of institutions and procedures for facilitating the advancement of those principles, including mechanisms for gathering information, fostering cross-border dialogue, and investigating incidents of noncompliance.[84]

The principles of labor protection to be promoted are, as stated in NAALC,[85]

1. freedom of association and protection of the right to organize;
2. the right to bargain collectively;
3. the right to strike;
4. prohibition of forced labor;
5. labor protections for children and young persons;
6. minimum employment standards, such as minimum wages and over-time pay, covering wage earners, including those not covered by collective agreements;
7. elimination of employment discrimination on the basis of grounds such as race, religion, age, sex, or other grounds as determined by each Party's domestic laws;[86]
8. equal pay for men and women;
9. prevention of occupational injuries and illnesses;
10. compensation in cases of occupational injuries and illnesses; and
11. protection of migrant workers.[87]

However, only three of the eleven principles are enforceable by sanctions if a country does not enforce them itself: occupational safety and health, child labor, and minimum wage technical labor standards.

As noted by Mary Jane Bolle, NAALC is essentially a noninvasive way of promoting worker rights in that it does not require any country to adopt new laws or conform to any international standards, only to enforce what is already on the books.[88] Another challenge is that NAALC is not fully operational in Canada, where provinces can opt out. Although adopted by the federal government in 1995, the intergovernmental agreement has been approved to date only by Alberta, Manitoba, Quebec, Nova Scotia, and Prince Edward Island.[89]

Many NAALC cases concern the rights of Mexican migrant workers in the United States. I will highlight one that was submitted through the Mexican National Administrative Office (NAO); NAALC establishes NAOs in each country to implement the agreement and serve as points of contact between national governments.[90] The example is Mexican NAO Submission 9802 (Apple Growers), which was filed with the Mexican NAO on May 27, 1998. The submission concerned migrant workers in Washington State employed in the apple industry and raised issues of freedom of association, safety and health, employment discrimination, minimum employment standards, protection of migrant workers, and compensation in cases of occupational injuries and illnesses. The Mexican NAO accepted this submission for review on July 10, 1998, and met with the submitters and workers on December 2, 1998. It reviewed the submission and issued a public report on August 31, 1999, recommending ministerial consultations to obtain further information on the agricultural sector workers' rights to freely associate and organize as well as on minimum standards regarding work, work discrimination, prevention of occupational injuries and illnesses, and protection of migrant workers.[91]

Besides the submissions, a public communication presented in 2016 to the Mexican NAO offers another look into the process. It concerned violations of labor standards set out in NAALC and the Canadian Charter of Rights and Freedoms by the government of Canada in the hiring of workers for Canada's Seasonal Agricultural Workers Program (SAWP). In the communication, the United Food and Commercial Workers Union of Canada sought to elicit a commitment from the Canadian government to cease discriminatory hiring practices in the program. According to the union, the government was to blame for the low participation rate of women in the program, at less than 3 percent of the thousands of agricultural migrants who participate in the SAWP every year. Canada, it was alleged, conveys the gender preferences of SAWP employers to the Mexican government, which tends to follow those preferences. The petitioners in this case, which was still pending in 2018, request that the Mexican NAO, following its investigation, recommend ministerial consultations regarding the Canadian government's failure to respect its own labor and discrimination laws as outlined under Article 22 of NAALC.

According to some analysts, NAALC has had success in shedding light on labor violations in each of the NAFTA nations through unfavorable publicity and exerting soft political pressure.[92] In line with this optimistic view, Lance Compa and Tequila Brooks have found that the NAALC has had beneficial effects in several areas. They find that knowledge of Mexican, American, and Canadian labor law systems has substantially increased among the trade unions, management structures, governments, academics, practitioners, journalists, and NGO communities in each country. There also has been a significant uptick in cross-border engagement—formally practically non-existent—among those communities, including labor organizations, NGOs, and governments. And, Compa and Brooks note, a NAALC complaint system has been created, and its impact is beginning to be seen in specific cases and in a broader, "climate-changing way whose consequences are yet to be fully appreciated."[93]

Other accounts take on a more pessimistic tone, representing the NAALC as a toothless and ineffective institution, a politicized mediator of social policy in the very unequal political economies of North America.[94] In this volume, for example, Bada and Gleeson show the limitations of NAALC mechanisms to effectively protect low-wage migrant workers.

An overall evaluation of the NAALC procedures exceeds the scope of this essay. I will limit myself to pointing out that after an initial era of success, enthusiasm, and high expectations, it seems that those procedures have recently come to be seen as less effective in protecting the rights of workers in North America. Despite these reservations, NAALC remains a supranational political opportunity structure that could be used to mobilize transnational labor relations and protect the workers, as suggested by the Apple Growers case.[95]

Final Reflections

States do not determine their policies and practices toward migrant workers in a vacuum. Rather, they are immersed in an array of global and regional normative regimes that set standards for how to treat migrant workers, from international and supranational perspectives. Indeed, the current stage of globalization is characterized by the emergence of new actors in international politics, which until some decades ago was dominated by nation-states. These new actors have great power and international influence; they include intergovernmental institutions, international tribunals, financial agencies such as the International Monetary Fund and the World Bank, supranational structures like the European Union and the World Trade Organization, and global companies such as Microsoft and CNN. In this new polycentric power structure, nation-states now have to share the stage with a greater number of players in a rapidly growing global economy and react to nascent global activism.

As a result of these changes, the dividing line between domestic and foreign policy is becoming blurred. Through transnational relations, external actors are increasingly involved in the internal affairs of states. Because of economic interrelations, crises are no longer confined to one single country. The densification of communications and transport is linking economies and societies at a rate never before seen, and national societies, regions, and municipalities increasingly feel the impact of decisions often made in distant places.[96]

In another vein, transnational networks that generate and exchange information have formed and consolidated. Modern communication systems enable individuals and groups to access social and physical environments that they otherwise would never have known. They can overcome the geographical boundaries that previously prevented contact and gain access to new social and cultural discourses. Certainly, cultural exchange existed before. Rather, as David Held and Anthony McGrew contend, the scale, intensity, speed, and volume of global cultural communications are now unparalleled.[97]

Finally, the current phase of globalization has been marked by the emergence of international problems, or "global dangers," in Ulrich Beck's expression,[98] which cannot be solved by isolated states; among them are population explosion, deterioration of the environment, terrorism, water scarcity, energy shortages, hunger, epidemics, exploitation of deep seabed resources, and migration. Finding their solutions will necessarily lead to greater degrees of interdependence and require innovative approaches from state and nonstate actors, intergovernmental cooperation, and establishment of international regimes and supranational political organizations.

Already, an extensive set of institutions and normative regimes has arisen in response to the issues at hand, particularly those concerning human rights and justice. One such global issue is international migration and specifically the international migration of workers. I have outlined the international regimes that have been created to protect the rights of migrant workers in North America. Those regimes can use either hard law or soft law to achieve their goals. Hard-law instruments are more desirable in terms of enforcing migrant workers' rights because noncompliance can be punished. However, because of the challenge the instruments pose to state sovereignty (the sovereignty to undermine migrant workers' rights!), states avoid ratifying core international treaties, preferring instead to sign soft-law instruments that have limited influence in modifying how states treat migrant workers.

One can conclude that the connection between global and regional regimes is asymmetrical such that, for example, the political and economic weight of a country can easily lead to attitudes of exceptionalism. In addition, states still have the capacity to decide which international regimes to join (and under what terms) and which to reject. Furthermore, domestic rules determining specific obligations under international law vary among states.

International instruments and their monitoring bodies, in spite of these limitations, constitute viable supranational political opportunity structures. They can effectively mobilize migrant civil society and provide avenues for action that national and transnational advocacy groups can take to better protect North American migrant workers' rights.

Notes

1. Scholars began to notice the growing influence of international intergovernmental organizations in the late 1970s. Evan Luard, for example, has used the term "international government" to refer to this phenomenon; *International Agencies: The Emerging Framework of Interdependence* (London: Macmillan, for the Royal Institute of International Affairs, 1997), 1. However, it was not until the 1990s that the concept of "global governance" started to appear in the language of international institutions. An example of this is the Global Commission on Governance text titled *Our Global Neighborhood* (Oxford: Oxford University Press, 1995). This report was drafted by a commission created in 1992 with the support of the UN secretary-general Boutros Boutros-Ghali and was co-chaired by the Swedish prime minister Ingvar Carlsson and former Commonwealth of Nations secretary-general Shridath Ramphal. In the academic field, the concept of global governance was taking shape by the early 2000s; see, for example, Robert O. Keohane and Joseph S. Nye Jr., eds., *Governance in a Globalizing World* (Washington, DC: Brookings Institution Press, 2000).

2. See, for example, Lawrence Finkelstein, "What Is Global Governance?" *Global Governance* 1, no. 3 (1995): 367–372; and Andrew Hurrell, "Emerging Powers, Global Order, and Global Justice," paper presented at the International Legal Theory Colloquium "The Turn to Governance: The Exercise of Power in the International Public Space," Institute for International Law and Justice, School of Law, New York University, January 20, 2010.

3. See, for example, Ulrich Brand, "Order and Regulation": Global Governance as a Hegemonic Discourse of International Politics?" *Review of International Political Economy* 12, no. 1 (2005): 155–176.

4. See Jonathan Fox and Gaspar Rivera-Salgado's chapter 1 of this volume.

5. Ricardo Méndez Silva, "Gobernanza global y derecho internacional," in *Gobernanza global y cambio estructural del sistema jurídico mexicano*, edited José Ma. Serna de la Garza (Mexico City: UNAM, 2016), 163–177.

6. Armin von Bogdandy, "El derecho internacional como derecho público," *Hacia un nuevo derecho público: Estudios de derecho público comparado, supranacional e internacional* (UNAM: Mexico City, 2011), 113.

7. A discussion of these ideas can be found in Armin von Bogdandy, "Globalization and Europe: How to Square Democracy, Globalization, and International Law," *European Journal of International Law* 15, no. 5 (2004): 885–889.

8. Cartsten Stahn proposes functional criteria for legitimacy, arguing that functional factors like expertise, independence, and neutrality can legitimize the authority of international agencies and their impact on domestic legal systems. "Governance beyond the State," *International Organizations Law Review* 2, no. 1 (2005): 46.

9. Edgar Corzo and Jorge Ulises Carmona proposed such revisions in panel 4, on procedural law and justice, in the seminar "Gobernanza global y cambio estructural del sistema jurídico mexicano," February, 27, 2014, at the Instituto de Investigaciones Jurídicas, UNAM, Mexico City.

10. Margaret Keck and Kathryn Sikkink, *Activists beyond Borders: Advocacy Networks in International Politics* (Ithaca, NY: Cornell University Press, 1998), 1–2.

11. Ibid., 2.

12. Méndez Silva, "Gobernanza global y derecho internacional," 168–170.

13. See, for example, Cleveland, Lyon, and Smith, "Inter-American Court of Human

Rights Amicus Curiae Brief: The United States Violates International Law When Labor Law Remedies Are Restricted Based on Worker's Migrant Status," *Seattle Journal for Social Justice* 1, no. 3 (2002): 798–864.

14. David Trubek, Patrick Cottrell, and Mark Nance, "'Soft Law,' 'Hard Law,' and European Integration: Toward a Theory of Hybridity" (Jean Monnet Working Paper 02/05, Jean Monnet Program, NWY School of Law, New York, 2005), 5.

15. Gunther F. Handle, comments in "A Hard Look at Soft Law," *Proceedings of the 82nd Annual Meeting of the American Society of International Law*, April 20–23, 1988, Washington, DC (Washington, DC: American Society of International Law, 1988), 371.

16. Dinah Shelton, "Normative Hierarchy in International Law," *American Journal of International Law* 100, no. 2 (2006): 292.

17. Chinkin, comments in "A Hard Look at Soft Law" (American Society of International Law, Proceedings of the 82nd Annual Meeting, April 20–23, 1988, Washington, DC), 393.

18. Antto Vihma, "Analyzing Soft Law and Hard Law in Climate Change," in *Climate Change and the Law*, ed. Erkki J. Hollo, Kati Kulovesi, and Michael Mehling, 21 Ius Gentium: Comparative Perspectives on Law and Justice 21 (Dordrecht, Netherlands: Springer, 2013), 150–151.

19. Ibid.

20. Vihma notes that this idealist perspective makes the analysis susceptible to classic criticisms that realist scholars of international relations originally leveled at international law. In his work (ibid.), Vihma suggests a middle path between constructivist and rationalist paradigms to explain why states and other international actors have both utilitarian and normative motives in creating international regimes based on different combinations of hard and soft law.

21. Alexander Betts has used the global governance focus to examine the international normative regime concerning refugees. See Alexander Betts, *Survival Migration, Failed Governance, and the Crisis of Displacement* (Ithaca, NY: Cornell University Press, 2013).

22. The resolution was adopted by the General Assembly on December 18, 2014.

23. "Promotion and Protection of Human Rights, Including Ways and Means to Promote the Human Rights of Migrants," August 3, 2015.

24. The resolution was adopted by the General Assembly on December 18, 2009.

25. This document, "Violence against Women Migrant Workers," provides information on measures taken by member states and the UN system to address violence and discrimination against women migrant workers. It was adopted on July 29, 2011.

26. The resolution was adopted by the General Assembly on December 19, 2011.

27. "Violence against Women Migrant Workers" focuses specifically on women's access to justice; it highlights the impacts on women migrant workers of legislation, policies, and programs implemented by member states. It is dated July 23, 2013.

28. The resolution was adopted by the UN General Assembly on December 18, 2013.

29. "Promotion and Protection of Human Rights, Including Ways and Means to Promote the Human Rights of Migrants," dated August 7, 2014.

30. The resolution was adopted by the UN General Assembly on December 21, 2012.

31. The resolution was adopted by the UN General Assembly on December 20, 2010.

32. The report is dated July 25, 2013.

33. The resolution was adopted by the UN General Assembly on December 19, 2008.

34. The report is dated August 2, 2010.

35. The resolution was adopted by the General Assembly on December 20, 2012.

36. The report is dated August 9, 2013. This report, submitted by the UN secretary-general, considers the components of a human rights–based approach to migrants and migration, including the perspective of the post-2015 development agenda. It analyzes how a human rights perspective can enhance the design and implementation of international migration and development policies. The report provides examples of recent practices in integrating a human rights perspective into the design and implementation of migration and development policies.

37. The report is dated August 11, 2014.

38. Paragraph 4(k) and (m). In its Resolution A/RES/69/167 the General Assembly requested the secretary-general to submit to the General Assembly at its seventieth session a report on the implementation of the resolution. Thus, in his Report A/70/259, the secretary-general made a series of recommendations directed to states, in line with the corresponding resolution, addressing issues related to rights of migrants, of migrant workers, and more specifically, of migrant domestic workers.

39. "Health as an Integral Part of Development," dated November 29, 1979.

40. "Global Health and Foreign Policy," dated December 6, 2012, recognizes the responsibility of governments to urgently and significantly scale up efforts to accelerate the transition toward universal access to affordable and quality health care services.

41. "United Nations Literacy Decade: Education for All," dated June 18, 2002, proclaims the ten-year period beginning January 1, 2003, to be the "United Nations Literacy Decade."

42. Among the factors are the time at which the resolution was passed, the fundamental issues that ground the resolutions, and the vote taken on the resolution or the language of the resolution; Gabriella Rosner Lande, "The Changing Effectiveness of General Assembly Resolutions," *Proceedings of the American Society of International Law at Its Annual Meeting (1921–1969)* 58 (1964): 162–166.

43. See Inis L. Claude, "Collective Legitimization as a Political Function of the United Nations," *International Organization* 20, no. 3 (1966): 367–379.

44. The UNHRC is composed of representatives of forty-seven UN member states, elected by the UN General Assembly.

45. UN Human Rights Council, twenty-fourth session, Universal Periodic Review, *Report of the Working Group on the Universal Periodic Review, Canada*, A/HRC/24/11, June 28, 2013, 15–23.

46. UN Human Rights Council, eleventh session, Universal Periodic Review, *Report of the Working Group on the Universal Periodic Review, Mexico*, A/HRC/11/27, May 29, 2009, 20–27.

47. UN Human Rights Council, sixteenth session, Universal Periodic Review, *Report of the Working Group on the Universal Periodic Review, United States of America*, A/HRC/16/11, January 4, 2011, 13–27.

48. *Specific Groups and Individuals: Migrant Workers*, report submitted by Ms. Gabriela Rodríguez Pizarro, special rapporteur, in conformity with resolution 2002/62 of the Commission on Human Rights, E/CN.4/2003/85/Add.3, October 30, 2002, 17–18.

49. Another report on the situation of migrants in Mexico is *Specific Groups and Individuals: Migrant Workers*, report submitted by Ms. Gabriela Rodríguez Pizarro, special rapporteur, in conformity with resolution 2002/62 of the Commission on Human Rights, E/CN.4/2003/85/Add.2E/CN.4/2003/85/Add.2, October 30, 2002.

50. UN Office of the High Commissioner for Human Rights, *Working with the United Nations Human Rights Programme: A Handbook for Civil Society* (New York and Geneva: 2008), http://www.ohchr.org/EN/AboutUs/CivilSociety/Documents/Handbook_en .pdf.

51. A safe guide to identifying hard-law instruments of international law is found in Article 38 of the Statute of the International Court of Justice. The article states that in solving disputes according with international law, the court shall apply international conventions, whether general or particular, establishing rules expressly recognized by the contesting states; international custom, as evidence of a general practice accepted as law; and the general principles of law recognized by civilized nations.

52. Specific references to migrant workers can be found in paragraph 47(e) and (f) of General Comment No. 23 (2016).

53. UN Committee on Economic, Social, and Cultural Rights, General Comment No. 19: The Right to Social Security (Article 9 of the Covenant), February 4, 2008, E/C.12/ GC/19, http://www.refworld.org/docid/47b17b5b39c.html.

54. UN Committee on Economic, Social, and Cultural Rights, General Comment No. 14: The Right to the Highest Attainable Standard of Health (Article 12 of the Covenant), August 11, 2000, E/C.12/2000/4, http://www.refworld.org/docid/4538838d0.html [accessed June 29, 2018].

55. UN Office of the High Commissioner for Human Rights, "The International Convention on Migrant Workers and Its Committee," Fact Sheet No. 24 (New York: United Nations, 2005), 1.

56. Ibid., 4.

57. At this writing, the most recent report prepared by Mexico dates from 2010; Committee on the Protection of the Rights of All Migrant Workers and Members of Their Families, *Consideration of Reports Submitted by States Parties under Article 73 of the Convention, Second Periodic Report, Mexico*, CMW/C/MEX/2, January 14, 2010.

58. Committee on the Protection of the Rights of All Migrant Workers and Members of Their Families, *Concluding Observations of the Committee on the Protection of the Rights of All Migrant Workers and Members of Their Families, Mexico*, CMW/C/MEX/ CO/2, May 3, 2011, 3–6. In Mexico, reforming laws on the books does not necessarily modify the behavior of state and nonstate actors toward migrant workers in general or in particular. As Ana Lorena Delgadillo, Alma García, and Rodolfo Córdova Alcaraz show in chapter 5 of this book, migrants continue to be particularly vulnerable to the illegal and corrupt actions of many Mexican public authorities and to the violence of organized crime.

59. Ibid., Committee, *Concluding Observations*, 5.

60. Migrant workers also benefit from the protection offered by other relevant ILO standards, including those concerning fundamental rights at work and relating to other areas such as employment, labor inspection, social security, wages, occupational safety and health, and private recruitment agencies. The standards provide protection in sectors such as agriculture, construction, and the hotel and restaurant industries, which traditionally employ large numbers of migrant workers. Of particular importance for the protection of labor rights are the Freedom of Association and Protection of the Right to Organize Convention, 1948 (no. 87), and the Right to Organize and Collective Bargaining Convention, 1949 (no. 98). The former has been ratified by Canada and Mexico but not by the United States. The latter has not been ratified by any of the three states.

61. By January 2017, the Migration for Employment Convention (Revised), 1949 (no. 97), had been ratified by forty-nine states and the Migrant Workers (Supplementary Provisions) Convention, 1975 (no. 143), by twenty-three states. Neither of these conventions has been ratified by Canada, Mexico, or the United States.

62. Other international instruments of direct importance to migrants are the so-called Palermo Protocols, which require participating states to criminalize acts of trafficking and smuggling and establish a framework for international cooperation. These protocols have been ratified by Canada, Mexico, and the United States.

63. Declarations of this kind are typical examples of soft law.

64. The fundamental rights covered by this declaration are freedom of association and effective recognition of the right to collective bargaining, elimination of all forms of forced or compulsory labor, the effective abolition of child labor, and elimination of discrimination in employment and occupation.

65. ILO, *ILO Multilateral Framework on Labor Migration, Non-Binding Principles and Guidelines for a Rights-Based Approach to Labor Migration*, International Labor Office (Geneva: International Labor Organization, 2006).

66. Complaints may be brought against a member state by employers' and workers' organizations. As stated, "The CFA is a Governing Body committee, and is composed of an independent chairperson and three representatives each from governments, employers, and workers. If, after establishing the facts in dialogue with the government concerned, the CFA concludes that there was a violation of freedom of association standards or principles, it issues a report through the Governing Body and makes recommendations on how the situation could be remedied. Governments are subsequently requested to report on the implementation of its recommendations."

67. In the case of *Hoffman Plastic Compounds, Inc. v. National Labor Relations Board*, the US Supreme Court ruled in March 2002 that an undocumented worker, because of his immigration status, was not entitled to back pay for lost wages after he was illegally dismissed for exercising rights protected by the National Labor Relations Act. The Committee on Freedom of Association's decision in the *Hoffman Plastic* case can be seen as a counterpart to the Inter-American Court on Human Rights Advisory Opinion OC-18/03 of September 17, 2003, requested by Mexico, on the rights of migrant workers irrespective of their migratory status. I discuss the inter-American court's opinion in more detail later in this chapter, in my remarks about the inter-American system for the protection of human rights.

68. The complaints are dated October 18, 2002, and October 30, 2002, respectively.

69. ILO Convention No. 87, on the Freedom of Association and Protection of the Right to Organize Convention (1948), protects the right of workers "without distinction whatsoever" to establish and join organizations of their own choosing. ILO Convention No. 98, on the Right to Organize and Collective Bargaining Convention (1949), requires "adequate protection against acts of anti-union discrimination."

70. Complainants further argued that "from a human rights and labor rights perspective, workers' immigration status does not diminish or condition their status as workers holding fundamental rights"; ILO Committee on Freedom of Association, Report No. 332, November 2003, Case No. 2227 (United States)—Complaint date: 18-OCT-02, http://www.ilo.org/dyn/normlex/en/f?p=1000:50002:0::NO:50002:P50002_COM PLAINT_TEXT_ID:2907332#1. In this report the committee requests to be kept informed of developments.

71. Ibid.

72. There are other conventions that form the normative frame of the inter-American system, such as the Inter-American Convention to Prevent and Punish Torture (1985), the Inter-American Convention on the Forced Disappearance of Persons (1994), the Inter-American Convention on the Prevention, Punishment and Eradication of Violence against Women (1994), the Inter-American Convention on the Elimination of Discrimination against Persons with Disabilities (1999), and the Additional Protocol to the American Convention on Human Rights in the Area of Economic, Social, and Cultural Rights (1988).

73. Five of the IACHR's thematic reports directly or indirectly concern migrant workers: *Progress Report on the Situation of Migrant Workers and Their Families in the Hemisphere*, OEA/Ser.L/V/II.102 Doc. 6 rev., April 16, 1999; *Informe de progreso de la relatoría especial sobre trabajadores migratorios y miembros de sus familias* (2005); *Report on Immigration in the United States: Detention and Due Process*, OEA/Ser.L/V/II. Doc. 78/10, December 30, 2010; *Human Rights of Migrants and Other Persons in the Context of Human Mobility in Mexico*, OEA/Ser.L/V/II. Doc. 48/13, December 30, 2013; and *Human Rights Situation of Refugee and Migrant Families and Unaccompanied Children in the United States of America*, OAS/Ser.L/V/II. 155 Doc. 16, July 24, 2015.

74. Canada, Mexico, and the United States have received visits from the rapporteur on the Rights of Migrants on several occasions. Several such visits are described on the OAS website at http://www.oas.org/en/iachr/migrants/activities/visits.asp #US2014Sur.

75. This is defined in Article 1 of the Statute of the Inter-American Court on Human Rights, adopted by the General Assembly of the OAS at its ninth regular session, held in La Paz, Bolivia, October 1979, in Resolution No. 448.

76. *Jesús Tranquilino Vélez Loor v. Panama*, IACrHR, Judgment of November 23, 2010; *Nadege Dorzema et al. v. Dominican Republic*, IACrHR Judgment of October 24, 2012.

77. Juridical Condition and Rights of Undocumented Migrants, Advisory Opinion OC-18/03, Inter-Am. Ct. H.R. (ser. A), no. 18, September 17, 2003. This opinion was requested in connection with the US Supreme Court decision in *Hoffman Plastic Compounds v. National Labor Relations Board*.

78. This is an example of how an external actor, the Mexican state itself, can play a part in coalition building and immigrant organizing. In chapter 1 of this volume, Jonathan Fox and Gaspar Rivera-Salgado explain how, through its consular apparatus in the United States, the Mexican state has contributed to immigrant organizing and protection.

79. IACHR, Report No. 50/16, Case 12.834, Merits (Publication), Undocumented Workers, United States of America, November 30, 2016. The "merits stage" is when the IACHR must decide on the merits or substance of a case, that is, whether there were violations of human rights. The merits stage ends with approving a merits report with the conclusions about whether the facts of the case constitute human rights violations. If the commission finds that there were human rights violations, the merits report includes recommendations to the state.

80. The petitioners were the University of Pennsylvania School of Law, the American Civil Liberties Union Foundation, and the National Employment Law Project.

81. Because of their immigration status the presumed victims in this case had been denied full workers' compensation benefits following on-the-job injuries.

82. Ibid., 2.

83. The other side agreement is the North American Agreement on Environmental Cooperation.

84. Ruth Buchanan and Rusby Chaparro, "International Institutions and Transnational Advocacy: The Case of the North American Agreement on Labor Cooperation," *UCLA Journal of International and Foreign Affairs* 13, no. 1 (2008): 132.

85. "The following are guiding principles that the Parties are committed to promote, subject to each Party's domestic law, but do not establish common minimum standards for their domestic law. They indicate broad areas of concern where the Parties have developed, each in its own way, laws, regulations, procedures and practices that protect the rights and interests of their respective workforces"; Annex 1 on Labor Principles, https://www.canada.ca/en/employment-social-development/services/labour-relations/international/agreements/naalc.html#naalc.

86. "Elimination of employment discrimination on such grounds as race, religion, age, sex or other grounds, subject to certain reasonable exceptions, such as, where applicable, *bona fide* occupational requirements or qualifications and established practices or rules governing retirement ages, and special measures of protection or assistance for particular groups designed to take into account the effects of discrimination" (ibid.).

87. "Providing migrant workers in a Party's territory with the same legal protection as the Party's nationals in respect of working conditions" (ibid.).

88. Mary Jane Bolle, "NAFTA Labor Side Agreement: Lessons for the Worker Rights and Fast-Track Debate," *CRS Report for Congress* (October 9, 2001): 3.

89. David A. Gantz, "Labor Rights and Environmental Protection under NAFTA and Other U.S. Free Trade Agreements," *University of Miami Inter-American Law Review* 42, no. 2 (2011): 321.

90. Interestingly, under Article 16(3), submissions alleging NAALC violations by a NAFTA country are first filed with the NAO of another country. That is, submissions are filed with an office other than the one in which the alleged labor violation has occurred, and this has encouraged cooperation between labor and social movements across borders in the NAFTA region, producing "international labor solidarity." See Lance Compa, "NAFTA's Labor Side Agreement and International Labor Solidarity," *Antipode: A Radical Journal of Geography* 33, no. 3 (2001): 451–467.

91. Two other submissions, on North Carolina and H-2B visa workers, are examined in greater detail by Xóchitl Bada and Shannon Gleeson in chapter 3 of this volume. The authors also discuss the scope and limitations of NAALC's ability to protect low-wage migrant workers.

92. Gantz, "Labor Rights and Environmental Protection," 320.

93. Lance Compa and Tequila Brooks, *NAFTA and the NAALC: Twenty Years of North American Trade-Labour Linkage* (Alphen aan der Rijn, Netherlands: Wolters Kluwer, 2015), 147.

94. While not agreeing with their views, Buchanan and Chaparro describe such accounts; "International Institutions and Transnational Advocacy," 134–135.

95. See Tamara Kay, "Labor Transnationalism and Global Governance: The Impact of NAFTA on Transnational Labor Relationships in North America," *American Journal of Sociology* 11, no. 3 (2005): 715–756. In this article Kay examines how NAFTA and NAALC catalyzed cross-border labor cooperation and collaboration, that is, labor transnationalism, by creating a new political opportunity structure at the transnational level. The author suggests that while the emergence of national social movements requires nation-states, global governance institutions can play a pivotal role in the devel-

opment of transnational social movements—and thus, we can add, contribute to the consolidation of migrant civil society.

96. Dirk Messner, "La transformación del estado y la política en el proceso de la globalización," *Nueva Sociedad* 163 (1999): 73–74.

97. David Held and Anthony McGrew, *Globalización/antiglobalización: Sobre la reconstrucción del orden mundial* (Barcelona: Paidós, 2003), 43–44.

98. Ulrich Beck, *¿Qué es la globalización?* (Barcelona: Paidós, 1988), 67–71.

References

Beck, Ulrich. *¿Qué es la globalización? Falacias del globalismo, respuestas a la globalización.* Barcelona: Paidós, 1998.

Betts, Alexander. *Survival Migration: Failed Governance and the Crisis of Displacement.* Ithaca, NY: Cornell Press, 2013.

Bogdandy, Armin von. "El derecho internacional como derecho público." In *Hacia un nuevo derecho público: Estudios de derecho público comparado, supranacional e internacional*, edited by Armin von Bogdandy, 93–119. Mexico City: UNAM, 2011.

———. "Globalization and Europe: How to Square Democracy, Globalization, and International Law." *European Journal of International Law* 15, no. 5 (2004): 885–906.

Bolle, Mary Jane. *NAFTA Labor Side Agreement: Lessons for the Worker Rights and Fast-Track Debate.* Report, October 9, 2001. Washington, DC: Congressional Research Service.

Brand, Ulrich. "Order and Regulation: Global Governance as a Hegemonic Discourse of International Politics?" *Review of International Political Economy* 12, no. 1 (2005): 155–176.

Brower, Adam. "Rethinking NAFTA´s NAALC Provision: The Effectiveness of Its Dispute Resolution System on the Protection of Mexican Migrant Workers in the United States." *Indiana International and Comparative Law Review* 18, no. 1 (2008): 153–188.

Buchanan, Ruth, and Rusby Chaparro. "International Institutions and Transnational Advocacy: The Case of the North American Agreement on Labor Cooperation." *UCLA Journal of International and Foreign Affairs* 13, no. 1 (2008): 129–160.

Chinkin, Christine. Comments in "A Hard Look at Soft Law." *Proceedings of the 82nd Annual Meeting of the American Society of International Law*, 371–395. Washington, DC: American Society of International Law, 1988.

Claude, Inis L. "Collective Legitimization as a Political Function of the United Nations." *International Organization* 20, no. 3 (1966): 367–379.

Cleveland, Sarah, Beth Lyon, and Rebecca Smith. "Inter-American Court of Human Rights Amicus Curiae Brief: The United States Violates International Law When Labor Law Remedies are Restricted Based on Worker's Migrant Status." *Seattle Journal for Social Justice* 1, no. 3 (2002): 798–864.

Compa, Lance. "NAFTA's Labor Side Agreement and International Labor Solidarity." *Antipode: A Radical Journal of Geography* 33, no. 3, 2001: 451–467.

Compa, Lance, and Tequila Brooks. *NAFTA and the NAALC: Twenty Years of North American Trade-Labour Linkage.* Alphen ann den Rijn, the Netherlands: Wolters Kluwer, 2015.

Corzo, Edgar, and Jorge Ulises Carmona. Presentation in panel 4, on procedural law and justice, in the seminar "Gobernanza global y cambio estructural del sistema jurídico mexicano," February 27, 2014, Instituto de Investigaciones Jurídicas, UNAM, Mexico City.

Finkelstein, Lawrence. 1995. "What Is Global Governance?" *Global Governance* 1, no. 3 (1995): 367–372.

Gantz, David A. "Labor Rights and Environmental Protection under NAFTA and Other U.S. Free Trade Agreements." *University of Miami Inter-American Law Review* 42, no. 2 (2011): 297–366.

Global Commission on Governance. *Our Global Neighborhood*. Oxford: Oxford University Press, 1995.

Handle, Gunther F. 1988. Comments in "A Hard Look at Soft Law." *Proceedings of the 82nd Annual Meeting of the American Society of International Law*, April 20–23, 1988, Washington, DC, 371–377. Washington, DC: American Society of International Law, 1988.

Held, David, and Anthony McGrew. *Globalización/antiglobalización: Sobre la reconstrucción del orden mundial*. Barcelona: Paidós, 2003.

Hurrell, Andrew. "Emerging Powers, Global Order and Global Justice." Paper presented in the International Legal Theory Colloquium "The Turn to Governance: The Exercise of Power in the International Public Space," Institute for International Law and Justice, School of Law, New York University, January 20, 2010.

International Labor Organization (ILO). *ILO Multilateral Framework on Labor Migration, Non-Binding Principles and Guidelines for a Rights-Based Approach to Labor Migration*. International Labor Office. Geneva: ILO, 2006.

Kay, Tamara. "Labor Transnationalism and Global Governance: The Impact of NAFTA on Transnational Labor Relationships in North America." *American Journal of Sociology* 11, no. 3 (2005): 715–756.

Keck, Margaret, and Kathryn Sikkink. *Activists beyond Borders: Advocacy Networks in International Politics*. Ithaca, NY: Cornell University Press, 1998.

Keohane, Robert O., and Joseph S. Nye Jr., eds. *Governance in a Globalizing World*. Washington, DC: Brookings Institution Press, 2000.

Lande, Gabriella Rosner. "The Changing Effectiveness of General Assembly Resolutions." *Proceedings of the American Society of International Law at Its Annual Meeting (1921–1969)* 58 (1964): 162–166.

Luard, Evan. *International Agencies: The Emerging Framework of Interdependence*. London: Macmillan, for the Royal Institute of International Affairs, 1997.

Méndez Silva, Ricardo. "Gobernanza global y derecho internacional." In *Gobernanza global y cambio estructural del sistema jurídico mexicano*, edited by José Ma. Serna de la Garza, 163–177. Mexico City: UNAM, 2016.

Messner, Dirk. "La transformación del estado y la política en el proceso de la globalización." *Nueva Sociedad* 163 (September–October 1999): 71–91.

Shelton, Dinah. "Normative Hierarchy in International Law." *American Journal of International Law* 100, no. 2 (2006): 291–323.

Stahn, Carsten. "Governance beyond the State." *International Organizations Law Review* 2, no. 1 (2005): 9–56.

Trubek, David, Patrick Cottrell, and Mark Nance. "'Soft Law,' 'Hard Law,' and European Integration: Toward a Theory of Hybridity." Jean Monnet Working Paper 02/05. New York: Jean Monnet Program, School of Law, New York University, 2005.

UN Office of the High Commissioner for Human Rights. *The International Convention on Migrant Workers and Its Committee.* Fact Sheet no. 24, rev. 1. New York: United Nations, 2005.

———. *Working with the United Nations Human Rights Programme: A Handbook for Civil Society.* New York: United Nations, 2008. http://www.ohchr.org/EN/AboutUs/Civil Society/Documents/Handbook_en.pdf.

Vihma, Antto. "Analyzing Soft Law and Hard Law in Climate Change." In *Climate Change and the Law*, edited by Erkki J. Hollo, Kati Kulovesi, and Michael Mehling, 143–164. Ius Gentium: Comparative Perspectives on Law and Justice 21. Dordrecht, Netherlands: Springer, 2013.

CHAPTER 3

The North American Agreement on Labor Cooperation and the Challenges to Protecting Low-Wage Migrant Workers

XÓCHITL BADA AND SHANNON GLEESON

Mexico-US binational coalition building emerged as advocates in both countries deepened their interest in cross-border organizing strategies. These
efforts have slowly transformed US-Mexico relations from below. Before the
North American Free Trade Agreement (NAFTA) was signed in 1993, ties
between cross-border social constituencies were concentrated primarily in
the border region (Brooks and Fox 2002). In the 1980s, Mexico's economic
dependency deepened, and national policies were increasingly crafted to attract the attention of US political and economic elites. By the early 1990s,
trade unionists in both countries realized that they were confronting similar issues: anti-union policies, privatizations, and deteriorating living conditions and job security for workers. Years of local, regional, and national
campaigns to challenge such conditions shattered divides between sectors.
As the public debate around NAFTA popularized dialogues over the structural economic changes occurring in the two countries, the boundaries between international and domestic policy issues blurred. Domestic civil society actors across Mexico and the United States struggled to mitigate the
impacts of free trade and soon realized that a cross-border strategy was necessary, thus reinvigorating the internationalist wings of the labor and envi-
ronmentalist movements (Fox 2002).

The first binational efforts between labor organizations and nongovernmental organizations (NGOs) concerned with the conditions of working
people can be traced back to the multisectoral Coalition for Justice in the
Maquiladoras and a Campbell Soup organizing campaign. Founded in 1989,
the coalition brought together religious, environmental, labor, community,
and women's rights organizers active around binational integration issues
related to improving working conditions and living standards for workers
employed in Mexico's maquiladora industry (Williams 2002). In the Campbell campaign, the AFL-CIO affiliate Midwestern Farm Labor Organizing

Committee (FLOC) partnered with an agricultural worker union in Sinaloa affiliated with the official Confederation of Mexican Workers to combat the Campbell Soup Company's efforts to divide unions in the United States and Mexico (Barger and Reza 1994). These two pioneering efforts paved the way for subsequent cross-border labor organizing campaigns against violations of freedom of association laws—even if the resulting claims filed through the NAFTA labor side agreements yielded few tangible results in terms of influencing government policies or private employers. However, the continued relationship between civil society groups interested in labor rights would eventually open the door to sustained cross-border networks. Those coalitions became denser and tested new strategies to increase visibility and strengthen collaborative efforts to ensure labor standards enforcement in Mexico and the United States.

In this chapter we report on findings from a larger collaborative project that began in 2012 as an inquiry into the Mexican government's role as an intermediary to labor standards enforcement for low-wage and undocumented migrant workers in the United States. The 2004 memorandum of understanding signed by US Secretary of Labor Elaine Chao and Mexico's Secretary of Foreign Affairs Ernesto Derbez was well known, but we sought to examine the specifics of its implementation and the emergence of the Labor Counter/Ventanilla Laboral, a new initiative stemming from a 2014 memorandum of understanding signed by Mexico's Ministry of Labor and the US Department of Labor to support labor rights enforcement. The Ventanilla Laboral initiative was not, as some have suggested, simply an outgrowth of the 2004 memorandum of understanding; rather, a public petition submitted in 2011 to the North American Agreement on Labor Cooperation (NAALC) was crucial to its creation. The organization leading the coalition was the Centro de los Derechos del Migrante (CDM), a binational workers' rights NGO that began operations in 2005 in Zacatecas, Mexico, and now has offices in Baltimore, Mexico City, and Juxtlahuaca, Oaxaca, and has been active in implementing Ventanilla Laboral in the United States. Here we trace the emergence of the 2014 joint government declaration on migrant labor rights following ministerial consultations under NAALC and the importance it holds to transnational advocacy efforts.

Background

Immigrants commonly face labor and employment law violations and struggle to access social protections in host countries. While levying sanctions seems to improve employer compliance, at least with regard to wage and hour standards (Galvin 2016), few studies have examined the role of bilateral initiatives to address workplace violations. The present study adds to the growing inquiries on transnational labor advocacy networks (e.g., Compa 2001; Kay 2010; Vega 2000) as we examine the mechanisms for regional cooperation established in 1993 by NAALC, also known as the labor side accords under NAFTA.

We analyze the genesis and evolution of the first bilateral resolution enacted as a result of negotiations under NAALC and facilitated by the consular partnership program that was coordinated by the US Department of Labor and the Mexican consular network in the United States (Bada and Gleeson 2015). We assess to what extent this bilateral effort has been able to confront extant enforcement challenges and ultimately improve migrant workers' access to labor and employment protections. We also address different strategies pursued by cross-border civil society organizations aimed at improving enforcement standards and implementing these policy changes. What are the "boomerang effects" (Keck and Sikkink 1998), if any, experienced by the Mexican government in supporting a joint declaration that primarily complains about the lack of enforcement in US territory? Has Mexico been forced to make adjustments to labor practices involving migrant workers as a result of complaints brought by NAALC? What is the main function of these petitions in a transnational labor rights advocacy framework?

We first describe the ways in which NAALC, a toothless regional governance structure, nonetheless offered a political opening for innovative transnational labor advocacy networks to form and defend migrant labor rights in the region and beyond. In doing so, we identify best practices for worker advocacy, reflecting on their potential to challenge hegemonic systems (García Agustín and Jørgensen 2016). We also consider how the pressure to hold the Mexican government accountable to its diasporic workforce in the United States has shaped parallel efforts to advocate for workers who have remained in or returned to Mexico. Our work follows Tamara Kay's (2010) labor transnationalism framework, in which NAFTA is viewed as a catalyzing platform for transnational institutional fields seeking to connect local issues with larger regional and global trade problems. Instead of focusing on labor unions, we pay special attention to migrant worker rights networks, including transnational NGOs, worker centers—"community-based and community-led organizations that engage in a combination of service, advocacy, and organizing to provide support to low-wage workers" (Fine 2005)— and immigrant advocacy organizations. In our analysis of the most recent NAALC petitions on behalf of migrant workers, we analyze the cooperation among diverse cross-border actors who have decided to work together, acknowledging the transnational reality of migrant workers' movement across borders. Our work shows how even amid weak enforcement mechanisms, transnational labor advocacy can influence progressive policy change.

Since the late 1990s, migrant civil society organizations have ramped up their transnational advocacy on behalf of immigrant labor and human rights (Bada 2014; Berg and Rodriguez 2013; Gordon 2006). Despite their limitations, international enforcement mechanisms have created an important avenue for such direct advocacy that challenges hegemonic political closures. In this analysis, we follow Óscar García Agustín and Martin Bak Jørgensen's approach to studying the formation of transnational labor advocacy alliances, which begins, they contend, "with an understanding of the geographies of resistance, that is, how alliances and practices of solidarity are constituted at different scales, ranging from the local to the global" (2016:14). While international law plays no direct role in enforcing any national laws, regional and international governance structures are influential for norms setting and exercising political pressure from civil society alliances (Compa 2001; Kay 2010). Margaret Keck and Kathryn Sikkink's (1998) seminal work on global advocacy networks suggests that transnational organizations have the potential to hold human rights abusers accountable. Creating sustainable transnational advocacy models to improve labor rights enforcement is a more complex endeavor, as it requires dedication and long-term commitments from institutional actors working together in more than one country. Yet as Lance Compa (2001) demonstrates in his analysis of the pioneering Washington Apple Growers case submitted to NAALC in 1998, regional governance structures brought about by NAFTA have the potential to improve cooperation, consultation, and collaboration among social actors interested in advancing the transnational labor rights of migrant workers in the region.

In the United States, labor standards co-enforcement models are on the rise. Matthew Amengual and Janice Fine (2017) define co-enforcement as a series of ongoing, coordinated efforts on the part of state regulatory agencies and worker organizations to jointly produce labor standards enforcement. Drawing on Ian Ayres and John Braithwaite's 1992 work, Amengual and Fine conclude that with co-enforcement, a tripartite model emerges "under which non-governmental organizations gain access to information, a seat at the negotiating table with the firm and agency, and the same standing as the regulator to sue or prosecute under regulatory statutes" (2017: 131). Co-enforcement is mutually beneficial for migrant and other workers alike as well as for industry and the government. In their work comparing partnerships between worker organizations and regulators in California and New York, Fine and Gordon (2010) have found that when worker centers and unions have access to information about sectors that are difficult to penetrate, they have more incentives to cooperate in jointly policing labor markets and function as a necessary complement to marginal increases in the wage and hour staff investigators.

Bilateral Labor Cooperation in Historical Context

Bilateral cooperation in defense of migrant workers in the United States is not an entirely new phenomenon. In 1929, Ramón P. de Negri, Mexican secretary of industry, commerce, and labor, appointed a dedicated staff to organize Mexican workers in the jurisdictions of California, Texas, Arizona, and New Mexico. The looming effects of the US Depression concerned Mexican officials, prompting this reactive strategy, its ultimate goal being to promote the unification of the Mexican laboring classes in foreign territory (González 1999). Almost a century after de Negri's efforts at finding bilateral solutions to labor concerns, government enforcement agencies and pro-immigrant transnational civil society organizations are still experimenting with new models of co-enforcing labor standards today. Important issues for migrant workers include wage theft, occupational safety and health protections, and a rise in criminal international recruiters taking advantage of the lack of a transparent recruitment system to commit fraud. On the enforcement side, how employers perceive the credibility and efficacy of enforcement mechanisms is vital to compliance (Gunningham, Thornton, and Kagan 2005).

During the 1992 US presidential campaign, candidate Bill Clinton strongly criticized NAFTA as it was being drafted, arguing that the agreement would put in place no effective mechanisms to ensure compliance with Mexico's frequently violated labor standards. Mexico's laxity, critics argued, would pave the way for US-based companies to move operations across the border (Solomon 2001). In part to appease the opposition of US labor groups to NAFTA and in part to guarantee fast-track congressional approval of the trade agreement, the Clinton administration supported creating parallel accords aimed at improving working conditions and living standards in each of the three countries involved—Canada, Mexico, and the United States.

The remedies proposed under NAALC were of limited scope and rather toothless, and as a result few petitions have been submitted on behalf of migrant workers. For those petitions that were submitted, many labor unions invested in transnational labor cooperation have grown disappointed in the outcomes, as NAALC does not require any participating country to affirmatively reform or upgrade its labor laws, does not limit abusive practices by employers, and threatens lax government enforcement with only symbolic penalties (Kay 2010; Wishnie 2002). Submitting public petitions to NAALC also requires that highly organized civil society organizations monitor conditions for labor violations, report abuses, and submit coordinated petitions.

The final negotiated accord ultimately avoided any suggestion that it was intended to harmonize labor standards across the three countries or incorporate international labor laws dictated by the International Labor Organization (ILO). Rather than establish a multinational judicial process or appeals procedure that could yield compensatory damages for aggrieved workers in any of the three countries, the accord committed only to broadly promoting improvements in labor conditions. To do so, it relied on diplomacy and engagement with advocacy organizations rather than binding compliance mechanisms.

NAFTA and Labor Cooperation in North America

NAALC has created a network of agencies for administering international labor affairs, including the US Department of Labor's International Labor Affairs Bureau and Mexico's Cooperación Laboral Internacional within its Secretariat of Labor and Social Welfare (Secretaría de Trabajo y Previsión Social, STPS). NAALC also created the North American Commission for Labor Cooperation (NACLC), charged with enforcing the labor side agreement to NAFTA. The commission, now closed, was comprised of a policy-setting, cabinet-level council consisting of the three nations' labor secretaries and a trinational office that conducted research and provided other support to the council. The commission worked in close cooperation with the national administrative office (NAO) created by each government within its own labor ministry or department to handle public submissions. This institutionalization was designed to facilitate an even broader international framework of labor rights protection within free trade agreements (Perez-Lopez 1996). In the subsequent negotiations to develop the Central America–Dominican Republic Free Trade Agreement (CAFTA-DR), the United States went as far as incorporating core ILO labor rights into the agreement, a clause absent in NAALC (Russo 2011).

These trade agreements have had varying effects on labor standards enforcement efforts. Among Latin American and Caribbean countries that signed free trade agreements with the United States, the effects have been largely positive, leading to an average increase of 20 percent in inspectors and a 60 percent increase in actual inspections from 2009 to 2012. NAFTA, however, has not produced the same positive impacts in Mexico and the United States (Dewan and Ronconi 2018). Originally struck as a compromise to appease labor groups disappointed by NAFTA in the year following a presidential campaign during which a Democrat promised to protect domestic jobs, the labor side accords of 1993 have had paltry success in terms of defending labor rights.

NAALC is frequently dismissed by academic and legal advocates as a marginally effective mechanism for enforcing the existing labor laws of signing countries (Adams and Singh 1997; Armstrong 2005; Dewan and Ronconi 2018; PRODESC and CDM 2010; Russo 2011; Solomon 2001; Vega 2000). In practical terms, NAALC has eleven labor principles, none of which establishes enforceable common minimum standards for domestic laws in Mexico or any other signatory country (Linares 2006). The weakness of those standards is compounded by the insufficient capacities of enforcement agencies in the United States and Mexico. The US Department of Labor Wage and Hour Division, which enforces the Fair Labor Standards Act, has not significantly increased its number of investigators to keep up with a labor force that has grown from 22.6 million in 1948 to 135 million in 2014 (Galvin 2016). The lack of investigative resources has affected enforcement actions, which have decreased and are frequently delayed by months or years (USGAO 2009). Faced with this situation, the US Department of Labor has admitted that it cannot adequately investigate or prosecute allegations of abuse, especially in markets as large and diverse as agriculture and seasonal jobs (Russo 2011).

The United States is not unique in its enforcement woes. Basic labor standards are also notoriously poorly enforced in Mexico. As in the United States, the Mexican Secretariat of Labor and Social Welfare follows a claims-driven enforcement strategy, initiating sanctions only when inspectors detect violations (McGuiness 2000). Since NAFTA's passage, Mexican employers have operated with massive impunity, the result being that most complaints to NAALC's national administrative offices have disproportionately been lodged against Mexico: twenty-four out of thirty-nine since 1998, amounting to 61.5 percent of all submissions. Of the remainder, only seven are related to protecting migrant workers in the United States, and five of those deal with violations to temporary workers with H-2A and H-2B visas (USDOL n.d.).

While NAALC obligates each nation to provide migrant workers with equal labor law rights, in practice the United States excludes legal guest workers from some of its labor provisions under the Migrant and Seasonal Agricultural Worker Protection Act. For example, the act allows domestic and undocumented workers to sue their employers in federal court and provides for actual or statutory damages. However, it also explicitly excludes H-2A workers from its coverage (ILRWG 2013; Linares 2006; Russo 2011). Migrant workers in the service and construction industries also face a range of challenges in securing their rights, some common to those faced by all low-wage workers, some specific to the immigrant worker experience (Gleeson 2016). In seeking justice, many Mexican immigrant workers struggle to navigate the complex labor and employment laws. It is in this muddled rights context that the Mexican government has played an increasingly important role in reaching out to its emigrant citizens through its fifty-two consular jurisdictions across the United States.

Temporary Migrant Labor in the United States

While bilateral and multilateral agreements such as NAFTA reduce barriers to the free movement of capital, labor mobility has become more restricted in all free trade zones in the Americas and the European Union (Domenech 2016). The agricultural industry in the United States depends in large part on labor recruiters, formal and informal, to meet the labor demand for a critical sector of the economy that keeps American citizens fed at low prices (Mercier 2014). The International Labor Recruitment Working Group finds rampant abuses by recruiters: "Regardless of visa category, employment sector, race, gender, or national origin, internationally recruited workers face disturbingly common patterns of recruitment abuse, including fraud, discrimination, severe economic coercion, retaliation, blacklisting, and, in some cases, forced labor, indentured servitude, debt bondage, and human trafficking" (2013:30). Even for workers with temporary work visas, the government oversight needed to ensure that employers comply with state and federal labor laws is lacking.[1]

Today, in addition to the roughly 56,000 temporary agricultural workers admitted through the H-2A program, the United States admits about 69,000 internationals as H-2B workers each year to perform jobs across a growing number of employment sectors, including landscapers, domestic workers, carnival workers, forestry workers, seafood workers, hotel workers, maids, janitors, herders, computer programmers, engineers, nurses, and public school teachers (Justice in Motion 2016). It is difficult to determine the actual number of workers under H-2B visas due to the different approvals processes taking place across different government entities, but advocates estimate that 115,000 H-2B workers are present in the United States at any given time (Justice in Motion 2016). Between fiscal year (FY) 2000 and FY 2008, the number of employers who applied to hire H-2B workers—capped at 66,000 per year—increased 129 percent. In 2017, the first year of the Trump administration, the Departments of Homeland Security and Labor issued a one-time increase to the limit of H-2B nonimmigrant visas, agreeing to issue up to 15,000 additional visas through the end of FY 2017. In 2018, the omnibus spending bill passed by Congress authorized the Department of Homeland Security to adjust the cap again. These decisions were intended to help "American businesses that are likely to experience irreparable harm (permanent and severe financial loss) without the ability to employ all of the H-2B workers that they request" (USCIS 2017). Mexico continues to be the leading source of H-2B workers; in 2011 a total of 36,179 H-2B visas were issued to Mexican workers (USDOS 2012). In 2015, more than 70 percent of H-2B workers were from Mexico (Justice in Motion 2016).

While the numbers of H-2 workers surge, labor standards enforcement efforts are still lacking. The Department of Labor collected more than $1 million in back wages for temporary foreign employees between 2007 and 2011, but only twenty-two of those employees receiving restitution were H-2B workers. The total sum collected for H-2B workers was a mere $18,307.08, not surprising when these often abused workers, especially those in the fair and carnival industries, have been found to make as little as $1.61 per hour, way below federal minimum wage standards (CDM 2012).

Methods

We draw on a larger research project we conducted on transnational labor advocacy in Mexico and the United States that focuses on the consular partnership program implemented by the Mexican and US governments in 2004, including surveys of fifty-two Mexican consular offices in 2012. From 2013 to 2015 we conducted approximately 170 interviews with three groups of organizational actors in Mexico City and twenty-six US cities. They included civil society actors, US labor standards enforcement agency staff members, and Mexican embassy and consular staff members. The analysis here draws especially on ten interviews conducted in Baltimore, Mexico City, New York, Santa Fe, and Washington, DC, in 2014–2015 and some follow-ups in 2016 with leaders of transnational civil society organizations, as well as with two officials representing Mexico's Secretariat of Labor and Social Welfare who were familiar with the 2011 petition to NAALC.

Within our broader research effort, the analysis we present here is based on interviews with staff members in charge of labor affairs at Mexico's embassy in Washington, DC, and staff members of three organizations that have been involved with NAALC's petitions: the Centro de los Derechos del Migrante Baltimore and Mexico City offices, Justice in Motion—formerly Global Workers Justice Alliance—in its New York and Mexico City offices, and the North American Congress on Latin America in New York. Through these perspectives we examine the genesis and development of petitions to NAALC aimed at improving the conditions of temporary migrant workers. We highlight the importance of civil society organizations that petition and deploy multiple strategies to institutionalize partnerships with labor standards enforcement agencies in both countries. In doing so, they have pushed for greater transparency and accountability, but they face complex challenges to creating meaningful changes.

Findings: Building Cross-Border Labor Advocacy Coalitions

Despite its many flaws, NAALC sets a precedent in the hemisphere by incorporating labor standards into free trade negotiations, even if those standards were excluded from the binding elements of the agreement itself. Thus far, the most promising result of the NAALC process has been, Robert Russo finds, the "greater cooperation and inclusiveness among various NGOs and civil society groups, including previously marginalized groups such as unofficial Mexican unions and Mexican migrant workers in the United States" (2011:38). Within a framework of participatory democracy, NAALC has created fertile ground on which to experiment with a tripartite model of labor rights enforcement (Amengual and Fine 2017; Ayres and Braithwaite 1992; Dias-Abey 2016). This model empowers public interest groups to provide support in enforcing regulations; if carried out effectively, it has the potential to achieve enforcement by staking out a middle ground between deterrence and compliance in which employers may find it increasingly difficult to abuse workers without facing any consequence. Below we track some of the key petitions that have emerged in this framework.

2003 Petition: Farmworkers in North Carolina

In February 2003, the Central Independiente de Obreros Agrícolas y Campesinos (Independent Union of Agricultural Workers and Peasants), based in Mexico City, and the Farmworker Justice Fund, based in Washington, DC, jointly filed a petition with the Mexican NAO, thus launching the first attempt under NAALC to improve labor conditions of temporary migrant workers. The petitioners asked the labor commission to address the mistreatment of and labor law violations concerning H-2A guest workers from Mexico employed in North Carolina's agriculture industry. Among many other violations, key charges included blacklisting, denying them the freedom to associate or not associate in violation of Articles 3, 4, and 5 of NAALC, and denying them access to workers' compensation for work-related illnesses and injuries. In its petition, Farmworker Justice demanded outreach education to workers about their rights along with restitution (CIAOC and Farmworker Justice Fund 2003). Filing the petition added to the growing public scrutiny of farmworker conditions in North Carolina and pressured agricultural employers to respond to demands for reforms.

The petitioners filed the submission, but there was no formal governmental response from the labor commission. However, due to pressure from organizers and a boycott against implicated growers, by September 2004, the North Carolina Growers Association in Raleigh signed a historic labor agreement with the Farm Labor Organizing Committee. As an agricultural labor union, FLOC is unique in that it had been a pioneer in labor cross-border organizing beginning in the late 1980s when it fought Campbell Soup Company's efforts to divide and conquer unions in the United States and Mexico (Brooks and Fox 2002). The 2004 labor accords gave thousands of H-2A workers in North Carolina a collective bargaining agreement and settled the boycott of the Mt. Olive Pickle Company, which purchases cucumbers picked by the North Carolina Growers Association members' H-2A workers. FLOC went on to establish offices in Monterrey, Mexico, and North Carolina to serve its new members and administer the agreement with the growers association. The goal was to improve access to information for would-be H-2A workers. Here, publicity was vital in the "mobilization of shame" (Compa 2001), which raised political pressures that would eventually produce widely disseminated judgments in the court of public opinion. The petition demonstrates just how easily an otherwise weak international enforcement mechanism could be creatively exploited to advance advocacy efforts.

The resulting settlement paved the way for targeting fraudulent recruiters who preyed upon desperate workers trying to obtain legal employment contracts in a lax regulatory environment. The petitioners pushed for increased access to timely and transparent information for temporary workers prior to their migration (Gutiérrez Ramírez 2014). However, working to defend Mexican migrant labor rights in Mexico has become a risky endeavor; on April 9, 2007, Santiago Rafael Cruz, a union organizer for FLOC, was found dead in Monterrey. He had been brutally tortured and murdered, and his bound body was left inside the union offices. The Inter-American Human Rights Commission found sufficient evidence that the crime had been politically motivated, and it issued a protective order to keep FLOC staff and members safe in Mexico. Six years after the murder, the AFL-CIO (2013) reported that only one of the murderers has been captured and sentenced to prison, while the government of Nuevo León state has been unable to bring the three other at-large suspects to justice.

2005 Petition: Tree Planters in Idaho and Farmworkers in Texas and Arkansas

In 2005, the Northwest Workers' Justice Project of Oregon, the Andrade Law Office of Boise, Idaho, and the Brennan Center for Justice in New York submitted a new petition to the Mexican NAO raising concerns about the rights of migrant workers under the H-2B visa program in Idaho, Texas, and Arkansas. The petition cited issues such as forced labor, employment discrimination, equal pay for women and men, and prevention of occupational injuries and illnesses. The vast majority of the workers in this petition had been employed by Universal Forestry in Idaho, an employer that, among other violations, illegally collected and retained their passports. In Mexico, support for the petition came from six NGOs, including the Frente Auténtico del Trabajo (an independent labor union), the Red Mexicana de Acción Frente al Libre Comercio (an anti-NAFTA organization), and Sin Fronteras (an immigrant advocacy organization). In the United States, the petition was supported by four organizations: the Idaho Migrant Council, National Immigration Law Center, Oregon Law Center, and Pineros y Campesinos Unidos del Noroeste, a member union of the United Farmworkers of America with a history of implementing transnational labor advocacy strategies dating back to 1985 (Bada, Fox, and Selee 2006). Once again, the Labor Cooperation Commission did not issue any response under NAALC.

The group of ten individual petitioners consisted of one Panamanian and nine Mexican workers. All of them had suffered numerous violations of their labor law rights, "including the rights to earn the statutorily mandated minimum wage, to safe working conditions, to compensation for occupational injuries, to disclosure of the conditions of their employment at the time of hiring, to adherence by the employer to the promised conditions of employment, to safe transportation when the transportation was provided by the employer, and to safe and sanitary housing when the housing was provided by the employer" (Northwest Workers' Justice Project 2005:1). Several of the workers had been recruited in Tamaulipas by an agent of the employer who misrepresented the terms of employment. A worker was paid as little as one dollar per hour during periods of his employment. Moreover, the petitioners who worked on farms in Texas and Arkansas had been recruited in Veracruz and received no training to operate machinery. Following a forklift accident, one had his leg amputated up to the knee. None of the workers named in the petition had access to adequate legal counsel.

The relief requested was similar to that in the 2003 petition in North Carolina. Petitioners called for ministerial consultations, educational outreach to workers before and after migration, and that the US government "effectively enforce its labor law and to afford immigrants authorized to work in the United States a means to seek a remedy for violation of labor rights it recognized under its law by ceasing to deny work-authorized immigrants in the United States the opportunity to receive legal assistance from Legal Service Corporation grantees" (Northwest Workers' Justice Project 2005:13). Securing access to Legal Service Corporation (LSC) grantees was a key component of this petition because H-2B workers are not entitled to receive legal assistance from organizations funded by federal LSC support.

The Emergence of a Tripartite System, 2008

In 2004 Mexico's Secretariat of Foreign Affairs signed the first memorandum of understanding with the US Department of Labor to improve access to labor standards enforcement for Mexican migrant workers in the United States. The agreement was the seed that would eventually flower into an institutionally coordinated and coproduced regulatory enforcement framework in which educational outreach was the most important component. The Consular Partnership Program began in 2008 when Labor Rights Week launched a pilot program involving fifteen consulates in conjunction with the Department of Labor and other federal and state agencies to promote migrant worker rights. The program has now spread to more than fifty-two consular offices in the United States and Canada and to partnerships with a dozen mostly Latin American countries that either use the facilities of Mexican consulates or organize smaller events at their own consular offices to offer Labor Rights Week services to their constituents. The spillover effects outside the NAFTA space reflect the general diffusion of diaspora engagement described by Alexandra Délano Alonso (2014).

The institutionalization of the Consular Partnership Program across the United States and Canada arose in response to pressure mounted by the Advisory Board of the Institute for Mexicans Abroad. This citizen council is composed of representatives from migrant civil society who offer advice to Mexico's consular corps on migrant-related issues including health, education, trade, and labor (Bada and Gleeson 2014). While the institutional infrastructure for this broad, tripartite collaboration was initiated by way of a bilateral memorandum signed in 2004, the Consular Partnership Program was primarily focused on worker educational outreach on behalf of migrant workers outside of the temporary migrant programs. Such initiatives were valuable but limited in that they frequently failed to reach employees unable to easily travel to consular offices, such as H-2 workers with scarce resources to voice complaints to linguistically competent labor inspectors.

The Emergence of Transnational Advocacy: The CDM and GWJA

In September 2005, after offering a series of educational presentations to Mexico's consular corps on migrant worker rights in the United States, a US-trained attorney established the Centro de Derechos del Migrante in Zacatecas, Mexico. The organization's main focus is to improve the working conditions of low-wage workers in the United States. By setting its headquarters in Mexico, the CDM pursued an innovative, transnational approach: by providing migrant workers with training, legal services, and advocacy opportunities in their communities of origin, the CDM could help workers safely and effectively defend their US labor rights. Ultimately, the CDM moved its base to Mexico City and opened an outreach office in Oaxaca and a policy office in Baltimore.[2]

The Global Workers Justice Alliance, an immigrant worker advocacy organization in New York and also founded in 2005, appointed a female Mexican American lawyer to its staff in 2008 as its Mexico field director. Although she was based in New York, the lawyer frequently traveled to a satellite office in southern Mexico to document abuses experienced by H-2A and H-2B workers and to redouble efforts to recover their back wages.[3]

The Global Workers Justice Alliance, now named Justice in Motion, does not keep a physical office in Mexico, but it does hire a local organizer in Oaxaca to assist several grassroots advocacy organizations it supports in that state and provides them with training and tools to defend transnational workers. Budgetary constraints have prevented the alliance from retaining more local organizers on its payroll in Mexico, but it hired a young Mexican American woman as its capacity-building and communications manager. She travels frequently to Mexico to train and support local NGOs interested in pursuing targeted migrant labor advocacy campaigns. By late 2016, Justice in Motion had developed an active Defenders Network, adopting a portable justice model,[4] with forty immigrant advocacy NGOs operating in Mexico, Guatemala, Honduras, El Salvador, and Nicaragua.[5] They are not only addressing labor violations but also supporting cross-border humanitarian immigration work and family law, asylum, and unaccompanied minor cases, among other issues.

The sustained binational collaboration that began in 2005 eventually evolved into a larger coalition with the power to submit a new petition to NAALC. In November 2010, Mexico hosted the states-only Global Forum of Migration and Development in Puerto Vallarta. Binational advocates specializing in international labor recruitment practices gathered in Mexico City a few weeks before the forum began to attend a meeting of the People's Global Alliance on Migration, Development, and Human Rights. Hundreds of labor groups and advocates from the United States, Mexico, and Canada used the alliance gathering as a platform to discuss a common advocacy framework for improving labor standards and recruitment practices in the region and to present a unified front during the Civil Society Days at the forum. Strategies were discussed to regulate the international recruitment of temporary guest workers and improve labor standards compliance in the United States, including through NAFTA's side agreements. By then it was clear to many of the groups that the 2003 and 2005 petitions had not produced the requested remedies or consultations, so the CDM resolved that a new petition would require a broader cross-border coalition able to exert constant pressure and sustain media attention. It is important to stress that there is no global agreement from civil society, only regional cooperation. Civil society is still too regionally fragmented to operate on a truly global scale to improve global migration democratic governance.

2011 Petition

In September 2011, the CDM became the lead organizer of a new petition to NAALC on behalf of H-2A and H-2B workers. The petition stated, once again, that H-2 workers were experiencing multiple and systematic violations of minimum labor rights laws at the local, state, and federal levels in violation of several articles of NAALC. Among other suggestions, the petitioners proposed a series of enforcement measures in the United States—including funding and training more bilingual inspectors to enforce minimum wage, reimbursement, and overtime laws effectively—and asked the US Department of Labor to conduct outreach to workers' communities to promote an understanding of their workplace rights (CDM 2014).

As in the 2003 and 2005 petitions, the 2011 submission requested that Mexico's Secretariat of Labor and Social Welfare begin ministerial consultations with the US Department of Labor on the issues raised in the filing. Moreover, to remedy the violations, the petition requested "public information sessions with workers, worker advocates, and judicial and other government officials affected by the failure of the United States to promote the compliance with and enforcement of minimum labor standards with respect to migrant workers" (CDM 2011:13).

The 2011 petition was submitted on behalf of three plaintiffs who had already returned to Mexico and was supported by a binational coalition of fourteen organizations: the AFL-CIO, Interfaith Worker Justice of Chicago, and organizations in North Carolina, Pennsylvania, Oregon, Texas, Alabama, and New York. In Mexico, five NGOs joined the CDM in supporting the petition, among them grassroots worker centers and immigrant legal advocacy organizations. The CDM submitted a follow-up to the petition in August 2012, and in November 2012, Mexico's Secretariat of Labor and Social Welfare issued a first report.[6] In its review of the report, Mexico's NAO recommended that Mexico's Secretariat of Labor and Social Welfare request consultations with its US counterpart.

In the petition's follow-up, the CDM acknowledged the US Department of Labor's revised regulations for the H-2B visa program. The changes affected the process by which employers arrange for issuance of an H-2B visa as well as the rights of the guest workers hired under the program. While the

CDM affirmed that the changes were an improvement that would offer modestly better protection to H-2B workers, it expressed disappointment in the failure to implement these new policies. The failure predominantly stems from the long-standing lack of effective enforcement strategies in the United States (Fine and Gordon 2010). Scheduled to become effective on April 23, 2012, the changes were halted due to a lawsuit submitted by the US Chamber of Commerce and other business associations. Ultimately, a US federal judge sided with the challengers and issued an injunction to prevent the implementation of the new regulations, limiting the potential remedies for future workers hired under the H-2 visa program (CDM 2012).

2013 Diplomatic Shifts

In 2013, Mexico's Secretariat of Labor and Social Welfare inaugurated its first labor attaché office in Mexico's embassy in Washington, DC. According to officials familiar with the process, the decision was made because of "increased labor issues Mexico was handling with the United States."[7] When Mexican officials were initially deciding where to locate a labor attaché office most strategically, they settled on Ottawa, Canada, because most of its work entailed running the Canadian guest worker program. Labor issues in the United States seemed secondary at the time, especially when the North American Commission for Labor Cooperation's council closed operations in Washington, DC, in 2010. As a result, the international affairs offices within NAALC became the national administrative offices that handled all public communications online, thus reducing access to information for those with less digital access such as poor workers. A government official representing Mexico's embassy in Washington told us, "This doesn't mean that [because of] the closure of the NACLC's council, the system doesn't work; it only means that some communications [petitions] get [quicker] answers and others take longer."[8] Nonetheless, Mexico's inauguration of a labor attaché office in its embassy in the United States signaled a growing willingness on the part of the Mexican government to engage in binational cooperation with the United States.

Almost ten years after the first public petition was filed, Mexico's NAO finally issued a review and requested ministerial consultations. Meanwhile, the CDM continued working closely with the binational supporting coalition and strategized their next move. On February 18, 2014, the CDM decided to increase the pressure. It submitted a new supplement to the original petition to Mexico's NAO denouncing the ten months of inaction. The declaration strategically coincided with the annual North American Leaders' Summit, which took place on February 19 in Toluca, Mexico. Backing the new supplement was a broader coalition of thirty-five NGOs rallied together by the CDM, including the United Food and Commercial Workers of Canada and immigrant worker advocates from El Salvador, Guatemala, Costa Rica, and Panama.[9] The new supplement attracted significant press attention in Mexico. Two months later, the consultations finally took place in Washington between the US and Mexican labor departments, leading to agreements for bilateral labor cooperation in 2014. These agreements were particularly important because they required that bilateral public outreach forums be conducted in both countries. The last time NAALC had agreed to bilateral public outreach and public hearings concerning migrant workers was in 2001 during the Washington Apple Growers case, but those forums took place only in the apple-growing region of Washington (Compa 2001), not throughout both countries.

2014 Joint Declaration and Its Boomerang Effect

The 2014 joint declaration between the US Department of Labor and Mexico's Secretariat of Labor and Social Welfare led to the creation of an official work plan, announced in June 2014, to educate workers about their rights. The program is focused in the US states with the largest numbers of violations to the H-2A and H-2B guest worker program and on the enforcement of existing US labor laws. However, Mexican civil society organizations also saw the joint declaration as an opportunity to push for changes in Mexican labor laws that had historically facilitated abuse by private recruitment agencies.[10] As a result of those efforts, several Mexican states initiated modifications to their penal codes to classify recruitment fraud as a criminal activity. The organizations also succeeded in increasing federal protections against fraudulent international recruitment (Gutiérrez Ramírez 2014). In 2016, Michoacán became the first state to pass an amendment to Article 325 of its criminal code, "to punish recruiters who engage in fraudulent practices, without a right to bail" (USDOL and STPS 2016:9). In this case, we observe a "boomerang effect" as local NGOs bypassed their usual domestic government channels to change legislation; they directly engaged powerful international allies to bring pressure on their state governments from outside, in turn unblocking communication channels between the state and its domestic actors (Keck and Sikkink 1998). In a similar vein, a boomerang effect for nonmigrant workers in Mexico emerges in an NAALC petition submitted by the United Food and Commercial Workers of America to the US NAO in 2015. That petition alleged violation of freedom of association laws occurring in Mexico's Chedraui retail stores, a multinational grocery chain.

The United States has pledged to continue cooperating with Mexico to jointly enforce existing labor standards in the United States for undocumented workers as well as temporary guest workers, and Mexico has also modified several of its domestic labor laws regarding the recruitment of temporary workers. While clearly an indirect effect of the cross-border coalition that submitted the 2011 petition, the changes will likely be far more difficult to enforce. Nonetheless, they constitute important improvements, especially given the consequences of Mexico's 2012 labor law reforms. Of particular concern is the streamlining of Article 28 of the federal labor law, which further complicates compliance procedures and threatens to roll back hard-fought gains in preventing international recruitment fraud (Global Workers Justice Alliance 2015). Strategically, the changes provide a legislative basis for reform in the global guest worker recruitment industry,[11] which regularly exploits high- and low-skilled migrants bound to the United States (Park 2015; Preston 2015, 2016).

Mexico's labor law reforms have diminished hard-fought labor protections such as severance pay, and the Mexican labor enforcement agencies face great hurdles to effectively monitor compliance with federal minimum wage violations. Still, the federal government has been interested in demonstrating a public commitment to the defense of Mexican migrant labor rights in the United States. In an email, an attorney has explained to us that from 2010 to 2014, the Dirección General de Protección a Mexicanos en el Exterior (Legal Protection Directorate for Mexicans Abroad) of Mexico's Secretariat of Foreign Affairs had a contract with the US-based law firm for which she works to provide labor rights representation to Mexicans in the United States, modeled on the Mexican Capital Legal Assistance Project.[12] That Chicago firm, Hughes Socol Piers Resnick and Dym, working on its own or with US-based NGOs, filed federal lawsuits that recovered tens of thousands of dollars in damages for Mexican workers in agriculture and seafood processing due to violations of federal wage and hour laws and regulations governing temporary worker programs. The contract, despite its success, was not renewed under the administration of President Enrique Peña Nieto.[13] While the decision of Peña Nieto's administration to fund the lawyering program can be interpreted as yet another layer contributing to the tripartite model of co-enforcement, the lack of institutionalization of such initiatives leaves them highly vulnerable to diplomatic shifts and the changing will of different administrations.

As we have shown, the role of transnational governance structures in improving labor enforcement standards for migrant workers is limited, but NAALC petitions on behalf of H-2 workers show the potential for building or solidifying transnational labor advocacy networks and international regulations. Taken together, the petitions create contingent transnational political opportunity structures in less democratic domestic spaces such as Mexico. They also can bring publicity to a given labor issue and exert political pressure on government actors and employees, increase transparency and accountability because investigating the petitions leads to document sharing, and support organizing efforts when worker groups use varying strategies to pressure employers to come to the bargaining table.

Conclusion

Most labor movements are primarily oriented toward their own nation-states, but their advocates' petitions demonstrate how transnational labor advocacy networks create spaces where activists come together to mobilize and develop their overlapping interests and identities across borders (Kay 2010). In the cases that led up to the 2014 joint ministerial declaration, we find five elements that were crucial in exerting the political pressure that spurred both US and Mexican governments to act, considering the constraints of international governance structures in enforcing domestic labor laws.

1. The last straw breaks the camel's back. The 2011 petition submitted by the CDM benefited from two previous petitions submitted by binational/transnational coalitions to NAALC in 2003 and 2005 on behalf of H-2 workers in North Carolina, Idaho, Texas, and Arkansas.
2. The existence of a relatively functional bilateral Consular Partnership Program on labor enforcement cooperation was important. The 2011 petition ultimately benefited from even a tripartite co-enforcement model.
3. Long-term commitment to publicity and sustained pressure can be effective. Organizers kept up the pressure and increased the visibility of their cause by submitting two supplements to the petition that reminded NAALC of its obligation to respond and alerted it to the increasing size of the coalition that had originally supported the plaintiffs.
4. Parties from the Americas outside NAFTA filed a public submission, demonstrating the importance of coalitional politics. The coalition began with fourteen organizations in 2011 and had grown to thirty-five organizations by 2014. After two decades, NAALC was finally able to attract the attention of parties outside North America, thereby increasing the scope of the transnational labor advocacy network.
5. Effective strategy requires smart timing. The second supplement to the submission was sent during the so-called 2014 Three Amigos Summit in Toluca to guarantee maximum press coverage and public shaming.

Despite the unprecedented victories of securing binational consultations and the joint declaration, civil society groups focusing on transnational migrant workers continue to confront obstacles. Public accountability is seriously limited by the difficulties in producing structural changes to prevent wage theft and other labor violations across borders. Paradoxically, the publicity generated by transnational strategies both helps and detracts from grassroots organizing and efforts to build legitimacy with workers who are waiting to have their cases resolved. That is, calling attention to the scope of injustice can discourage victims of that injustice. That is a problem also encountered by many low-wage workers in worker centers across the United States (Gordon 2005). While worker centers strategically aim to pursue state and federal legislative bills favoring higher minimum wages, workers become easily frustrated when such legislation fails to ensure that the improved salary regulations are effectively enforced.

Dissatisfaction within Civil Society

By and large, advocates we interviewed believe that forcing the Mexican and US governments to conduct direct educational outreach to workers was a good first step. During the outreach programs held across both countries, "more than 2,300 workers and 1,000 employers across 15 states attended the 29 events in the United States. . . . The eleven events held in Mexico reached approximately 1,600 people, including those who were interested in working in the United States on H-2 visas and those who had previously worked on H-2 visas" (USDOL and STPS 2016:8–9). In the events held in the United States, inspectors from the US Department of Labor Wage and Hour Division received sixteen potential referral cases for screening by the relevant district office, including potential Fair Labor Standards Act complaints and potential reinvestigations. Considering that only twenty-two H-2B workers received back wages between 2007 and 2011, finding sixteen potential cases for redress is a tiny step in the right direction. However, the events were historic in that they arose from close consultation among the two governments and all the NGOs named in the petition, revealing an opportunity to solidify a tripartite model of cooperation for enforcement.

Still, the CDM and Justice in Motion, two of the petitioners who joined the 2011 coalition, remain dissatisfied with the outcome. While they recognized the historic nature of the outreach events, they expressed concern that most of the recommendations were largely ignored, specifically, increasing the number of bilingual wage and hour inspectors, targeting industries that employ large numbers of H-2B workers for investigations, and improving language access and legal representation for H-2 workers. In practice, the joint declaration committed to hold the outreach events only once, failing to effectively institutionalize the tripartite model of coproduced enforcement that had begun so ambitiously. The lack of commitment was problematic, especially given the deep investment on the part of civil society organizations that had worked to gain the trust of migrant workers over years of cross-border advocacy and legal support.

In addition, the surprising decision to hold several "know your rights" workshops for workers, *with employers present*, did little to improve an environment unconducive to claims-making. The goal of the outreach events, according to both governments, was "to have migrants become agents of change who know their rights and demand such rights be respected, report fraudulent and illegal activity, and are able to provide this information to other migrants" (USDOL and STPS 2016:8), yet its programmatic decisions demonstrate the Mexican government's severe lack of understanding of the obstacles low-wage workers face for claims-making and of the power of employers. The resulting framework ultimately shifts responsibility back to migrants themselves and allows the government to easily get off the hook and blame the victims for failing to know their rights.

As observed, the journey to securing the NAALC provisions has taken more than a decade, but it has renewed the coalition's commitment to move forward. The CDM met with all stakeholders who participated in the original petition to decide the next steps to take beyond reaching the modest educational outreach goals. Organization leaders admit that they remain ambivalent about ultimately issuing stronger measures like sanctions, but they have not ruled out the option entirely. The CDM has continued other advocacy efforts as well, such as submitting a petition to NAALC alleging gender discrimination in the recruitment of H-2A and H-2B workers.

Continued Government Assurances

In 2014, the US Department of Labor and Mexico's Secretariat of Labor and Social Welfare issued a joint declaration confirming their intention to improve the information provided to Mexican immigrants in the United States with H-2A and H-2B temporary work visas. The goal was to inform the workers about their rights under US labor and employment law and to provide their employers with guidance regarding compliance. The joint declaration resulted from more than a decade of advocacy efforts by Mexican and US civil society organizations that submitted three public petitions—in 2003, 2005, and 2011—to Mexico's NAO on behalf of H-2 workers. In the claims, advocates alleged that the United States failed to effectively enforce various labor laws for H-2A and H-2B workers, and they cited scores of common abuses.

In practical terms, after an initial complaint, the NAO evaluates the opposing nation's labor law and produces a report that recommends nonbinding policy changes. At best, the NAO's evaluations merely create bad publicity for employers and governments without necessarily prompting them to improve enforcement mechanisms. In effect, there have been no real enforcement sanctions under NAALC since it went into effect in 1994 despite the rampant wage theft immigrant workers suffer. None of the available sanctions under NAALC has been implemented, not enacting monetary enforcement assessments or suspending trade benefits for signatory governments who fail to meet internationally recognized labor standards.[14] Nevertheless, including social actors from diverse institutional fields within this labor advocacy network may be the key to developing cohesive collective identities and interests among transnational labor advocacy groups interested in defending migrant worker rights in the region.

Lessons Learned and Moving Forward

In sum, our findings reveal that NAALC has prompted greater transnational cooperation and inclusiveness among various NGOs and civil society groups in North America. The coalition is a mix of prominent anti-NAFTA groups, newer and less visible groups, independent Mexican unions, agricultural unions, and transnational organizations such as the CDM, FLOC, Pineros y Campesinos Unidos del Noroeste, Frente Auténtico del Trabajo, and the Global Workers Justice Alliance, among many others. The alliances and coalitions of immigrant labor advocates that have decided to escalate pressure and demand bilateral government action using NAFTA's labor side accords have not patiently waited for results. Rather, their petitions are one tactic in a repertoire that includes boycotts, solidarity across borders, lawyering strategies, educational outreach using the Consular Partnership Program, and a stronger push to secure a seat at the table with labor standards enforcement agencies and inspectors in Mexico and the United States. Their efforts have led to a boomerang effect in which Mexico has had to address its own lack of enforcement to protect migrant workers who are recruited in its territory by fraudulent means.

While NAALC has not been able to improve labor rights enforcement for migrant workers due to its nonbinding structure, its trilateral adjudication process has allowed innovative North American labor advocacy networks and coalitions to spring up, with the potential for building larger transnational labor movements in the future. The coalitions have gone above and beyond traditional labor union strategies of the past (Kay 2010), and they have taken advantage of political opportunities to implant multilayered coalitions—including worker centers, binational NGOs, and immigrant advocates—in the regional governance enforcement regulatory framework initiated by NAFTA. Therefore, NAFTA's and NAALC's indirect effects have enabled potentially long-lasting transnational labor advocacy networks. Those are important outcomes that legitimize advocates' strategies and give us hope for the future of transnational labor alliances and coalitions in North America.

Notes

The authors thank Cathleen Caron, Lance Compa, Margit Fauser, Kate Griffith, Rachel Micah-Jones, and Kevin Middlebrook for providing valuable suggestions for framing this chapter.

1. For a comprehensive overview of the temporary foreign labor visa system in the United States, please refer to the Global Workers Justice Alliance publications webpage, http://www.globalworkers.org/our-work/publications/visas-inc.

2. CDM staff member, conversation with Xóchitl Bada at the CDM fund-raiser and program, Chicago, December 6, 2012.

3. Interviews were conducted with former staff members of the Global Workers Justice Alliance and staff members of the CDM in Mexico City and the United States in August 2014, June 2015, August 2015, and October 2016.

4. Portable justice is a model pursued by several transnational advocacy organizations based on the ideas that all migrants have the right to justice across borders and that there is a need to leverage local resources to support access to justice for migrant workers wherever the workers go.

5. Justice in Motion staff member, interview by the authors, New York, July 20, 2017.

6. The report was issued through a Mexican NAO public communications review (MEX 2003-1, MEX 2005-1 and MEX 2011-1 pursuant to NAALC).

7. Mexico's Secretariat of Labor and Social Welfare staff member, interview by the authors, Mexican embassy, Washington, DC, May 15, 2015.

8. Ibid.

9. By then, the United Food and Commercial Workers was very familiar with bilateral cooperation with Mexico, since it was one of the few labor unions that supported the Consular Partnership Program from its inception in 2008. The program had made modest investments in worker education programs in more than a dozen cities chosen for the first Labor Rights Week pilot program.

10. Global Workers Justice Alliance staff member, interview by the authors, Mexico City, July 2015.

11. CDM staff member, interview by the authors, Washington, DC, August 14, 2014.

12. Susan Gzesh of the law firm Hughes Socol Piers Resnick and Dym, Chicago, email to the authors, April 13, 2018.

13. Ibid.

14. The assessments and sanctions are set forth in Articles 39 and 41 of the NAALC agreement.

References

AFL-CIO. 2013. "Resolution 47: Justice for Santiago Rafael Cruz." AFL-CIO Convention. August 26. Los Angeles, CA. https://aflcio.org/resolutions/resolution-47-justice-santiago-rafael-cruz.

Adams, Roy J., and Parbudyal Singh. 1997. "Early Experience with NAFTA's Labour Side Accord." *Comparative Labor Law Journal* 18 (2): 161–181.

Amengual, Matthew, and Janice Fine. 2017. "Co-Enforcing Labor Standards: The Unique Contributions of State and Worker Organizations in Argentina and the United States." *Regulation and Governance* 11 (2): 119–142.

Armstrong, Jeffrey R. 2005. "A Seat at the Table: A Critical Analysis of the Right to Foreign Nation *Parens Patriae* Standing." *Florida Journal of International Law* 17:39–57.

Ayres, Ian, and John Braithwaite. 1992. *Responsive Regulation: Transcending the Deregulation Debate*. Oxford: Oxford University Press, 1992.

Bada, Xóchitl, Jonathan Fox, and Andrew Selee, eds. 2006. *Invisible No More: Mexican Migrant Civic Participation in the United States*. Washington, DC: Woodrow Wilson International Center for Scholars.

Bada, Xóchitl, and Shannon Gleeson. 2015. "A New Approach to Migrant Labor Rights Enforcement: The Crisis of Undocumented Worker Abuse and Mexican Consular Advocacy in the United States." *Labor Studies Journal* 40 (1): 32–53.

Barger, W. K., and Ernesto M. Reza. 1994. *The Farm Labor Movement in the Midwest*. Austin: University of Texas Press.

Berg, Ulla Dalum, and Robyn Magalit Rodriguez. 2013. "Transnational Citizenship across the Americas." *Identities: Global Studies in Culture and Power* 20 (6): 649–664.

Brooks, David, and Jonathan Fox. 2002. "Movements across the Border: An Overview." In *Cross-Border Dialogues: U.S.-Mexico Social Movement Networking*, edited by David Brooks and Jonathan Fox, 1–68. La Jolla: Center for U.S. Mexican Studies, University of California, San Diego.

CDM (Centro de los Derechos del Migrante). 2011. "Petition on Labor Law Matters Arising in the United States submitted to the National Administrative Office (NAO) of Mexico under the North American Agreement on Labor Cooperation." September 19. Baltimore and Mexico City.

———. 2012. "Supplement to Petition on Labor Law Matters Arising in the United States Submitted to the National Administrative Office (NAO) of Mexico under the North American Agreement on Labor Cooperation." August. Baltimore, MD: CDM.

———. 2014. "Supplement to Public Communication. Mex 2011-01 on Labor Law Matters Arising in the United States submitted to the National Administrative Office (NAO) of Mexico under the North American Agreement on Labor Cooperation." February 18. Baltimore, MD: CDM.

CIOAC (Central Independiente de Obreros Agrícolas y Campesinos) and Farmworker Justice Fund. 2003. "Petition to the National Administrative Office in Mexico under the North American Agreement on Labor Cooperation Regarding the Failure by the United States to Implement and Effectively Enforce the Labor Laws Applicable to Agricultural Workers under the H-2A program in the State of North Carolina, United States of America." February. Mexico City: CIOAC; Washington, DC: Farmworker Justice Fund.

Compa, Lance. 2001. "NAFTA's Labor Side Agreement and International Labor Solidarity." *Antipode* 33 (3): 451–467.

Délano Alonso, Alexandra. 2014. "The Diffusion of Diaspora Engagement Policies: A Latin American Agenda." *Political Geography* 41:90–100.

Dias-Abey, Manoj. 2016. "Sandcastles of Hope? Civil Society Organizations and the Working Conditions of Migrant Farmworkers in North America." PhD diss., Ontario: Queen's University.

Dewan, Sabina, and Lucas Ronconi. 2018. "U.S. Free Trade Agreements and Enforcement of Labor Law in Latin America." *Industrial Relations: A Journal of Economy and Society* 57 (1): 35–56.

Domenech, Eduardo. 2016. "Políticas y prácticas de control de las migraciones en el espacio sudamericano: Una mirada crítica." Paper presented at the seminar "Nuevas movilidades del Hemisferio Occidental: Desafíos para el nuevo siglo," August 30–31, Centro de Investigación y Docencia Económica, Mexico City.

Fine, Janice. 2005. "Worker Centers: Organizing Communities at the Edge of the Dream." Economic Policy Institute (blog). December 13, 2005. https://www.epi.org/publication/bp159/.

Fine, Janice, and Jennifer Gordon. 2010. "Strengthening Labor Standards Enforcement through Partnerships with Workers' Organizations." *Politics and Society* 38 (4): 552–585.

Fox, Jonathan. 2002. "Lessons from Mexico-U.S. Civil Society Coalitions." In *Cross-Border Dialogues: U.S.-Mexico Social Movement Networking*, edited by David Brooks and Jonathan Fox, 341–418. La Jolla: Center for U.S. Mexican Studies, University of California, San Diego.

Galvin, Daniel J. 2016. "Deterring Wage Theft: Alt-Labor, State Politics, and the Policy Determinants of Minimum Wage Compliance." *Perspectives on Politics* 14 (2): 324–350.

García Agustín, Óscar, and Martin Bak Jørgensen. 2016. *Solidarity without Borders: Gramscian Perspectives on Migration and Civil Society Alliances*. London: Pluto.

Gleeson, Shannon. 2016. *Precarious Claims: The Promise and Failure of Workplace Protections in the United States*. Oakland: University of California Press.

Global Workers Justice Alliance. 2015. *Reglas del reclutamiento: Países de origen. Análisis comparativo de leyes de reclutamiento para trabajadores en el exterior en México, Guatemala, El Salvador, Honduras y Nicaragua*. New York: Global Workers Justice Alliance.

González, Gilbert G. 1999. *Mexican Consuls and Labor Organizing: Imperial Politics in the American Southwest*. Austin: University of Texas Press.

Gordon, Jennifer. 2005. *Suburban Sweatshops: The Fight for Immigrant Rights*. Cambridge, MA: Harvard University Press.

———. 2006. "Transnational Labor Citizenship." *Southern California Law Review* 503 (80): 503–588.

Gunningham, Neil A., Dorothy Thornton, and Robert A. Kagan. 2005. "Motivating Management: Corporate Compliance in Environmental Protection." *Law and Policy* 27:289.

Gutiérrez Ramírez, Paulina del Pilar. 2014. *Estudio de evaluación del Reglamento de Agencias de Colocación de Trabajadores (RACT)*. Mexico City: Instituto de Estudios y Divulgación sobre Migración.

ILRWG (International Labor Recruitment Working Group). 2013. *The American Dream Up for Sale: A Blueprint for Ending International Labor Recruitment Abuse*. Report, February. https://fairlaborrecruitment.files.wordpress.com/2013/01/the-american-dream-up-for-sale-a-blueprint-for-ending-international-labor-recruitment-abuse1.pdf.

Justice in Motion. 2016. "H-2B VISA." http://globalworkers.org/sites/default/files/H -2B_Visa_2015update.pdf.

Kay, Tamara. 2010. *NAFTA and the Politics of Labor Transnationalism.* New York: Cambridge University Press.

Keck, Margaret, and Kathyrn Sikkink. 1998. *Activists beyond Borders: Advocacy Networks in International Politics.* Ithaca, NY: Cornell University Press.

Linares, Juan C. 2006. "Hired Hands Needed: The Impact of Globalization and Human Rights Law on Migrant Workers in the United States." *Denver Journal of International Law and Policy* 34:321–352.

McGuiness, Michael J. 2000. "The Politics of Labor Regulation in North America: A Reconsideration of Labor Law Enforcement in Mexico." *Journal of International Economic Law* 21 (1): 1–40.

Mercier, Stephanie. 2014. *Employing Agriculture: How the Midwest Farm and Food Sector Relies on Immigrant Labor.* Chicago: Chicago Council on Global Affairs Immigration Initiative.

Northwest Workers' Justice Project. 2005. "Petition on Labor Law Matters Arising in the U.S. Submitted to the NAO of Mexico under the NAALC Regarding the Failure of the U.S. to Effectively Enforce Laws Protecting the Rights of Immigrant Workers." April 13. https://www.brennancenter.org/sites/default/files/legacy/d/download _file_8911.pdf.

Park, Haeyoun. 2015. "How Outsourcing Companies Are Gaming the Visa System." *New York Times,* November 10. https://www.nytimes.com/interactive/2015/11/06/us /outsourcing-companies-dominate-h1b-visas.html.

Perez-Lopez, Jorge F. 1996. "Conflict and Cooperation in U.S.-Mexican Labor Relations: The North American Agreement on Labor Cooperation." *Journal of Borderlands Studies* 11 (1): 43–58.

Preston, Julia. 2015. "Large Companies Game H-1B Visa Program, Costing the U.S. Jobs" *New York Times,* November 10. http://nyti.ms/1OBwIDj.

———. 2016. "Laid-Off Americans, Required to Zip Lips on Way Out, Grow Bolder." *New York Times,* June 11. http://nyti.ms/1OiASBb.

PRODESC and CDM (Proyecto de Derechos Económicos, Sociales y Culturales and Centro de los Derechos del Migrante). 2010. *A Regulatory Framework for the defense of migrant workers in the United States and Mexico.* Mexico City: PRODESC, CDM. http:// www.prodesc.org.mx/index.php/es/2014-04-21-22-18-4/manuales.

Russo, Robert. 2011. "A Cooperative Conundrum? The NAALC and Mexican Migrant Workers in the United States." *Law and Business Review of the Americas* 17 (1): 27–38.

Solomon, Joel. 2001. "Trading Away Rights: The Unfulfilled Promise of NAFTA's Labor Side Agreement." *Human Rights Watch Americas Division Report* 13, no. 2(B), April. New York: Human Rights Watch. https://www.justice.gov/sites/default/files/eoir /legacy/2013/06/14/mexico_0401.pdf.

USCIS (US Citizenship and Immigration Services). 2017. "One-Time Increase in H-2B Nonimmigrant Visas for FY 2017." Press release. Washington, DC: USCIS. https:// www.uscis.gov/working-united-states/temporary-workers/one-time-increase -h-2b-nonimmigrant-visas-fy-2017.

USDOL (US Department of Labor). n.d. "Submissions under the North American Agreement on Labor Cooperation (NAALC)." Washington, DC: USDOL. https://www.dol .gov/ilab/trade/agreements/naalc.htm. Accessed November 23, 2016.

USDOL and STPS (US Department of Labor and Secretaría de Trabajo y Previsión Social). 2016. Public Report on Outreach Events Pursuant to U.S.-Mexico Ministerial Consultations on Public Communications MEX 2003-1, 2005-1, and 2011-1 under the North American Agreement on Labor Cooperation. September. Washington, DC: USDOL. https://www.dol.gov/sites/default/files/documents/ilab/reports/Pu blic%20Report%20-%20H-2%20Events%20%28FINAL%20for%20Publication %29.pdf.

USDOS (US Department of State). 2012. FY2012 Non-Immigrant Visa Statistics, Non-Immigrant Visa Issuances, by Visa Class and by Nationality. Washington, DC: USDOS. https://travel.state.gov/content/dam/visas/Statistics/Non-Immigrant-St atistics/NIVDetailTables/FY12NIVDetailTable.pdf.

USGAO (US Government Accountability Office). 2009. "Department of Labor: Wage and Hour Division's Complaint Intake and Investigative Processes Leave Low Wage Workers Vulnerable to Wage Theft." Testimony Before the Committee on Education and Labor, House of Representatives. Washington, DC: USGAO. https://www.gao .gov/assets/130/122107.pdf.

Vega, Griselda, 2000. "Maquiladora's Lost Women: The Killing Fields of Mexico—Are NAFTA and NAALC Providing the Needed Protection?" *Journal of Gender, Race and Justice* 4:137–158.

Williams, Heather. 2002. "Lessons from the Labor Front: The Coalition for Justice in the Maquiladoras." In *Cross-Border Dialogues: U.S.-Mexico Social Movement Networking*, edited by David Brooks and Jonathan Fox, 87–112. La Jolla: Center for US-Mexican Studies, University of California, San Diego.

Wishnie, Michael J. 2002. "Immigrant Workers and the Domestic Enforcement of International Labor." *University of Pennsylvania Journal of Labor and Employment Law* 4:529–552.

PART II

MEXICO

CHAPTER 4

Mexican Migrant Federalism and Transnational Rights Advocacy

ADRIANA SLETZA ORTEGA RAMÍREZ

Since the first weeks of the Donald Trump administration in early 2017, amid executive orders on immigration, building the wall, and strengthening border security, migratory activism by Mexican state governments has re-emerged in the following ways:

- The governments of Baja California and Tijuana are expanding their state health services to Haitians, Africans, and Asians waiting to request asylum in the United States at the San Ysidro border crossing.
- The government of Puebla is expanding access to legal advice and services for undocumented immigrants and their American-born children in its offices in Los Angeles, New York City, and Passaic, New Jersey.
- San Luis Potosí and Nuevo León have announced actions to welcome and provide economic support to their states' returning migrants deported from the United States.
- The Conferencia Nacional de Gobernadores (National Conference of Governors) has been in dialogue with the National Governors Association in the United States regarding defending Mexican immigrants who fear deportation.

Since the 1980s, local governments of Mexico's federative entities have developed a "migratory diplomacy" through international strategies focused on their émigrés and emigrant organizations in the United States. The governments of federative entities in Mexico have historically focused on serving their diasporas in the United States alongside Mexican consulates; however, in recent years they have had to expand from service provision to a wider range of policies and programs. As a result, the Oficinas Estatales de Atención a Migrantes (OFAMs, State Migrant Assistance Offices) are now adopting transnational rights advocacy.

In previous research I have documented that programmatic priorities for OFAM policies and programs include: service provision, collection and investment of remittances, development of migrant and civil society organizations, promotion of temporary work visas in the United States and Canada, and international and institutional outreach (Ortega 2013; Velázquez and Ortega 2010). In this chapter I discuss the OFAMs' transnational rights advocacy in a changing migratory context and problematic federalism in Mexico.

Theoretical Framework of Migratory Federalism and Methodology

In migration studies, migration policies and the role of governments in general have been so underestimated that migration issues have only recently begun to be explored by the disciplines of political science, public administration, and international studies (Hollifield 2000). Policy, politicians, and bureaucrats have been the "missing elements" in the theory of migration (Massey 2015), although they are essential to any discussion of migration today.

The departure point in this chapter is a broad conceptualization of migration policies as the sum of public policy actions related to migration flows and, in accordance with Lelio Mármora (2002:50, 51), as specific governmental responses to distinct migration flows with immediate consequences. The difficulty in this approach lies in grouping these actions together, given the diversity of criteria within governmental systems that the various agencies use to implement migration policies.[1]

In the twenty-first century, municipal, state, and provincial migration policies that diverge from those of national governments—which traditionally have held a monopoly over policy on migration and naturalization of migrants—have become more visible. International comparison studies have shown that the roles of subnational governments and intergovernmental governance arrangements around migration vary across different models of so-called immigration federalism and federal migration governance (Joppke and Seidle 2012; Spiro 2001).

A systemic analysis of migration reveals how micro, meso, and macro processes intersect and feed into one another. Migrant agency exists in a global political context; it follows patterns established by the social networks that connect territorial spaces and the transnational practices of the stakeholders involved, including those of the exploitative migration industry. As a result, analysis of migration policies tends toward a pessimistic assessment of the different factors, hidden agendas, and undesirable outcomes involved in crafting such policies (Castles 2004).

Government policies and decisions around international migrations stem in part from geopolitics and foreign policy and in part from domestic political processes (Mármora 2002; Ortega 2014). Governance theory concerns the ways in which different spheres of governance address different migration flows, with refugees addressed multilaterally, low-skilled and unauthorized labor migrants regionally, and highly skilled migrants unilaterally. This perspective also addresses macro, national, and local spheres (Betts 2011).

Following Felipe Filomeno's (2017) theoretical model for local migration policies, I look at the relational intergovernmental processes through which these policies are developed, avoiding the reification of localities and the assumption that local migration policies are unique products of a self-explanatory process based on unique and successful case analysis.

My analysis complements transnational perspectives on the challenges of defending migrant rights through federative diplomacy,[2] an area within international studies dedicated to subnational governments and their strategies in the international arena. Federative diplomacy views globalization as well as bilateral and multilateral relations through the lens of the interests of local governments (Michelmann 2009; Muro Ruiz 2017). In a previous study I argue that migration federalism and diplomacy in the Mexican case is a window into the jurisdictional issues raised by federal, state, and municipal interactions in migration policy (Ortega 2013). From the federalist perspective, the principle of subsidiarity is especially important due to the distinct scales involved in governing migrations (macro, meso, and micro) and the particular legal jurisdictions that serve as spheres of authority, power, and governmentality.

A systemic approach would address these interrelated elements and scales through an analytical model, intersecting federal migration policy and international relations, along with diaspora and community organizing, influence in state migration policies, legislation, and transnational advocacy. Mexican states have been increasingly adopting transnational rights advocacy for their migrant populations, particularly in the sphere of service provision, by issuing ID documents, providing legal advice and services, helping with investing remittances, and working to secure access to education, health care, and work permits in the United States or Canada. Federal migration policy focuses on regulation and control, particularly on federal admission of migration flows and selectivity through categories and requirements. Meanwhile, the international relations scale involves elements of international law, foreign policies, and global migration and development forums where new agendas are adopted to guide governments.

I employ a longitudinal methodology of observation and data collection about federalism and the migration policies of Mexican states since 2000. I compare the previous results of a national study of state migration policies (Ortega 2013) with data updated to 2015 to look at adaptations to the changes in migration flows in Mexico and to the national legal framework. The research draws on official documents, especially legal and state documents, reports from international and Mexican civil society organizations, and interviews with government officials and activists.

Changing Migration Dynamics and National Migration Legislation

Mexico is situated geopolitically and geostrategically in the midst of substantial international migration flows, placing the issue of migration on national and international agendas in various arenas of government. The different migration flows within Mexico posit challenges for governmental institutions, which often demonstrate ambivalence about their roles and frequently operate under reactive logics. Migration flows, by contrast, respond to the broader dynamics of the global political economy and the unequal economic integration of North America after the implementation of NAFTA in 1994.

Mexico is connected through different migration flows, including

- Mexicans living permanently abroad, the majority of whom (97 percent) are in the United States;
- unauthorized Mexican migration to the United States;
- Mexican seasonal workers in the United States and Canada;
- returning Mexican migrants and deportees;
- migrant minors, not only those who are in transit from Central America but also US-born Mexicans;
- cross-border migrants on Mexico's northern and southern borders;
- foreign migrants in transit to the United States, mostly from Central America;
- victims of crimes associated with migration, such as human trafficking and smuggling;
- people internally displaced by the violence of criminal drug trafficking organizations in Mexico;
- seasonal and permanent foreign immigrants;
- refugees and asylum seekers in Mexico and Mexico-US border areas; and
- naturalized immigrants in Mexico

The confluence of North American and Mesoamerican migratory dynamics has created a regional migration system with Mexico, where the contradictions of North America and Mesoamerica converge, at its center. This is a vast, interdependent system. International migration systems theory explains how countries exchanging relatively large numbers of migrants experience feedback mechanisms that connect the movement of persons to concomitant flows of goods, capital, ideas, and information, creating the economic, cultural, and political ties and network of relations that sustain the international migration system (Massey et al. 2005:60).

In their analysis of the North American migration system, Douglas Massey and his colleagues (2005:66, 68) document the strong immigration pull of the United States and Canada and the large volume of Mexican migration headed north. The authors anticipate the contradictions that would develop within the migration system between Canada, the United States, and Mexico, foreseeing that an expansive free trade agreement in the region would tend to accelerate the economic drivers of migration, including labor factors, and they question what would happen if Canada and the United States continued to impose restrictive migration policies upon Mexico while at the same time stimulating Mexican participation in the movement of goods, capital, and information.

Evidently, to the extent that the flows of goods, investments, lines of communication, and transportation expanded under NAFTA, so too did the interdependencies within regional labor markets in need of migrant labor. Formally, NAFTA contemplated only seasonal migration flows of persons, businesses, and certain professionals, leaving the administration of migration within the purview of each of the signatory countries. Nonetheless, in its implementation, NAFTA generated the systemic conditions for regional growth of migration flows in North America and then Mesoamerica, attracting people from Central America through Mexico to cross the US border. NAFTA relied on a highly segmented and selective migration system based on the requirements of increasingly integrated labor markets.

In his January 28, 1992, State of the Union address, delivered in the midst of the negotiations that would lead to NAFTA's signing, President George H. W. Bush promised, "We will work to break down the walls that stop world trade. We will work to open markets everywhere. And in our major trade negotiations, I will continue pushing to eliminate tariffs and subsidies that damage America's farmers and workers. And we'll get more good American jobs within our own hemisphere through the North American free trade agreement and through the Enterprise for the Americas Initiative." The commitment to free markets was absolute. Unlike other regional economic agreements, NAFTA, by excluding migration from its formal governance structure yet spurring flows of people between the three countries, generated the conditions for accumulated labor migration in response to market demands. Labor mobility, flexibility, and precarity were the logical results of tariff reduction and demand for economic competition, and migrant workers paid the costs of being inserted into this economic model.

Since NAFTA's inception, the Mexico-US, Canada-US, and Mexico-Canada migration corridors have had increased flows consubstantial to levels of economic integration, with the United States as the strongest pole of immigrant attraction due to its economy and segmented labor markets. The Mexico-US migration corridor is the largest in the world, giving rise to a diaspora concentrated in the United States of more than 25 million people, of whom 12 million were born in Mexico. In 2014 about half of those—an estimated 6.6. million—were living undocumented (Baker 2017).

With 11.1 million immigrants not authorized to be in the country, the United States has the largest number of irregular migrants in the world. Despite public acknowledgments from the administrations of George W. Bush and Barack Obama that the immigration system is broken, its government has postponed updating its immigration system for years. Many countries with large-scale immigration have had to make legal and administrative reforms, including redefining the roles of states, provinces, and cities to adjust to the new realities of migration (Joppke and Seidle 2012), while the United States has simply continued accumulating undocumented immigrants, mostly from Mexico and the rest of Latin America.

The Mexico-Canada migration corridor had greater activity from 1994 to 2009, but the flow decreased after the Canadian government imposed a visa requirement for Mexicans after 9,511 Mexicans submitted asylum applications in 2009 and 9,400 did so in 2008. Most of the resulting investigations found the migrations to be economically motivated and not covered by asylum. The imposition of the visa impeded the growth of that particular migration corridor and decreased seasonal Mexican tourism to Canada from 270,000 Mexican tourists in 2008 to 123,000 in 2010, according to the Tourist Industry Association of Canada. Predictably, the number of asylum applications fell dramatically, with the Immigration and Refugee Board of Canada receiving only 120 asylum petitions in 2015.

NAFTA generated the conditions for what scholars predicted would be a "migration hump": flows would increase for fifteen years after its implementation before stabilizing and then declining (Mahendra 2014; Martin 2005). Accordingly, statistics reveal two major changes in migration patterns: the decrease in the rate of emigration and the increment of migrants returning to Mexico.

Following the 2008 US economic crisis, demographic experts like René Zenteno (2012) and Jeffrey S. Passel, D'Vera Cohn, and Ana González-Barrera (2012) began to call attention to "zero migration," the null migration flows between Mexico and the United States from 2009 to 2012. Zero migration arose either from a decrease in emigration and the return migration to Mexico voluntarily following the 2008 US economic crisis or by force through the policies to escalate deportation under the administrations of George W. Bush and Barack Obama. The data represent a significant change in the trend of Mexicans emigrating to the United States between 1970 and 2005.

In this same postcrisis period, international migration through Mexico became more visible, and the Mexican government has been systematizing statistics that show substantial growth in the numbers detained by the Instituto Nacional de Migración (INAMI, Mexico's National Migration Institute). The annual flow of Central Americans between 2008 and 2009 crossing through Mexico oscillated between 150,000 and 180,000 each year, while that number grew to 342,00 in 2015. INAMI data show that detentions have also risen, jumping from the roughly 100,000 annual figure of the early 2000s to 198,000 in 2015. The detention of migrants in transit, the majority of whom are from Central America, has grown to such an extent that civil society organizations comparing the 2009–2015 deportation statistics of Mexico and the United States insist that Mexico tends to deport more Central Americans than the United States does (Berumen, Narváez, and Ramos 2012; CONAPO 2016:100; UPM 2016a).

Children and adolescents are among the most vulnerable migrant flows. In 2014, for example, there was a serious humanitarian crisis of unaccompanied Central American and Mexican migrant children at the Mexico-US border. In 2010, US authorities apprehended 18,331 unaccompanied children; in 2014, the figure reached 68,541, and the child migrant crisis was not over. Between 2013 and 2015, Mexican immigration authorities strengthened deportations of children by 270 percent, with 9,600 deported in 2013 and 37,000 Central American minors deported in 2015. In the same year, 29,500 unaccompanied children went through the United States as part of the Refugee Resettlement Program. Data show that the number of children being detained wasn't declining; rather, the detentions were being spread out between Mexico and the United States (CONAPO and BBVA Research 2016:103, 104; UPM 2016b).

What do the volumes of emigration, transit, return, and immigration in Mexico represent? On one hand, they reveal most of the systemic regional character of migrations. People don't randomly migrate; rather, their paths represent collective trajectories along north-south routes that respond to conditions of structural violence and historical events. Meanwhile, federal immigration enforcement policies in Mexico and the United States are expressed through "detentions" and "removals/returns," which are, in practice, deportations perpetrating additional systematic violence against populations with prior motivations to migrate.

On the other hand, the principle of subsidiarity in the spheres of migration governance implies decision making and responsibility in other spheres of authority. Where is authority and governmentality exercised in the area of migration? What should be "governed" in global, multilateral, regional, national, provincial, and/or local spheres? And what public and private stakeholders should be involved?

In North America, the lack of trilateral and regional migratory mechanisms has led to a reliance on market forces such as labor markets and the "migration industry," which includes smugglers, traffickers, and criminal organizations. Formally, each of the three countries regulates migration and exercises selection processes unilaterally.

Canada, the United States, and Mexico have all had to deal with the consequences of their increasing migration flows, and the governments of local areas, especially those being transformed and challenged by migration, have taken part in regional migratory governance, although with different models. For example, in the United States there are highly competitive and conflictive intergovernmental relations between the federal government, polarized anti-immigrant cities and states, and pro-immigrant and sanctuary cities and states. In Canada, however, the model tends to be one of cooperation between the federal government and the provinces on migration issues, while in Mexico, the federal government's centralized hegemony dominates (Ortega and Velázquez 2014).

In addition, Mexico has been pressured internationally to modernize its migration legislation and migrant human rights enforcement because international organizations have expressed grave concerns to the Mexican state regarding the abuse and violation of migrant human rights at the federal, state, and local levels. These were aired in 2013 and 2015 by the Inter-American Commission on Human Rights and in 2011 by the Committee on the Protection of the Rights of All Migrant Workers and Members of their Families (CMW 2011; IACHR 2013, 2015). Nonetheless, government agencies have faced obstacles in collaborating and coordinating around migrant issues, clearly revealing their failure to internalize human rights norms despite the Mexican government being a signatory to the most important international mechanisms for defending migrant human rights (Martínez and Ortega 2015).

In terms of human rights, Mexican foreign policy in recent decades has passed from a statist to a more liberal approach, embracing the multilateralism of international organizations. The shift has fostered activism by Mexican diplomats in positions of leadership and encouraged the signing and ratification of useful agreements and mechanisms in the area of human rights (Saltalamacchia 2015). Since 2000, the Mexican government has opened itself up to international scrutiny, responding to transnational pressure in the area of human rights and employing an active policy from outside to inside, whereby multilateral activism compels and fosters internal changes to improve enforcement of human rights standards (Anaya 2012, 2014).

In the international arena, Mexico has belatedly incorporated the principles of international legal instruments into its migration policies. One of the main reasons for this delay stems from postrevolution nationalistic Mexican legislation approved in the Constitution of 1917, which was still in effect until the first decade of the twenty-first century. The legislation was traditionally very restrictive of the rights of foreigners in Mexico, in contrast to a Mexican foreign policy designed to defend migrant rights in the United States and in the world. This dynamic explains why the Mexican government was diplomatically active in negotiations for the International Convention on the Protection of the Rights of All Migrant Workers and Members of Their Families but did not ratify it until almost a decade later (table 4.1).[3]

The ratification of the convention requires submitting to a periodic review and commits Mexico to update its legislation and efforts with respect to migrant human rights.[4] In preparation for Mexico's first review, the federal authorities organized forums in October 2005. The resulting document, *México frente al fenómeno migratorio* (Mexico facing the migratory phenomenon, SRE 2014a), would serve as the basis for the Mexican position in the discussions around immigration reform in the United States at that time. The document makes explicit demands about migrant rights in Mexican foreign policy and about updating the normative framework around foreign-born immigrants in Mexico. Consultations with federative entities continued throughout 2006 with the declared purpose of formulating "a comprehensive and explicit Mexican policy" (INAMI 2006:9, 10). However, legal and institutional changes were complicated in the years following 2006, when the Felipe Calderón administration strengthened its military response to organized crime and drug trafficking routes to the United States that, among other effects, extended awareness of violence against irregular migrants.

The massacre in San Fernando, Tamaulipas, in August 2010 confirmed what the Comisión Nacional de Derechos Humanos (National Human Rights Commission) had warned of the previous year: escalating violence against migrants committed by organized crime along the routes to the US border (CNDH 2009). Similar crimes have been well documented. Salvadoran journalist Oscar Martínez (2010) describes violence against Central American migrants in Mexico in his book about traveling along migration routes through Chiapas state and Ixtepec, Oaxaca; the states of Tabasco and Veracruz and cities Río Bravo and Juárez, Chihuahua; the Sonoran border with Arizona; and Tijuana, Baja California. The title of Martínez's work *Los migrantes que no importan* (The migrants who don't matter) is particularly strik-

Table 4.1. Legal migration framework in Mexico, 1999–2012

Date of ratification or passage	Treaty or law
	International legal instrument
1999	International Convention on the Protection of the Rights of All Migrant Workers and Members of Their Families, 1990
2000	Convention Relating to the Status of Refugees, 1951
2000	Protocol Relating to the Status of Refugees, 1967
2003	Protocol to Prevent, Suppress, and Punish Trafficking in Persons, Especially Women and Children, supplementing the UN Convention against Transnational Organized Crime, 2000
2003	Protocol against the Smuggling of Migrants by Land, Sea, and Air, supplementing the UN Convention against Transnational Organized Crime, 2000
	National migration legislation
Jan. 27, 2011	Ley Sobre Refugiados y Protección Complementaria (Law on Refugees and Complementary Protection)
May 25, 2011	Ley de Migración (Migration Law)
June 9, 2011	Constitutional reform around human rights
June 13, 2012	Ley General para Prevenir, Sancionar y Erradicar los Delitos en Materia de Trata de Personas y para la Protección y Asistencia a las Víctimas de Estos Delitos (General Law on Prevention, Sanction, and Eradication of Crimes around the Trafficking of Persons and for the Protection and Assistance of Victims of These Crimes)

ing, as are these lines from his prologue (Martínez 2010:17): "Íbamos y volvíamos de esta ruta a la otra y la barbarie era estruendosa. Siempre pasa, siempre, a todas horas, y todos los saben, lo que ocurre es que esta gente no importa en este país." (We would come and go from one route to another amid outrageous barbarity. It is always happening, always, at all hours, and everyone knows it, it's just that these people don't matter in this country.)

What is the scope of this indifference? In its recommendations to Mexico, the International Committee on Migrant Workers refers to the deterioration of human rights, ongoing crimes and violence against migrants, and paradigmatic cases of the massacre of San Fernando in August 2010 and the kidnapping of forty migrant workers in Oaxaca in December of the same year (CMW 2011).[5] International observers have made clear recommendations: train and sanction immigration officials and the Policía Federal Preventiva (Federal Preventive Police); effectively coordinate federal, state, and municipal authorities around migration; and involve civil society. The central problem is that Central American migrants in transit have not mattered enough to any of the three tiers of government (municipal, state, and federal), which have been deaf to the migrants' pain and unwilling to assume responsibility for intergovernmental coordination.

The Ley de Migración (Migration Law) was being drafted when the massacre of San Fernando took place. The international attention garnered by the massacre accelerated the legislation, which the Mexican House of Representatives and Senate passed unanimously without any changes after a formal process of only a few months. Some were suspicious of the rapid pace. During a forum in Michoacán in September 2010, some academics and members of civil society organizations warned against rushing to approve new laws, urging that time should be taken to carefully design new migration policies (IC 2010:86, 113). In discussing the draft of the bill, forum participants considered the relative advantages of various reforms—to general law, federal migration law, and constitutional law—and the need to comprehensively re-create the legal framework for new migration policies. The actual framers, by contrast, considered changes only to federal law.

Moreover, the bill was narrowly focused. The bill originally included a section about the emigration and repatriation of Mexicans, but it was not included in the final version, which on the whole failed to consider the different migration flows in Mexico despite the country's large volumes of both emigration and repatriation. In practice, then, the Ley de Migración ended up being an immigration law instead of a comprehensive law including international emigration (Durand 2013). The law grants primacy to federal authorities and is designed to reorganize and centralize Mexican migration policy, deviating from the course of state migratory federalism that had been dominant since 1980.

Centripetal and Centrifugal Forces in Mexican Migratory Federalism

The Mexican political system has historically tended toward centralism, despite its formal federal structure that recognizes the sovereignty of the states and the basic unit of the *municipio libre* (independent municipality). The political system has traditionally been hierarchical and centralizing (*centripetal*), with power flowing from a strong president in the federal capital and mirrored by the authoritarianism of governors over their respective state territories and the powers of the municipalities within them. As a result, the processes of decentralization, federalism, and democracy have been contentious in Mexico. Although by law migration is the exclusive domain of Congress (according to Article 73 of the Constitution),[6] migration between Mexico and the United States is not just a national or federal issue, given the historic regionalization of Mexican emigration (Durand 2016:41, 43).

Mexican states and municipalities on the northern border as well as those with a high incidence of migration in the Mexican midwest and the Bajío have had to deal with migration and its consequences throughout history (Durand 2016:127, 128; Fitzgerald 2006). However, the modern involvement of Mexican states in terms of consular protection for their citizens was initiated by the Secretaría de Relaciones Exteriores (SRE, Secretariat of Foreign Affairs) in the 1990s. Throughout the Mexican economic crisis of the 1970s, the migration flows from the various regions of Mexico started to diversify, and the volume of emigration expanded and intensified until the 1990s. Roger Díaz de Cossío, the first director of the SRE's Programa de Comunidades en el Exterior (Program for Communities Abroad), writes in his memoirs,

> We started to raise awareness among the governors. Genaro Borrego, then governor of Zacatecas, was the only one who had been able to build strong contacts with Zacatecans in Los Angeles. . . . I remember that one time in Jalisco I told the governor: "Sir, did you know that the biggest source of income for your state is sending your citizens from the United States, bringing in close to $800 million dollars annually?" He and his cabinet looked shocked. And we went on. "There isn't a single person in your government dedicated to serving them." And like that, little by little, we were able to get some states to open offices to attend to their émigrés. Many governors started to make trips to Los Angeles and Chicago.[7] (Díaz de Cossío 2010:20–21)

Through these precedents, the federative entities in Mexico incorporated migration policies pertaining to their émigrés in the United States into their government agendas. OFAMs started to appear formally at the end of the 1980s in some states, and from 2000 on, most Mexican states had them. The state offices were created in a context of democratic openness, highly competitive party politics, revival of Mexican federalism, initiatives by governors, expansion of international emigration, and steady growth of remittances (Ortega 2013).

Some state governments created innovative programs or legislation around migration that would inspire national progress on the issue. The pioneers addressing migration in public programs and government structures were Michoacán, Zacatecas, and Guanajuato (Velázquez and Ortega 2010). Michoacán started collaborating with educational authorities in California in 1982 to assure that migrant children would be admitted during the appropriate school year and then went on to establish the federal Binational Migrant Education Program. Michoacán was also a pioneer in establishing the Secretaría del Migrante (Michoacán Migrant Secretariat) as a primary state government structure in the governor's cabinet, and other Mexican states including Guerrero have imitated its governmental structure and programs.

The government of Zacatecas set a precedent by financially supporting the purchase of a building for the Casa del Zacatecano, a community center for Zacatecan migrants, in East Los Angeles. The state has been an innovator in programs that match remittance investment such as One-for-One, Two-for-One, Three-for-One programs that would later be adopted by the federal government through the Secretaría de Desarrollo Social (Secretariat of Social Development). Zacatecas also adopted legal modifications in its constitution to recognize binational residency and the political rights of émigrés.

In Guanajuato, the state government has supported Casa Guanajuato community centers for its migrants in the United States since 1994 and has given seed grants to Guanajuatan civil society organizations. The model of creating *casas* to represent Mexican state governments has been copied by other federative entities as well.

Since 2005, legislative progress around migration has been made at the state level also in Sonora and Durango. Sonora specifically addresses problems confronted by migrants in transit to the United States as well as migrant children. One of the most progressive laws, the Ley de Interculturalidad, Atención a Migrantes y Movilidad Humana (Interculturality, Migrant Services and Human Mobility Law), was adopted by the government of Mexico City in 2011. The law is implemented by a program of the same name, the Programa de Interculturalidad, Atención a Migrantes y Movilidad Humana, which addresses different migrant populations in Mexico City: indigenous immigrants, émigrés, and documented as well as undocumented foreigners including asylum seekers. Mexico City has linked its migration policy to its international agenda through its membership in the International Intercultural Cities Network, which is supported by the Council of Europe (COE 2014).

These state innovations can be considered *centrifugal* forces in Mexican migrant federalism because the states have generated their local migration policies and, in contrast to immigration federalism in the United States (Gulasekaram and Ramakrishnan 2016), have not presented any constitutional controversies or federal challenges. Simultaneously, though, Mexican federal authorities have unleashed *centripetal* forces, as in establishing the federal Unidad de Política Migratoria (Migration Policy Unit) after the approval in 2011 of the Ley de Migración. The unit's mission is to "design and propose the strategies, programs, and actions that make up a comprehensive and coherent migration policy anchored by the Mexican State" (UPM 2015). Therefore, despite significant state actions, the federal government maintains its tendency to centralize and make decisions hierarchically.

The Ley de Migración finds practical expression in the Programa Especial de Migración 2014–2018 (Special Migration Program). The only reference in the program to the role of the federative entities is a mention of the need to adapt state migration laws with the Ley de Migración (SEGOB 2014). The Migration Policy Unit officials in charge of implementing the Special Migration Program recognize that three years after its launch, there still were neither formal nor informal mechanisms for working with the federative entities (Berumen interview). In other words, they expect that in response to a centralized order, the states will themselves adapt their policies and programs around migration to those of the federation.

Notwithstanding the states' compliance with federal laws, there is great diversity among them in terms of migration policies. Map 4.1 presents four categories to distinguish Mexican states by their current migration legislation and institutions:

1. States with migration legislation and OFAMs: Baja California, Ciudad de México, Chihuahua, Durango, Estado de México, Guanajuato, Hidalgo, Michoacán, Oaxaca, San Luis Potosí, Sonora, and Tlaxcala.
2. States with some legislation mentioning the migrant population: Aguascalientes, Campeche, Chiapas, Morelos, Nayarit, Puebla, Tabasco, Tamaulipas, Yucatán, and Zacatecas.
3. States with OFAMs but no migration legislation: Coahuila, Colima, Guerrero, Jalisco, Nuevo León, Querétaro, and Veracruz.
4. States without OFAMs or related legislation: Quintana Roo, Baja California Sur, and Sinaloa.

The specific analysis of local legislation and OFAMs reveals that most of the states are selective about which migrant populations they serve, preferring to assume responsibility for their émigrés but leave the safety and rights of foreign migrants in the hands of federal authorities, in accordance with Mexican migration law. The OFAMs have begun to dichotomize "migrants who matter" with those whom they prefer not to serve. Incorporating other migrant populations such as foreign immigrants and asylum seekers would mean taking on more challenges and expanding their services. Table 4.2 clas-

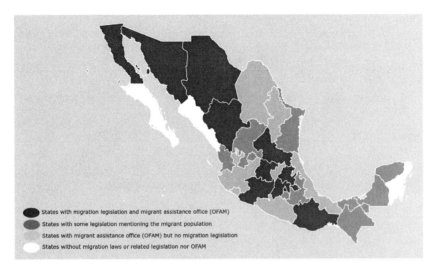

States with migration legislation and migrant assistance office (OFAM)
States with some legislation mentioning the migrant population
States with migrant assistance office (OFAM) but no migration legislation
States without migration laws or related legislation nor OFAM

Map 4.1. Mexican states' migration legislation and migrant assistances offices. Courtesy of Instituto de Estudios y Divulgación sobre Migración, Mexico City.

sifies the OFAMs based on the migrant populations they serve, with three cases—Michoacán, Oaxaca, and Jalisco—that are somewhat contradictory because their legal frameworks address both domestic and foreign-born migrants but still prioritize their own émigrés. In Michoacán and Jalisco, specifically, the favored émigrés are the only migrant population included in the mechanisms for public participation that were designed to support migrant federations and organizations in the United States.

In their decision not to serve all migrants, the OFAMs reflect Martínez's (2010, 2014) observation that Mexican society chooses to ignore and obscure the problems of violence against Central American migrants to avoid responsibility. Since the OFAMs are government bodies specializing in serving and supporting migrants and have staffs sensitive to the problems faced by these populations, it is surprising that they do not take a more proactive role in combating serious problems of migrant violence and violations of migrant rights. They could also be more proactive in adopting the international migrant law signed by Mexico and the national migration legislation (table 4.1).

Meanwhile, following the San Fernando massacre of August 2010, a majority of the Mexican states still are not adopting migrant human rights perspectives in their legislation, institutions, or public policies. Their priorities continue to center on their émigrés. Only Mexico City and four states out of thirty-two have suitable legislation, OFAMs, and public services for the diverse migrant populations: Baja California, Chihuahua, Durango, and Sonora.

Table 4.2. Migrants "who matter"

2015 OFAM service populations		
State émigrés only		Nationals and foreigners
Aguascalientes	Oaxaca	Baja California
	Puebla	
Campeche	Querétaro	
Coahuila	State of México	Chiapas
	Tabasco	
Colima	Tlaxcala	Chihuahua
		Durango
	Veracruz	Mexico City
		Nuevo León
Guanajuato	Yucatán	San Luis Potosí
Guerrero	Zacatecas	Sonora
Hidalgo		
Jalisco		Tamaulipas
Michoacán		
Morelos		
Nayarit		

Note: Determination of the migrant population served is derived from analysis of the legal framework upon which the OFAMs are based and public information about the people who use their programs and services.

Transnational Advocacy by the OFAM: Pressure and Achievements

Attending to émigrés through the OFAMs has implied extraterritoriality for the subnational governments in Mexico. Transnational and international pressure led to OFAM improvements and expansion of services. Transnational pressure has stemmed from the demands of émigrés by way of their hometown associations and diaspora organizations. In 2016, nine of thirty-two Mexican states had outreach staffs or offices in the United States to service their émigrés. Some states also had offices in other parts of Mexico or at transit points along the US border. The Michoacán Migrant Secretariat, for example, has a presence in its main office in Morelia but also in Tijuana, Chicago, and California. Likewise, the Dirección General de Atención a Migrantes de Veracruz (Veracruz General Directorate for Migrant Assistance) operates its central office at Xalapa but also an office in Reynosa, Tamaulipas, near the McAllen, Texas, border primarily to assist deported migrants from Veracruz and migrants from Veracruz living in Tamaulipas (DGAM Veracruz 2017).

Another expansion has involved *casas* in the United States, community centers following the Guanajuato model promoted while Vicente Fox was governor of that state and presiding over its historically high migration flows, and the Casa del Zacatecano in East Los Angeles, supported initially by Zacatecas's government budget. In the Puebla case, the founder of the nonprofit Casa México in New York, Isabel Navarro, remembers beginning her organizing efforts in the late 1960s, then in 1973 becoming the first Mexican woman elected to the city's school board. A large number of people from Mexico in general, and Puebla in particular, arrived in the 1980s, people who "venían sin nada" (came with nothing). She explains how the governor of Puebla at the time, Melquiades Morales, began visiting New York in the 1990s, which led to greater financial and institutional support for those from Puebla and the creation of the Casa Puebla (Navarro interview).

Casas Puebla in New York and New Jersey opened in response to migratory circuits between Puebla and the metropolitan New York area. Other Mexican states determine where to open offices abroad based on the concentration of their migrant populations and political pressure from those populations' organizations. Since 2010, the number of Mexican state offices in the United States has grown within two primary areas, Southern California, particularly Los Angeles, and the Chicago metropolitan area; an office opened in Southern California because of the number of émigrés living there and in the Chicago area because of political pressure from Mexican émigré organizations. If the offices were established solely along population lines, Texas cities like Houston, Dallas, and San Antonio would have more Mexican state offices than Chicago has, as Texas is the US state with the second-highest Mexican population (Pew Research Center 2016). Only the state of México has an office in Texas, located in Houston, though the state of Puebla had a *casa* in Houston from 2003 to 2005.

In 2016 Mexico City and the state governments of Colima, Durango, Guanajuato, México, Michoacán, Oaxaca, and Puebla had offices in the Los Angeles area (SRE 2013). In 2014 in the Chicago area, there were outreach migrant offices for Mexico City and the states of Durango, Guerrero, Guanajuato, Jalisco, México, Michoacán, and Zacatecas (SRE 2014b). These extraterritorial OFAMs deploy federative diplomacy on migration issues—migration diplomacy, or more technically, migration "paradiplomacy" (Tavares 2016)—because although Mexican consulates advocate for Mexican immigrants in the United States and engage in migration diplomacy, the extraterritorial OFAMs employ their own paradiplomacy along with the consulates.

These state offices outside Mexico have served as bridges connecting populations from each state, and in general they have focused on transactions involving state and municipal documents such as birth, marriage, and death certificates, school diplomas, and records of municipal residence. They carry out programs in accordance with migrant priorities such as the Three-for-One program for co-investment of remittances and support of organizational cultural festivals. More broadly, OFAMs and Mexican states' *casas* in the United States have adapted to the needs and demands of the migrant populations that use their services.

The SRE and Mexican consulates have collaborated in various ways with the extraterritorial OFAMs. The consulate in Los Angeles has collaborated with Mexican state offices to develop strategies and activities for their communities. During the years when the OFAMs were first proliferating outside Mexico, the SRE responded cautiously, wary of opportunistic governors and local politicians approaching their states' émigrés. It was difficult to reach formal agreements for specific collaborations or trainings, and few states followed Mexico's federal guidelines on foreign policy and formal consular protocols (Chávez interview; SRE 2013, 2014). Gradually, the SRE has been opening spaces for collaboration with state governments in which they aid each other in distributing official documents, such as registration forms issued by state governments needed for consular services, and providing consular protection and case management for missing and arrested persons in the United States.

Despite the growing cooperation, challenges persist, including institutional difficulties such as staff continuity, budgets in Mexican pesos rather than dollars, and political changes in Mexico. For such reasons, the OFAMs and *casas* have remained low-profile actors with differing levels of interaction with organized émigrés. A unique and especially successful case, however, is Casa Michoacán in the Pilsen neighborhood of Chicago. The *casa* hosts the Federación de Clubes Michoacanos en Illinois (Federation of Michoacán Hometown Associations in Illinois), and the government of Michoacán contributed to the building's purchase. The *casa* offers a variety of services and activities for the migrant population and hosts a liaison to the Michoacán Migrant Secretariat, which provides documents and services from Michoacán to its migrants. Programs and services available at the *casa* also are financed with resources from the City of Chicago, the Illinois state government, and the office of Alianza Américas, a transnational advocacy network (Arreola interview). In sum, the *casa* is a space where an array of migrant rights campaigns, events, services, and programs converge and are made accessible to those from Michoacán and other migrant groups in the area.

Other *casas* and Mexican states' offices in the United States have had to designate themselves as official governmental spaces and distance themselves from conflicts among organizations of their own states' émigrés. They generate their own complementary services that do not compete with the *casas* registered by migrant organizations like the Casa de Durango in Los Angeles, the Casas Guanajuato located around the United States, or the Casa Puebla–New York. In these cases, government and organizational offices are separate, with representatives of the Durango state government operating in the South Gate area of Los Angeles, for example, distinguishing themselves from the civil society organization and community space of Casa Durango in Lynwood, California.

Some OFAMs have been proactive in incorporating transnational rights defense strategies in the United States and Mexico, including migration diplomacy and international cooperation. The most visible examples are the OFAMs of Michoacán and Chiapas, the Michoacán Migrant Secretariat and the Chiapas Secretariat for Development of the Mexican Southern Border and Liaison for International Cooperation. These states traditionally have received strong transnational and international pressures to improve their governmental responses to migration flows and adopt a migrant rights agenda rather than one limited to migrant services.

Michoacán's émigrés have historically exerted strong political pressure, and the region has consistently experienced large-scale migrations for decades. Between 2000 and 2010, it was one of the top three Mexican states in terms of its numbers of migrants and returning and circular migrants. Between 2010 and 2014, Michoacán had the third-largest number of repatriated minor migrants. Moreover, it is among the top recipients of remittances of all the Mexican states, bringing in $2 billion per year (CONAPO and BBVA Research 2015:82, 84–87, 115, 158, 168).

The Michoacán Migrant Secretariat has an organizational structure set up to account for the various problems its migrant populations encounter by embracing a transversal orientation in its programs. Unlike the other OFAMs that provide general counseling, referrals, or accompaniment, Michoacán's government provides specialized services for cases such as international restitution and custody of minors, enforcement of criminal sentences for transferred prisoners, waiver applications, and advice for recovering lost wages in the United States. Furthermore, it offers representation to émigrés from Michoacán appearing before national and foreign authorities to defend their human and civil rights (SM, 2012, 2016a, 2017).

Michoacán's secretariat cooperates significantly with different stakeholders, including other Mexican states' OFAMs, around specific programs and with Mexican federal government agencies to manage migrant initiatives such as the Three-for-One program.[8] It has signed agreements and run programs with public and private universities and other educational institutions in Michoacán and the United States. The programs include a partnership with the psychology department of the Universidad Michoacana de San Nicolás de Hidalgo and a program to help nursing professionals from Michoacán pay to get certified in the United States. Michoacán's secretariat also cooperate with national and transnational civil society organizations; examples are their support for temporary workers in the United States and Canada through the Global Workers Justice Alliance and United Food and Commercial Workers-Canada (SM 2016b). The agreements constitute formal, interinstitutional instruments to carry out initiatives and provide services together with other entities, whether public, private, or from civil society. The agreements can also allow for cooperation in networks that, from a governance perspective, play a central role in implementing public policies.

Chiapas is another unique case in terms of migration policy. The state operates under tremendous pressure from a variety of sources including critical civil society organizations in communities around Chiapas as a result of the armed 1994 conflict with the Ejército Zapatista de Liberación Nacional (Zapatista National Liberation Army), the vigilance of international observer missions, the presence of UN High Commissioner for Refugees and International Organization for Migration offices in Tapachula, and serious problems of violence against migrants and transnational human smuggling and trafficking rings. As a recipient of international funds for local development, the state of Chiapas has since 2009 incorporated the development agendas of the United Nations and the UN Development Program into its constitution and the structure of its Secretaría para el Desarrollo de la Frontera Sur y Enlace para la Cooperación Internacional (Chiapas Secretariat for Development of the [Mexican] Southern Border and Liaison for International Cooperation). This secretariat is Chiapas's OFAM and link to resources in and outside Mexico. Since 2014 the government of Chiapas also has had a prosecutor specializing in crimes against migrants.

The Chiapas Secretariat for Development of the Southern Border and Liaison for International Cooperation is structured to advocate for and defend migrant human rights as part of the state's focus on serving international migrants, cross-border populations from Guatemala, and émigrés from Chiapas to the United States, particularly to Florida. Additionally, the state carries out development projects along its southern border with Guatemala and has established formal relations with other countries and foreign authorities in the region in sister-city and other international cooperation projects (SFS 2015).

The government of Chiapas provides numerous migrant services. In 2015 it reported aiding foreign migrants principally from Guatemala, Ecuador, Nicaragua, Honduras, and El Salvador as well as following 4,861 cases of vulnerable migrants from Chiapas and their families and distributing 96,128 pesos for transporting the bodies of those deceased in the United States. But its objectives also include promoting a human rights agenda and activities, as seen in its work with the Comisión Nacional de Derechos Humanos on the campaign Niñas, Niños y Adolescentes en Movimiento (Children and Adolescents in Motion), which sought to raise awareness of the rights of migrant children and adolescents, and with the UN campaign Te Acompañamos (We're with You) about migrant rights. With support from the UN High Commissioner for Refugees and the International Organization for Migration, it also develops training procedures for state and municipal officials. Finally, Chiapas is in charge of investment projects and promotion of commerce through efforts such as the Feria Internacional Mesoamericana (Mesoamerican International Trade Show) and its special economic zones (SFS 2015).

Michoacán and Chiapas have been pressured for transparency more than other Mexican states have by the stakeholders involved in their migrant initiatives. They therefore provide more information about budgets, process, and results, and each has responded to the pressure through active engagement with migrant rights.

Conclusions

Local territories and states in Mexico challenged by international migration flows confront dilemmas in deciding how to respond to, design policies around, and secure services for migrant populations moving through North America and Mesoamerica, particularly those who are vulnerable and whose migration status is irregular. In Mexico's regional migration system, the principle of subsidiarity in spheres of governance, decision making, and responsibility plays a significant role. At the same time, the processes of centralization of federal migration policy and innovation by states as they adopt a migrant human rights perspective represent, respectively, centripetal and centrifugal forces in migration federalism.

Over a period of thirty years, Mexico has moved with difficulty through a process of recognizing human rights, but its experience with regard to the rights of migrants is relatively recent. While the OFAMs have consolidated their operations since 2000, in recent years most Mexican states have encountered more evident dichotomies between national émigrés and foreign migrants. Despite the recommendations of international organizations, demands from human rights activists and organizations, changing migration dynamics, and increasing violence against migrants in Mexico, most OFAMs prefer to continue to focus on their own states' émigrés.

The actual implementation of federal migration law since 2011 has revived the aspiration for a unified Mexican migration policy, that is, for a migratory centralism. The Programa Especial de Migración aims for all states to harmonize their legislation with federal migration law, thus preventing the OFAMs from becoming more proactive as they follow federal mandates. After five years, only Mexico City and four states of thirty-two had developed legislation or programs to protect migrants without explicitly discriminating between Mexican nationals and foreigners. Three of the four states are situated along the US-Mexico border, so they confront the realities of migrant populations on a daily basis. The case of Mexico City is also relevant because it hosts the vast majority of foreigners living in Mexico. As such, the second paragraph of its new constitution proposes a welcoming identity as a city of "interculturality and hospitality" (Mexico City 2017).

Within the federal government, the perspective persists that the federative entities shouldn't exceed their authority, despite the fact that some OFAMs have more than twenty years of experience in programs and services for migrants. As the phenomenon of migration in Mexico becomes more complex and the context of violence against migrants persists, it becomes increasingly difficult to implement a framework that organizes the states and municipalities via mandate. While some OFAMs like those of Mexico City, Baja California, Michoacán, and Chiapas are generating their own projects and alternatives for migration governance, few OFAMs have changed, preserving their tendency toward service provision and a target population limited to their own states' émigrés.

The dichotomy that many OFAMs draw between national migrants and foreigners is rooted in nationalism, stating a preference for Mexican citizens instead of foreigners, and the ways governments choose to exercise their enforcement powers. Distinguishing between migrants who matter and those who do not is based on the discriminatory treatment and invisibility of migrants in disregard for and indifference to atrocities, particularly of those irregular Central Americans migrants en route to the United States through Mexico. North America's and Mesoamerica's regional migratory systems converge in Mexico and are associated with violence against transit migrants. Such violence gained international notoriety following the 2010 massacre in San Fernando, which Ana Lorena Delgadillo, Alma García, and Rodolfo Córdova Alcaraz discuss in chapter 5 of this volume. A global resurgence of nationalism and xenophobia presents a challenge that could play out in Mexico, especially in the states and localities where the human rights agenda is not extended to the diverse migrant populations, making prevention and anticipation of violations a necessity.

In this chapter I have examined the progress and limitations of various OFAMs, but the chapter can also serve as a map of opportunities and challenges for civil society organizations with agendas of transnational rights defense and advocacy for laws, norms, and collaborative mechanisms that allow for policy transformation and local impact.

The particular experiences of the offices of Mexican states in the United States serving their émigrés and the Michoacán Migrant Secretariat and Chiapas Secretariat for Development of the Mexican Southern Border and Liaison for International Cooperation are illustrative of the innovations that states can actually implement to develop a progressive migrant rights agenda in Mexico. The diversity of stakeholders and scales involved can be dealt with through governance, federative diplomacy, and international and transnational cooperation for local development. Migrant human rights violations and crimes cannot be resolved through the legal framework alone or through the centralized and hierarchical Mexican political processes that persist alongside and undermine the migratory diplomacy of Mexican states in the United States.

Notes

1. Studies about migration policies have traditionally been done from within immigrant-receiving countries, leading many of them to focus on migration enforcement and regulation (see Beine et al. 2016; Meyers 2000). International organizations such as the OIM have also privileged a conceptualization of migration policy as the management of migratory flows, although in recent years they have started to adopt a "migration governance perspective" to include the different actors involved (see Betts 2011; Galstyan 2010; IOM 2005, 2010, 2015).

2. Federative diplomacy is also known as "paradiplomacy" (Tavares 2016).

3. Mexico ratified the convention with legal reservations about its own constitutional Article 33, which states that the Mexican president may expel a foreign person.

4. During the updates, the articles of the Ley General de Población of 1979 that penalized foreigners in irregular immigration with jail time and fines had to be stricken from the books (SEGOB/INAMI 2002:261–263).

5. The International Committee on Migrant Workers is a formal mechanism monitoring compliance of the International Convention on the Protection of the Rights of All Migrant Workers and Members of Their Families by signatory states.

6. Section XVI of the article specifies that among the powers of Congress is the issuing of laws regarding nationality, legal status of foreigners, citizenship, naturalization, colonization, emigration, and immigration.

7. Translations are by the author except as otherwise noted.

8. The OFAMs do maintain hierarchical relations with the municipalities of their states but solely for the purposes of advertising the OFAMs' programs or referring cases to them.

References

Interviews by the Author

Arreola, Lourdes, governmental liaison of the state of Michoacán based in Chicago, May 30, 2012, Chicago.
Berumen, Salvador, adjunct general director of migration policy, Secretaría de Gobernación, February 16, 2017, Mexico City.
Chávez, Betina, general director of political coordination for the Secretaría de Relaciones Exteriores, September 27, 2009, Mexico City.
Navarro, Isabel, founder of Casa México in New York, June 26, 2102, New York.

Published Sources

Anaya, Alejandro. 2012. *El país bajo presión: Debatiendo el papel del escrutinio internacional de derechos humanos sobre México*. Mexico City: Centro de Investigación y Docencia Económicas.
———. 2014. "Política exterior y derechos humanos durante el gobierno de Felipe Calderón." In *Balance y perspectivas de la política exterior de México*, edited by Humberto Garza Elizondo, Jorge A. Schiavon, and Rafael Velázquez, 365–388. Mexico City: Colegio de México, Centro de Investigación y Docencia Económicas.
Baker, Bryan. 2017. Estimates of the Unauthorized Immigrant Population Residing in the United States: January 2014. Washington, DC: Office for Immigration Statistics, US Department of Homeland Security. https://www.dhs.gov/sites/default/files/publications/Unauthorized%20Immigrant%20Population%20Estimates%20in%20the%20US%20January%202014_1.pdf.
Beine, Michel, Anna Boucher, Brian Burgoon, Mary Crock, Justin Gest, Michael Hiscox, Patrick McGovern, Hillel Rapoport, Joep Schaper, and Eiko Thielemann. 2016. "Comparing Immigration Policies: An Overview from the IMPALA Database," *International Migration Review* 50 (4): 825–1076.
Berumen, Salvador, Juan Carlos Narváez, and Luis Felipe Ramos. 2012. "La migración centroamericana de tránsito irregular por México. Una aproximación a partir de registros administrativos migratorios y otras fuentes de información." In *Construyendo estadísticas: Movilidad y migración internacional en México*, edited by Ernesto Rodríguez, Luz María Salazar, and Graciela Martínez, 89–134, Mexico City: Centro de Estudios Migratorios, Unidad de Política Migratoria, Secretaría de Gobernación, Instituto Nacional de Migración, and Tilde.
Betts, Alexander. 2011. *Global Migration Governance*. Oxford: Oxford University Press.
Bush, George H. W. State of the Union. January 28, 1992. Reprint, American Presidency Project, University of California, Santa Barbara. http://www.presidency.ucsb.edu/ws/index.php?pid=20544.
Castles, Stephen. 2004. "Why Migration Policies Fail." *Ethnic and Racial Studies* 27 (2): 205–227.
CNDH (Comisión Nacional de Derechos Humanos). 2009. *Informe especial sobre casos de secuestro en contra de migrantes*. Mexico City: Comisión Nacional de Derechos Humanos. http://www.cndh.org.mx/sites/all/doc/Informes/Especiales/2009_migra.pdf.
CMW (Committee on the Protection of the Rights of All Migrant Workers and Members of Their Families). 2011. *Concluding Observations of the Committee on the Protection of*

the Rights of All Migrant Workers and Members of Their Families. Fourteenth session, CMW/C/MEX/CO/2, Mexico City, April 4–8. https://tbinternet.ohchr.org/_layo uts/treatybodyexternal/Download.aspx?symbolno=CMW%2fC%2fMEX%2fCO%2 f2&Lang=en.

COE (Council of Europe). 2014. *Mexico City: Results of the Intercultural Cities Index*. Mexico City: COE. https://rm.coe.int/16802ff6d2.

CONAPO (Consejo Nacional de Población). 2016. *Prontuario sobre movilidad y migración: Dimensiones sobre el fenómeno migratorio en México*. Mexico City: Secretaría de Gobernación and Consejo Nacional de Población. http://www.politicamigratoria.gob.mx /work/models/SEGOB/Resource/2801/1/images/Prontuario%20sobre%20m ovilidad%20y%20migraci%C3%83%C2%B3n%20internacional.pdf.CONAPO and BBVA Research (Consejo Nacional de Población/Banco Bilbao Vizcaya Argentaria Research). 2015. *Yearbook of Migration and Remittances, Mexico*. Mexico City: Secretaría de Gobernación, CONAPO, and BBVA Research. https://www.gob.mx/cms/up loads/attachment/file/72780/Anuario_Migracion_y_Remesas_2015.pdf.

———. 2016. *Yearbook of Migration and Remittances, Mexico*. Mexico City: Secretaría de Gobernación, CONAPO and BBVA Research. https://www.bbvaresearch.com/wp -content/uploads/2016/06/1606_Mexico_AnuarioMigracion_2016.pdf.

Díaz de Cossío, Roger. 2010. "Recuerdos del principio." In *Mexicanos en el exterior: Trayectoria y perspectivas (1990–2010)*, edited by Instituto Matías Romero de Estudios Diplomáticos, 17–24. Mexico City: Secretaría de Relaciones Exteriores.

DGAM-Veracruz (Dirección General de Atención a Migrantes-Veracruz). 2017. Organigrama, Dirección General de Atención a Migrantes, Gobierno del Estado de Veracruz. Chart. Xalapa, Mexico: Secretaría de Gobierno del Estado de Veracruz. http:// segobver.gob.mx/migrantes/organigrama.php.

Durand, Jorge. 2013. "La 'desmigratización' de la relación bilateral: Balance del sexenio de Felipe Calderón." *Foro Internacional* 5 (3–4): 750–770.

———. 2016. *Historia mínima de la migración México-Estados Unidos*. Mexico City: Colegio de México.

Filomeno, Felipe Amin. 2017. *Theories of Local Migration Policy*. Cham, Switzerland: Springer.

Fitzgerald, David. 2006. "Inside the Sending State: The Politics of Mexican Emigration Control." *International Migration Review* 40 (2): 259–293.

Galstyan, Kristina. 2010. *Migration Management and Human Rights*. Yerevan, Armenia: Antares, International Organization for Migration. http://publications.iom.int/sys tem/files/pdf/migration_management_eng.pdf.

Gulasekaram, Pratheepan, and S. Karthick Ramakrishnan. 2016. "The President and Immigration Federalism." *Florida Law Review* 68 (1). https://scholarship.law.ufl .edu/cgi/viewcontent.cgi?article=1273&context=flr.

Hollifield, James. 2000. "The Politics of International Migration: How Can We 'Bring the State Back In'?" In *Migration Theory: Talking across Disciplines*, edited by Caroline Brettell and James Hollifield, 137–185. New York: Routledge.

IACHR (Inter-American Commission on Human Rights). 2013. *Human Rights of Migrants and Other Persons in the Context of Human Mobility in Mexico*. Washington, DC: Organization of American States. http://www.oas.org/en/iachr/migrants/docs /pdf/report-migrants-mexico-2013.pdf.

———. 2015. *Situation of Human Rights in Mexico*. Washington, DC: Organization of American States. http://www.oas.org/en/iachr/reports/pdfs/Mexico2016-en.pdf.

IC (Iniciativa Ciudadana para la Promoción de la Cultura del Diálogo). 2010. *Foro nacional para la construcción de una política migratoria integral y democrática en el México del bicentenario: Diálogo, propuestas, ponencias y otros documentos.* Conference proceedings and CD. Morelia, Mexico, September 23.

INAMI (Instituto Nacional de Migración). 2006. *Hacia una política migratoria del estado mexicano.* Mexico City: Secretaría de Gobernación.

IOM (International Organization for Migrations). 2005. *World Migration Report 2005: Costs and Benefits of International Migration.* Geneva: IOM. http://publications.iom .int/system/files/pdf/wmr_2005_3.pdf.

———. 2010. *World Migration Report 2010: The Future of Migration: Building Capacities for Change.* Geneva: IOM. http://publications.iom.int/system/files/pdf/wmr_2010 _english.pdf?language=en.

———. 2015. *World Migration Report 2015: Migrants and Cities, New Partnerships to Manage Mobility.* Geneva: IOM. http://publications.iom.int/system/files/wmr20 15_en.pdf.

Joppke, Christian, and Leslie Seidle. 2012. *Immigrant Integration in Federal Countries: Forum of Federations.* Montreal: McGill-Queen's University Press.

Mahendra, Edo. 2014. *Trade Liberalisation and Migration Hump: NAFTA as a Quasi-Natural Experiment.* Working Paper Series 98. Oxford: International Migration Institute, Oxford University. https://www.imi.ox.ac.uk/publications/wp-98-14.

Mármora, Lelio. 2002. *Las políticas de migraciones internacionales.* Buenos Aires: Paidós.

Martin, Philip. 2005. *NAFTA and Mexico-US Migration.* University Park: Pennsylvania State University. http://citeseerx.ist.psu.edu/viewdoc/download?doi=10.1.1.474.14 45&rep=rep1&type=pdf.

Martínez, José Álvaro, and Adriana Sletza Ortega. 2015. "Internalización de normas internacionales en materia de derechos de migrantes: El caso de Chiapas." *Norteamérica* 10 (1): 191–213. http://www.revistanorteamerica.unam.mx/index.php/nam/ar ticle/view/229.

Martínez, Oscar. 2010. *Los migrantes que no importan: En el camino de los centroamericanos indocumentados por México.* Barcelona: Icaria.

———. 2014. *The Beast: Riding the Rails and Dodging Narcos on the Migrant Trail.* London: Verso.

Massey, Douglas. 2015. "A Missing Element in Migration Theories." *Migration Letters* 12 (3): 279–299.

Massey, Douglas, Joaquín Arango, Graeme Hugo, Ali Kouaouci, Adela Pellegrino, and J. Edward Taylor. 2005. *Worlds in Motion. Understanding International Migration at the End of the Millennium.* Oxford: Oxford University Press.

Mexico City. 2017. Constitución Política de la Ciudad de México. http://www.cdmx.gob .mx/storage/app/uploads/public/59a/588/5d9/59a5885d9b2c7133832865.pdf.

Meyers, Eytan. 2000. "Theories of International Immigration Policy: A Comparative Analysis." *International Migration Review* 34 (4): 1245–1282.

Michelmann, Hans. 2009. *Foreign Relations in Federal Countries.* Montreal: McGill-Queen's University Press.

Muro Ruiz, Eliseo. 2017. "La diplomacia federativa de los gobiernos locales y los consulados mexicanos en Estados Unidos de América, en un multiculturalismo latino." *Revista de la Facultad de Derecho de México* 67 (269): 29–56. http://www.revistas .unam.mx/index.php/rfdm/article/view/30192/28052.

Ortega, Adriana Sletza. 2013. "Federalismo migratorio en México: Las oficinas estatales de atención a migrantes en un modelo comparativo nacional." *Migraciones Internacionales* 7 (1): 101–130.

————. 2014. "Políticas migratorias." In *Treinta claves para entender el poder: Léxico para una nueva comunicación política*, vol. 3, edited by J. S. Galicia and C. Cansino, 325–332. Puebla, Mexico: Piso 15.

Ortega, Adriana, and R. Velázquez. 2014. "Migratory Federalism in North America after NAFTA." In *The External Relations of Local Governments in North America after NAFTA: Trends and Perspectives*, edited by Rafael Velázquez Flores, Earl Fry, and Stéphane Paquin, 143–162. Mexico City: Programa Interinstitucional de Estudios sobre la Región de América del Norte-Colegio de México, Konrad Adenauer Foundation, Universidad Autónoma de Baja California.

Passel, Jeffrey S., D´Vera Cohn, and Ana Gonzalez-Barrera. 2012. *Net Migration from Mexico Falls to Zero—and Perhaps Less*. Hispanic Trends. Washington, DC: Pew Research Center. http://www.pewhispanic.org/2012/04/23/net-migration-from-me xico-falls-to-zero-and-perhaps-less/.

Pew Research Center. 2016. "Unauthorized Immigrant Population Trends for States, Birth Countries and Regions." Hispanic Trends. Washington, DC: Pew Research Center. http://www.pewhispanic.org/interactives/unauthorized-trends/.

Saltalamacchia, Natalia. 2015. "Entre liberales y estatistas: México en la gobernanza global de los derechos humanos." In *México y el multilateralismo del siglo XXI: Reflexiones a los 70 años de la ONU*, edited by Guadalupe González, Olga Pellicer, and Natalia Saltalamacchia, 209–235. Mexico City: Siglo XXI, Instituto Tecnológico Autónomo de México, and Senado de la República.

SEDEREC (Secretaría de Desarrollo Rural y Equidad para las Comunidades). 2016. *Programa ciudad hospitalaria, intercultural y de atención a migrantes en la Ciudad de México*. Mexico City: Gobierno de la Ciudad de México. http://www.sederec.cdmx.gob.mx /programas/programa/ciudad-hospitalaria-intercultural-y-de-atencion-migrantes -en-la-ciudad-de-mexico.

SEGOB-INAMI (Secretaría de Gobernación-Instituto Nacional de Migración). 2002. *Compilación histórica de la legislación migratoria en México 1821–2002*. Mexico City: Secretaría de Gobernación.

SEGOB (Secretaría de Gobernación). 2014. Programa Especial de Migración 2014–2018. Mexico City: Secretaría de Gobernación. http://www.gobernacion.gob.mx/es_mx /SEGOB/edicion_impresa_PEM.

SFS (Chiapas, Secretaría para el Desarrollo de la Frontera Sur y Enlace para la Cooperación Internacional). 2015. *Estado analítico del ejercicio del presupuesto de egresos. Clasificación por unidad responsable*. Tuxtla Gutiérrez, Mexico: Gobierno del Estado de Chiapas. http://www.spdfs.chiapas.gob.mx/transparencia.html.

SM (Michoacán, Secretaría del Migrante). 2012. *Manual de procedimientos de la Secretaría del Migrante*. Morelia, Mexico: Gobierno del Estado de Michoacán. http://mi grante.michoacan.gob.mx/wp-content/uploads/2012/08/manualprocedimientos .pdf.

————. 2016a. *Facultades de cada área de la Secretaría del Migrante*. Morelia, Mexico: Gobierno del Estado de Michoacán. http://laipdocs.michoacan.gob.mx/formatos/24 /2016/trimestral/3.Facultades_de_cada_area_SEMIGRANTE_2doTrimestre.pdf.

————. 2016b. *Convenios de coordinación, de concertación con el sector social o privado*. Morelia, Mexico: Gobierno del Estado de Michoacán. http://laipdocs.michoacan .gob.mx/formatos/24/2016/trimestral/33.Convenios_de_coordinacion_SEMI GRANTE_2doTrimestre.pdf.

————. 2017. Asesoría: Coordinación de Políticas Públicas y Programas Transversales.

Morelia, Mexico: Gobierno del Estado de Michoacán. http://migrante.michoacan .gob.mx/asesorias/.

Spiro, Peter. 2001. "Federalism and Immigration: Models and Trends." *International Social Science Journal* 53 (167): 67–68.

SRE (Mexico, Secretaría de Relaciones Exteriores). 2013. *Directorio de oficinas de estados mexicanos*. Los Angeles: Consulado General de México. https://consulmex.sre.gob .mx/losangeles/index.php/avisos/52-representacion-estados-enlaces.

————. 2014a. *Mexico frente al fenómeno migratorio*. Mexico City: Secretaría de Relaciones Exteriores. https://sre.gob.mx/sre-docs/dh/docsdh/2014/fenomeno.pdf.

————. 2014b. *Directorio de oficinas de representación de algunos estados de la república en Chicago*. Document ARJ/20.03.104. Chicago: Mexico, Secretaría de Relaciones Exteriores.

Tavares, Rodrigo. 2016. *Paradiplomacy: Cities and States as Global Players*. Oxford: Oxford University Press.

UPM (Unidad de Política Migratoria). 2015. Misión y vision. México: Secretaría de Gobernación. http://www.politicamigratoria.gob.mx/es_mx/SEGOB/mision_y_vi sion_UPM.

————. 2016a. *Estadísticas Migratorias: Síntesis 2016*. Mexico City: Secretaría de Gobernación. http://www.politicamigratoria.gob.mx/work/models/SEGOB/CEM/PDF /Estadisticas/Sintesis_Graficas/Sintesis_2016.pdf/.

————. 2016b. Eventos de menores presentados ante la autoridad migratoria, según continente, país de nacionalidad, grupos de edad, condición de viaje y sexo, 2015. Mexico City: Secretaría de Gobernación. http://www.politicamigratoria.gob.mx /es_mx/SEGOB/Estadistica.

Velázquez Rafael, and Adriana Sletza Ortega. 2010. "Políticas públicas de los gobiernos subnacionales de México en asuntos de migración." In *Perspectivas migratorias: Un análisis interdisciplinario de la migración internacional*, vol. 1, edited by Jorge Schiavon and Jorge Durand, 493–551, Mexico City: Centro de Investigación y Docencia Económicas.

Zenteno, René. 2012. "Saldo migratorio nulo: el retorno y la política anti-inmigrante." *Coyuntura Demográfica* 2:17–21.

CHAPTER 5

Rebuilding Justice We Can All Trust:
The Plight of Migrant Victims

ANA LORENA DELGADILLO, ALMA GARCÍA,
AND RODOLFO CÓRDOVA ALCARAZ

At present, around 250 million people live in a country other than the one in which they were born, and more than 750 million live in their country but not their city of birth. One of every seven people in the world today, therefore, is a migrant (IOM 2016). Throughout history, the movement of people at this scale has never been seen. At the same time, restrictive policies linking migrants with terrorism have put migration at the center of the global security agenda. Moreover, the narrative that paints migrants as a threat to perceived "national identity" has returned in recent years in Europe and the United States, most notably in the Trump administration (Wallace 2017).

Thousands of migrants fall victim to crime and human rights violations during their transits. Many thousands die or disappear along the way. However, systematized global data about the number of crimes and human rights violations suffered by migrants in transit is still lacking.[1] The best figures on migrant disappearances come from the Missing Migrants Project of the International Organization for Migration (IOM). The corridors from Central to North America and from North Africa to Europe are the world's most dangerous for migrants.

August 2010 witnessed the most heinous instances of such dangers when 72 bodies were found in the Mexican city of San Fernando, Tamaulipas. One year later, 195 cadavers were found in the same municipality. In 2012, in Cadereyta, Nuevo León, which borders Tamaulipas, 49 torsos were found strewn about close to the main highway connecting the two states. Some of those killed were migrants,[2] and the government has yet to identify them all. Where did they come from? Who are their families? Who committed these terrible crimes and why?

Abuses committed against migrants are nothing new; one could even argue that they have been an intrinsic element of the treacherous migratory route through Mexico known as the "vertical border." Shelters and migrant centers have documented crimes and human rights violations since 2002, and despite national migratory policies meant to deal with the issue, they continue to take place, as demonstrated by the two reports on migrant kidnappings issued by Mexico's national human rights commission, the Comisión Nacional de Derechos Humanos (CNDH 2009).

In their analyses, nongovernmental organizations (NGOs) have established a direct relation between the intensification of migratory control as part of Mexico's plan for its southern border, Plan Frontera Sur, and violations of individual rights, above all of the rights to integrity and freedom. In the process of enforcing laws and detaining and deporting migrants, the Mexican government does not fulfill its obligations with regard to asylum and refugee rights (Semple 2017). Between July 2014 and June 2015 alone, migrant detentions increased 73 percent compared to the same period one year earlier, from 97,000 to 168,000 (Knippen, Boggs, and Meyer 2015). The conditions that have provoked large-scale massacres persist, and based on recent information collected by the Foundation for Justice and the Democratic Rule of Law (Fundación para la Justicia y el Estado Democrático de Derecho, FJEDD) and other shelters along the migrant trail, one could even say that they have intensified. Organizations have continued to document cases such as that of the nine Guatemalans who disappeared in Tamaulipas in 2014 and the attack against members of a group of migrants in Caborca, Sonora, in June 2015.

Mexico's national crime and impunity statistics confirm the dangerous conditions for people in Mexico. In September 2016 in Mexico, 2,187 people were killed — one every twenty minutes — according to statistics from Mexico's national public safety authority, the Secretariado Ejecutivo del Sistema Nacional de Seguridad Pública, and 2017 was the deadliest year of the previous twenty (SESNSP 2016). Impunity levels shed additional light on conditions, as an estimated 94 percent of all crimes committed in Mexico in 2015 were either not reported or left uninvestigated, according to a national poll on crime victims and perceptions of public safety conducted by Mexico's national statistics institute, the Instituto Nacional de Estadística y Geografía (INEGI 2016). The two most frequently cited reasons for crimes going unreported were that it would be a waste of time and that victims lacked confidence in the authorities. The level of impunity in Mexico doesn't allow people to feel safe, in the sense that if they are the victims of crimes, the state cannot guarantee that the crimes will be punished.

Responding to the lack of trust in justice, particularly in cases of serious human rights violations such as the large-scale massacres of migrants, grassroots and human rights organizations in Central America and Mexico have advocated for the passage of public policies by the Mexican state. Principal among the successes are the creation of the federal Comisión Forense (Forensic Commission), the Mecanismo de Apoyo Exterior Mexicano de Búsqueda e Investigación (Mechanism for External Support), the Unidad de Migrantes de la Procuraduría General de la República (Migrant Unit of the Attorney General's Office), the Plan Nacional de Desarrollo (PND, National Development Plan), and the Programa Especial de Migración (Special Migration Program), which brings all of the policies related to migrants under the same framework and includes judicial access for migrants as one of its five objectives. All the initiatives and entities aim to reinstill trust in justice so that everyone in Mexico can feel safe.

Our objective herein is first to outline the transnational strategies adopted by groups of migrants and family members to exercise their rights to justice, truth, and reparations. We do so from the perspective of our work at the Foundation for Justice and the Democratic Rule of Law (Foundation for Justice), an organization created in 2011 to work closely with victims of gross human rights violations. We analyze how policies are working and the impacts they are having on people's well-being in terms of human rights. Our work puts us in touch with survivors of serious human rights violations who have sought justice and used various methods to push the Mexican state to improve in those areas. Based on these elements, we have developed recommendations for how the state can implement comprehensive actions to address migrant rights.

We begin by focusing on the ways migrant families organize themselves, what they have been through, and the strategies they have employed in coordination with human rights organizations, specifically with the Foundation for Justice. With regard to the transnational avenues migrants are taking to exercise their rights, we examine the work of two networks to which the Foundation for Justice and Rule of Law belongs as well as efforts of groups formed by migrants' family members. Of particular interest is the collaborative work that went into creating the Forensic Commission, a special policy umbrella for migration, the Transnational Mechanism for Access to Justice, and the inclusion of migrant rights in the National Development Plan. This last achievement is particularly significant since the plan is the government's most important public policy document, guiding the development of all institutional programs during each six-year presidential term.

In examining the strategies that victims have followed to accelerate justice, we focus on two processes: the identification of those found dead in Tamaulipas and Nuevo León and the criminal investigation by local and federal prosecutors to find those responsible. Two parallel processes are at work at the Foundation for Justice: the strategy we followed to spur public policy debate and the policies that were ultimately crafted and adopted as a result of our work and pressure, particularly with regard to the search for disappeared persons and judicial access. Actions the Foundation for Justice has undertaken along with the committees and groups of migrants' families from and in Honduras, El Salvador, and Guatemala and other networks forced the state to create unprecedented public policies. The history of this work can be divided into two periods, 2011–2013 and 2014–2018, to more clearly identify and elaborate upon the elements related to the strategies and policies that resulted.

Through this work we have come to identify concrete actions the Mexican state can take to make progress in implementing the policies to protect and guarantee access to justice for migrants and their families. We focus on what the government can do in terms of policy design, but above all in applying policies already in place with equal commitment to everyone to confront the violence and human rights violations that migrants have suffered for years while crossing through Mexico. We go beyond Mexico as well, to examine actions that some Central American governments can take to accelerate the Mexican state's implementation of policies related to justice, truth, and reparations. Such measures would send a message that human rights will be protected so people can feel safe and regain trust in the justice system.

Our methodology consists of nothing more than presenting the testimony of those working at and with the Foundation for Justice, a Mexican-based organization that has promoted the rights of migrants who have been killed or disappeared, working hand in hand with their families in Central America. It is a reconstruction of the process of developing a civil society regional network specialized in reclaiming and demanding migrant rights through our viewpoint as participants. This, of course, carries all the limitations and subjectivities implicit in narrating what follows in our own words.

How Do the Committees and Groups of Families Organize? And What Are Their Strategies?

In chapter 1 of this volume, Jonathan Fox and Gaspar Rivera-Salgado introduce the concept of migrant civil society to refer to *migrant-led membership organizations and public institutions.* This concept would be more useful in explaining how the participating committees, groups, and families organize if we tweak it slightly. According to the International Organization for Migration, an international migrant is a person who has lived in a different country from which he or she was born for at least one year. Most of the people who are part of the committees promoting migrant rights are not and never have been migrants themselves, but still they have strong links to migration, and the committees wouldn't exist if their family members hadn't disappeared during their transits to the United States. In other words, although the concept of migrant civil society doesn't exactly describe the committees or the NGOs that are working closely with them, it could if we understand migration as not only an individual process but more a family or community one. In this same vein, the International Convention on the Protection of the Rights of All Migrant Workers and Members of Their Families of 1990 could also provide an interesting framework in the sense that it stipulates that the families and not only the migrants themselves have rights.

The history of the Comité de Familiares de Migrantes del Progreso Yoro (COFAMIPRO, the Committee of Families of Migrants from El Progreso, Yoro), in Honduras, starts with a natural disaster: Hurricane Mitch, which shook the countries of Central America in 1998 and caused devastation throughout the region. In Honduras alone an estimated 1.5 million people were affected, more than 7,000 dead, 8,000 missing, and 11,000 injured (CEPAL 1999). A year later the country was still recovering, and despite efforts by the government and the international community, many people's whereabouts were still unknown.

Other organizations arose alongside COFAMIPRO in response to the crisis. In September 1999 a community radio station, Radio Progreso, invited mothers to participate in a program to help find their family members and to create a space where the community could address migration and its consequences. The radio program was initially called *Sin Fronteras* (Without Borders), though its name eventually was changed to *Abriendo Fronteras* (Opening Borders). The radio station documented cases of missing people, their ages, and the communities from which they left. A group of the missing people's mothers, wives, and daughters formed COFAMIPRO in 1999 and invited others to speak out about those who had disappeared—and not only those who were in the path of Hurricane Mitch's destruction. They also took up the cause of disappeared women who were taken by criminal gangs from their home communities to Guatemala to work and those who had gone in search of the "American Dream" due to the conditions of extreme poverty that arose after the natural disaster.

Since 1999, COFAMIPRO had documented more than 800 cases of missing persons, the majority of whom disappeared along the migratory route; in some cases, family members have been found, but they are the minority. The committee's objectives are to find family members who have disappeared en route to the United States; to hold state institutions accountable through legal complaints, protests, and proposals for their responsibility to search for lost migrants; and in coordination with other organizations, to raise the population's awareness about the phenomenon of migration.

A similar organization arose in El Salvador when the families of missing migrants started, like all families do, to search for their missing loved ones without any support from the state. In 2002 several families in El Salvador came together around the Central American Resource Center (CARECEN), an organization founded in the 1980s to assist the thousands of refugees fleeing the civil wars in Central America (CARECEN 2015). CARECEN's founders in Washington, DC, saw the necessity of supporting the refugees and created the organization, which initially focused on direct legal assistance but evolved over time to providing support to Latin American communities in the United States. Even El Salvador's own Ministerio de Relaciones Exteriores (Ministry of Foreign Affairs) would direct the family members of disappeared persons to CARECEN for assistance. After several years, the family members of missing Salvadorans migrants crossing through Mexico started to organize autonomously, and by 2003 they elected a board of directors. By 2006 they decided to use the name Comité de Familiares de Migrantes Fallecidos y Desaparecidos de El Salvador (COFAMIDE, Committee of Family Members of Deceased and Disappeared Migrants from El Salvador) and incorporated their organization to make it official.

Another committee with which the Foundation for Justice works was created in 2014 in response to the massacre in Tamaulipas. On May 13, 2012, television stations broadcast the news that forty-nine torsos had been found along the national highway between Monterrey and Reynosa. The victims had been staying in a house run by *coyotes* (migrant smugglers) in Nuevo Laredo, Tamaulipas, a week before, and days later their bodies were found cut to pieces. Authorities, who did not know that some of the victims were migrants on their way from Honduras, Guatemala, and El Salvador to the United States, declared that the victims were criminals. Despite the immense pain of having the remains of their relatives delivered to them, Honduran victims' families soon decided to organize to demand justice, truth, and reparations and help family members of other missing migrants. In 2014 they named their organization the Comité de Familiares Desaparecidos del Centro de Honduras (COFAMICENH, the Committee of Family Members of the Disappeared of Central Honduras).

More recently, a committee was formed in Guatemala to unite families of migrants with whom the Foundation for Justice had been working since 2012. The Asociación de Familiares de Migrantes Desaparecidos de Guatemala (AFAMIDEG) started working in 2015 and was legally established in February 2018. The association brings together people from different Mayan cultures, like Kakchikel, Mam, Quiché, Xinca, and Ladina. One of its aims is to push government at local, national, and regional levels to implement search procedures to find missing migrants from Guatemala.

Something that has been constant during these past years in Mexico is that authorities usually follow the same script when a tragedy like this happens. In the Tamaulipas massacre and similar cases, authorities followed a deliberate strategy of justification, that is, of framing the violence as gang-related, at the expense of devising effective security plans (Chong 2012). Mexico has since 2006 been deploying its army and navy to carry out public safety work and fight organized crime, duties that go beyond either institution's mandate. Their deployment generated direct confrontation not just between state agencies and organized crime but also among drug cartels fighting to maintain control over territories and smuggling routes for migrants and drugs. The number of deaths and disappearances in the country has increased exponentially ever since. To justify all the killings, the federal government claims that the majority are gang-related and not directed against innocent civilians.

The Mexican government has doubled down on this strategy. At the end of 2017, the Mexican Congress enacted the Ley de Seguridad Interior proposed by President Enrique Peña Nieto; the law expanded the army's mandate to include public safety and investigation work. Saying that the law will perpetuate the violence that makes Mexicans feel unsafe is an understatement; from 2007 to 2017 in Mexico, 220,000 people were killed and at least 33,000 more went missing (SEGOB 2017). The decision by the executive and legislative branches to increase military involvement goes against the perception of 84 percent of respondents to public opinion surveys that the army hasn't helped to decrease the violence in their communities, and it also goes against what UN agencies recommend. The militarization of public safety suggests that the government wants to perpetuate an atmosphere of violence and impunity in which Mexicans are living.

The Foundation for Justice emerged from this context. Its founding members recognized that among all the victims, migrants were exceptionally vulnerable because they could be disappeared or be killed in Mexico without their families ever knowing what happened to them. We thus reasoned that the only way to make substantial changes would be through regional work across Central America, and that is why the Foundation for Justice pushed to create the Red Regional Verdad y Justicia (Regional Network for Truth and Justice). We initially wanted to prove that it was possible to get organized and set up transnational collaborations between civil society organizations and local committees in Central America. Better data were needed, so the Foundation for Justice first documented cases of missing migrants in Guatemala, Honduras, Mexico, and El Salvador. Then we talked about combining search and remains-identification efforts and research with the organizations described above. We also developed a set of objectives, as follows:

along with local stakeholders, to support consolidation of local and regional committees of the family members of migrant victims of human rights violations so that family members can be protagonists in defending their rights to truth and justice; to establish regional mechanisms to search for missing migrants; with the Equipo Argentino de Antropología Forense (EAAF, Argentine Forensic Anthropology Team) and other stakeholders, to create protocols to identify and search for migrants; and to implement a regional legal framework that benefits all stakeholders seeking access to justice and the right to truth.

It is important to highlight that the Foundation for Justice followed the trail blazed by the EAAF, one of the pioneering organizations that adopted a regional approach to resolving the identification of remains; its work began in 1984 to recover and identify remains of disappeared victims of Argentina's military dictatorship of the 1970s and early 1980s. The Border Plan carried out by the EAAF supported the consolidation of Forensic Information Data Banks, a governmental and nongovernmental mechanism, where cases of migrants missing in transit are documented locally. These banks record genetic information that can be crossed with remains found in morgues of the countries of transit and destination. The idea was to exchange information in order to identify the remains of migrants who may have died during their journeys and were recorded as anonymous by forensic services and municipal cemeteries in the United States and Mexico. By 2011, 1,132 cases of missing migrants and 3,061 DNA samples had been registered under the EAAF project, and as a result 162 migrants' remains had been identified.

The Foundation for Justice came up with its objectives in support of missing migrants from analyzing nearly 350 cases, the majority of which shared common characteristics. One that stood out is that family members would go to their country's foreign affairs branch to file missing persons reports, but then nothing would happen because the information was shared only between the participating countries' foreign affairs officials. The Attorney General's Office in Mexico and its counterparts in the Central American countries, whose staffs would be more equipped to take action, were left in the dark. In some cases the families of migrants were told that Mexico had not responded, and most were told they would be called with any news, but that did not happen in a single case. They were also informed that their home governments couldn't do much because the migrants had disappeared in another country. By mid-2018 there was no verifiable evidence of what happened with the reports families filed with their home countries' foreign affairs offices. There is even less information about any investigations that may have been launched in response to the hundreds of detailed reports filed by various agencies.

Finally, in sketching the history of migrant activism, we should note that the committees, family groups, and regional networks are staffed by diverse sets of organizers. The overwhelming majority of them are women directly affected by the disappearance of family members. Men participate, too, but not nearly as many. Faced with structural injustice and a lack of answers, people become defenders of their own rights, a phenomenon that undoubtedly has an impact on their lives, communities, and in the long run, societies. Although many leaders have been involved since the committees were created, many others are new activists seeking to engage. They are carrying out a form of transnational activism, as understood under the conceptual framework developed by Margaret Keck and Kathryn Sikkink (1999), who analyze how networks of activists come together through cross-border strategies to push for policy changes at the state level or to pressure international institutions. The Foundation for Justice, for example, has staff in four countries: Mexico, Honduras, Guatemala, and El Salvador. The lawyers who work in the three Central American countries operate from a psychological-legal approach but also work with the organizations and groups that are part of the Regional Network for Truth and Justice. This scope creates a huge challenge in terms of funding, but ultimately the Foundation for Justice is committed to a transnational approach to enacting policies that enable people to achieve justice and feel safe.

Strategies and Public Policies, 2011–2013

Beginnings of the Foundation for Justice
and the Forensic Commission

The foundation's work with the committees started in 2011, one year after the EAAF and other organizations and institutions—COFAMIDE, El Salvador's Foreign Relations Ministry, and la Procuraduría para la Defensa de los Derechos Humanos (Attorney General's Office for Human Rights) in El Salvador—signed an agreement creating the first forensic data bank (Godoy 2010).

In establishing the Regional Network for Truth and Justice, the foundation recognized the need for a transnational mechanism to allow families to seek justice in the country where the migrant was reported missing. Mexican authorities, however, sharply rejected the proposal. They said they couldn't open the door for foreigners to seek justice, fearing a barrage of cases due to the country's level of insecurity. They took this stance despite its putting at risk many international treaties Mexico has signed, such as the American Convention on Human Rights (Pact of San José), the Inter-American Convention on Forced Disappearance of Persons, the International Convention on the Protection of the Rights of All Migrant Workers and Members of Their Families, the Convention against Torture and Cruel, Inhumane, or Degrading Treatment or Punishment, and the International Convention for the Protection of All Persons from Enforced Disappearance.

The foundation realized that upon the discovery of remains in clandestine graves, a transnational legal umbrella was required to identify them and properly pursue criminal investigations. A transnational process was necessary to avoid the mistakes committed by the Mexican government, which would often deliver remains to the wrong families in Central America. We requested that the Inter-American Commission on Human Rights (IACHR), an autonomous affiliate of the Organization of American States, deliver precautionary measures to be adopted by Honduras, Ecuador, Guatemala, El Salvador, and Mexico. However, the IACHR responded that there were no precedents for measures issued to several countries at the same time or for measures that did not imply a risk to the integrity and life of the persons, and therefore the request was denied. The IACHR failed to take action even though people with missing family members are experiencing something similar to torture as long as they are not receiving any information or support from their home governments.

Finding that meeting our objectives would be a more complex undertaking, the Foundation for Justice, along with the EAAF and the committees, changed our approach and proposed something more limited and benign to authorities: performing a humanitarian action and identifying the remains from the three massacres in San Fernando and Cadereyta. Our assessment was that identifying the remains could start the families on their path to truth, justice, and reparations. In addition, the foundation noted that one way to pressure states, specifically Mexico, where those crimes and human rights violations took place, was by getting them into a neutral negotiating space from which the organization could start a conversation and put migrant rights on the table. To this end, the foundation, with the EAAF and its associated network of actors, asked for a hearing before the IACHR. As a result, a session called "Situation of Missing Migrants and Unidentified Remains in Mexico" took place at the IACHR headquarters in Washington, DC, on March 23, 2012.[3]

Representing civil society organizations as the petitioners were the Argentine EAAF, Salvadoran COFAMIDE, the Honduran COFAMIPRO, Mexican migrant refuge Casa del Migrante de Saltillo of Frontera con Justicia (Border of Justice), Humanidad sin Fronteras (Humanity without Borders), Voces Mesoamericanas Acción con Pueblos Migrantes (Mesoamerican Voices of Action for Migrant Peoples), and the Foundation for Justice.

The organizations were petitioning for

1. the immediate creation of a technical commission made up of international forensic staff to collaborate with its Mexican counterparts in identifying discovered remains requiring special effort due to their complexity (the commission would aid Mexico in the short term to increase the number of identified remains found in August 2010 and April 2011 in the Mexican municipality of San Fernando, Tamaulipas);
2. the opening of a dialogue with the Mexican government to create national and regional mechanisms that would include civil society in their leadership structures to facilitate the exchange of information about unidentified remains and missing persons, Mexicans as well as Central American migrants who went missing in Mexico (the mechanisms would directly benefit the search for the disappeared among the unidentified remains, particularly in the cases of missing migrants); and
3. actions by the technical commission and the national and regional mechanisms to facilitate the adoption of protocols and good forensic practices for identifying remains in complicated cases in Mexico and the region, thus facilitating the exchange of information and significantly increasing the possibility of providing answers to the thousands of family members of disappeared persons. (COFAMIDE et al. 2012)

The Mexican state's rebuttal to the petition was a lesson in evading responsibility for disappearances and massacres: a barrage of statistics about technology, the number of fingerprints on file, hired experts, forensics and ballistics units, and genetic labs and DNA registries, among other diversions. Such information was offered as a sufficient response to what the organizations were asking, an official response that was absurd, to put it mildly. Beyond that, the state denied that disappearances were systemic in the country but did mention that family members of the 2010 San Fernando massacre victims were compensated and cited the forensic tests state agents had performed. In other words, the government provided many facts but little substance.

The IACHR's special rapporteur on migrants visited Mexico in summer 2011. He was aware of the precautionary measures that had been requested and denied earlier that year; the Mexican government's resistance demonstrated to him some of the institutional barriers faced by migrant families. During his visit he met with the mothers of some missing migrants and listened to the challenges and obstacles they faced. He also met with organizations from Mexico and the region that presented him with a detailed report about the state of migrants' human rights (González 2013). What stands out from the subsequent report issued to the Mexican state is the need to identify victims' remains and sanction perpetrators of massacres. These goals were reaffirmed at the hearing, as the IACHR pressed the Mexican state to look into creating a mixed commission to identify migrants and establish an internationally coordinated national forensic database.

The hearing in March 2012 opened the door to negotiations with the Mexican state to create what would become, in September 2013, the Forensic Commission. Its objective was to identify and determine the causes of death for remains potentially related to killings of migrants: 72 found on August, 23, 2010, in San Fernando; at least 193 found between April and May 2011 in several clandestine graves in San Fernando; and 49 found in Cadereyta, Nuevo León, on May 14, 2012 (Mexico, Procuraduría General 2013). Before the formation of the Forensic Commission, several family members of people killed in the three massacres received remains without any information about how to confirm the identities of the deceased or causes of death or even how to get permission from the state to cremate the remains. Sending unidentified remains not only violates the victims' rights to justice and truth but directly conflicts with practices and customs of indigenous communities for whom holding a wake is fundamental. Doing so is a violation not just of civil and political rights but also of cultural and social rights.

The Forensic Commission would not have been created without a change in the federal administration, institutional personnel, and federal public policy cycle. In July 2012, three months after the hearing, Peña Nieto came into office, and there was a shakeup at the Attorney's General Office, opening a window of opportunity for the organizations and committees to enter.

Work with Other Networks and Organizations on Mexico's Plan Nacional de Desarrollo

An important element of this early period was the creation of the PND-Migración collective in August 2012. It formed as an alliance of fifty migrant and human rights organizations and networks advocating for the migration section of the 2013–2018 National Development Plan to focus on human rights, sustainable development, and social inclusion. The National Development Plan is a cornerstone public policy document that each new administration, as mandated by law, constructs to guide policies during its six-year term.

The collective created an Agenda Estratégica Transnacional (Strategic Transnational Agenda) with six objectives and more than thirty action items to shape the National Development Plan. The agenda was developed with the participation of all the organizations and networks at the first Encuentro Transnacional (Transnational Summit) in February 2013, and later approved by consensus. The Foundation for Justice participated actively in that summit, ensuring that the language outlined actions that would facilitate the pursuit of justice. Once the agenda was created, we started the process of lobbying the Senate and the Secretaría de Gobernación, the office that handles Mexico's internal affairs, as well as the Secretaría de Relaciones Exteriores (Secretariat of Foreign Affairs), the Attorney General's Office, and, most importantly, the Secretaría de Hacienda y Crédito Pública (Secretariat of Finance and Public Credit), which is charged with coordinating the drafting of the National Development Plan. The forum to discuss migration was particularly noteworthy during that period of advocacy, as the organizations and networks urged the government to adopt the ideas presented in the groups' Strategic Transnational Agenda. The forum was organized by the Unidad de Política Migratoria (Migration Policy Unit), which is charged with designing all of the country's policies on migration.

Substantial changes were made in the National Development Plan's proposals for migrants and their families as a result of our efforts. Of particular note is that for the first time in Mexico's history, a plan of this type included access to justice for foreign-born migrants. Plan Objective 5.4 establishes that the state should "protect the interests of Mexicans outside of the country as well as the rights of foreigners in our national territory" (Mexico, Presidencia de la República 2013). It should be said that the draft version of Objective 5.4 included protection only for Mexicans outside the country but was changed as a result of our work.

Another important result of advocacy around the 2013–2018 National Development Plan was the mandate to create the Special Migration Program. The plan incorporated the collective's proposal to link all national public policies related to migration under a common umbrella; in doing so, it set another precedent for the country. The Secretariat of Finance and Public Credit's original draft of the National Development Plan proposed four strategies and fourteen action items for Objective 5.4, which the secretariat called the Objetivo Migrantes (Migrant Objective). The final version of the plan, however, has five strategies and thirty-three lines of action. Of the five strategies, three are directly related to the Strategic Transnational Agenda. And of the thirty-three lines of action that ended up in the National Development Plan, twenty are proposals contained in one form or another in the agenda.

Beyond the specifics of how many strategies and lines of action were incorporated, a substantial change in the treatment of migrant rights within the National Development Plan can be seen more broadly due to the work of civil society networks and organizations. The 2013–2018 plan laid the foundation not only for the Special Migration Program but also for specific policies around access to justice. The government published the National Development Plan in June 2013 and the decree creating the Forensic Commission three months later.

To summarize, the change in administration opened a small window for making policy originating in the proposals of civil society actors and of the migrant family groups in particular. One reason for this was that new political interlocutors assumed power and sought to distance themselves from the previous administration of Felipe Calderón. A second was that the beginning of a new public policy cycle created space for positioning our proposals. As a result, the family committees and groups were able to draft public policies to meet people's needs and, with the Forensic Commission specifically, to develop a policy without parallel anywhere in the world. As we have shown, the strategies employed by victims and organizations defending their rights include

a. the creation of a local forensic data bank pushed by the EAAF as a mechanism that combines governmental and nongovernmental efforts to compile forensic information on missing migrants in their countries of origin that can be compared with genetic profiles from unidentified remains found in the countries of transit and destiny;

b. documentation of cases to methodically identify the most pressing needs of families and migrant communities, especially in the search for people and justice;

c. elaboration of solid technical proposals based on the long-standing demands of migrants and their families, translating their identified needs into public policy proposals;

d. advocacy work in transnational coalitions to shape national public policy;

e. alliance with key actors in the UN and IACHR systems;

f. political advocacy at the highest levels to position our previously agreed-upon proposals;

g. communication campaigns alongside advocacy efforts to apply pressure at key moments; and

h. strategic litigation in cases to facilitate the migrant population's access to rights.

In the face of attempts by some sectors in Mexico, including state agents, to discredit many of the institutions in the UN and IACHR systems, it is worth considering whether the proposals would have translated into policy and government action if not for the contributions of such institutions (*Animal Político* 2015). As with any analysis of this nature, the answer is complicated and requires consideration of the overall political context, the government transition, and the influence that we as organizations have in decision making. A response involves weighing not just the relevance of multilateral systems but also the diverse factors that influence decision makers. In any case, there can be no doubt that the alliances with the UN, the IACHR, and their rapporteurs were important. Nor can there be any doubt that their contributions have been indispensable on this and other issues and that society as a whole stands to lose when they are attacked. Their relevance makes them potentially key actors in advancing rights in the Americas and in global struggles.

Strategy and Public Policies, 2014–2018

The Special Migration Program as a New Framework for Migrant Policy

Following the creation of the National Development Plan and the Forensic Commission, we recognized that both achievements, while fundamental to our objectives, were just starting points for other changes we wanted to introduce. The next step was to devise a strategy to make progress on two fronts: ensuring timely follow-through on the National Development Plan and Forensic Commission initiatives and pushing for concrete policies aimed at ensuring effective investigations and reparations for victims.

The National Development Plan mandated the creation of the Special Program for Migration. Using the experience gleaned from the National Development Plan process, we decided to begin advocating that the Special Migration Program include our proposals and adopt a human rights focus. Building upon our joint work, the networks and organizations convened the second Transnational Summit in August 2013, from which the Transnational Budgetary and Programmatic Agenda emerged. The agenda addressed the Secretariat of Finance and Public Credit's criteria for implementing elements of the National Development Plan and would ideally constitute the basis for the Special Migration Program.

The government, for its part, was in the process of developing the program, an effort led by the Migration Policy Unit. However, the unit did not convene civil society organizations to gather input into the Special Migration Program until October 2013. That convocation, moreover, did not meet the minimum requirements established for civil society consultations. In particular, its agenda lacked the necessary breadth of issues, and there were insufficient opportunities to discuss how to integrate them. Fortunately, after arduous negotiations in New York during the second High-Level Dialogue on International Migration and Development—with officials of the Mexican government and in Mexico with the Migration Policy Unit—we were able to alter the process for providing input during the consultation.

Having achieved this commitment to a process that we as a collective had agreed upon, the next item of negotiation was the number of forums to be held. By the end, we were able to secure five government-organized forums in Mexico and two more organized by the networks of Migration for the Americas Collective (COMPA) in the United States that were also considered official forums — another important precedent. We used these forums to position the elements of the Transnational Budgetary and Programmatic Agenda.

The final phase of the COMPA work around the Special Migration Program was initiated after the forums were held. That phase involved technical meetings with five or six representatives of the collective, who negotiated to include human rights–based language in the program. The achievements of such efforts can be seen throughout the program and especially in the area of access to justice in its fifth strategic objective, "strengthen access to justice and security for migrant persons, their families, and those who defend their rights" (SEGOB 2014). This objective lays out four strategies, all of which directly tie into our work:

1. to design mechanisms to prevent and reduce crimes and human rights violations against migrants, their families, and those who defend their rights;
2. to provide information, assistance, and effective protection to migrants and human rights defenders;
3. to enable complaint mechanisms and guarantee access to justice and reparations for migrants and human rights defenders; and
4. to strengthen the institutional capacities for denunciation, investigation, and sanction of corrupt practices around migration.

One of the metrics for progress on the fifth strategic objective is the "proportion of judgments issued in cases in which the crime's victim is a migrant" (SEGOB 2014), but little has been done yet to measure success using that metric — or at least public information about such efforts is scarce — and thus far we have not seen any independent evaluations of the program.[4] Still, the work in crafting the Special Migration Program, which was published in April 2014, is important because the program groups all of the state's public policies around migration under one common logic and coordination process. Furthermore, it obligates the state to create new policies based on the Special Migration Program's main points and gives the relevant networks and organizations a clear blueprint of what the policies should be, including those related to access to justice and reparations.

The Transnational Justice Mechanism as a Next Step for the Forensic Commission

With regard to the Forensic Commission the biggest challenge has been to implement its mandate. The commission has a political component and a technical component. By mutual agreement with the organizations and committees, the Foundation for Justice is the civil society representative to the state to foster more efficient processes of identification, notification, and delivery of remains. For their part, the Argentine forensic anthropology group, the EAAF, is civil society's representative during the technical work, which is carried out alongside the attorney general's forensic teams. During its first months, the Forensic Commission identified a lack of uniform criteria for identifying remains, leading the organizations to propose the creation of an identification protocol, the Protocolo para la Notificación de Identificación de Restos de Personas Localizados en San Fernando, Tamaulipas y en Cadereyta, Nuevo León, which was adopted by the commission in June 2014. The protocol helps guide the actions of public servants involved in the identification of remains and notification of families and will also be a reference point to guide family members, their representatives, and NGOs involved in those procedures. In October 2014 two local public prosecutors' offices were added to the commission, those of Tamaulipas and Nuevo León, the states where the three massacres occurred (Mexico, Procuraduría General de la República 2013).

By February 2017 the parties had worked together to identify and return the remains of 66 out of the total of 346 victims of the three massacres. Much of the foundation's work focuses on following up on the agreements reached in Forensic Commission meetings in which several administrative units of the Attorney General's Office participate. This is an enormous challenge because it involves working and coordinating not only with public agencies in Mexico but also with the governments of the migrant massacre victims' countries of origin.

The other component of our strategy has to do with developing a transnational mechanism to access justice. To accomplish this, the Foundation for Justice returned to what worked previously: advocacy within the bodies of the UN and IACHR systems. At the beginning of 2015, the Foundation for Justice, along with the committees of Central America, asked for a subject-matter hearing in front of the IACHR to present proposals to the state. In March of that year, the hearing took place, and the foundation proposed a mechanism for addressing problems encountered during searches and criminal investigations, as identified by the Regional Network for Truth and Justice.[5] The problems included the following:

   a. the difficulty of filing a report in Mexico about a missing loved one or of making sure that the complaints filed in the migrant's own country reached Mexico's federal or state prosecutors;
   b. the difficulty or impossibility for family members residing in the victims' countries of origin to be recognized as victims and become part of and contribute to the preliminary investigations;
   c. during searches and investigations, the difficulty of expediently obtaining evidence from another country, such as fingerprints of a missing person or other information relevant to the search or identification process, due to the lack of forensic banks in several countries in the region and lack of procedures and efficient mechanisms for the flow of forensic information between countries; and
   d. the difficulty, during the preliminary investigations and throughout the investigation process, of establishing what occurred and identifying those responsible, due to the challenges of gathering evidence from the victims' countries of origin or following lines of investigation that entail cross-border activity and operations of criminal structures. (FJEDD et al., 2015)

During the hearing, the Mexican state agreed to create a regional mechanism, following the recommendations of civil society organizations and bodies of the IACHR and the UN. A negotiation followed with the Attorney General's Office's community service and human rights office, the Subprocuraduría de Servicios a la Comunidad y Derechos Humanos, to create the mechanism. On December 18, 2015, World Migrant Day, the agreement was signed, creating the Unidad de Investigación de Delitos para Personas Migrantes (Unit for Investigation of Crimes against Migrants) and the Mecanismo de Apoyo Exterior Mexicano de Búsqueda e Investigación (Mexican Support Mechanism for External Searches and Investigations) and establishing the functions and structures of both (Mexico, Procuraduría General de la República 2013).

The Foundation for Justice's mechanism proposal was simple: Mexico has embassies in many countries, and these embassies can be used as gateways for families of migrants to establish direct contact with the Mexican institutions in charge of searching for migrant victims and bringing justice for them. That way, people would not be forced to travel to Mexico or contact their countries' foreign affairs offices to initiate and follow the proceedings—a process that has proven inadequate for many years. Making use of technology, a family member could now contact the prosecutor in Mexico, access the file, and follow up on the investigation.

The agreement declares that the mechanism should involve a combination of actions, measures, and institutions aimed at facilitating access to justice for migrants and their family members; likewise, it outlines the procedures for searching for missing migrants and investigating crimes committed by or against migrants, and it directs, coordinates, and supervises the administration of effective and appropriate reparations.[6] The mechanism, run through the Unit for Investigation of Crimes against Migrants, is made up of the unit's head, investigators, analysts, police, and unit staff members along with those added for support by the Attorney General's Office outside of the country. In other words, migrants' families can use Mexican embassies in their own countries to access justice and search for missing persons. Through this channel they are able to make a report, request a search, present evidence, receive follow-ups on cases, file pleadings or petitions, secure assistance in exercising rights recognized under the Ley General de Víctimas (Crime Victims Law), seek protective measures, connect a detained migrant with a family member or public defender, and file a complaint.

In September 2016, after much pressure from the committees and organizations, the first nineteen disappearance reports filed in Honduras entered Mexico's Attorney General's Office through the Mexican Support Mechanism for External Searches and Investigations. The reports were delivered during the unit head's visit to Honduras to comply with an agreement reached with COFAMIPRO and COFAMICENH in July of that year. Their filing marked the first time that the Mexican state received legal complaints directly from family groups and committees outside of Mexico, thus abolishing the discriminatory principle that had existed in Mexico for decades and prevented migrants from accessing justice. In December 2016, reports came in from El Salvador through a process organized hand in hand with COFAMIDE and in January 2017 from Guatemala through a process led by family groups working with the Equipo de Estudios Comunitarios y Acción Psicosocial (Community Studies and Psycho-Social Action Team).

Unfortunately, the Mechanism for External Support is not yet operating as it was intended to, in failing to permanently staff Mexican embassies to assist families when they need help. It is still incumbent upon the Migration Unit within the Attorney General's Office to travel to Central American countries and establish the necessary legal communication between families and the authorities in charge of investigating crimes.

Finally, a special mention needs to be made of the Enforced Disappearance and the National System to Search for People Act, enacted at the end of 2017. The law was sought for many years by the committees of families of missing people and represents the end result of their work and of many recommendations from UN agencies and committees. Although the law is positive in many ways, such as forcing Mexican consulates abroad to play an active role by working closely with the National Search Commission and the

Mexican Support Mechanism for External Searches and Investigations, we will need to see how it is implemented on the ground, which is where most of the laws in this country tend to fail.

Conclusion

Fox and Rivera-Salgado state in chapter 1 of this volume that an increasing number of migrant organizations pursue agendas in the countries of origin and destination. In our work we have witnessed such migrant organizations promote change in their fight for justice, truth, and reparations that make them and us feel safe in *all* the countries along the migration route.

Our work did not begin in 2011, the year the organization first set out our strategies and considered how to translate them into public policy. Rather, we are building on a process that was started two decades ago by the committees in Central America and then by the EAAF at a transnational level. Without their efforts, the Foundation for Justice would not exist. Our work began as soon as the family members of missing migrants started to search for their loved ones and make minimal demands for justice. In some cases, such efforts originated informally several decades ago and have been taking place in an organized fashion since 1999 with the creation of the first migrant families committee. Their path has been complicated by closed-minded authorities, lack of political will to create meaningful changes, and outright denial of what is taking place in the country. Nonetheless, it is clear that the strategies developed have grown more sophisticated with time and are leading to the resolution of cases and creating structural changes in the country.

The public policies created in Mexico in the 2010s are novel in terms of democratic planning and access to justice; indeed, they are without precedent or parallel anywhere in the world. From our viewpoint, there is no better preventive policy than employing comprehensive development strategies to address dire economic conditions in Central America so people won't have to migrate in the first place. Until the structures of inequality, lack of access to quality jobs and opportunities, and impunity are addressed, any crime prevention strategies will be insufficient. These policies, we feel, should be combined with a robust investigative component in Mexico and the Central American countries. While one may think that more policies to prevent crime would not involve the creation of forensic commissions to investigate crimes already committed, in reality the two procedures respond to two different necessities and rights structures. Creations like the Forensic Commission are in the present context crucial to advancing rights to justice, truth, and reparations for the families of the thousands of migrants who die and disappear along migratory routes throughout the world, not just in Mexico. Nonetheless, policy creation is just a first step. What is needed next is adequate and consistent implementation of those policies, which is where the state continues to come up short. Therefore, some of our work has focused and will continue to focus on identifying and correcting the system's shortcomings in order to turn what is written on paper into a reality for the migrants and their families in the region. It is the only way we can move to a place in which all people can trust the justice system and feel safe.

Based on our work at the Foundation for Justice, we have already identified some areas for improvement to ensure the proper implementation of these policies. With regard to Mexico's National Development Plan and Special Migration Program, we recommend that those charged with oversight and coordination of implementation develop the necessary tools to guarantee that the institutions involved carry out their mandates. With regard to access to justice, we provide some recommendations below. With regard to the Attorney General's Office, a reform to Article 102 of the Mexican Constitution is urgently needed to transform the office into an autonomous agency. Through the coalition #FiscalíaQueSirva we have proposed an initiative to create an independent prosecutor's office that investigates crimes and prosecutes criminals in which the prosecutor is the most capable person available and not the friend of any president and has proper staff and civic checks and balances. Only with that kind of institution people will be able to trust in the Mexican justice system.

With regard to the Forensic Commission we recommend the following steps:

1. Expand the commission to the entire migratory route through Mexico and even to other countries in the region. This should not require additional work by authorities and would be an important development given the violence that continues to plague the country and to which the migrants are subjected during their transits through Mexico. It is also a demand of the family committees and groups that work together under the umbrella of the Regional Network for Truth and Justice.

2. The Attorney General's Office should coordinate efficiently with the different administrative units involved in criminal investigations and the identification of remains, specifically the Subprocuraduría de Investigación Especializada en Delincuencia Organizada, a unit for investigating organized crime; Subprocuraduría de Derechos Humanos, a unit focused on human rights; and Subprocuraduría de Asuntos Jurídicos y Asuntos Internacionales, a legal and international affairs unit.

3. Mexico's Secretaría de Relaciones Exteriores should be an ongoing partici-

pant to facilitate coordination with other countries, as should the Comisión Especial de Atención a Víctimas (Special Commission for Victims' Assistance) to process reparations to families.

4. The countries of Central America, particularly Honduras, Guatemala, and El Salvador, should design a protocol similar to Mexico's to regulate the processes of notification and delivery of remains.

With regard to the Mexican Support Mechanism for External Searches and Investigations, we recommend the following:

1. The Attorney General's Office should assign attachés to each of the Central American embassies to work with the Mexican Support Mechanism for External Searches and Investigations. There is only one attaché in Guatemala who is responsible for all of Central America and the Caribbean. That is a limitation, as the attaché is supposed to be the first agent whom crime victims and their family members can approach in their countries of residence.

2. The Attorney General's Office should modify operating procedures that limit and contradict the mission of the Mexican Support Mechanism for External Searches and Investigations and integrate into it the proposals made by families and organizations.

3. The countries of Central America, specifically Honduras, Guatemala, and El Salvador, should create a mechanism similar to Mexico's to conduct parallel processes to pursue justice for victimized migrants, search for missing migrants, and provide reparations.

4. The countries of the region should implement a regional coordination mechanism to help guarantee those three rights for people regardless of their countries of residence or migratory status.

We want to emphasize that there is still much important work to be done with organized migrant civil society in the United States. One factor that may have hampered such work is the Mexican government's official narrative that the massacres are just tit-for-tat retaliations between so-called criminals, which desensitizes not just immigrants in the United States but also general society in both countries to the murders. Another challenge is how to weave together common agendas that may originate in separate spheres, in this case the push to develop the communities of origin and the desire to enforce the rights of the disappeared. In reality, there is a connection between the many individual agendas and initiatives that lends itself to collaboration among existing entities, as seen in the Migration for the Americas Collective and others. That kind of cooperation becomes all the more vital in addressing crimes and human rights violations against migrants on both sides of the border.

Notes

1. FJEDD et al. 2014. In this report the civil society organizations highlight the importance of the Mexican state creating statistical data about missing migrants.

2. As of March 2018, the federal Forensic Commission had identified sixty-eight bodies: one from El Salvador, thirteen from Honduras, sixteen from Guatemala, and thirty-eight from Mexico.

3. A full recording of the session can be found at OAS 2012.

4. According to official data from 2014 to 2016, a total of 5,824 complaints of crimes against migrants were registered in Chiapas, Coahuila, Oaxaca, and Sonora states and at the federal level. Only 1 percent had been punished by 2017 (Suárez et al. 2017, 4).

5. The following organizations participated at the hearing: the FJEDD, EAAF, COFA-MIDE, COFAMIPRO, COFAMICENH, Mesa Nacional para las Migraciones en Guatemala (MENAMIG), the Centro Diocesano para los Derechos Humanos Fray Juan de Larios, the Casa del Migrante de Saltillo, Coahuila, the Centro de Derechos Humanos Victoria Diez, and Fuerzas Unidas por Nuestros Desaparecidos(as) en Coahuila (FUUNDEC). A recording of the hearing is available at IAHCR 2015.

6. Mexico, Procuraduría General de la República 2013.

References

Animal Político. 2015. "Relator contra la Tortura acusa ataques personales de Relaciones Exteriores." April 1. http://www.animalpolitico.com/2015/04/relator-contra-la-tortura-acusa-ataques-personales-de-relaciones-exteriores/.

CARECEN (Central American Resource Center). 2015. "History." http://www.carecendc.org/about/history/.

CEPAL (Comisión Económica para América Latina y el Caribe). 1999. *Honduras: Evaluación de los daños ocasionados por el huracán Mitch, 1998*. New York: United Nations. http://www.cepal.org/publicaciones/xml/1/15501/l367-1.pdf.

Chong Magallanes, Jahtziri. 2012. "Cuerpos en Cadereyta, resultado de pugna entre cárteles: Poiré." *MVS Noticias*, May 14. http://www.noticiasmvs.com/#!/noticias/cuerpos-en-cadereyta-resultado-de-pugna-entre-carteles-poire-508.html.

CNDH (Comisión Nacional de los Derechos Humanos). 2009. *Informe especial sobre los casos de secuestro en contra de migrantes*. Mexico City: CNDH. http://www.cndh.org.mx/sites/all/doc/Informes/Especiales/2009_migra.pdf.

———. 2011. *Informe especial sobre el secuestro de migrantes en México*. Mexico City: CNDH. http://www.cndh.org.mx/sites/all/doc/Informes/Especiales/2011_secmigrantes.pdf.

COFAMIDE (Comité de Familiares de Migrantes Fallecidos y Desaparecidos de El Salvador) et al. 2012. *Situación de las personas migrantes no localizadas y restos no identificados en México*. Testimony at a hearing of the Inter-American Commission on Human Rights, March 23, Washington, DC. Posted at FJEDD website, http://fundacion

justicia.org/cms/wp-content/uploads/2013/06/ANEXO-17-INFORME-CIDH-Mi
grantes-no-localizados-y-restos-no-identificados-en-Me_xico.pdf.

FJEDD (Fundación para la Justicia y el Estado Democrático de Derecho). 2013. Red regional verdad y justicia para personas migrantes. Webpage. Mexico City: FJEDD.
http://fundacionjusticia.org/red-regionalverdad-y-justicia/.

FJEDD et al. 2014. "Informe alternativo presentado al Comité contra la Desaparición
Forzada en vista del examen del informe de México durante la 8a sesión del comité,
del 2 al 13 de febrero de 2015." http://fundacionjusticia.org/cms/wp-content/up
loads/2015/02/Informe-Adicional-a-CED-Dic-2014.pdf. Mexico City: FJEDD.

FJEDD et al. 2015. "Avances y obstáculos en garantizar los derechos de las personas
migrantes, mexicanas y no mexicanas, en tránsito hacia Estados Unidos, víctimas
de delitos y graves violaciones a sus derechos humanos en México y de sus familiares." Posted at FJEDD website, http://fundacionjusticia.org/cms/wp-content/up
loads/2015/04/Informe-para-CIDH-marzo-2015-2.pdf.

Godoy, Emilio. 2010. "Banco genético para los inmigrantes desaparecidos." Periodismo-
Humano. http://periodismohumano.com/migracion/banco-genetico-para-los-inmi
grantes-desaparecidos.html.

González, Felipe. 2013. "Informe sobre la situación general de los derechos de los migrantes y sus familias." http://www.oas.org/es/cidh/migrantes/docs/pdf/informe
-migrantes-mexico-2013.pdf

Hope, Alejandro. 2016. "Un muerto cada 20 minutos." *El Universal*, February 11, 2017.
http://www.eluniversal.com.mx/entrada-de-opinion/columna/alejandro-hope/na
cion/seguridad/2016/10/24/un-muerto-cada-20-minutos.

IAHRC (Inter American Human Rights Commission). 2012. *Situación de personas migrantes no localizadas y restos no identificados en México*. Sesiones por tema, session
144. Washington, DC: OAS, Comisión Interamericana de Derechos Humanos.
https://www.oas.org/es/cidh/audiencias/TopicsList.aspx?Lang=es&Topic=20.

———. 2015. *Acceso a la justicia para personas migrantes*. Video, public hearing, March
20. Washington, DC: OAS, Comisión Interamericana de Derechos Humanos.
https://www.youtube.com/watch?v=-gpnhUKgkeo.

INEGI (Mexico, Instituto Nacional de Estadística y Geografía). 2016. *Encuesta nacional
de victimización y percepción sobre seguridad pública principales resultados*. Mexico City:
http://www.inegi.org.mx/saladeprensa/boletines/2017/envipe/envipe2017_09
.pdf.

IOM (International Organization for Migrations). 2016. "Global Migration Trends Fact-
sheet." Berlin: IOM Global Migration Data Analysis Center. http://gmdac.iom.int/gl
obal-migration-trends-factsheet.

Keck, Margaret E., and Kathryn Sikkink. 1999. *Activists beyond Borders*. Ithaca, NY: Cornell University Press.

Knippen, José, Clay Boggs, and Maureen Meyer. 2015. *Un camino incierto: Justicia para
delitos y violaciones a los derechos humanos contra personas migrantes y refugiadas en
México*. Washington, DC: Washington Office on Latin America. https://www.wola
.org/wp-content/uploads/2015/11/Un-camino-incierto_Nov2015.pdf.

Mexico, Presidencia de la República 2013. Plan Nacional de Desarrollo 2013–2018.
Diario Oficial, May 20. http://www.dof.gob.mx/nota_detalle.php?codigo=5299465
&fecha=20/05/2013.

Mexico, Procuraduría General de la República. 2013. "Convenio de colaboración para
la identificación de restos localizados en San Fernando, Tamaulipas y en Cadereyta,

Nuevo León que se llevará a cabo por conducto de una Comisión Forense." *Diario Oficial*, September 4. http://www.dof.gob.mx/nota_detalle.php?codigo=5312887& fecha=04/09/2013.

———. 2014. "Adenda al convenio de Colaboración para la identificación de restos localizados en San Fernando, Tamaulipas y en Cadereyta, Nuevo León que se llevará a cabo por conducto de una Comisión Forense." *Diario Oficial*, October 23. http://dof .gob.mx/nota_detalle.php?codigo=5365261&fecha=23/10/2014.

———. 2015. "Acuerdo A/117/15 por el que se crea la Unidad de Investigación de Delitos para Personas Migrantes y el Mecanismo de Apoyo Exterior Mexicano de Búsqueda e Investigación y se establecen sus facultades y organización." *Diario Oficial*, December 18. http://www.dof.gob.mx/nota_detalle.php?codigo=5420681&fecha= 18/12/2015.

SEGOB (Mexico, Secretaria de Gobernación). 2014. *Programa Especial de Migración*. Mexico City: SEGOB. http://www.gobernacion.gob.mx/es_mx/SEGOB/edicion_im presa_PEM.

———. 2017. *Registro Nacional de Datos de Personas Extraviadas o Desaparecidas*. Mexico City: SEGOB. http://www.gob.mx/sesnp/acciones-y-programas/registro-nacional -de-datos-de-personas-extraviados-o-desaparecidas-rnped.

Semple, Kirk. 2017. "La política migratoria de Estados Unidos empuja al límite al sistema de asilo mexicano." *New York Times*, August 7. https://www.nytimes.com/es /2017/08/07/asilo-mexico-refugio-migracion-eeuu/.

SESNSP (Mexico, Secretariado Ejecutivo del Sistema Nacional de Seguridad Pública). 2016. "Informe de víctimas de homicidio, secuestro y extorsión 2016." Tables. Mexico City: SEGOB, SESNSP. http://secretariadoejecutivo.gob.mx/docs/pdfs/vic timas/Victimas2016_092016.pdf.

Suárez, Ximena, Andrés Díaz, José Knippen, and Maureen Meyer. 2017. *El acceso a la justicia para personas migrantes en México: Un derecho que sólo existe en el papel*. http:// fundacionjusticia.org/cms/wp-content/uploads/2013/06/Accesoalajusticia_Ver sionweb_Julio2017.pdf.

TRIAL et. al. 2012. *¡Enforced Disappearance Is Torture!* Alternative report to the Comité contra la Tortura on Mexico periodic reports 5 and 6. Posted at FJEDD website, http://fundacionjusticia.org/cms/wp-content/uploads/2014/03/Desaparici %C3%B3n-forzada-tambi%C3%A9n-es-tortura_TRIAL.pdf. Geneva: TRIAL.

Wallace, B. 2017. "The Trump Administration's Dark View of Immigrants." *New Yorker*, February 11. http://www.newyorker.com/news/benjamin-wallace-wells/what-mo tivates-the-immigration-ban?mbid=social_twitter.

CHAPTER 6

With Dual Citizenship Comes Double Exclusion: US-Mexican Children and Their Struggle to Access Rights in Mexico

MÓNICA JACOBO-SUÁREZ

In recent years, deportation and immigration policies in the United States have taken an anti-immigrant focus significantly affecting Mexican immigrants. Since 2009, 2.8 million Mexican citizens have been forced to move back to Mexico, the main destination for US deportations, according to numbers of the Mexican Ministry of the Interior (SEGOB 2017). In fact, since 2014 fewer Mexicans are migrating to the United States than moving back to Mexico (Gonzalez-Barrera 2015). Different from previous returning waves, the recent flow to Mexico is characterized by a growing number of family units that include Mexican-born as well as US-born children of migrants. This last group, US-Mexican children, are citizens of both countries and will likely have a transnational future. Yet, once in Mexico, they must actively exercise their civil rights to access basic services such as education and health care and integrate into society. I focus on these US-Mexican children and the role dual citizenship plays in their Mexican integration process. My analysis illustrates the intersection of three phenomena central to this volume: the role of civil society in advocating for the rights of migrants; the response of an "origin state," Mexico, to its returning diaspora; and the actions taken by the US government with regard to their US children abroad.

As dual nationals, US-Mexican children question the concept of citizenship and the rights associated with it. Citizenship is the most desired legal status a member of a society can obtain; in its basic form, it entails the right to have rights (Román 2010). US-Mexican children would be expected to have greater access to rights and opportunities as citizens of two countries. However, I find that the opposite is often true for a majority of US-born children who have moved to Mexico due to the deportation of at least one of their parents. In the United States, their parents' unauthorized status significantly constrains the opportunities these children have in spite of their coveted citizenship status. Once in Mexico, they are routinely denied the support to which they are entitled, given the difficulties associated with securing the necessary documents to claim citizenship. Overly bureaucratic processes and discretionary practices grant the US-Mexican children in Mexico something like what Patricia Landolt and Luin Goldring, in chapter 8 of this volume, call "precarious status."

In the Mexican context, return migration represents a citizenship dilemma. On the one hand, migrants and their offspring born abroad have rights and privileges granted by the Mexican Constitution. On the other hand, they cannot effectively access those rights because of documentation issues and the lack of reintegration programs. While Mexico has launched a few programs to assist returning migrants, little attention is paid to their long-term needs such as education, employment, and health care. In that regard, US-Mexican children are particularly vulnerable. Unlike adult returnees, children require immediate school access, may not have a good command of Spanish, and depend on their parents or tutors to navigate the bureaucratic system. More important, being born in the United States may cause them to be excluded from basic services and resources (Escobar, Lowell, and Martin 2013; Jacobo 2017; Medina and Menjívar 2015) unless they had also been registered by their parents as Mexican nationals at birth, an uncommon practice among returning families.

For years, scholars, migrant civil society, media, and returnees have shone a light on important bureaucratic obstacles to reintegration in Mexico, some of them affecting binational children directly (Ángel 2016; IMUMI 2014; Lakhani and Jacobo 2016; Landa 2015). This pressure first led Mexico to simplify requirements for accessing elementary and secondary education for students coming from the United States. In 2016 Mexico's federal government took a more comprehensive approach to securing rights for the US-Mexican population by launching Soy México, a program to help US-born children of Mexican descent register their Mexican citizenship and to provide them with nationally accepted ID documents that are a basic requirement for accessing pretty much any services in Mexico. Roberta Jacobson, then US ambassador to Mexico, declared that Soy México is based on an agreement between Mexico government and the Maryland-based nonprofit National Association for Public Health Statistics and Information Systems (NAPHSIS), which helps verify birth certificates issued in the United States and thus speed up nationality registration in Mexico (Jacobson 2016). The program demonstrates that a home country can tap resources in a destination country to secure the rights of their shared citizens. The Mexican government operates Soy México through the national population registry. While Soy México can have an important impact on the American-Mexican population in Mexico, there is very little information on it, as the Mexican government's agreement with the association is considered classified.[1]

I analyze the bureaucratic and administrative barriers that US-Mexican children encounter in attempting to claim their rights as citizens in Mexico. Drawing on the political science literature, I find that return migration undercuts the traditional concept of citizenship by raising questions about the exclusion and inclusion of nationals. Because national institutions in Mexico are not designed to consider international mobility, regulations and government practices prevent citizens from effectively exercising their rights while creating a distinction between the Mexicans born in the national territory and those born abroad. As dual citizens, the situation of US-Mexican children raises theoretical and pragmatic questions for the United States and Mexico: How might their experiences with exclusion or marginalization in the United States interfere with their adaptation process in Mexico? How might their social exclusion in Mexico interfere with a potential reintegration in the United States? What efforts should the governments of Mexico and the United States undertake to secure the well-being of the citizens they share? And ultimately, whose responsibility are these children?

To answer such questions I consider the relationship between migration and the concept of citizenship, as well as the rights of Mexican migrants in general in the United States and in Mexico and the rights and exclusions of US-Mexican children specifically in the two nations. I also study the impact of government efforts such as Soy México to increase access for this population, potential roadblocks to becoming more inclusive of its dual citizens, and challenges ahead.

Citizenship and Migration

Citizenship is intrinsically related to the nation-state, which in its basic form consists of a territory, a population linked to that territory, and a system of rights that regulates the people of that territory (Joppke 2010). Citizenship is considered the most basic of all rights, and being a citizen is the most desired legal status because the subject is protected under all constitutional provisions (Román 2010). As a political concept, citizenship consists of three interrelated dimensions: the status of equality and political freedom, equal rights and obligations for all members, and collective membership in a political community. This last aspect, collective membership within what is generally understood as the nation, implies that each person is a citizen of one country in which he or she has both rights and obligations (Faist 2015).

The number of people holding more than one citizenship has increased worldwide since governments began allowing citizens to belong to more than one nation-state. In 1990 only 25 percent of European and Latin American states allowed dual nationality; by 2010 75 percent had approved the practice (Harpaz 2015). Among the variety of factors that have contributed to the expansion of dual and multiple citizenship are increasing international migration flows, the intergenerational transmission of citizenship, and increased naturalization rates of immigrants who are not required to give up their nationality of origin. Thus, migration encourages the creation of new forms of citizenship as nation-states continue to accept these new groups of citizens. This expanding citizenship process can occur in various ways. First, through the *ius soli*, territoriality principle, an individual acquires citizenship of the country where he or she was born, which opens the door for the children of immigrants to acquire the nationality of the country to which their parents migrated; for example, US citizenship is granted to children born in the United States to Mexican parents. Second, citizenship is granted through naturalization, one of the longest and most difficult mechanisms to acquire citizenship—and one that encounters resistance from and stirs fear among the country's nationals. Third, migration extends citizenship beyond the territorial limits of a state, such as when a child acquires the nationality of immigrant parents through the principle of *ius sanguinis*, right of blood. The children born in the United States to Mexican immigrant parents are an example of this extension, as the right of blood grants the children Mexican citizenship (Faist 2007, 2015). Consequently, the logic of exclusive membership in one nation is being replaced by that of multiple and overlapping memberships (Cook-Martin 2015; Mateos 2015).

The proliferation of dual citizenship raises questions about exclusion and inclusion within a political community when individuals transcend the territorial boundaries of a state. From a theoretical perspective, dual citizenship undercuts two basic assumptions about the nation-state: that a congruence exists among a territory, a nation, and the state authority and that a supposed homogeneity of the population exists with respect to characteristics such as class and geography (Faist 2015). In the same way, international migration flows raise questions about the classical concept of citizenship. Migration challenges the homogeneity associated with the nation-state, as the newcomers are a source of religious, ethnic, cultural, and linguistic diversity. And an individual's citizenship in two countries—due to his own migrant trajectory or that of his parents—creates doubts over what it means to be a partial member of a political community. Hovering in the background is the question of whether dual citizenship is an effective instrument for integrating migrants.

Pablo Mateos (2015) asserts that states use dual citizenship as a mechanism of inclusion or exclusion, as a "geopolitical tool," while for migrants, dual citizenship represents a form of capital that can, through *ius sanguinis*, be activated across generations. However, to assume that dual citizenship automatically brings greater benefits and opportunities to migrants is to oversimplify the condition. Poverty, language, the migration status of family members, and access to services are just some of the factors that play crucial roles in determining the opportunities a citizen has in his or her country. The importance of such factors can be seen in what happens to children of immigrants in the United States, particularly those of Mexican descent. US-born Mexican children are vulnerable due to the high incidence of unauthorized status among their parents, which often limits their chances of learning, accessing services, and getting well-remunerated jobs in spite of being citizens. Frank Bean, Susan Brown, and James Bachmeier (2015) argue that social membership, understood as both legal and social citizenship, strongly conditions structural integration among migrants in the United States. Considering US-born Mexican children, the authors find that parents' unauthorized status directly affects the children's social integration and results in their exclusion from many arenas of societal participation, whether by law, social disapprobation, or both. Proposing a membership exclusion model, Bean, Brown, and Bachmeier contend that initial denial of social citizenship based on migration status puts immigrants in such marginal social and economic positions that the material integration of their children is hampered, even if the children are US citizens.

Therefore, US-Mexican citizens in the United States are likely to encounter exclusion consistently over their lifetimes. About four million children in the United States live in families with at least one undocumented parent, and Mexicans are overrepresented among those children (Yoshikawa 2011). Parental unauthorized status also affects the integration of US-born children in their schooling. From the students' perspective, anxiety, shame, and fear may be triggered when they are asked to have school paperwork signed by their parents because they think they may get deported (Suárez-Orozco and Suárez-Orozco 2001). As for the parents, undocumented status plays a role in their reluctance to fill out paperwork for child care subsidies or to participate in their children's school events more actively, both of which are extremely important for families living in poverty. In a large-scale study, Yoshikawa (2011) has found that undocumented status pervasively affects everyday life, as in not availing oneself of resources that require identification. Subsidies are often the only way low-income parents can access child care centers, whose programs have been shown to be most effective in boosting children's early cognitive skills. However, subsidy programs require verification of employment, and undocumented parents are likely to be paid in cash. The two largest federally funded sources of child care subsidies require other documentation such as tax returns. Undocumented status is associated with greater economic hardship and worse working conditions, all reducing parents' abilities to engage in stimulating learning activities with their children.

Although constitutionally they are equal members of US society, citizen children of undocumented parents have less access to a variety of resources. The resources can be formal, such as public programs, or informal, such as social network supports; they can be material, such as the stable income that a living wage brings, or psychological, such as the parents' well-being that is essential for the emotional development of children (Yoshikawa 2011). Because unauthorized immigrants lack effective membership in so many sectors, their integration and that of their citizen children is problematic. US-born children of Mexican descent, or "US-Mexican children," as they often are called in the United States, therefore challenge the traditional concept of citizenship in illustrating what Ediberto Román (2010) calls "gradations of membership." To the extent that levels of membership exist, with less powerful groups having less favored status, subordinate forms of citizenship derive from the desire of the favored or majority groups to maintain their preferred status within their societies. Román explores how citizenship, a construct that is universally associated with equality among those within a society, can simultaneously entail seldom-explored exclusionary practices. On the sending-country side, US-Mexican children are also citizens of Mexico, and as such, they have full rights and are entitled to access to all the services offered in Mexico.

Mexican Migrants' Rights in the United States and Mexico

Mexican migration to the United States is a unique phenomenon because of its long history, its massive volume, and the proximity of the countries (Becerra-Ramírez 2000; Durand 2016). The US-Mexico border is an extremely important migratory corridor (Durand and Arias 2014). Mexican migrants in the United States are the largest national minority and constitute the largest group within the unauthorized population (Durand 2016). Indeed, legal status has played a crucial role in their integration and that of their offspring, directly affecting legal and social rights (Bean, Brown, and Bachmeier 2015). Legal residents have greater access to these rights than undocumented migrants, but they are still restricted from the right to vote, something reserved for citizens. Hence, the Mexican population in the United States is stratified in relation to the effective exercising of rights (Escobar 2015).

As for Mexico, its response to its US diaspora has changed significantly over time, moving from indifference to a model of "state extension" (Bada 2014; Bada and Gleeson 2015). Alexandra Délano Alonso, in chapter 11 of this volume, argues that Mexico justified supporting its diaspora as a governmental responsibility to protect its citizens who, as was increasingly evident, were settling in the United States permanently. Thus, a turning point occurred in 1997 when Mexico amended its Ley de Nacionalidad (Nationality Act) to allow dual citizenship for its diaspora. The purpose of the law was two-fold: to strengthen the rights of its citizens living in the United States and to build relations between those citizens and the Mexican government. The law was intended to strengthen their rights by encouraging their US naturalization without requiring them to renounce their Mexican citizenship, as was required before the law was amended (Becerra-Ramírez 2000; Escobar 2015; Harpaz 2015). In light of the increasing restrictions on noncitizens' rights in the United States over recent decades (Massey and Pren 2012; Durand 2015), and particularly since 2017 under the administration of Donald Trump, US naturalization has become particularly vital to protect the Mexican community. The 1997 changes to the law were intended to strengthen Mexico's bonds with its citizens living in the United States, accounting for 98 percent of all Mexicans living abroad, by implementing two forms of dual citizenship; one allows citizens to maintain Mexican nationality after acquiring a second one, and the other allows intergenerational transmission of Mexican citizenship to children born abroad to Mexican parents.

Mexico's dual citizenship laws thus targeted its diaspora in the United States, not returning migrants and their families. Mexico has reacted slowly to its returning diaspora even though significant numbers of deportations occurred during the George W. Bush and Barack Obama administrations and now under Trump's. Deportation proceedings, coupled with militarization of the border and a series of measures that limit migrants' access to rights in the United States, have caused many of those returning to Mexico to see their return as permanent (Durand 2016). Since 2008, the increasing numbers of Mexicans returning from the United States have formed a critical mass, calling attention to issues such as documentation and access to services. The return flow encompasses people of all kinds of backgrounds and therefore differing reintegration needs. Those referred to as Dreamers (from the Development, Relief, and Education for Alien Minors Act) are young people of working age with at least a high school education who face multiple bureaucratic obstacles to entering universities in Mexico and having their educational credits earned outside of Mexico recognized. There is also an adult population for whom labor reintegration is urgent because they often return with economic dependents. And there is the binational population, mainly children born in the United States who face difficulties claiming their rights despite the 1997 amendment granting them Mexican citizenship.

Regardless of the differences, each group of returnees faces a common challenge: exercising the right to identity, which translates into having a legal document accrediting them as Mexican citizens. Securing that right opens the door for exercising all other rights and accessing services. For those born in Mexico, obtaining official identification cards such as that of the IFE (Instituto Nacional Electoral) is a relatively easy process if they have Mexican birth certificates or registration cards called CURPs (Clave Única de Registro de Población).[2] For Mexicans born abroad without such documents, though, such as US-Mexican children, obtaining an official identification requires registering as a Mexican national. The registration can be obtained at Mexican consulates abroad or in civil registries in Mexico. However, doing so from abroad is easier because once in Mexico, the applicant usually has to get an apostille for all necessary documentation.[3] Families who have recently returned from the United States commonly lack accurate information to complete the registration process that would secure Mexican nationality for their children. Many, especially those who have undergone processes of forced return, do not have apostilles for their birth certificates, which are essential documents for the administrative procedure. Moreover, testimonies collected by scholars demonstrate how corrupt or misinformed state and local authorities sometimes offer their help in exchange for payment or advise families to register their children as if they were born in Mexico, a different process from registering Mexican citizenship (Escobar, Lowell, and Martin 2013; IMUMI 2015; Jacobo and Landa 2015; Lakhani and Jacobo 2016; Medina and Menjivar 2015). As a result, thousands of US-Mexican children have seen their integration into Mexico delayed until their parents find a way to overcome a convoluted and confusing bureaucratic system.

Although dual nationality has been allowed for almost two decades, and registration of Mexican nationality is necessary to access services in Mexico, the number of families that have registered their children in both countries is modest. The 1997 amendment took effect in 1997, and between 2000 and 2003 around 87,000 citizenship registrations were issued (Escobar 2015). In a 2016 report, the Instituto Nacional de Estadística, Geografía e Informática (INEGI) concludes that about 290,000 US-born children entitled to dual citizenship were living in Mexico without having registered their Mexican nationality (INEGI 2016). For children, one of the most detrimental consequences of lacking a Mexican-issued ID relates to school access, an urgent need when they move to Mexico. For decades, excessively bureaucratic procedures were required by the federal Secretariat of Public Education for children who were born abroad and studied outside the Mexican education system. The bureaucratic problems increase as children and youth advance in their education. For instance, there is no standardized procedure for recognizing credits for foreign university studies by autonomous universities in

Mexico; in many cases, no clear criteria or contact points are established within the universities to assist in transferring the credits, complicating the process of educational insertion for young people coming from the United States who wish to continue their studies in Mexico (Ángel 2016).

As country of origin, Mexico has responded so far with isolated efforts to reintegrate its returning diaspora, such as providing food and medical aid at points of repatriation, setting up returnees with employers, and offering support in some states to secure apostille certificates for identity documents. However, the government has established no comprehensive policy or reintegration program to coordinate processes and documents across levels of government or systematically attend to the needs of the returning diaspora. Considering the growing number of the US-Mexican population living in Mexico—about 600,000 children in 2018 (Jensen et al. 2017)—it is important that the Mexican government facilitate the registration process for them.

US-Mexican Children: Dual Citizenship as Double Exclusion

International migration and transnational trajectories do not necessarily translate into broader and better opportunities for US-Mexican youth and children. In fact, they often face a double exclusion in spite of being citizens of two countries. On each side of the US border, their integration is affected by several factors, including their immigration status and that of their parents, their family's socioeconomic status, and their language proficiency in English and Spanish. In the United States, parental legal status plays a crucial role in defining educational, social, and economic opportunities for children of immigrants, particularly for US-Mexican youth. Research shows that unauthorized status hampers material integration for children of Mexican immigrants. Oftentimes, its limiting effects reach up to the second and third generations (Bean, Brown, and Bachmeier 2015). In poor families, the imperative to work falls disproportionally on boys, pressuring them to enter the labor force as early as possible to the detriment of their education (ibid.: 53). Immigration status manifests in many other areas as well, but for children and youth, education is of paramount importance. Indeed, the authors hypothesize that educational attainment for students whose parents remain undocumented would be lower than that of those whose parents' status is legalized. In conjunction with low socioeconomic status among Latino families, poor school attainment further compromises family members' economic and professional development.

The flow of return migration to Mexico that began during the Obama administration demands consideration of US-Mexican youth and children from a transnational perspective. Once in Mexico, they may encounter additional forms of discrimination and exclusion in various areas. Since school is the greatest site of socialization for children, securing access to and receiving adequate education are crucial for US-Mexican children's well-being. How, then, is the transition process from the US education system to the Mexican one? To what extent are the rights of US-Mexican children realized once they arrive in Mexico? A first challenge the children face is overcoming invisibility within the classroom and the educational system. Research conducted over the course of a decade by Ted Hamann, Víctor Zúñiga, and Juan Sánchez has shown that the unique needs of "transnational students"—the term they use to refer to both US-born and Mexico-born children of Mexican descent— are often neglected by their teachers in Mexico (Zúñiga and Hamann 2006, 2009, 2015; Hamann, Zúñiga, and Sánchez 2006). While conducting extensive interviews at schools in northern Mexican states, the researchers found that transitional students were not perceived as different from their peers without migratory experience because they resembled each other physically. As a result, teachers and school authorities did not realize that US-Mexican students who had moved from the United States were trained to speak and write English, familiar with a different curriculum, and accustomed to different pedagogical practices. All these factors hampered their adaptation to the Mexican education system.

Mexicans who have not had transnational experiences often expect US-Mexicans to be Spanish monolingual, identify as Mexican, and fit into such social and cultural norms in Mexico as liking spicy foods, knowing the Mexican national anthem, and playing soccer (Despagne and Jacobo 2016). The pressure to deny one's multiple identities is not exclusive to students of Mexican descent in Mexico's schools. Patricia Baquedano-López, in chapter 9 of this volume, illustrates how Maya students in California fight the dynamics of cultural and linguistic assimilation while resisting assimilation into the broader Latino category. Yet social and cultural distance from a heritage country, as many encounter in the United States, may hinder the adaptation process for US-Mexican children in Mexico. Depending on the length of time they have lived and attended school in the United States, children could experience cultural, linguistic, and identity shock upon settling in Mexico. While many of the children have visited Mexico or returned for short stays before moving there with their families, others have never been there (Zúñiga and Hamann 2015; Zúñiga and Vivas-Romero 2014). Qualitative studies conducted in various states throughout Mexico identify discriminating attitudes from peers and even teachers based on students' lack of command of written Spanish or their "strange" accent (Despagne and Jacobo 2016;

Hamann, Zúñiga, and Sánchez 2006; Vargas and Lugo 2012; Zúñiga 2013). Social discrimination they suffer in Mexico acquires greater relevance because it reenacts discrimination they experienced previously in the United States, for lacking a command of the English language, for not looking white, or because of their parents' legal status or national origin. And yet, despite a pressing need, Mexico has no explicit educational policies for transnational students or language programs supporting Spanish literacy, much less bilingual classes so that US-Mexican students who possess a good command of English can keep developing their language skills. The double exclusion—first in the United States, then in Mexico—suppresses their educational opportunities and therefore their chances for advancement in Mexico.

In addition to stereotypes and social discrimination that may befall US-Mexicans in Mexico, many also encounter government structures and processes that restrict their formal access to education. While students do not need to be citizens to enroll in elementary school in Mexico, they must possess valid proof of identity. For those with foreign birth certificates, this entails obtaining an apostille and a certified translation of that certificate. Since 2013, civil society organizations have identified dozens of cases in which US-Mexican children were not permitted to enroll in school because their birth certificates lacked the apostille certificate and were not translated by certified translators (Jacobo 2017). To transition to secondary school, students also need a CURP, a unique registration number that functions similarly to a Social Security number in the United States. A CURP is necessary to access various types of public services, including education, medical care, and personal identification documents such as passports and driver' licenses. However, requesting CURPs is part of the growing bureaucracy parents must navigate in dealing with what should be one of the simplest of processes—registering their US-Mexican children in public schools. How do the barriers to obtaining these documents put US-Mexican children in Mexico at risk of not accessing education and other services? In 2015, approximately 480,000 US-Mexican students were attending primary and secondary schools in Mexico (Aguilar and Jacobo 2019). Unlike their Mexican-born peers, 49 percent of foreign-born students did not have CURPs in 2014 (Jacobo 2017). The lack of required documentation presents a real obstacle to foreign-born students seeking to fully integrate into society.

From a transnational perspective, US-born children of Mexican descent have dual nationality and therefore are entitled to full rights in both Mexico and in the United States. But access to these rights in Mexico has been hampered by bureaucratic obstacles to acquiring necessary documents, by the lack of adequate integration programs in schools, and by stereotypes. After sometimes harsh discrimination in the United States and deportation, parents often face economic limitations and then problems navigating bureau-cratic institutions, which in turn restricts their ability to advocate for their children. In many ways, structures that limit opportunities for children of immigrants in the United States continue to limit opportunities for depor-tees and their children back in Mexico. The obstacles can intersect when Mexican government officials and school leaders perpetuate stereotypes vis-à-vis US-Mexicans and are not well-informed on policies or the rights of citi-zen children. US-Mexican children are left in precarious legal status, citizens of both countries though they may be. While the term "precarious status" has primarily been applied to noncitizens, as in Landolt and Goldring (this volume) and Délano's analysis of the Dreamers (this volume), here I reveal how discretionary practices and convoluted regulations may re-create pre-cariousness for citizens as well. Organized efforts from migrant civil society, academia, and deportees to advance returning migrants' rights often cen-ter around securing educational access for all returning youth and children, US- and Mexican-born, while certain initiatives have favored US-Mexican children.

Fighting for the Right to Education and Identity

Education is a universal right recognized in Mexico's legal framework, in-cluding its constitution, General Education Law, Migration Law, and Spe-cial Migration Program. All children in Mexico have a right to free public education irrespective of their nationality. Migrants may access educational services provided by the public and private sectors regardless of their immi-gration status, as provided in Mexico's Ley de Migración, Article 8, of 2011. However, many US-born children who come to Mexico with their returning migrant families have not been able to enroll in school because they lack identity documents.

Since most such children arrived in Mexico as minors, enrolling in school is an immediate need but also a process that exemplifies the legal and prac-tical barriers to effectively exerting their rights. It is no wonder, then, that the fight to secure the rights of US-Mexican citizens started in the education realm. Civil society organizations made specific demands once they started identifying cases of denied and conditional school access among returning families; qualitative studies began to proliferate that demonstrated that transnational students, whether born in Mexico or in the United States, ex-perienced bullying once their linguistic and cultural differences were made apparent in the classroom. In 2013 the Instituto para las Mujeres en la Mi-gración (IMUMI), a pro-immigrant nonprofit organization, took the lead in advocating for US-Mexican children's rights by lobbying the Mexican Secretariat of Public Education. IMUMI (2014) elaborated a diagnostic that identified specific administrative and normative barriers and estimated the economic cost of delaying and denying educational access to foreign-born children. Lacking apostilles for their foreign birth certificates, the institute found, was one of the main reasons Mexican school authorities deny enrollment. Other reasons include making access to school conditional on parents' supplying the required documentation during a specific time frame and even withholding issuing completion certificates once foreign-born students successfully enrolled. Identifying the apostille requirement as one of the biggest hurdles in school access across states and municipalities in Mexico, IMUMI proposed that the Department of Public Education eliminate apostilles and certified translations as requirements for school enrollment (IMUMI 2014).

For eighteen months IMUMI tried to pressure the office to eliminate the apostille requirement without success. Having limited resources, the institute sought alliances with scholars and with deported youth who were influential with the media in the United States and Mexico. As a result, 2015 marked a turning point in the fight for returnee rights. The media started to cover deportation stories more frequently, and educational access was a demand often mentioned by deported youth, in particular the validation of higher education credits. Among the growing number of deported youth, one woman, Nancy Landa, articulated specific complaints and demanded solutions from the Office of Public Education. Her grassroots efforts and direct confrontation of the secretary of education in various international media outlets led to the formation of the Committee on Education and Identity within the office. Landa invited IMUMI and a few scholars (including this author) specializing in the issue to join the working group.

After three months of negotiations with federal authorities, the group succeeded in having the first regulatory piece modified on June 15, 2015. The Acuerdo Secretarial 286 established that no apostille or official translation of foreign documents would be required for validation of any education level up to high school completed outside of Mexico (SEP 2015a).[4] In the same manner, the Normas de Control Escolar 2015–2016, the standards that regulate primary and secondary education, were amended in September 2015. For the first time, the standards explicitly stated that foreign birth certificates, without an apostille or official translation, are valid identity documents for enrolling foreign-born students (SEP 2015b). School authorities would no longer require birth certificates for school access or deny issuance of official school certificates to foreign-born students. The amended standards established that students should be enrolled in school even if, for any reason, they do not have birth certificates or any official identification. The amendments apply to all foreign-born children, not only those of Mexican descent. The issue of validating higher education credits, one of the petitions that led to the formation of the working group, was not included among the amendments.

Despite the normative changes, many cases of denied school access were still reported after the 2015 amendments were adopted because school authorities were not trained in how to implement them. Implementation continued to be uneven at the state and local levels for at least a year after the amendments went into effect. More important, the amendments affected only education; proving Mexican citizenship through a birth certificate with an apostille was still a requirement for accessing other public services such as health care and social security. Civil society groups demanded a more comprehensive solution—streamlining Mexican citizenship registrations for all foreign-born children of Mexican descent. In cases of migrants' forced return to Mexico, it is crucial for their registration to be facilitated in Mexico since only a small of percentage of families register as Mexican citizens while in the United States. Some progress has been made. In September 2016, Mexico's interior secretary Miguel Ángel Osorio Chong signed an agreement with the Maryland-based nonprofit National Association for Public Health Statistics and Information to create the Soy México program. Announced as a temporary agreement, the program removed the apostille requirement for foreign birth certificates used to register Mexican nationality. Originally the agreement was to take effect on its announcement date, September 22, 2016, and conclude on December 31, 2016, but Soy México continued and became part of a wider government strategy to reintegrate the growing return population (Jacobo 2017; Jensen et al. 2017).

Soy México was implemented to facilitate registration for Mexican citizenship of US-born children of Mexican parents, in particular those who lack apostilles for their birth certificates. Soy México's ultimate purpose, therefore, is to enforce the rights of the US-Mexican population. Replacing the apostille is the Registro de Población Nacional (RENAPO), a national registry that electronically verifies the US-issued birth certificates of children who apply for dual citizenship. US-Mexicans can go to any state civil registry in Mexico, submit their US birth certificates without apostilles, and request verification from RENAPO, which searches the US birth records database. The procedure is offered to registrants for free, as the verification costs are absorbed by the Mexican government. Once a birth record is found in the US database, confirmation is sent to the civil registry where the Mexican nationality registration was requested. A Mexican birth certificate is then delivered to the applicant's family along with a CURP so binational children are registered with Mexican nationality.

Soy México responds to the reality of a child population that is binational but lacks official documentation needed to exercise their rights as citizens in Mexico. It also responds to the demands of a growing population of those whose return to Mexico appears to be more permanent than temporary. Soy México is the first joint effort between Mexico and the National Association for Public Health Statistics and Information to attend to a returning diaspora that now includes US citizens. Mexico's obligation to its returning citizens is stated as a central principle of the program: "Return migration is part of human nature and history of nations. Ensuring legal identity and dual nationality of Mexicans is a higher duty, for the government of Mexico it is justice, security, and protection" (SEGOB 2016). Soy México indicates a change in Mexico's official discourse and actions toward its diaspora. The federal government has transitioned from gradually granting rights to Mexicans abroad to recognizing the importance of a growing return population that includes dual citizens.

The agreement, if implemented successfully, opens potential for the US-Mexican binational population to expand on both sides of the border. Dual citizenship is, in Mateos's terms (2015), a form of capital widening the range of opportunities available to individuals who possess it. Ensuring the legal identity of the binational population in both countries would allow dual citizens, when they reach eighteen years of age, to live, work, and study on both sides of the border and access market opportunities legally. That is a significant step, Yossi Harpaz (2015) argues, as dual citizens living in Mexico have privileged access to the United States, one that is not based on the principle of selection and replaces the use of social networks that have characterized the undocumented population. The importance of ensuring the legal identity of the binational population in Mexico is obvious; binational children there cannot be ignored, numbering some 422,000 in 2014 according to my estimates based on Mexico's educational census of that year (Jacobo 2017). For the US government, there is a clear need to ensure that these US citizens are educated and have access to services in Mexico, since their citizenship allows them to return to the United States if they so choose. Soy México is the first foreign government program to have an agreement with the National Association for Public Health Statistics and Information to provide US birth certificates and other personal documents, perhaps leading the United States to take the issue seriously as well.

Whose Citizens Are These? The Challenges Ahead

Clearly, policies aimed at migrant communities need to be examined from the perspective of the origin and destination states while considering the role of their civil societies. Mexico and the United States are inevitably linked through international migration and a shared, complex history. Migration patterns have changed drastically over recent years, and now people moving south of the border outnumber those trying to reach the United States. As a consequence of a long history of migration, the return population in Mexico now includes US-born children of Mexican descent, some of whom have never lived in Mexico. Only a couple of decades ago, dual and multiple citizenships were not countenanced by nation-states. Now, however, possessing more than one citizenship is a possibility and indeed a reality for a growing number of international migrants. Despite the militarization along the US-Mexico border, as well as several legal initiatives to restrict access for undocumented immigrants, the Mexican diaspora constitutes the largest immigrant group in the United States. Mexico has thus adopted a gradual strategy to recognize and reconnect with its citizens abroad. From the amendment made to the Nationality Act in 1997 to the Soy México program, the Mexican government is moving toward extending and expanding Mexican citizenship beyond the national territory. Soy México also reveals the recognition of a shared responsibility between the United States and Mexico with regard to their dual citizens. In both sovereign states, dual citizenship is a means to achieving their goals: for the United States, granting citizenship is a way to encourage naturalization and integration in an era of increasing restrictions targeting noncitizen immigrants; for Mexico, dual citizenship allows it to connect with and provide rights for its diaspora.

Although legally recognizing Mexican citizenship is the first step to integrating returning children, there are no comprehensive reintegration programs geared toward families. Children do not exist in a vacuum; as minors, they depend on their parents or guardians to feed them, take them to the doctor, enroll them in school, and ultimately help them navigate Mexican life. Therefore, addressing the integration needs of adults is a crucial part of securing their entire family's adaptation. Without programs that target families and specifically parents, US-Mexican children are at risk of reproducing cycles of exclusion. Mexico's response to return migration has been slow and triggered by pressure from civic groups and the international context. The election of Donald Trump forced the Mexican government, after a century of migration's absence from its public agenda, to respond. The Mexican population in the United States and the returning diaspora are now being discussed at every governmental level. Will this attention translate to effective reintegration programs and binational policies? Or will US-Mexican children continue to experience precariousness in Mexico? Time will tell. For now, the official discourse in Mexico transcends borders and seeks collaboration from its neighbor, as Osorio Chong (2016) illustrates in announcing Soy México: "Let's say yes to the strengthening of friendship between Mexico and the United States. . . . [For] more than 200 years we have shared values and principles; we are linked together by our past, present, and future, because Mexico cannot be explained without the United States and the United States cannot be explained without Mexico."

Mexico's ability to integrate US-born children, in turn, must be included on the agenda of US policy makers. Soy México is a first effort to guarantee legal identity, but many issues still may hinder its effective implementation. There is little information on how the Mexican government will reach out to the eligible population within the limited time frame of the program. Since the program operates on demand—that is, US-Mexicans must make the requests—return families first need to be informed of its existence. Also, the birth certificate verification process is available only in Mexican consulates in the United States and in state civil registries in Mexico, which might be a considerable barrier for families living in smaller communities. Moreover, capacity is limited for completing the verifications, since only a couple of people within RENAPO, the national registry, are authorized to request the verifications. That is, state registries cannot do the verification process themselves but rather send the requests to the two authorized people at RENAPO. In order to certify the status of the 600,000 children who are eligible for binational citizenship, civil registries would have to reach out to a dispersed population. Another limitation is that only thirty-six US states agreed to share their data on birth certificates through NAPHSIS. Therefore, RENAPO can verify only birth certificates from the US states that participate in the Soy México temporary agreement. Texas, a state with an important Mexican diaspora, did not sign. No information has been made public on the number of children who have completed the process of dual nationality, and Mexico's government has not yet informed the public about efforts to negotiate with the other states.

US-Mexican children represent a new stage in US-Mexico migration history. For the Mexican government, the US-Mexican population living in national territory constitutes a challenge, but this population also raises serious issues for the US government in terms of securing its rights. US-Mexican children are dual citizens and as such are likely to have a transnational future, yet their often involuntary return to Mexico creates uncertainty around their educational opportunities. They might return to the United States at some point, and therefore the quality of their Mexican education should be of interest to the United States. To Mexico, integrating this bicultural and bilingual population represents a long-term challenge, one that requires resources the country may need to develop. Steps taken in the educational sphere have targeted school access and transition between educational levels. Curricula, teacher training, Spanish literacy programs, and high-level English classes have been absent from the discussion. For many of the children, transition to living in Mexico is difficult; once in the public education system, they are pretty much on their own to learn cultural codes, understand lessons, catch up with curricula, and develop Spanish literacy skills. Unless teachers and schools in Mexico develop effective strategies to facilitate their transition and guarantee effective learning, US-Mexican children will continue to be socially excluded at school.

In fact, the right to education, secured through bureaucratic changes, does not translate to equal opportunity in the classroom, and unequal conditions at school are likely to affect students' opportunities in adulthood. Thus, achieving equality of educational opportunity for US-born Mexican children requires more than modifying regulations and ensuring their effective implementation, an area in which Mexico still has much room to improve. Equitable opportunity for binational children also requires investment across the different government levels. Whose economic responsibility are these children? If they can decide to work in the United States after enjoying the benefits of Mexico's free education, then the United States must consider taking steps to ensure educational access and quality for all its citizens, even those beyond its own territory. Many US-Mexican children have spent most if not all of their lives in the United States, attended US schools, adopted English as their preferred language, and moved to Mexico because of their parents' situations. Without action, the bicultural and bilingual capital these children have may erode and further compromise their well-being and future opportunities. They are entitled to come back to the United States in the future, but what kind of job opportunities will they have if they are not college graduates or lose their English proficiency? In such scenarios, the benefits derived from their US citizenship would not translate into better opportunities. Dual citizenship would not translate into access to tangible rights but rather reproduce exclusion and create societal membership gradations affecting US-born Mexicans' inclusion in both Mexico and the United States.

Notes

1. A. Hernández, officer at the US embassy in Mexico, interview with the author, November 2016.

2. A CURP is a unique number that is assigned to every individual, including foreigners, living in Mexico; it is used to request various types of public services such as education.

3. The apostille is a stamped seal used on documents to verify their authenticity so they can be accepted in other countries. The apostille system was established in 1961 in the Hague Convention.

4. Geographically, 75 percent of the US-born students enrolled in K–12 education in Mexico are concentrated along the border and in states with historically high emigration rates—Jalisco, Guanajuato, Puebla, Michoacán—and in Mexico City.

References

Aguilar, Rodrigo, and Mónica Jacobo. 2019. "Migración de retorno infantil y juvenil en México: Cambios demográficos y desafíos educativos." In *Políticas públicas y migración de retorno*, edited by Silvia Giourguli, 183–218. Mexico City: Colegio de México.

Ángel, Hiram. 2016. "Mexican Universities and Returned Students from the United States: The Case of the University of Guadalajara." Conference paper presented at the annual meeting of the American Education Research Association, April 7–12, Washington, DC.

Bada, Xóchitl. 2014. *Mexican Hometown Associations in Chicagoacán: From Local to Transnational Civic Engagement.* New Brunswick, NJ: Rutgers University Press.

Bada, Xóchitl, and Shannon Gleeson. 2015. "A New Approach to Migrant Labor Rights Enforcement: The Crisis of Undocumented Worker Abuse and Mexican Consular Advocacy in the United States." *Labor Studies Journal* 40 (1): 32–53.

Bean, Frank D., Susan K. Brown, and James D. Bachmeier. 2015. *Parents without Papers: The Progress and Pitfalls of Mexican-American Integration.* New York: Russell Sage Foundation.

Becerra-Ramírez, Manuel. 2000. "Nationality in Mexico." In *From Migrants to Citizens: Membership in a Changing World*, edited by T. Alexander Aleinikoff and Doublas Klusmeyer, 312–334. Washington, DC: Carnegie Endowment for International Peace.

Cook-Martin, David. 2015. "El pasaporte del abuelo: Orígenes, significado y problemática de la ciudadanía múltiple." In *Ciudadanía múltiple y migración*, edited by Pablo Mateos, 145–170. Mexico City: Centro de Investigaciones y Estudios Superiores en Antropología Social and Centro de Investigación y Docencia Económicas.

Escobar, Agustín, Lisa Lowell, and Susan Martin. 2013. "Diálogo binacional sobre migrantes mexicanos en Estados Unidos y México." Mexico City: Centro de Investigaciones y Estudios Superiores en Antropología Social.

Escobar, Cristina. 2015. "Derechos extraterritoriales y doble ciudadanía en América Latina." In *Ciudadanía múltiple y migración*, edited by Pablo Mateos, 173–215. Mexico City: Centro de Investigaciones y Estudios Superiores en Antropología Social and Centro de Investigación y Docencia Económicas.

Despagne, Colette, and Mónica Jacobo. 2016. "Desafíos actuales de la escuela monolítica mexicana: El caso de los alumnos migrantes transnacionales." *Sinéctica* 47 (July–December): 1–17. https://sinectica.iteso.mx/index.php/SINECTICA/article/view/645.

Durand, Jorge. 2015. "Migración y ciudadanía. El caso norteamericano." In *Ciudadanía múltiple y migración*, edited by Pablo Mateos, 217–241. Mexico City: Centro de Investigaciones y Estudios Superiores en Antropología Social and Centro de Investigación y Docencia Económicas.

———. 2016. *Historia mínima de la migración México-Estados Unidos.* Mexico City: Colegio de México.

Durand, Jorge, and Patricia Arias. 2014. "Escenarios locales del colapso migratorio: Indicios desde los altos de Jalisco." *Papeles de Población* 20 (81): 165–192.

Faist, Thomas. 2007. *Dual Citizenship: From Nationhood to Societal Integration*. Avebury, England: Ashgate.

———. 2015. "Migración y teorías de ciudadanía." In *Ciudadanía múltiple y migración*, edited by Pablo Mateos, 25–56. Mexico City: Centro de Investigaciones y Estudios Superiores en Antropología Social and Centro de Investigación y Docencia Económicas.

Gonzalez-Barrera, Ana. 2015. *More Mexicans Leaving Than Coming to the US*. Washington, DC: Pew Research Center. November. http://www.pewhispanic.org/files/2015/11/2015-11-19_mexican-immigration__FINAL.pdf.

Hamann, Edmund, Víctor Zúñiga, and Juan Sánchez. 2006. "Pensando en Cynthia y su hermana: Educational Implications of United States-Mexico Transnationalism for Children." *Journal of Latinos and Education* 5 (4): 253–274.

Harpaz, Yossi. 2015. "La doble nacionalidad como herramienta geopolítica, régimen de movilidad y forma de capital." In *Ciudadanía múltiple y migración*, edited by Pablo Mateos, 267–290. Mexico City: Centro de Investigaciones y Estudios Superiores en Antropología Social and Centro de Investigación y Docencia Económicas.

IMUMI (Instituto para las Mujeres en la Migración). 2014. "Propuesta de eliminación del requisito de acta de nacimiento apostillada para la inscripción de niñez extranjera a educación básica en México." Mexico City: IMUMI. http://imumi.org/sep/apostilla.html.

———. 2015. "Acceso a la educación de la niñez migrante binacional en México." Mexico City: IMUMI. http://imumi.org/sep/video.html.

INEGI (Mexico, Instituto Nacional de Estadística, Geografía e Informática). 2016. "Resultados del procesamiento de información de la Encuesta Intercensal 2015." Coordinación Interinstitucional Especializada.

Jacobo, Mónica. 2016. "Migración de retorno y políticas de reintegración al sistema educativo mexicano." In *El sistema migratorio mesoamericano*, edited by Carlos Heredia. Serie Perspectivas Migratorias 4. Mexico City: Colegio de la Frontera Norte and Centro de Investigación y Docencia Económicas. https://www.academia.edu/28837414/Migraci%C3%B3n_de_retorno_y_pol%C3%ADticas_de_reintegraci%C3%B3n_al_sistema_educativo_mexicano.

———. 2017. "De regreso a 'casa' y sin apostilla: Estudiantes México-Americanos en México." *Sinéctica* 48: 1–18.

Jacobo, Mónica, and Nancy Landa. 2015. "La exclusión de los niños que retornan a México." *Nexos*, August 1. http://www.nexos.com.mx/?p=25878.

Jacobson, Roberta. 2016. Registro de población México-americana. Mexico City: SEGOB. https://www.gob.mx/segob/prensa/roberta-s-jacobson-embajadora-de-los-estados-unidos-de-america-en-mexico-en-el-programa-soy-mexico-registro-de-nacimiento-poblacion-mexico-americana.

Jensen, Bryant, Rebeca Mejía-Arauz, and Rodrigo Aguilar. 2017. "Equitable Teaching for Returnee Children in Mexico." *Sinéctica* 48:1–20.

Joppke, Christian. 2010. *Citizenship and Immigration*. Cambridge, England: Polity.

Lakhani, Nina, and Mónica Jacobo. 2016. "Uprooted: Returned to a Country They Barely Know." *The Guardian*, July 13.

Landa, Nancy. 2015. "La no validación de estudios como política de educación en México." *Animal Político*, April 14. http://www.animalpolitico.com/blogueros-blog-invitado/2015/04/14/la-no-validacion-de-estudios-como-politica-de-educacion-en-mexico/.

Massey, Douglass, and Karen Pren. 2012. "Unintended Consequences of US Immigration Policy: Explaining the Post-1965 Surge from Latin America." *Population and Development Review* 38 (1): 1–29.

Mateos, Pablo. 2015. "Ciudadanía múltiple y extraterritorial: Tipologías de movilidad y ancestria de euro-latinoamericanos." In *Ciudadanía múltiple y migración*, edited by Pablo Mateos, 81–110. Mexico City: Centro de Investigaciones y Estudios Superiores en Antropología Social and Centro de Investigación y Docencia Económicas.

Medina, Dulce, and Cecilia Menjivar. 2015. "The Context of Return Migration: Challenges of Mixed-Status Families in Mexico's Schools." *Ethnic and Racial Studies* 38 (12): 2123–2139.

Osorio Chong, Miguel Ángel. 2016. "Miguel Ángel Osorio Chong, Secretario de Gobernación en el Programa Soy México, Registro de Nacimiento de la Población México-Americana." Press release. https://www.gob.mx/segob/prensa/las-fronteras-geo graficas-deben-ser-un-punto-de-encuentro-e-intercambio-el-secretario-de-gober nacion.

Román, Ediberto. 2010. *Citizenship and Its Exclusions: A Classical, Constitutional, and Critical Race Critique*. New York: New York University Press.

SEGOB (Mexico, Secretaría de Gobernación). 2016. *#SoyMéxico: Registro de Nacimiento de la Población México-Americana*. Video, 3:57. Mexico City: SEGOB. https://www .youtube.com/watch?v=V5U300fRd-o.

———. 2017. Unidad de Política Migratoria. Boletínes Estadísticos Anuales. Mexicanos Repatriados 2000–2016. http://www.politicamigratoria.gob.mx/es_mx/SEGOB /Boletines_Estadisticos.

SEP (Mexico, Secretaría de Educación Pública). 2015a. Acuerdo número 07/06/15 por el que se modifica el diverso 286 por el que se establecen los lineamientos que determinan las normas y criterios generales a que se ajustarán la revalidación de estudios realizados en el extranjero. *Diario Oficial de la Federación*, June 15. Mexico City: SEP.

———. 2015b. Normas específicas de control escolar relativas a la inscripción, reinscripción, reinscripción, acreditación, promoción, regularización y certificación en la educación básica. Mexico City: SEP. http://www.sepyc.gob.mx/documen tacion/1.1.3%20NORMAS%20ESPECIFICAS%20DE%20CONTROL%20ESCO LAR%20CICLO%202015-2016.pdf.

Suárez-Orozco, Carola, and Marcelo Suárez-Orozco. 2001. *Children of Immigration*. Cambridge, MA: Harvard University Press.

Vargas, Alethia, and Eduardo Lugo. 2012. "Los que llegan, regresan y se quedan." In *Movilización, migración y retorno de la niñez migrante: Una mirada antropológica*, edited by Gloria Ciria Valdéz Gardea, 13–38. Hermosillo, Mexico: El Colegio de Sonora.

Yoshikawa, Hirokazu. 2011. *Immigrants Raising Citizens: Undocumented Parents and Their Young Children*. New York: Russell Sage Foundation.

Zúñiga, Víctor. 2013. "Migrantes internacionales en las escuelas mexicanas: Desafíos actuales y futuros de política educativa." *Sinéctica* 40:1–11.

Zúñiga, Víctor, and Edmund Hamann. 2006. "Going Home? Schooling in Mexico of Transnational Children." *CONfines* 2 (4): 41–57.

———. 2009. "Sojourners in Mexico with US School Experience: A New Taxonomy for Transnational Students." *Comparative Education Review* 53 (3): 329–353.

———. 2015. "Going to a Home You Have Never Been To: The Return Migration of Mexican and American-Mexican Children." *Children's Geographies* 13 (6): 643–655.

Zúñiga, Víctor, and María Vivas-Romero. 2014. "Divided Families, Fractured Schooling, in Mexico: Educational Consequences of Children Exposition to International Migration." *Cahiers/Cuadernos CEMCA* 6:1–18.

PART III

CANADA

CHAPTER 7

Transnational Labor Solidarity versus State-Managed Coercion: UFCW Canada, Mexico, and the Seasonal Agricultural Workers Program

ANDREA GALVEZ, PABLO GODOY, AND PAUL MEINEMA

The Seasonal Agricultural Workers Program (SAWP) between Mexico and Canada is still considered a model of binational, legal, and orderly migration despite two decades of analyses and reports underlining its fundamental flaws. Specifically, the SAWP restricts labor mobility and imposes precarious migratory status on the workers it covers, creating a second class of citizens consistent with the Canadian agricultural sector's history of allowing "unfree labor" (Pentland 1959).[1] The SAWP's legitimacy stems from its being intertwined in a transnational structure that creates a delimited legal and social space where labor practices evolve under restricted conditions. A fundamental element of the SAWP's success is the generalized perception that the migrant workers in the program are "privileged." They have an opportunity, so it is argued, to escape rural poverty and unemployment and enter the Canadian labor market. As a result of such persuasive framing, it becomes extremely difficult to mobilize public opinion, public officials, and stakeholders to transform and reform the fundamentally flawed program.

Confronted with this reality, migrant workers imagine, create, and share strategies of resistance. Their success in doing so also depends on the resources, support, and visibility of other social actors such as United Food and Commercial Workers Canada (UFCW Canada) that are willing to support the workers' cause. UFCW Canada has worked to expose the program's flaws; present provincial, national, and international legal challenges to modify the juridical conditions that limit workers' freedoms; finance support and legal aid for workers; and run organizing drives (where the law permits) to transform decision-making processes that had been controlled exclusively by employers and governments. As union representatives and activists working for UFCW Canada, we analyze the role of the Mexican government through its Secretariat of Labor and Social Welfare and Secretariat of Foreign Affairs in managing Mexican migrant workers in Canada. UFCW Canada has focused on improving migrant workers' labor and living conditions, promoting equal rights for workers and access to formal institutions. We discuss the logic behind the resistance from employers and state authorities to UFCW Canada's intervention. We document the work that the labor movement, academia, and migrant workers have done to create effective political and legal advocacy platforms, and we examine the limits imposed by the current SAWP framework to renegotiate institutional arrangements. The union has had to develop transnational strategies to overcome the legal, juridical, and political barriers the workers face in exercising their rights; moreover, in developing these strategies, UFCW Canada has itself become a viable transnational actor. The union has advanced the interests of migrant workers, while the response of the Mexican government has been to resist the establishment of a transnational coproduction regime that could guarantee stricter enforcement of labor standards.

The Role of Mexico in a Transnational Regime of Labor Relations Management

The Seasonal Agricultural Workers Program was created in 1966 to respond to the increasing demand for labor in the Canadian agricultural sector. The agreement, signed originally by several Caribbean countries, was extended to Mexico in 1974. Access to the program is reserved to employers in the agricultural sector.[2] Two ministries, Citizenship and Immigration Canada (CIC) and Employment and Social Development Canada (ESDC), simultaneously administer the program. The SAWP agreement, or memorandum of understanding, includes administrative and operational directives and a contract to be signed jointly by the worker and the employer. The operative management in Canada is assured by provincial employers' associations; they are nonprofit organizations run and financed by the employers. To qualify for a temporary work permit under the SAWP, the applicant must be of legal age, satisfy the Canadian immigration security and health requirements, and sign the work contract. The labor contract, Agreement for the Employment in Canada of Seasonal Agricultural Workers from Mexico, establishes general labor and living conditions for SAWP workers (ESCD 2016a). This contract is negotiated every year by the governments of Canada and Mexico as well as by the employers, under the conditions set forth in the memorandum of understanding. Although a representative of the Mexican government signs every individual contract between employer and employee, it nonetheless constitutes a private employer-employee agreement under Canadian law and provincial labor codes.[3]

SAWP workers are recruited in Mexico through the offices of the State

Employment Service under the direction of the General Coordination of the National Employment Service, an agency of the Secretariat of Labor and Social Welfare. The National Employment Service, acting on behalf of the applicant, files for a temporary work visa before the Canadian embassy in Mexico City. If the application is approved, the worker receives authorization to reside temporarily in Canada. The temporary resident visa is linked to the work permit and granted on the condition that the worker live on the employer's property. The temporary permit authorizes the worker to perform agricultural functions solely for the employer designated in the contract. An employee's stay in Canada is permitted only as long as the work relationship is maintained, even though all temporary visas expire on December 15. That is, a worker terminating his employment in September would have to leave before the visa expiration date. The worker can return to Canada the following year as long as "he is named" by the employer. Up to 80 percent of workers are in the "named" category, and the rest of the free slots in the program are assigned by the General Coordination of the National Employment Service. The SAWP gives priority to married men between the ages of eighteen and forty-five from rural areas and with experience as farmworkers.[4] Their families are not allowed to travel with them. Workers are distributed across nine provinces, with higher participant rates in Ontario, Quebec, and British Columbia.

Under this bilateral scheme, the Mexican government assumes the cost of selecting, recruiting, and placing workers. Until 2017, it followed precise indications supplied by the employers, including "the labor profile (experience, required abilities and physical characteristics, among others) as well as the gender of the workers."[5] Mexico is responsible for recruiting and selecting workers, providing labor and migratory paperwork, receiving and processing applications requested by Canadian employers, coordinating and processing medical examinations, providing advisory and support services, and planning and coordinating flight tickets. All SAWP activities done by the Secretariat of Labor and Social Welfare had a cost of more than $2.2 million, 62 percent of the total SAWP budget (Muñoz Carrillo 2011:30). For the same year, Mexican consular services spent more than $790,000, 23 percent of the SAWP's annual budget, for the following activities: "receipt and approval of applications for workers by Canadian employers; inspection of working conditions, housing, payment and treatment provided by employers; management and support to workers before Canadian employers and public and private Canadian institutions due to accidents, death, repatriation or early return, medical coverage, discounts, taxes; mediation and conflict resolution between workers and employers; as well as coordination of return flights to Mexico" (Muñoz Carrillo 2011:30).

Under the SAWP memorandum of understanding, the Canadian government agrees to grant Mexican workers the same rights as Canadian workers. During their stay in Canada, migrant workers are protected from discrimination and assured of their equality before the law by the Canadian Charter of Rights and Freedoms as well as by provincial human rights charters. Still, a closer look at the SAWP employment agreement and the SAWP operative guidelines reveals the outsized role played by Mexican authorities, specifically the government agent who will

> be stationed in Canada to assist in the administration of the program; receive a copy of the rules of conduct, safety and discipline that the worker may be aware of and observe such rules; sign the Employment agreement; approve the accommodation in absence of an appropriate government authority responsible for health and living conditions; recover monies due to the worker in case of absence or death; approve health insurance compensation; receive notification in case of injury of death; receive record of hours worked and wages paid; approve transportation arrangements made by the employer; approve transfers or loans of workers between employers; approve the worker's lieu of residence, approve deductions made from the worker's pay check, provide information regarding fiscal obligations; approve employer's request to prematurely cease the worker's employers; establish the distribution of transportation costs in case of early cessation of employment; rescind the employment agreement in case of breach, access worker's personal information; designate a private insurance company for the worker, assist workers in the filling of official forms and sign the employments agreement. (ESDC 2016a)

The Mexican government argues that this long list of responsibilities represents a public subsidy for the worker and the employer, totaling almost $3.6 million in 2011 (Muñoz Carrillo 2011). The oversight element of the program has been considered one of the best practices in labor migration and a key to the SAWP's success. Analysis of such subsidies allows us to distinguish between, on the one hand, selection, recruitment, and placement costs and, on the other, management, inspection, legal representation, mediation, and conflict resolution costs. While the first set of costs clearly benefits workers and employers, it is less clear how the second set is in the best interests of the employees. The latter costs, primarily related to intervention, might not be that effective (or advantageous to the worker) within a complicated network of migration and labor relations management structures. With this in mind, the Mexican government is not only acting as a private recruiter in its own territory but also developing extraterritorial functions that stretch far beyond ordinary consular representation. The SAWP's level of intervention is more robust than that of another Canadian program aimed at migrant workers, the low-skilled branch of the Temporary Foreign Worker Program (TFWP), which guarantees only consular representation.[6] Muñoz Carrillo (2011:29) notes that workers under the TFWP are hampered by "the lack of control and supervision mechanisms that allow a mutual evaluation about the workers' performance as well as regarding the worthy treatment and working conditions offered by the employers, along with a serious lack of mechanisms of support towards the workers during their stay in Canada as well as conflict resolution between the worker and the employer." The employer suffers from "lack of mediation and conflict resolution." Such activities fall within the scope of provincial Canadian institutions to which workers have de jure access.

On the ground, third-party consular liaison officers, apart from their recruitment and selection roles, are intermediaries between the employer and the employee, acting as a bureaucratic filter between formal Canadian institutions and the worker: "In the event that differences arise between the employer and the TFW [temporary foreign worker], the contract will guide the resolution of disputes. In cases of demonstrable breaches of the employment contract, and where no resolution, including possible compensation, has been made, the TFW, the liaison officer or the employer can contact the Ministry of Labor in the province/territory where the work is being performed" (ESDC 2016b). This third party is legally recognized within the institutional and contractual frame of the SAWP, an official role that significantly changes the traditional employer-employee labor relation scheme.

The memorandum of understanding and the SAWP employment agreement allow for a parallel legal regime of labor relations management. In this regime, the employer is not subject to the standard consequences of breaching labor or living conditions, since the authority in charge of inspecting, approving, and solving work-related conflicts acts outside the legal framework and institutionality that protect domestic workers. The liaison agents responsible for worker protections are classified as worker representatives but also as mediators and arbitrators, which muddies their task. Meanwhile, because these government agents are pressured to maintain or increase their country's participation in the program, they engage in a race to the bottom vis-à-vis worker protections, prioritizing the smooth functioning of the program. In this case, a country's pursuit of its national interests can involve neglecting the interests of its citizens (Verma 2003). Valenzuela (2018:70) explains how Mexico's foreign affairs and labor secretariats "want Canadian farms to keep on asking for Mexican workers, as a way to increase government granted positions through the Program. This is largely possible if some violations to workers' civil and labor rights are allowed." Verma (2003) notes that the kind of competition between countries to remain in the SAWP is indeed welcomed by the Canadian government. To this effect, she cites a brief in which Canadian officials interpret it "as a useful development in the sense that the competition aids Canadian producers in bargaining conditions with the Caribbean authorities."[7]

Apart from the desire to keep the program running smoothly, other factors could lead to slack worker protection. Verma (2003) explains, "The second potential for conflict of interest arises from the state interest that the Government agents represent which is to maintain their respective country's participation in the program, and obtain as many placements as possible in order to maximize the return of remittances." The remittances are not negligible—$38 million in 2010—and have a tremendous impact in the rural, marginalized communities that send the workers through the program (Muñoz Carrillo 2011).

A second and very important element of the SAWP employment agreement is the worker's capacity to benefit from the established labor protection regulations and gain access to legal recourses. The program's conditions and arrangements, established by the Canadian authorities, are based on Canada's immigration regulations. However, these rules also have an impact on labor relations between worker and employer, in overlapping with labor regulations: "The articulation between two distinct bodies of rules, with very different functions and objectives, has a repercussion on the application of role of labor law protection. . . . The labor relation temporary status and the limits placed on labor mobility can have consequences on the capacity to mobilize their labor rights and the efficacy of their legal recourses of employment protection" (Gesualdi-Fecteau 2013:251).

To sum up, we have identified the Mexican government's three main functions within the SAWP: selection and recruitment, representation and arbitration in work-related issues, and acting as a bridge between the worker and Canadian institutions. Under the memorandum of understanding, the Mexican government is the only actor entitled to provide those services to the worker, apparently eliminating the need for competing private and state actors. In the case of representation and arbitration in work-related issues, the liaison agent simultaneously usurps the role of unions and workers' organizations and the role of labor tribunals. As a bridge, the liaison agent alternately acts as a worker advocate and as an institutional representative, not only diminishing the workers' capacity to have their labor standards enforced but also excluding legitimate agents from doing so. Laura López-Sanders (2014) examines the dynamics between brokers and immigrant workers and concludes that the intermediaries' mediation in post-hiring functions affects the balance of power and exacerbates existing inequalities. As embedded brokers, liaison agents can threaten workers, who must comply or risk losing their jobs. Liaison agents cannot be said, therefore, to be fully protecting worker rights.

Simply stated, the Mexican government's intervention in private employer-employee agreements does not benefit the worker. In contrast, the agricultural sector does benefit from the program, fitting with the Canadian policy of actively regulating the agricultural labor market. Following the categories proposed by Manolo Abella (2006), the SAWP simultaneously increases the flexibility of the labor market, brings support structures to a specific industry, increases Canada's competitive edge in agriculture, and minimizes the cost of providing social welfare benefits to an equivalent population of local workers.

In the end, workers enjoy fewer benefits. For example, limited access to Canadian institutions has affected their health and security. Maxim Amar and colleagues (2009) note that access to the Quebec health system is compromised by important linguistic, geographic, and organizational barriers. Without the political will and any compromise from the health administration, the stakeholders' good intentions are not sufficient to guarantee, de facto, the workers' rights to health, integrity, and life.

The Labor Movement Response

The Mexican government has a role in shaping a particular workforce through two functions: migration management and labor relations management. The role of the labor movement and specifically UFCW Canada in organizing migrant workers can be viewed through the lens of the labor movement's relations to the body of norms and rules that apply to this particular workforce and new transnational actors modifying the rules and generating novel organizing possibilities. Within the broader discussion about coproduction we can read the history of the union's involvement with SAWP workers as a progressive development of capacities oriented to enforce labor standards. These standards have failed to achieve their potential due to the systematic refusal of state authorities to recognize the union's relevancy in a national and transnational labor regulation regime. Coproduction,[8] or co-enforcement,[9] is particularly relevant to SAWP regulations. Workers in the program face such traditional labor enforcement challenges as agricultural exceptionalism, lack of resources to guarantee inspections, poor legislation, and geographical limitations, along with institutional, legal, and cultural barriers that prevent them from enjoying their full labor rights (Carpentier and Fiset 2011).

From a broader perspective, the SAWP and its peculiar labor relations management structure are entwined in a long-standing Canadian tradition of agricultural exceptionalism, defined as the sum of legal instruments designed to exclude the agricultural sector from legislation regarding social protection, labor law, and access to health and safety (McWilliams 1999). Indeed, the development of temporary foreign worker programs since the end of the nineteenth century represents a larger strategy of labor market state regulation geared toward recruiting and retaining a workforce in such a way as to benefit the agricultural sector. This strategy gives rise to "unfree labor" (Pentland 1959). The inability of workers to negotiate working conditions and the obligation to work for a single employer are the products of extra-economic state coercion. Victor Satzewich (1989:90) finds that these arrangements imply "an explicit recognition that the operation of market mechanisms for the allocation and distribution of labor power are ineffectual." Kerry Preibisch notes that under this particular arrangement, "the State, private intermediaries and the employers collude in the discipline of migrant labor" (2011:76). We can interpret the formation of migrant workers' organizations as attempts to break free from a discipline that has transnational expressions, origins, and consequences.

Organized labor has historically achieved only temporary successes in organizing migrant farmworkers, mainly because of farm employers' resistance, the mobilization of rural residents and local enforcement agencies to counter union activities, and the slow response of federal and state administrations in extending labor protections to agriculture (Kahmann 2002). In the SAWP, the migratory status of the farmworkers and the precariousness of their employment increase the risks and costs of organizing. In response, UFCW Canada has focused its activities since the mid-1990s on modifying the political, economic, and social arrangements made between states, capital, and society that determine workers' access to fundamental rights. The union's scope is thus wide; it attempts to reduce workers' economic and other costs to entering the Canadian labor force while increasing their benefits, activities that go well beyond securing contracts or signed union cards. Meanwhile, the state resists workers' organizing efforts to improve their labor conditions. Preibisch (2011) describes the role of the government in weakening workers' power and negotiating position. UFCW Canada, in turn, resists by trying to correct imbalances in the SAWP's production policies and developing expertise to better enforce labor standards in the transnational coproduction regime.

UFCW Canada's role in promoting all temporary foreign workers' rights — not exclusively those of farmworkers — must be read within the context of a profound shift in the Canadian workforce that poses challenges that have not been addressed yet by Canadian regulatory labor bodies. While the agriculture-focused SAWP has been around for more than forty years, the immigration reform of 2002 made radical changes to Canadian immigration, with important consequences for the labor market. In 2005 the top five occupations brought into Canada under the Temporary Foreign Worker Program were musicians and singers, actors and comedians, film producers and directors, other technical occupations in motion pictures, and specialist physicians. By 2008 the mix had changed significantly. At the top of the list were food-counter attendants, kitchen helpers, and cooks; construction tradesmen and laborers; janitorial workers; and musicians and singers. The number of new arrivals changed as well. In 2007 Canada gained more temporary foreign workers than new permanent residents for the first time in its history (Nakache 2010). UFCW Canada has become ubiquitous, with members present in every sector of the food industry, including in the fields, processing plants, warehouses, stores, and restaurants but also in retail, health care, hospitality, security, financial services, and nonfood manufacturing. The early, effective organizing of TFWs in these sectors represents the best and most progressive way of securing decent wages and working conditions for both domestic and foreign workers. Canadian demographics, politics, and policies are shaping this new workforce, and the wisest position the labor movement can adopt is to integrate them into its global organization strategy. Agricultural workers' organizing efforts have provided the union with precious experience, institutional knowledge, and hard-learned lessons on national and transnational mobilization that could later be integrated in a broader supply-chain campaign.

Since 2002 UFCW Canada has provided free and anonymous services to migrant farmworkers in Canada through a network of ten support centers run in collaboration with the Agricultural Workers Alliance. The services are not conditioned on union membership since labor laws in most provinces deny agricultural workers the right to form a union. For more than fifteen years the centers have assisted workers in need of immediate assistance with work-related conflicts, occupational injuries, health concerns, and bureaucratic procedures. They are located in the heart of rural areas with high concentrations of migrants, and their hours are tailored to workers' schedules. The support centers have filled a void left by Canadian institutions and Mexican consular staff; they provide legal and other resources that were previously denied or unknown to workers. Tanya Basok (2003) points out that workers are denied the protections granted by Canadian society but also the knowledge required to exercise the juridical rights. The primary function of the support centers is to facilitate access to this knowledge, that is, to become a bridge between Canadian institutions and the worker. Here, the mediator/representative conflict of interest that defines the government agent's role is absent. On the contrary, support centers are a means to achieve trust and stable relations between the workers and the union, so it is paramount that the centers deliver diverse, excellent, and useful services.

As a result, workers tend to have favorable views of the centers and trust that the union is helping them when the Canadian and Mexican governments refuse to do so (Valarezo 2007). By providing the services outside the regulatory framework of the SAWP, the union is actively diminishing the program's harmful impacts and effectively reducing the economic and noneconomic costs of migration for workers. Faced with a lack of citizenship and representation, workers view social and workers' organizations as means to overcome the institutional barriers that prevent them from fully exercising their rights. In the process, crucial, urgent networks are created that allow for more information and experiences to be shared among workers. Yet such potentially transformative organizing and educational power could be harnessed only because workers first approached the centers with concrete demands. Providing safe and resourceful spaces for workers allowed the Agricultural Workers Alliance to reach a membership of more than 13,000 less than ten years after its founding in 2007, making it the biggest farmworker union in North America. Through the support center model, the union and the alliance had a direct impact on labor standards enforcement. They developed capacities that, Matthew Amengual and Janice Fine (2016:7) note, "could only be partially substituted by the state and only at a very high cost." These crucial, on-the-ground resources have been systematically ignored by federal authorities, although some provincial institutions have developed occasional partnerships with the AWA and UFCW support centers. In 2012 the Quebec Labor Standards Board granted a settlement of 250,000 Canadian dollars to Guatemalan workers for a collective complaint filed in 2009 by forty workers at Agricultural Workers Alliance center. That action forced employers across Quebec to immediately lower what they charged for housing to migrant workers to the provincial maximum rate, saving the workers hundreds of thousands of dollars in the years since. Although provincial legal assistance was free, it was possible to make the complaint only because the alliance's staff provided brochures, education on the labor code, and assistance translating and filing the complaints while reassuring the workers of confidentiality and anonymity in the process.

While the outreach and support center services focus on providing immediate relief and access to rights for workers under the SAWP system, UFCW Canada has invested resources in bringing the plight of migrant workers to public scrutiny, as the arrangements between Canada and employers for temporary foreign workers are possible only when such a parallel legal regime is legitimated by society. Canadian immigration policy has evolved to incorporate legal regimes tailored to certain groups of workers. These discriminatory legal regimes differentiate between those considered "more foreign" from those protected fully by the state (Glenn 1998). In this case, protections are curtailed for migrant farmworkers because they are foreign and have temporary employment. By demonstrating that the SAWP depends on controlling a flexible workforce, UFCW Canada can deconstruct the criteria used to justify discrimination. Working to uncover the origins and dynamics of temporary foreign worker programs increases the political cost of such arrangements and paves the way for making stronger, fairer, and more formal arrangements that eliminate the need for temporary fixes. While Canadian academia pointed to structural flaws of the SAWP long before the union got involved, the legal challenges, reports, and support centers garnered important media coverage and progressively convinced people that this was not, as authorities pretended, a "win-win" situation.

Local UFCW union members across Canada have shown solidarity, particularly those that represent both migrant and domestic workers. They have resisted the efforts of employers to pit one group against the other. In 2007 a greenhouse employer tried to get the Quebecer workers to vote to exclude migrant workers from the bargaining unit in exchange for a raise. The union staff asked its members, "If there is a group of workers that are paid less and have no protection, who do you think will be fired next year?" The members quickly voted decisively in favor of the migrants. While the migrant worker exclusion clause could have been challenged and defeated in the provincial courts because of its unconstitutionality, the legal costs were saved and hostility between the workers avoided. The same solidarity logic has been applied in union discourse about temporary foreign worker programs. Beyond concerns for social justice and equality, unions argue, the Canadian workforce is directly affected by the deterioration of wages and treatment made possible by the asymmetry of global economies and labor markets.

Labor costs also include compliance with social standards. While enforcement regarding minimal standards, health and safety, and housing regulations is very lax within the program, UFCW Canada's efforts have shown that employers do react to private, societal supervision and the fear of bad press. In the summer of 2007 René Mantha, director of the Quebec Fondation des entreprises en recrutement de main-d'œuvre agricole étrangère (FERME, Employers' Recruiting Migrant Workers Foundation), sent an internal letter to its affiliates urging them to respect minimum labor standards because, as he put it, "the summer has started, the union is around and young untrained journalists are looking for a hot topic to cover."[10]

While the exclusion of migrant workers and the discriminatory conditions they endure are socially legitimated, the legal framework constructed around the program—the memorandum of understanding, employment agreement, and immigration and labor regulations—normalizes its exploitative nature (Irving 1990). As a result, since the late 1990s UFCW Canada has invested significant resources in promoting stronger labor, health, safety, and social protections and fairer migratory regulations.[11] In the process, it has secured health and safety coverage and training for both domestic and migrant farmworkers in Ontario; the right for farmworkers in Ontario and Quebec to unionize before the courts, though this was later revoked by the government; a rent reduction in collective contracts for Guatemalan farmworkers after the Agricultural Workers Alliance filed a human rights complaint; compensation for unfair dismissal and unjust repatriation of workers; and increased responsiveness from various provincial labor boards to provide better information to migrant workers. These actions to redress exploitation have not always been welcomed by the Canadian government, which has increasingly stepped forward to defend and maintain discriminatory conditions by overturning progressive legal decisions through executive actions and legislative processes.

The legal challenges presented by UFCW Canada have consistently been based on Article 15(1) of the Charter of Rights and Freedoms, which guarantees that everyone enjoys equal protections and benefits under the law without discrimination, and on provincial human rights charters. Time and time again, however, the federal and provincial governments have resisted implementing court-mandated changes by citing national interests, expressed as the power to interfere in the agricultural sector to protect its competitive advantage.

Migrant farmworkers are even less visible in the parliamentary system, where they lack electoral representation. This injustice could and should be eliminated through granting permanent residency for SAWP workers; in the meantime, UFCW Canada has insisted on representing them to negotiate living and working conditions at annual meetings of Canada, Mexico, and the employers. Beginning in 2006, UFCW Canada has secured contracts in Manitoba, Quebec, Alberta, and British Columbia that fixed the SAWP's fundamental flaws surrounding the inherent deportability of the recruited workers, a condition studied by Mezzadra and Neilson (2013:146): "The migrant is a deportable subject, whose position in both the polity and the labor market is marked by and negotiated through the condition of deportability, even if actual removal is a distant possibility or the fact." Collective agreements for temporary migrant workers negotiated by UFCW Canada are intended to diminish the impact of skewed labor relations by offering a broader and fairer regulatory scheme that eliminates elements of precariousness. One such element is the SAWP employer's prerogative to terminate employment at any time. The collective agreements negotiated by the union give workers seniority rights and assurances that while the job might be seasonal, the work relationship is longer-lasting. A second element of precariousness is the lack of resources available to the worker in labor disputes. The collective agreements establish expedited, neutral arbitrations, paid for by the employer and the union, that give workers access to formal labor protection mechanisms. The agreements ensure that the costs of accessing these mechanisms will not skyrocket if the worker returns to his community without an official resolution, and they increase workers' wages so their union dues will not affect their living conditions.

More broadly, in the fight to minimize precariousness, UFCW Canada has entered into transnational discussions with migrant workers, local actors, organizations, and other nonfederal Mexican authorities. Starting in 2006, the union began developing a presence in Mexico's legislative spaces to voice migrant workers' concerns and mobilize support, increasing the transparency and accountability of the program. At the same time, as a way to overcome systematic resistance from the federal government, UFCW Canada developed collaborative and cooperative agreements with local governments by reaching out to representatives in Mexico City and the states of Guerrero, Michoacán, Oaxaca, and Tlaxcala. The union has provided local functionaries with information about workers' benefits and rights so they would transmit it effectively to the workers themselves. The union's local authority strategy has multiplied the number of actors involved in the process and made access to information easier for workers in communities of origin. Moreover, the union's presence in Mexico has allowed for networking and collaborating with migrant rights and labor rights organizations, many of them critics of temporary worker programs in Central America, Mexico, and the United States. As a result of allying with progressive critics, the union can have more direct input to policy proposals and in discussions with Mexican civil society over how to improve this "model of managed migration" (STPS 2015). Finally, the local approach has allowed the union to reach out to distant communities and mobilize workers who are no longer participants of the SAWP to add their voices to collective complaints such as those centered on gender discrimination.

Hitting a Wall: Transnational State-Led Resistance to Union Organizing

Farm-by-farm certification has a direct impact on wages and living conditions in each bargaining unit, but such a painstaking regulatory approach is not a viable means to address the SAWP's structural flaws. That is why the union steps in. While states are rightly investing resources in diminishing migration costs for employers and workers, the only long-term investment to secure a balanced labor relations management scheme has been made by the union. The government's agent cannot and should not be interfering in this particular dimension, but very close attention should be paid to the practices developed by UFCW Canada since the mid-2000s and the serious, measurable impact they have had on the lives of SAWP participants, unionized or not. Through its legal challenges, outreach, services, and campaigns, UFCW Canada has diminished the costs of access to rights and social justice for thousands of migrant workers, thereby strengthening and improving the program despite institutional resistance from employers and authorities in both countries. The states have justified their resistance, including refusal to grant permissions to join unions, and their reluctance to divulge information about their negotiations by citing national interests. Asked to provide every communication between Mexican and Canadian authorities as well as employers regarding union activities under the SAWP, Mexico's Secretariat of Foreign Affairs demurred, requesting that the information be declared reserved and confidential: "Bringing to light the requested documents would generate a present, probable, and specific damage to the bilateral relation between Mexico and Canada and would undermine the mutual trust principle that rules the relation. The distribution of the located documents without the opinion of the government of Canada would provoke a negative reaction from such government to the dialogue sustained between both countries around this and other issues."[12] The requested and eventually disclosed documents included a SAWP meeting proposal regarding the "legal implications of unionization in the agricultural sector" as well as a two-page email between the Canadian Ministry of Employment and Skills Development and the Mexican embassy that was completely blacked out.

We have examined the role of the Mexican authorities in migration management and labor relations management only as they concern the SAWP's legality. However, beginning in 2006, UFCW Canada has documented systematic anti-union activities by Mexican authorities in Manitoba, Quebec, and British Columbia.[13] Supporting workers' exercise of their right to unionize in Canada goes beyond the roles of Mexico's foreign relations or labor offices; organized workers and the union were asking only for a neutral position that would not require Mexico to make a positive intervention in a foreign state with considerably limited resources to uphold freedom of association. When we consider Mexico's anti-union activities in light of Verma's "race to the bottom" framework, we can say that the Mexican government actually deployed human and political resources to infringe on the workers' right and to ensure the smooth functioning of the program. As an example, consular staff used the Mexican internal data system, Sistema de Información de Movilidad Laboral (SIMOL, Labor Mobility Information System), to inform labor officials that active union supporters were to be blacklisted. Actively imposing restrictions on the workers' right to organize in effect reduces the employers' compliance costs. We find, therefore, a third role for the Mexican government in the scheme—as a scab. It acts as such only after workers mobilize outside the realm of migratory and labor constrictions imposed by the SAWP and access the body of norms usually accessible to all other workers. The conditions provided by the union, or more exactly, the access to these protections and institutions rendered possible by a lowering of its costs provoke a reaction from the Mexican state, which fights to bring the workers back under the control of the employer and the Canadian and Mexican governments under this parallel regime.

Mexican public officials' anti-union activities thus represent a transnational interference to which workers have little power to respond. After all, the Mexican government can blacklist them from the program, authorize their repatriation, or place them under constant surveillance. Leah Vosko (2015:1372) argues that the blacklisting functions "as a modality of deportability among temporary migrant workers" in which the sending state plays an obscure but central role. Vosko reviews UFCW Local 1518's legal battle to hold employers and Mexican officials accountable for anti-union activities during its organizing drives in British Columbia. At the time, the British Columbia Labor Relations Board concluded that Mexican consular officials in Vancouver threatened workers with blacklisting for any union involvement and worked with Mexico's Secretariat of Labor and Social Welfare to prevent union supporters or those perceived to be union supporters from returning to Canada. Although Mexico could not be formally tried because of its sovereign immunity, the findings allowed the board to cite improper interference in the organizing process and dismiss a union decertification vote request.[14] Although Mexico suffered no legal consequences for its interference, it definitely paid a political cost, as revelations that Mexican officials had forged documents to conceal their improper interference tarnished the government's reputation. Vosko (2015:1377) stresses that the decision denouncing Mexico's interference while at the same time granting state immunity "meant that Mexican officials could continue to blacklist with impunity under the SAWP [and] demonstrated the utility of workers' deportability in supporting the sending state's strong incentive, at odds with upholding labour rights among its own nationals, to appease host state employers to safeguard its stature in this model program."

The clash between UFCW Canada's efforts to diminish migration and labor costs and the sending country's interference is not specific to the Mexican case. Another example shows how this dynamic hurts the worker. In a 2010 letter to the Guatemalan ambassador in Canada, the Guatemalan consul general in Montreal pushed for workers' housing fees to be *increased*:

> The system [allowing employers to overcharge rent despite provincial regulations] had worked very well and had indubitably contributed to the success of the Guatemalan program since, depending on the contract period, an employer with Guatemalan workers could recover through housing fees an amount higher than his initial investment (transportation fees, housing arrangements). If at the *individual level* the Guatemalan was disadvantaged vis-à-vis the Mexican worker (earning at most 45 [Canadian dollars] less than a Mexican), the system granted us *a tangible competitive advantage* illustrated by the fact that in 2009, more Guatemalans than Mexicans travelled for the first time. . . . In 2009, the Union [UFCW Canada], on behalf of Guatemalan workers, presented a complaint before the Human Rights Commission denouncing the practice, according to them discriminatory, of charging rent to Guatemalans when Mexicans were exempted. However, this law . . . can also be considered discriminatory as its hinders Guatemalans' *competitiveness* in the labor market in relation to the Mexican workers.[15] (Emphasis added)

As with the former example, the consular staff framed its stance as being in the "best interest" of its nationals in collective terms; that is, by granting Guatemalans a competitive advantage, it would secure the highest possible number of positions. UFCW Canada's intervention to diminish costs for the workers or extend legislation protection provisions to them are thus read as a frontal attack on this competitive advantage. That explains why Mexican consular reports merely admonish farms where workers have been physically and verbally abused and those that have conducted unauthorized repatriations and transfers and committed labor and housing legislation violations.[16] The violations, were they to be dealt with through formal complaint mechanisms, would translate to higher operating costs for the employers, the consulate, and the program but would definitely improve the individual situation of each worker and send a strong message to employers to improve their practices. Still, diminishing employer costs remains the top priority, leading various actors with diplomatic immunity to coerce workers or allow employers to outsource illegal hiring practices.

Another example of the SAWP's lack of compliance with provincial, national, and international law is the gender discrimination bias that has plagued the program since its origins. Statistics confirm that women represented less than 3 percent of the total participants in 2012, while Canadian women's participation in the agricultural sector hovered around 28 percent. Provincial labor codes and legislation on discrimination clearly prohibit gender-based discrimination in recruiting and placing workers, but the

SAWP mechanism has allowed employers to outsource this illegal discriminatory practice to the Mexican government:

> Canadian employers DO have the choice to hire men or women for positions that are not occupied by workers named by the employer. The Seasonal Agricultural Workers Program Mexico-Canada (SAWP) is a labor coordination program that depends entirely on the request for the agricultural workforce by Canadian employers, which is why the only entities that define the labor profile (experience, required skills, physical characteristics, among others) as well as the sex of the workers are the Canadian employers themselves.[17]

Attempts have been made to rectify the situation, but complaints filed against employers before provincial human rights tribunals have not yet ended the practice. The complaint filed by UFCW Canada against the Mexican Secretariat of Labor and Social Welfare before the Consejo Nacional para Prevenir la Discriminación (CONAPRED 2014) underwent a mediation process, with sides agreeing that progressive steps were to be taken to completely eliminate gender discrimination by 2021. While the authorities declared to have eliminated discriminatory hiring criteria including gender, civil status, and age, women's participation in the program has not increased. In a simultaneous process, the National Administrative Office of Mexico, under the North American Agreement on Labor Cooperation, accepted UFCW Canada's complaint against the Canadian government in August 2016 (ACLAN 2016). The labor movement has once again relied on transnational legal instruments to combat the SAWP's opacity and lack of democratic mechanisms.

Other illegal hiring procedures include easily dismissing older or sick workers through nonrenewal contract clauses. Mexico's labor secretariat blatantly ignores the practice of some Canadian provinces to grant continuous service protection to seasonal workers after a certain number of years, which forces their employers to renew yearly contracts except for just and sufficient cause. Instead, workers under the SAWP are simply informed that their contracts were not renewed, and then they are replaced by younger, stronger job candidates. Once again, López-Sanders's (2014) description of brokers' functions applies to our case: the Mexican government, as an external broker, shields employers from the legal risks of hiring.

Conclusion

Labor mobility systems not only channel workforces from one region or sector to another; they themselves constitute structures that distribute economic, social, and political costs among employers, intermediaries, and workers at the micro level and between states and communities at the macro level. The institutional design of each system includes political and sociological premises that have direct impacts on the asymmetry of such distribution. The Seasonal Agricultural Workers Program has been held up as a model of managed migration because it clearly diminishes the economic costs of migration for employers and workers alike, eliminating expensive or fraudulent intermediaries and providing juridical certainty to its participants. However, this rosy analysis has failed to encompass a broader view of how the reduction of other costs, mainly those associated with the management, control, and surveillance of workers, is fundamental to the program's success and adversely affects workers and their communities of origin. The SAWP allows Canadian employers to outsource the significant legal and economic costs of labor relations to Mexican authorities that recruit, manage, and control the Mexican migrant workforce. At the same time, Canadian federal and provincial governments outsource costs associated with social protection and access to health and justice to Mexico, where families and communities assume the burden. This particular arrangement limits workers' access to justice, health care, and social protections and is the result of carefully designed policies advantageous for the governments and the employers.

The UN Department of Economic and Social Affairs (DESA 2013) states, "Seasonal agricultural workers programs illustrate how the search for labor market flexibility is made compatible with the objective of avoiding settlement of unskilled workers through a combination of measures attaching different limitations and conditions for admissions. The most common elements are quotas, age ceiling, the specification of qualified countries of origin, the obligation to leave after the agricultural season is over, and the denial of rights to family reunification." The main idea is that while state-managed migration has enormous advantages compared to privately managed migration, proper mechanisms of democratization, representation, and verification by the labor movement or workers' organizations must be included to guarantee a more symmetric distribution of migration costs.

A new model of coproduction that can address the transnational challenges of labor enforcement for migrant workers is feasible. However, it will require bringing expert stakeholders and every available resource, including political will, to the table to construct a stronger, healthier program through collaborative governance (Ansell and Gash 2008). UFCW Canada's efforts to enforce labor standards have been hampered by the institutional resistance of Canadian and Mexican authorities to developing a partnership and allowing the union to complement government enforcement capacity. Amengual and Fine (2016) argue that to understand the potential of co-enforcement (or coproduction of enforcement), it is necessary to recognize the irreplaceable capabilities of government and society as well as the need to cultivate political support for partnerships; the mere presence of capable societal organizations does not mean they will be mobilized for enforcement. This challenge may require high-road firms that could help impose the union's presence on labor management arrangements.

While the SAWP's economic benefits for migrant workers and Canadian communities are evident, we should consider what kind of society Canada is designing through its temporary foreign worker programs. The productivity of temporary agricultural workers has guaranteed Canada's increasing competitiveness in the regional market without occasioning a proper redistribution of its benefits. After more than forty years, Canada needs a new model that will grant migrant workers rights that are already recognized in international and national instruments: decent working conditions; legal representation; freedom of association and collective bargaining; social benefits portability; and health, social inclusion, and development. Extending the analysis of the SAWP beyond migratory policy to the dimension of labor management policy allows us to properly discern UFCW Canada's role in balancing the power relations between worker and employer while actively designing practices that overcome the limits imposed by the program. By recognizing the systematic failure of the Canadian and Mexican governments to protect the fundamental rights of SAWP workers, UFCW Canada's unique contribution to labor standards enforcement within the program becomes clear, as does the necessity of granting the union or the workers a seat at the negotiating table.

Finally, the Canadian government imposes a perverse dynamic under which any union attempt to bring workers out of the normative body of the SAWP and into the legal, formal channels of protection encounters a strong reaction from the country of origin. In denying migrant workers full citizenship rights and real protections, Canada delegates its responsibilities to third parties that cannot effectively protect the workers' national rights without jeopardizing their employability. In that sense, Mexico's position against UFCW Canada is predictable and almost understandable, while Canada's tacit or explicit encouragement of the situation can be explained only by the deliberate decision to favor one industry at the expense of noncitizens' rights. One must not forget that the same Mexican institutions—the Secretariat of Labor and Secretariat of Foreign Affairs—that fight unions in the program have a more labor-friendly role in the United States, where they share resources and activities with many local unions, including the UFCW's. Thus, the anti-union stance responds to very specific dynamics imposed by the SAWP and not to an institutional position; by not having to be a broker to US employers, consular authorities can effectively participate in labor standards enforcement by recognizing, collaborating with, and effectively exploiting the power of workers organizations. Alexandra Délano Alonso, in chapter 11 of this volume, notes that Mexican consulates in the United States have established partnerships and shared resources with labor unions to allow them to reach new populations and extend services including labor protections as means for workers to gain full access to civic, social, economic, and political rights. Promisingly, the American UFCW launched Labor Rights Week in collaboration with the Instituto de los Mexicanos en el Exterior, and the Mexican consular staff has supported some UFCW organizing drives in the United States, achieving real coordination between labor union leaders and the Mexican consulate (Bada and Gleeson 2015).

Notes

1. Clare Pentland has defined "unfree labor" as "relations of production in which labor power is acquired and retained through the use of extra-economic coercion, or in which labor is constituted as part of the private property of another" (1959, xxiii).

2. The agricultural sector includes apiary products, fruits, vegetables (as well as the canning or processing of these products if grown on the farms), mushrooms, flowers, nursery-grown trees including Christmas trees, greenhouses and nurseries, pedigreed canola seed, sod, tobacco, cattle, dairy products, ducks, horses, minks, poultry, sheep, and swine.

3. The standard contract includes the following provisions: the established wage must correspond to the highest of either the provincial minimum wage, the wage established by ESDC, or the wage paid to Canadians for the same work; the period of employment lasts from a minimum of six weeks to a maximum of eight months, during which the worker has the guarantee of working a minimum of 240 hours within a period of six weeks or less; the employer provides free housing—in some provinces, an administrative fee is charged in lieu of housing—and makes sure workers are enrolled in private health insurance programs that will complete or substitute for the provincial public system; in case of work-related accident or illness, the worker is protected by the provincial health and safety boards, entirely financed by the employer; the employer and the worker equally share the cost of the air transport between Mexico and Canada.

4. The signature of a conciliation agreement between UFCW Canada and the Mexico Department of Labor and Social Welfare resulted in the elimination of gender, age, and civil status requirements in the SAWP. This measure has not yet had a direct impact on the profile of the SAWP workforce.

5. Answer of the General Coordination of the National Employment Service to access to information request no. 1001400028012.

6. The TFWP was designed to bring in highly skilled workers for temporary contracts and for the same reason had very low regulations. In 2002, however, the Canadian labor market faced a real shortage, and the Liberal government opened the TFWP for industries needing lower-skilled workers such as the agricultural sector. The reform in the TFWP was done without adjusting regulations to those sectors' dirty, dangerous, and difficult conditions. When Guatemalan agricultural workers arrived in Que-

bec under the agricultural branch of the TFWP, Mexican workers and authorities feared that Guatemala would eventually displace Mexico as the main country of origin, as employers benefited from lower costs under the TFWP. Despite the initially rapid growth of Guatemala's participation, both programs have managed to peacefully coexist since 2000. Guatemalan-Canadian relations under the TFWP could not be more different than Mexican-Canadian relations under the SAWP. The latter are based on bilateral agreements and a combination of public and private stakeholders, while the former are based solely on the participation of private employers and recruiters operating with no coordination between the states involved. The trend of hiring Guatemalan farmworkers under the low-skilled TFWP has challenged the SAWP model by offering employers even less regulation, although it does come at a cost: all recruitment operations are, ostensibly, financed by the employers themselves.

7. Verma quotes a September 20, 1974, confidential brief for a meeting on September 23 between External Affairs and the acting director of Manpower and Immigration on expansion of the Caribbean Seasonal Workers Program; National Archives of Canada, RG 118, vol. 81, accession 85–86/071, file 3315-5-1, part 8, p. 4.

8. Elinor Ostrom (1996) defines "coproduction" as the process through which inputs used to produce a good or service are contributed by individuals who are not "in" the same organization.

9. Amengual and Fine (2016) define "co-enforcement" as the ongoing, coordinated efforts of state regulators and worker organizations to jointly produce labor standards enforcement.

10. René Mantha, general director of FERME, evidence presented in QC LRB 2010. Details on court and labor board decisions are listed in the References section "Legal Decisions and Cases."

11. Cases include the following: MB LB 2007; ON HRT 2015; ON SC 2003, 2005, 2013; QC CLP 2009; QC LRB 2010; SCC 2001, 2011.

12. Ministry of Foreign Relations, answer to IFAI request 000500071014, June 30, 2014.

13. Undue interference by Mexican consular officials was documented before labor tribunals in Manitoba (MB LB 2007), Quebec (QC LRB 2006), and British Columbia (BCCA 2015; BCLRB 2012).

14. In BCCA 2015, Mexico was asking for all evidence related to its anti-union actions to be suppressed, but it was unsuccessful. The court upheld Mexico's sovereign immunity while considering that its actions could be used to understand whether the decertification vote was influenced. In BCLRB 2012a, Mexico argued successfully that as a sovereign state, it was immune from the proceedings of a Canadian-based labor board. In BCLRB 2012b, former employees of the Mexican consulate in Vancouver declared that Mexican authorities saw anti-unionism as a way to protect Mexico's position in the SAWP. In BCLRB 2014, the tribunal concluded that Mexican officials colluded with the employer to block visa reapplications of union members and therefore participated in improper interference in a decertification process.

15. Letter from general consul of Guatemala in Montreal Federico Urruela Arenales to Haroldo Rodas, Guatemalan ambassador in Ottawa. Note N15-CG-007-2010. After UFCW Canada presented a complaint regarding the illegality of the pay disparity in the temporary foreign worker programs under provincial legislation, the Quebec Labor Standards Commission forced employers to stop the practice and reimburse undue deductions. The letter from Urruela to Rodas calls for mobilizing Guatemalan re-

sources to support employers' request to modify the legislation and raise the housing fee limitation.

16. Mexican Secretariat of Foreign Relations response to access to information request folio 0000500014214, communication PME 111852, between the Mexican consulate in Vancouver and the Dirección General de Protección a Mexicanos en el Exterior regarding actions taken against farms that violated the conditions of the program.

17. Mexican Secretariat of Labor and Social Welfare response to access to information request 1001400028012, regarding whether Canadian employers had the ability to choose the gender of their potential, unnamed workers.

References

Books, Articles, and Reports

Abella, Manolo. 2006. "Policies and Best Practices for Management of Temporary Migration." Paper presented at the United Nations International Symposium on International Migration and Development, Turin, June 9. http://www.un.org/esa/popu lation/migration/turin/Symposium_Turin_files/P03_SYMP_Abella.pdf.

Amar, Maxim, Geneviève Roberge, Andrée Larue, Lucie Gélineau, and Yvan Leanza. 2009. *Rapport de recherche évaluation: Les travailleurs agricoles migrants mexicains et guatémaltèques de l'Île d'Orléans. Portrait des besoins de santé, de l'accessibilité et des trajectoires d'utilisation des services de santé*. Montreal: Centre de santé et services sociaux et centre affilié universitaire. http://www.csssvc.qc.ca/telechargement.php ?id=655.

Amengual, Matthew, and Janice Fine. 2016. "Co-Enforcing Labor Standards: The Unique Contributions of State and Worker Organizations in Argentina and the United States." *Regulation and Governance* (January). http//:doi.org/10.1111/rego.12122.

Ansell, Chris, and Allison Gash. 2008. "Collaborative Governance in Theory and Practice." *Journal of Public Administration Research and Theory* 18 (4): 543–571.

Bada, Xóchitl, and Shannon Gleeson. 2015. "A New Approach to Migrant Labor Rights Enforcement: The Crisis of Undocumented Worker Abuse and Mexican Consular Advocacy in the United States." *Labor Studies Journal* 40 (1): 32–53.

Basok, Tanya. 2003. "Human Rights and Citizenship: The Case of Mexican Migrants in Canada." Working paper 72, Center for Comparative Immigration Studies, University of California, San Diego.

Carpentier, Marie. 2003. "L'applicabilité de la Charte des droits et libertés de la personne aux travailleurs migrants." Montreal: Commission des droits de la personne et des droits de la jeunesse.

Carpentier, Marie, and Carole Fiset. 2011. "La discrimination systémique à l'égard des travailleuses et travailleurs migrants." Montreal: Commission des droits de la personne et des droits de la jeunesse.

DESA (UN Department of Economic and Social Affairs). 2013. International Migration Policies. Government Views and Priorities. ST/ESA/SER.A/342. New York: DESA Population Division. http://www.un.org/en/development/desa/population/publi cations/pdf/policy/InternationalMigrationPolicies2013/Report%20PDFs/z _International%20Migration%20Policies%20Full%20Report.pdf.

ESDC (Employment and Social Development Canada). 2016a. *Agreement for the Employ-*

ment in Canada of Seasonal Agricultural Workers from Mexico. Ottawa: ESDC. http://www.esdc.gc.ca/en/foreign_workers/hire/seasonal_agricultural/documents/mexico.page.

———. 2016b. "Hire a Temporary Worker through the Seasonal Agricultural Worker Program: Program Requirements." Ottawa: ESDC. http://www.esdc.gc.ca/en/foreign_workers/hire/seasonal_agricultural/requirements.page.

Gesualdi-Fecteau, Dalia. 2013. "Les droits au travail des travailleurs étrangers temporaires 'peu spécialisés': (petit) voyage à l'interface du droit du travail et du droit de l'immigration." In proceedings of the 20th Conference des juristes de l'État, "Redéfinir la gouvernance publique." Cowansville, Canada: Editions Yvon Blais. http://www.conferencedesjuristes.gouv.qc.ca/files/documents/4d/52/dalia-gesualdi-fecteau.pdf.

Glenn, H. Patrick. 1998. "L'étranger et les groupements d'État." *McGill Law Journal* 43 (4): 165–180.

Irving, Andre. 1990. "The Genesis and Persistence of the Commonwealth Caribbean Seasonal Agricultural Workers Program in Canada." *Osgoode Hall Law Journal* 28 (2): 243–301.

Kahmann, Marcus. 2002. *Trade Unions and Migrant Workers: Examples from the United States, South Africa, and Spain*. Brussels: European Trade Union Institution. http://library.fes.de/pdf-files/gurn/00316.pdf.

López-Sanders, Laura. 2014. "Embedded and External Brokers." *American Behavioral Scientist* 58 (2):331–346.

McWilliams, Carey. 1999. *California: The Great Exception*. Berkeley: University of California Press.

Mezzadra, Sandro, and Brett Neilson. 2013. *Border as Method, or, the Multiplication of Labor*. Durham, NC: Duke University Press.

Muñoz Carrillo, Luis Manuel. 2011. "Programa de Trabajadores Agrícolas Temporales México-Canadá: Costos y beneficios." Washington, DC: George Washington University. http://www.gwu.edu/~ibi/minerva/Spring2011/Luis_Munoz_Spanish_version.pdf.

Nakache, Delphine. 2010. "The Canadian Temporary Foreign Worker Program: Regulations, Practices, and Protection Gaps." Presented at the workshop "Producing and Negotiating Precarious Migratory Status in Canada," Research Alliance on Precarious Status, York University, Toronto, September 16.

Ostrom, Elinor. 1996. "Crossing the Great Divide: Coproduction, Synergy, and Development." *World Development* 24 (6): 1073–1087.

Pentland, Clare. 1959. "The Development of a Capitalist Labor Market in Canada." *Canadian Journal of Economics and Political Science* 25:450–461.

Preibisch, Kerry. 2011. "Migrant Workers and Changing Work-place Regimes in Contemporary Agricultural Production in Canada." *International Journal of Sociology of Agriculture and Food* 19 (1): 62–82.

Satzewich, Victor. 1989. "Unfree Labor and Canadian Capitalism: The Incorporation of Polish War Veterans." *Studies in Political Economy* 28:89–110.

STPS (Mexico, Secretaría del Trabajo y Previsión Social). 2015. "2015 Season of the Mexico-Canada Seasonal Agricultural Workers Program Begins." Press release, January 9. Ottawa: Embassy of Mexico. https://embamex.sre.gob.mx/canada/index.php/en/press/press-releases/1292-jan15/11465-ptat15begins.

Valarezo, Giselle. 2007 "Out of Necessity and into the Fields: Migrant Farmworkers

in St. Rémi, Quebec." Master's thesis, Queen's University, Ontario. https://qspace
.library.queensu.ca/bitstream/1974/1087/1/Valarezo_Giselle_V_200710_MA.pdf.
Valenzuela Moreno, Karla Angélica. 2018. "La protección consular mexicana y la pre-
carización del trabajo de las y los trabajadores agrícolas temporales en Canadá."
Norteamérica 13 (1): 57–78. http://www.revistanorteamerica.unam.mx/index.php
/nam/article/viewFile/309/337.
Verma, Veena. 2003. *The Mexican and Caribbean Seasonal Agricultural Workers Program:
Regulatory and Policy Framework, Farm Industry Level Employment Practices, and the
Future of the Program under Unionization.* Ottawa: North-South Institute. http://
s3.amazonaws.com/migrants_heroku_production/datas/95/Verma_2003_original
.pdf?1311163747.
Vosko, Leah F. 2015. "Blacklisting as a Modality of Deportability: Mexico's Response to
Circular Migrant Agricultural Workers' Pursuit of Collective Bargaining Rights in
British Columbia, Canada." *Journal of Ethnic and Migration Studies* 42 (8): 1371–1387.
http://doi.org/10.1080/1369183X.2015.1111134.

Legal Decisions and Cases

ACLAN (Acuerdo de Cooperación Laboral de América del Norte, Mexico National
Office). 2016. Public Communication MEX 2016-2, receipt of communication by
UFCW Canada against the Canadian government. Mexico City.
BCCA (British Columbia Court of Appeal). 2015. United Mexican States v. BCLRB. Case
32. Victoria.
BCLRB (British Columbia Labor Relations Board). 2012a. Sidhu & Sons Nursery Ltd.
[Certain Employees of] and Floralia Plant Growers Limited [Certain Employees of]
and Sidhu & Sons Nursery Ltd. and Floralia Plant Growers Limited and UFCW, Local
1518 and United Mexican States and Consulado General de México in Vancouver,
February 1. Vancouver.
———. 2012b. Testimony, Sidhu & Sons Nursery Ltd. [Certain Employees of] and
United Food and Commercial Workers International Union, Local 1518, February
23, 24, 27, 28. Cases 61942 and 61973. Vancouver.
———. 2014. Sidhu & Sons Nursery Ltd. [Certain Employees of] and United Food
and Commercial Workers International Union, Local 1518. Cases 61942 and 61973.
Vancouver.
CONAPRED (Consejo Nacional para Prevenir la Discriminación). 2014. File CONA-
PRED/DGAQR/405/14/DQ/I/DF/Q303, regarding complaint by UFCW Canada
against Secretariat of Labor and Social Welfare. Mexico City.
MB LB (Manitoba Labour Board). 2007. United Food and Commercial Workers Union,
Local No. 832 v. Mayfair Farms (Portage), Ltd. Case 81887. Winnipeg.
ON HRT (Ontario Human Rights Tribunal). 2015. Raper v. Foreign Agricultural Re-
source Management Services. Case 269. Toronto.
ON SC (Ontario Superior Court), 2003. Fraser et al. v. Attorney General of Canada. Case
No. 03-CV-257806CM2, November 12.
———. 2005. Fraser v. Canada (Attorney General). Case 47783. Toronto.
———. 2013. L'Écuyer c. Côté. Case 973, Montreal.
QC CLP (Quebec Commission des Lesions Professionelles). 2009. Sanchez-Castillo
c. Légumière YC, Inc. Case 2485. Montreal.

QC LRB (Quebec Labor Relations Board). 2006. TUAC 501 c. La Légumière YC, Inc. Case 0466. Montreal.

———. 2010. Travailleurs et travailleuses unis de l'alimentation et du commerce (TUAC), section locale 501 c. L'Écuyer. Case 191. Montreal.

SCC (Supreme Court of Canada). 2001. Dunmore c. Ontario (Attorney General). Case 94. Ottawa.

———. 2011. Ontario (Attorney General) v. Fraser. 2011. Case 2. Toronto.

CHAPTER 8

Assembling Noncitizen Access to Education in a Sanctuary City: The Place of Public School Administrator Bordering Practices

PATRICIA LANDOLT AND LUIN GOLDRING

Public education holds a near-sacred place in secular liberal democracies, imparting civic values and offering the promise of social mobility. In nation-states with high rates of immigration, public education is meant to transform the children of newcomers into informed and productive citizens (Gerstle and Mollenkopf 2001; Tyack 2001). Education policies and practices determine who is entitled and who can claim access to this core element of social citizenship. Laws and regulations establish the parameters of access, but practices of access are always variable. As a result, citizens' and noncitizens' formal rights and substantive claims to education are historically specific, socially constituted, and variable in practice. The potential for eroded social membership is ever present, with profound long-term consequences for marginalized groups and society (Gonzáles 2015; TRC 2015).

In this chapter we examine the case of access to education for precarious legal status migrants in the Toronto School District. In 2007 the Toronto District School Board (TDSB) passed a policy to ensure access to education for all children regardless of immigration status. Evaluations of the TDSB's policy are mixed. Grassroots activists find that precarious status families continue to be asked for documentation, are denied access, and experience a level of scrutiny that instills fear and pushes them into the shadows (Aberman, Villegas, and Villegas 2016; F. Villegas 2013). School administrators, frontline staff, and teachers report challenges but claim to be making a genuine effort to ensure a smooth enrollment process and access to a fulfilling educational experience for all city residents regardless of legal status.

A wide range of scholarship has addressed the variation in the effectiveness, consistency, and experiences of access to state entitlements for noncitizens. One line of argument focuses on face-to-face interactions and organizational dynamics within bureaucracies. It emphasizes the systemic variation generated by discretionary gatekeepers in highly bureaucratized settings (Alpes and Spire 2014; P. Villegas 2013; Willen 2012); the "accidents" built into any technology of government and regulation (Nyers 2006); the role of bureaucratic cultures and fiscal pressures (Satzewich 2013); and differences between local actor and policy frames versus national policy framing (Marrow 2012). Other research compares across cases and explains the gap between policy and practice as a product of contextual variation in resources, demographics, institutional and political cultures, and overlapping jurisdictions (Gleeson 2012; Varsanyi et al. 2012). The literature provides distinct entry points to explain variation: face-to-face interactions, laws and policies, and institutional practice. Less developed, however, is a satisfactory account of how face-to-face encounters, organizational contexts, and macrostructural forces come together to produce contingent and variable yet systemic experiences of access that in turn affect noncitizen legal status trajectories.

We draw on critical border studies and assemblage theory to connect frontline, institutional, and organizational dynamics and macro-level regulations and laws that generate indeterminacy and heterogeneity in experiences of noncitizenship. We use data from interviews with public school principals and vice principals as a point of entry for examining how routinized encounters between administrators and precarious legal status families and students shape noncitizenship. We argue that administrator bordering practices—the practices they develop to delimit membership and negotiate access to state entitlements—at the point of admission *and after* enrollment produce variable and unpredictable experiences of inclusion and exclusion. Bordering practices at enrollment dissociate requests for IDs and other paperwork from screening based on immigration status and physically and temporally displace bordering. After enrollment, status-blind bordering obfuscates the systemic and distinct qualities and vulnerabilities of precarious legal status. As an ensemble, these bordering practices have implications for the experiences and trajectories of noncitizenship.

Noncitizenship Assemblages

We are interested in developing a conceptual framework of precarious noncitizenship that can attend to indeterminate and heterogeneous experiences and legal status trajectories of noncitizenship (Landolt and Goldring 2016). We work with the concepts of precarious legal status, noncitizenship assemblages, and bordering practices to build the framework. Precarious legal status is a global phenomenon (Morris 2003). It is marked by any of the following: the absence of a permanent right to remain in a national territory;

lack of permanent work authorization; limited or no access to social citizenship rights and entitlements; and deportability (Goldring, Berinstein, and Bernhard 2009). These conditions generate the *liminal* qualities of temporariness, limited and mediated rights, revocability, and deportability that characterize precarious legal status (cf. Menjívar 2006). Myriad institutional mechanisms may generate precarious legal status, and these will vary across cities, regions, and countries. In addition to unauthorized entry, precarious legal status can involve a temporary entry followed by permit expiry or denied refugee claim—so that one is shuttling between authorized and unauthorized situations—and illegalization (Black et al. 2006; Crépaud and Nakache 2006; De Genova 2002; Goldring, Berinstein, and Bernhard 2009; Saad 2011; Schweitzer 2014; Vickstrom 2014). The production of legal status precarity is systemic but leads to variable experiences of substantive citizenship, membership, and inclusion.

Estimates of the precarious legal status population in Canada, including the nonstatus population, vary considerably and are not based on systematic empirical data. In 2006 the nonstatus population was said to range from 20,000 to 500,000 (Jimenez 2006). Analysts agree that the number of temporary residents who arrive or are present in Canada in any given year has risen dramatically since the 1990s (Elgersma 2014; Foster 2012). Some will renew permits, become permanent residents, or leave the country, but others remain without authorized status. In 2015 the Toronto Census Metropolitan Area population was more than 5.9 million. About half of the population is foreign-born, speaks a mother tongue other than English or French, and is racialized as nonwhite (TCF 2016). Given general demographic trends,[1] it is likely that the Greater Toronto Area is home to a comparatively large share of precarious status residents and that this population is characterized by working-age individuals and families (cf. Hudson et al. 2017; Hynie, Ardern, and Robertson 2016). While residential concentration based on income and racialization has risen in Toronto (Hulchanski 2010), there is no basis for determining the distribution of precarious legal status students among schools. Extrapolating from neighborhood composition and country of origin data on Toronto residents suggests a likely concentration of precarious legal status students in the city's working-class, immigrant gateway neighborhoods.

We argue that noncitizenship experiences of rights and access as well as trajectories of precarious legal status are assembled; they are produced by constellations of action occurring across multiple scales, arenas, jurisdictions, and institutions through the structurally mediated practices of individuals (Landolt and Goldring 2016; Ong and Collier 2005; Sassen 2006; P. Villegas 2012). The notion of assemblage illuminates how disparate and conflicting policies, power relations, institutions, and actors interact to produce different experiences of noncitizenship as well as variable legal status trajectories and relations between noncitizenship and citizenship. Experiences and trajectories vary in terms of *presence*—the terms shaping the right to remain in a given national territory—and *access* to sociolegal rights and entitlements such as education, health care, city services, labor markets, and legal protections. Breaking down noncitizenship assemblages, we discern three dimensions. First, to help noncitizens remain in the country and to access entitlements, individuals and institutions negotiate the formal systems and substantive practices through which noncitizens are conferred or denied rights. Second, noncitizens exercise agency in choosing to make claims (or choosing not to make claims) to formal and substantive rights. Third, the individuals and institutions with which noncitizens interact draw on narratives of deservingness and moral worth to make discretionary decisions about these claims that may encourage or discourage further claims-making. As these different dimensions are assembled—or come together—they may blur or brighten the formal and substantive boundary between citizenship and noncitizenship, intersect with categories of precarious legal status and other dimensions of social location, and generate heterogeneity in noncitizenship experiences and trajectories of legal status.

Finally, we draw on the concept of bordering practices to specify the systemic importance of face-to-face encounters that mediate the conditions of precarious noncitizen access to state entitlements and the right to remain in the national territory. Bordering practices deploy the border as a rhetorical and administrative tool that intersects with other social markers of differentiation and inequality and marks the noncitizen body as foreign. They are a politics of delimitation and classification that specify movement, membership, inclusion, and exclusion within and between nations (Pratt 2005). Bordering practices make the border geographically mobile so that it begins to saturate ordinary sites and social interactions with the exclusionary exercise of sovereignty and territoriality (Johnson et al. 2011; P. Villegas 2014). As such, bordering practices reveal the link between seemingly mundane encounters and systemic experiences of noncitizenship and trajectories of precarious legal status. In the process, they work to routinize interactions between administrators and precarious legal status noncitizens.

We focus on the case of public school administrators, who in their professional practice implement the conditions noncitizens must meet to remain present and secure access to education. We argue that school administrators engage in bordering practices. Pulling together the formal and substantive threads of action related to educational access, school administrators play a pivotal role in assembling variable experiences of precarious noncitizenship.

They interpret and enact provincial and school board policies and procedures of access, setting the terms of precarious legal status students' enrollment and their educational experience postenrollment. School administrators also make decisions about what other state entitlements such as health care,[2] social welfare, and law enforcement might be accessed by precarious legal status students and in what manner. School administrators can contribute to routing precarious legal status students along variable legal status trajectories in part because the students come into contact with other arms of the state via the school. We demonstrate how administrators' bordering practices, guided by their understandings and beliefs about social citizenship, state entitlements, and precarious legal status, have direct, immediate, and cumulative impacts on precarious legal status students' experiences and legal status trajectories of noncitizenship.

Research Methods

The case study of the Toronto District School Board is designed to extend our understanding of the assemblages of noncitizenship with a focus on secondary border zones. The TDSB offers seemingly favorable conditions for precarious legal status students and families to access education. A clear multi-jurisdictional legal framework and a school board–level set of policies and procedures explicitly formalize access to school for all children in the City of Toronto regardless of immigration status. Moreover, the TDSB is a highly regulated and unionized work setting in which both management and union workers have a long-standing commitment to equity and social justice, as demonstrated by formal statements and professional development practice. Institutionally and politically, it offers the best-case scenario of a liberal, equity-oriented welcome for precarious legal status noncitizens.

Between 2012 and 2016 we conducted eighty semistructured, in-depth interviews with institutional actors at various levels of the educational system. We interviewed school board trustees and superintendents, school administrators such as principals and vice principals, guidance counselors, settlement workers, and teachers. In 2015 we also interviewed parents and youth who had precarious legal status when they registered or attempted to register themselves or their children in the TDSB. Examining the multiscalar landscape of institutional contact points and the experiences of precarious legal status families moving through the system captures the systemic contingencies of noncitizenship assemblages as they are constituted in the education system.

In this chapter we focus on principals and vice principals because they represent crucial contact points between citizens and noncitizens that are both highly bureaucratized and discretionary (Marrow 2012; Pratt 2005; Spire 2008). Principals and vice principals mediate and bridge domains of bureaucratic power within the TDSB and across different arenas of state entitlement. School administrators receive ongoing professional development from the TDSB on a range of strategic policy mandates including managing precarious status noncitizen student enrollment. They put into practice a massive array of school board strategic mandates, oversee long-standing policies and procedures, manage labor relations across multiple unions, and manage budgets to ensure the fiscal health of their schools. Principals and vice principals also set the cultural and political tone in their schools. They work to raise the reputation of the schools and students and advocate for their schools to secure scarce board resources. Given their institutional location and professional role, school administrators are therefore crucial to shaping policy vis-à-vis precarious status noncitizens.

We analyze data from nineteen semistructured interviews conducted with school administrators between 2012 and 2016. The principals and vice principals we interviewed were career TDSB professionals, all with at least fifteen years of experience working in the Toronto District School Board. Most had taught for years before moving into administration. While some had changed schools several times, others had been in administration at the same school for many years. The majority had worked in the same Toronto neighborhoods for the greater part of their careers. Principals and vice principals knew their students well and were very knowledgeable about the economic and social profiles of the neighborhoods in which they worked. Many had chosen to work in neighborhoods they described as stigmatized, misunderstood, and marginalized. Their profiles varied; some were themselves immigrants and people of color, while others were children of immigrants of European descent, and a small number were Anglo-Canadians with limited personal experiences of immigration. In spite of the variation, there was a striking degree of narrative consistency in respondents' evaluations of TDSB policy and practice with regard to students with precarious legal status.

The TDSB Context for Access to Education

The Toronto District School Board was formed in 1998 as part of the urban amalgamation of six municipalities into the City of Toronto. Seven school boards were merged to create the TDSB, resulting in a gigantic school board, the largest in Canada and the fourth-largest in North America; its organizational structure, sociodemographic composition, and ethnoracial character are complex and politically charged. The TDSB manages approximately 600 schools and serves 245,000 elementary and high school students each year. Thirty percent of students were born outside of Canada, and 70 percent of students live in households where both parents were born outside of Canada. More than 120 languages are spoken by TDSB families, and 66 percent of students learned or speak languages other than English at home. No single language group predominates; the top ten languages are Chinese, Tamil, Urdu, Bengali, Gujarati, Somali, Spanish, Arabic, Vietnamese, and Tagalog. Seventy percent of homes have at least one parent with a university or college education. Despite the high educational attainment, there is considerable income insecurity. Fifty percent of primary school students live in low-income households.[3] Poverty is racialized: 50 percent of racialized families live in poverty, in contrast with 18 percent of white and 36 percent of mixed-race families (TDSB 2012).

The legal framework that organizes access to education for precarious legal status migrants in the province of Ontario was articulated in the 1990s and formalized in 2007 (F. Villegas 2013). Canada's 1989 ratification of the UN International Convention on the Rights of the Child jump-started a decade of Canada-wide children's rights advocacy. In 1993 education advocates lobbied for the inclusion of a new provision in the Ontario Education Act (OEA) to advance nonstatus children's access to education. As a result of their efforts, Section 49.1 was added to the OEA, stating, "A person who is otherwise entitled to be admitted to a school and who is less than eighteen years of age shall not be refused admission because the person or the person's parent or guardian is unlawfully in Canada" (Ontario Government n.d.). In 1999 education advocates secured a further amendment to the OEA to specify the legal status conditions under which a precarious legal status individual who is otherwise required by Ontario law to be in school would be exempt from paying enrollment fees. The amendment distinguishes between fee-paying international students and all other children living in the province. Also in 1999, the newly created TDSB adopted an Equity Foundation Statement to ensure that the curriculum, educational opportunities, and school workplace actively comply with the Ontario Human Rights Act (TDSB 1999). The equity framework further articulated the rights of all students to participate fully in public education.

Despite the legal and policy framework, school access for precarious status students was informal and uncertain throughout the 1990s and 2000s. Families met with difficulties when enrolling students, and obstacles to access were dealt with on a case-by-case basis. School board–level understanding and application of the framework established by the Ontario Education Act were inconsistent. No system was in place to help local schools navigate the procedural application of the law, a lack that led to further variations and inconsistencies across wards and schools depending on the experience, preparation, and disposition of local administrators.

The gap between law and practice came to a head in 2007 with high-profile cases in which precarious legal status students were apprehended to bait parents who had received deportation notices (NOII 2006; F. Villegas 2013). Their arrests galvanized the emergent no-borders movement No One Is Illegal (NOII) to focus its city-level activism on fighting for policy changes at the TDSB. NOII joined forces with the Education Rights Taskforce to mobilize a multisectoral coalition that eventually included individuals in the health sector and the legal community as well as teachers unions—among them the District 12 Ontario Secondary School Teachers Federation and the Elementary Teachers of Toronto—and elected school board trustees. Absent from the coalition were ethnospecific organizations and parent groups (F. Villegas 2013). Building on momentum from the 2007 mobilization, grassroots education activists working with the NOII met regularly with relevant TDSB offices to discuss obstacles and new challenges in precarious legal status access to enrollment and schooling to ensure the robust implementation of the policy.

The 2007 mobilization led to the passage of Policy P.061 SCH, Students without Legal Immigration Status. Referred to by many as "Don't ask, don't tell," the policy reaffirmed the conditions of access set by the Ontario Education Act and offered school administrators and staff specific directives for enrolling students without full immigration status. Directives were designed to do away with school-level discretion and inconsistencies. The implementation agreement included annual communication to all school administrators about the OEA and access rights, annual staff sensitivity training, a list of alternative mechanisms for documenting students when no official documentation was available, and reaffirmation that schools would not provide student information to immigration authorities and that the TDSB opposed immigration authority access to students while in school (Ontario Government n.d.). The policy also reaffirmed that schools actually needed to verify date of entry to Canada for all students for two reasons: first, to secure provincial funding for English-language learner instruction and second, to ensure that international students paid fees for school access.

Two strategic mandates of the TDSB complicate the motivation behind and implementation of the 2007 "Don't ask, don't tell" policy. First, the school board actively recruits fee-paying international students at all levels, from kindergarteners to twelfth-graders. It charges international students, of whom there were an estimated 1,500 enrolled in 2014, up to $14,000 per year to study in Toronto. The fiscal and political pressure to ensure that international students pay fees requires that school administrators verify student legal status and time in Canada. The requirement poses a problem for precarious status noncitizen students, who as visitors typically have six-month visas and are also considered fee payers, not residents. As a result, precarious status noncitizen families that plan to overstay their visas and remain in Toronto are often encouraged by local school administrators to keep their children out of school for up to six months to fall out of status and thus avoid paying international student fees. Second, the school board secures federal and provincial funding for services and programs that serve the immigrant newcomer population. Eligibility for services and programs is based on legal status and time in Canada. Federally funded Settlement Worker in the School programs are made available only to secure legal status immigrants with less than three years in Canada, that is, recent permanent residents. English-language funding, however, is available to all students regardless of legal status but requires information about their time in Canada. Both mandates thus require school administrators to collect relevant information about immigration status, and both undercut a policy meant to extend access to schooling for precarious legal status students.

Access Assembled: The Routinized Encounters of School Administrators

Our analysis of interviews with school administrators focuses on their philosophies on school access, the actual enrollment process, how they view the postenrollment educational experiences of precarious legal status students, the relationship between the school and other institutional arenas, and the transition to colleges or universities. Each theme sheds light on the character of school administrators' bordering practices and the indeterminate impacts of those practices on noncitizenship experiences and trajectories.

Administrators' Understandings of Access

School administrators across the city agreed that every child who lives in Toronto has a right to enroll in school regardless of legal status. A principal stressed the link between the school board's expectations and student access: "I say that the TDSB is obviously looking . . . to offer education to everyone, and whether you are an international student, or a landed immigrant, whether you are a refugee claimant waiting for your immigration to come through . . . the expectation is that you are in school and the expectation . . . at the board is: do whatever . . . to ensure you are in school" (Int54).[4]

Administrators also stressed the connections between the 2007 TDSB policy on access to schooling, the provincial Education Rights Act, and their personal philosophies and professional commitments to equity and access.

A high school principal explained, "Having experienced the TDSB for thirty years . . . our mandate is to welcome every student under the age of eighteen who wants to be here. That guiding philosophy . . . is not a new one. So I find the policy [passed in 2007] is consistent with that philosophy" (Int60).

Another respondent made connections across jurisdictions. He positioned himself and other administrators as playing a similar role as government agents who deal with immigrants: "I think that the kids have a right to an education. The TDSB and every board in this province, and every government agent in this country, that has deal[t] with immigrants has a duty, a legal duty, to make sure that these kids are being educated" (Int59).

We found that school administrators across neighborhoods and schools were unwavering in their commitment to educational access for precarious status noncitizens. They saw an unambiguous alignment of their personal philosophies and professional roles with the equity and access policies of the TDSB, provincial legislation, and national law.

Enrollment Practices

We asked administrators to explain their schools' enrollment process. They consistently described enrollment straightforwardly as a set of procedures designed for ease of access. One principal recounted, "We don't ask students, we don't ask questions. . . . All a kid needs to tell us to register in this board . . . [is] something with an address on it, something that says this is the parent of this child or the legal guardian of this child. And that's it!" (Int59).

The belief that enrollment was a clear-cut process was echoed by another principal: "Well, in the TDSB, basically we want to educate every child. The main requirement is if they live in the catchment area. So, they have to show that they actually have an address. . . . They have to show somewhere that they are paying to live at that address, whether a rental agreement or an ownership or whatever, and contact information, so basically things that prove they live in the neighborhood, that prove they are who they say they are" (Int19). School administrators dissociated requests for papers such as those that establish residence and confirm student and legal guardian identification from requests to disclose immigration status.

Of course, the bureaucratic contradictions imposed by the TDSB's internationalization strategy were not lost on respondents. One principal in particular talked about the dissonance between not asking about legal status and the need to establish whether a student is eligible to pay international fees:

> You know, in order for the board to ascertain whether a kid that is showing up at their door is not the kind that can pay international fees . . . that needs

to be registered, right? They have to ask the question, they have to ask about status, right? . . . And so people have been forced to disclose their status. Now, the TDSB has never turned . . . away any kid. But the very fact is that they are forced to ask this question because they are potentially . . . fee-paying students, right? (Int59)

School administrators also explained that asking new students for paperwork stemmed from the need to secure English-learner funding from the province. A vice principal elaborated on that point:

My understanding is that if a child comes here to be enrolled, we enroll them. . . . I don't care about [the child's status], period. The only reason that paperwork would come into play for your precarious legal status would be to get ESL [English as a Second Language] funding. So, you come, you're enrolling your child, and I ask if you have documentation. If they give me the documentation, I check it off on a form that has to be filed with the board—that has to go to the ministry that gives us ESL funding. (Int57)

Another procedure that requires some degree of disclosure is English and math grade-level assessments. One principal described the procedure as follows: "Students that are coming from another country, they do go for an assessment . . . they will have their prior learning assessed just so they're placed in the right slot. That's not so much about their status as it is about, should we put you in grade nine math or grade ten?" (Int5). In this case, evaluative requirements that require disclosure are understood as inclusionary; they ensure school success for every student.

Again, school administrators view this paperwork as unrelated to concerns over a student's immigration status. What precarious legal status families might see as an intimidating gauntlet of papering, administrators see as a vital, streamlined process. One principal explained how she understood enrollment and, more important, the welcoming schooling experience that followed:

So, generally, they come to the school, the family's new to the country. . . . They're directed to the reception center, they get an appointment, they're told what documents that they have to bring to the reception center, which [are] . . . proof of address and birth certificate. And . . . they go to the reception center, usually within a day or two, they have the testing [for language instruction and grade placement]. . . . But before anything, I introduce them to all the important people. I tell the parents, y'know, we're gonna take good care [of you]. And I say, y'know, if you have any problems, you come to this person or this person, and . . . usually a parent or someone comes who speaks some

English so that . . . you get the message, 'cause we want to make sure they feel at home and that they feel comfortable. 'Cause it's pretty scary, coming to a new country, coming to a big high school. It's kinda scary. (Int57)

From the administrators' perspective, therefore, a speedy and well-documented enrollment is the key to ensuring a warm welcome and school success.

Interviews with school administrators confirmed that enrollment requires multiple forms of papering and that there is considerable variation in procedures across schools and among families. A tension emerges between routinized encounters and impromptu practices of bordering. Documentation is required to establish: whether a student should pay international student fees, legal guardianship, immunization record, proof of residency in the school catchment, and math and English-language grade levels. Some of this papering takes place at the local school, and other parts involve going to the school board's central office or an assessment center. There was variation in how administrators managed these requirements: Some had a finely tuned, on-the-spot enrollment practice managed by well-trained staff, while others preferred to refer families to the central office for complete documentation reviews. In response to our interview questions, administrators expressed confidence that they were welcoming of immigrant and refugee families from every country and condition imaginable and applying their long-standing inclusive practices to all migrant families regardless of status. Steadfast in their certainty that legal status does not matter to their or the school board's educational mission, administrators rarely acknowledged the specific vulnerabilities of precarious legal status. According to them, they operate in an enrollment universe in which immigration status does not matter, and thus they do not ask about it.

Schooling Postenrollment

The vast majority of precarious legal status students enrolled in the TDSB will experience legal status changes while in school. We conceptualize this systemic contingency as the "chutes and ladders" of immigration and legal status trajectories (Goldring and Landolt 2013). Students and their families may transition from precarious authorized legal status to secure status, from authorized to unauthorized status, and may cycle through multiple categories of precarity. This flux means that families—parents and to a lesser extent their children—are often striving to obtain more secure legal status or working to avoid an erosion of status. Therefore, they are constantly aware of the potential impact of mundane procedures—such as enrolling in school—on their status or living situation.[5]

Given this context, we asked administrators about precarious legal status students' experiences postenrollment. Interviews revealed that intense scrutiny at the enrollment threshold was followed by a status-blind treatment of precarious legal status students after enrollment (Bonilla Silva 2006). School administrators were quick to explain that once a student was enrolled, legal status was irrelevant: "Once they're in, they're in: a full student. . . . But the precariousness doesn't really play out when they are in school. It may play out maybe at the enrollment juncture, but once we get over that, they're a full student" (Int72).

Administrators drew a clear borderline between pre- and postenrollment, and they were at pains to explain that their interactions with individual students were never about immigration status. One principal described her steadfast refusal to consider the student experience through the lens of legal status:

> We're serving kids who come through the door, and if, depending [on] what happens politically, budgets are different and you have less resources to go around, that's an issue for all students. . . . We don't have a school improvement plan for status students versus non—we just have a school improvement plan. We want students to get their number of credits to graduate—all students. I don't ever look at, oh, what are my suspension rates for my status versus non? We're trying to keep school safe for everybody. We want everybody to pass all of their classes. We want all of our students to be safe, to be fed, and so really, I don't ever stop to think about what is the status of the student who's sitting in my office who needs discipline or who needs help or who needs whatever. It's the student who's there at that moment. (Int5)

Indeed, her evaluations of the student population as a whole focused on shared barriers to schooling that required an even-handed treatment of the entire school population, devoid of legal status considerations.

> You know, our students that don't have status would have some of the same challenges as my general population. This is a school, in terms of socioeconomic status, where there are a lot of needs for the student population in general, and so we would meet the needs of all students regardless of their status as best as we can. So, whether it's access to be able to participate in a field trip that costs money . . . you know, there wouldn't be barriers that are unique to students because of their immigration status. (Int5)

Administrators' bureaucratic commitment to accountability, transparency, and privacy deepened their desire to avoid focusing on student legal status. Asked about their own individual encounters with precarious legal status students, many administrators began by emphasizing that there was often no need for them to know a student's legal status.

> Because this is a privacy issue . . . we have no way to even track which students have what status as far as I know. As far as I know, I can't run a report and say, "List me all the students who are refugee claimants. List me all the students who are nonstatus." I don't think that I have the ability to do that. So, it would be hit or miss. I don't keep a list. So, as far as having to track them, and be the—I mean, the student comes to us with X issue. Whether it's to guidance, to the teacher's attention through guidance, or to me, directly to me—the only reason that I would have to find that [status] out is if I cared to look at their index card to find out what their status was. So, it's never really . . . been on the radar. (Int57)

Administrators interpreted and operationalized the TDSB equity policy quite literally: treat all students the same regardless of their legal status. Status-blind interactions and programming were designed to mitigate externally created social and economic differences and even the playing field. Two administrators, though, did recognize a link between legal status precarity and "emotional challenges" that might impact student success. One principal explained,

> If these students are in your school and their situation is precarious, emotionally it takes a really serious toll on them. Some of them, they can't function. They are a basket case, they're crying, they're worrying constantly, you know, "I may have to go back." . . . Yeah, this could really impact on their academic performance. Sometimes they are amazing students and really committed to getting stuff done and doing whatever it takes to be successful. . . . At other times, they are . . . aware of what they are dealing with, and they just take it in their stride. (Int56)

However, recognizing that legal status precarity could affect student behavior did not translate into a systemwide evaluation of what living with precarious legal status might mean in relation to schooling.

Multijurisdictional Schooling

The school is a multijurisdictional site that comes into contact with various arms of the state. In a large school with a complex student population, school administrators inevitably interact on a weekly or even daily basis with Toronto Public Health, Toronto Police Services, and Child Protection Services; of these, only the public health apparatus has a clearly articulated policy of access and nondisclosure for all Toronto residents regardless of status. Schools may also come into contact with border enforcement through the Canadian Border Services Agency. We asked school administrators how they handled interinstitutional contacts and processes given the presence in schools of students with precarious legal status. School administrators argued that legal status became an issue only when the school policy hit an externally imposed roadblock to access for a student with precarious legal status.

> It becomes confusing to the system from our perspective to know what status kids are. It ends up being an issue only when we advocate for them in a normal way and we hit a roadblock. So, it's actually somebody else who has to say no for us to know that the status is an issue. So, let's say we hook him up with public health, right? So, we call the public health nurse, we take him to the clinic or if somebody there goes, "Whoa, there's an issue here because of their status," then we realize. But . . . we're not conditioned to be concerned about their status. We tend to treat them all the same. (Int23)

Thus even when thinking through interinstitutional contact points, school administrators steadfastly distanced themselves from legal status as a relevant dimension of evaluation.

School administrators' status-blind framework was also reflected in the ways they responded to disciplinary and truancy concerns. An administrator explained her approach to discipline:

> To be honest with you, I don't think I distinguish [among students] . . . in any way. If we have a policy in effect and . . . if a kid gets into a fight or does something against our policy or procedure, there's progressive discipline. Now it usually starts off with a chat, then it escalates to something a little bit more serious [such as calling the police]. . . . So, yeah, I don't think I distinguish. (Int53)

Administrators' narratives failed to include the cascade of adverse impacts that might result from disciplining students with precarious legal status. They ignored the probability that a disciplinary action could involve Toronto police, which has a standing practice of working with the Canadian Border Services Agency (NOII 2015). The failure to see precarious legal status as a dimension of exclusion and vulnerability is evident in the TDSB's policy on truancy. The TDSB requires that student absences of more than fifteen consecutive days be reported. As a principal explained, if after a fifteen-day absence the school has not received a transfer notice from another school, administrators will probably alert the social worker "because then Children's Aid might be involved" (Int25). Evaluations of truancy thus revealed a similar lack of awareness regarding legal status as a site of vulnerability. Administrators did not recognize potential connections between the immigration system and child welfare services that might exacerbate vulnerability of students or parents with precarious legal status.

Administrators' status-blind approach to schooling was governed by the school board's equity framework, their own awareness of the economic challenges that a growing number of TDSB families faced, their professional management training, and their heightened concern for privacy and confidentiality. Status-blind interactions obfuscated the border between citizen and noncitizen and in so doing denied the specific forms and experiences of vulnerability associated with precarious legal status. Furthermore, administrators did not consider whether the institutions with which they interacted and to which they shuttled students were governed by anything approximating an access policy for families with precarious legal status. The status-blind ethos of school administrators thus allowed them to leave unexamined the personal and legal implications of turning them over to other institutional arenas for health, discipline, or truancy concerns.

Moments of Crisis in Status-Blind Administration

We asked administrators to discuss situations in which awareness of students' immigration status couldn't be avoided, notably of deportation orders. In these cases, a status-blind framework was not sustainable. Most administrators reported some direct experience with cases in which families in legal status crises turned to them for help. They dealt with these on a case-by-case basis and were more than happy to write letters of support for families working toward stays of deportation. As administrators recalled, their letters emphasized the character and work ethic of the student in question: "There was one case where some teachers got together and wrote letters, as one particular child has been there and loved school and was really helpful. They did try, but in my understanding—and by the time we were aware of things—it was really too late" (Int19). Another administrator also emphasized how the school rallied to offer support for a well-regarded student:

> There's one girl in particular who has claimed refugee status—and this just came to me last week—but she's got a hearing, and there [are] concerns that she might be sent back home. So, we're hoping that because she's done so well

here for the last year, really well in her classes, that will work in her favor in keeping her here—that she's very much focused, she's integrated into Canadian society, she's got long-term plans of staying here and contributing to society. So, that would hopefully help. I know there was a situation too when I was at [another school] with another student and again, great student, but unfortunately, she was deported back to Mexico. (Int21)

Because status was revealed only during crises, deportation proceedings were often too far along to preserve the student's ongoing presence and access to education.

Long-Term Implications of Status-Blindness

We asked administrators about the transition to postsecondary education as a way of gauging the long-term impacts of precarious legal status on educational outcomes. Most administrators were not knowledgeable about those issues and suggested that we speak to guidance counselors. They did not see that their status-blind equity framework could generate potential barriers for students' access to postsecondary education. The principal we quote here captured the general thrust of most high school administrators' responses when asked whether there was targeted support for precarious status students interested in attending college or university.

> I can't make a good distinction for how we do it [postsecondary counseling] for these students as opposed to how we do it for any student, because we largely don't view the label [*laughs*] when the student walks through the door. We don't say, "This is the advice we give to people with precarious legal status" as opposed to "This is the advice we give to any other person." We deal with all of these things in the same particular way. We invite the colleges and the universities in to talk about their programs. When they get into conversations— and it's usually about financial aid—then it's the college people who are really good at, you know, explaining what you can do with OSAP [Ontario Student Assistance Program], what you can't do with OSAP. When people come to us and say, "I would love to go to college, but I can't afford to go to college," then, you know, maybe that's a more individual conversation with a guidance counselor. And again, it's around tapping what resources people can qualify for. (Int60)[6]

Consistent with the equity agenda, administrators recognized income but not legal status as a potential barrier. Principals and vice principals seemed unaware of three status barriers to postsecondary education: the online application system for university requires legal status disclosure, precarious legal status students qualify only for international student fees, and these students are not eligible for any provincial study loans or scholarships.

Conclusion

We examined the bordering practices of school administrators in the Toronto District School Board to analyze how noncitizenship is assembled in one institutional arena—access to education. We drew on critical border studies, particularly the concept of bordering practices, and assemblage theory to situate our analysis of face-to-face, seemingly routine encounters between citizen actors and precarious status noncitizen families. Our analysis offers a window into how facets of the system come together to assemble access to education and postenrollment experiences for precarious status noncitizen students. The policies and actions we examined include federal immigration policies, provincial education policies, and school board policies regarding access to education, equity, discipline, and truancy; principals' and vice principals' personal interpretations of the policies; and finally, the administrators' discretionary actions based on evaluations of students' character.

Our analysis makes several empirically based conceptual contributions. Recent scholarship disrupts notions of bright borders and bordering practices as uniform or temporally and geographically static. Instead, the literature examines the proliferation of borders in terms of their clarity of demarcation, location(s), scale, temporality, and multiple purposes. We add to this scholarship by identifying distinct types of bordering practices that occur at admission and postenrollment. Carefully unpacking tensions between specific types of bordering practices, the administrative rationales that drive them, how administrators interpret the practices, and their potential implications leads to an empirical and conceptual understanding of how the practices can generate indeterminacy and heterogeneity in noncitizen experiences and trajectories.

Our detailed analysis of administrators' actions allows us to identify distinct bordering practices associated with two temporal phases. At the time of enrollment, administrators engage in practices of *dissociation* that divorce requests for various identification and health-related documents from the idea that such requests constitute a legal status barrier. At this stage, they also engage in a second set of geographic and temporal border *displacement* practices that send families to other sites to determine eligibility and placement. School administrators occlude the border between citizen and noncitizen by separating the request for proof of legal status from other identification checks and papering practices. Proof of residence, guardianship, and immunization are reduced to routinized clerical checks disconnected from legal status. Administrators thus displace and reorganize the border as they send families in precarious legal status to different school board offices. Doing so also hides their role in capturing fee-paying international students for the board. This bureaucratic exercise seems to distance the school administrator from the bordering practices to which the noncitizen students are submitted. As precarious status noncitizen families move around the system presenting different pieces of paper to different arms of the state, the enrollment process becomes an exercise in the geographic displacement and jurisdictional fragmentation of the border that can generate unpredictable and diverse experiences for students and their families.

After enrollment, administrators engage in a third type of bordering practices. Their status-blind practices *obfuscate* the border by ignoring the specificity of noncitizen legal status situations or the vulnerability that permeates the conditionality of presence and access. The practices are premised on treating all students the same, which conflates equality and equity. Poverty and racism are recognized fault lines of social inequality that can be mitigated through special programs, but legal status goes unrecognized. The "Don't ask, don't tell" policy elides vulnerability within a narrative of access and equity while leaving room for discretion or favoritism when problems arise in a seemingly ad hoc manner. Students of good character—deemed studious and hard-working—elicit more sympathy and support than others. However, even in those cases, not knowing about a student's legal status situation means that when problems arise in the form of truancy, discipline issues, anxiety, or a deportation order, there may be little chance for meaningful intervention.

Postenrollment status blindness ignores the most dramatic barriers that precarious status students with postsecondary aspirations face. Principals and vice principals we interviewed did not seem to be aware that precarious legal status might present a barrier to accessing postsecondary education. A principal in a low-income and racialized neighborhood said his school helped low-income students cover the cost of applying to postsecondary institutions; that assistance was consistent with the administrator's interpretation of the board's equity agenda. What such administrators fail to see is that students are asked for their status when they use the online portal for applying to universities in Ontario. The drop-down menu offers "Canadian Citizen," "Permanent Resident," "Study Permit," and "Other" as options. Using this last classification can lead to admission but as an international student, with correspondingly high fees. Administrators also seemed unaware that public financial aid is available only to citizens and permanent residents. That oversight can produce a situation in which academically strong students are advised to apply to university but are unlikely to be able to afford application costs or tuition. In short, students in precarious legal status are told that they are like everyone else, but when the time comes to continue their educations, they are typically left behind, with low-wage jobs as their only option.

Noncitizen access to public goods and services will continue to be an arena of advocacy and contention. Sanctuary city declarations in Canada, as in the United States, represent local efforts to redraw the boundaries of substantive membership by offering material access to city services for all residents. We contribute to critical analyses of supposedly inclusionary bordering practices by considering their limits in a best-case scenario. Our analysis shows that while local politics and institutional procedures may offer favorable conditions for extending rights to entitlements for noncitizens (Fox and Rivera-Salgado, chapter 1 of this volume), routinized encounters and the discourses of deservingness that animate these face-to-face encounters play a crucial role in mediating the practice of rights and access to public services for noncitizens. Administrators are guided by a commitment to providing access but must navigate a policy environment that generates bordering practices that rely on dissociation, displacement, and status-blindness. Identifying specific types of bordering practices is crucial for understanding the potential for uneven experiences and trajectories of noncitizenship. The recurrent requests to show documents at various stages in the enrollment process make it probable that some noncitizen students will experience delayed access or be excluded from schooling. If these students do enroll, the failure to acknowledge their precarious legal status as a dimension of inequality means that schools, students, and their families cannot openly address a key source of vulnerability. As a result, this vulnerability persists. Indeterminacy and heterogeneity are a systemic feature of the contemporary assemblage of noncitizenship. We recognize the importance of policies that expand access to education and other services. However, our analysis points to the importance of finding ways to ensure the safety of students and their families while recognizing the specificity of legal status vulnerabilities, anticipating their effects more systematically, and developing strategies to mitigate them that do not rely on obfuscation.

Notes

1. In 2015 the population of nonpermanent residents in Canada was 771,572, with 42 percent, 326,762, residing in Ontario (Statistics Canada 2016).

2. A provincial health card or equivalent is required to access state-funded, free health services. Citizens, permanent residents, and some categories of temporary

workers and refugee claimants have a health care entitlement. Some clinics and service providers offer care to the "medically uninsured," a designation that includes those without authorized status (Hynie, Ardern, and Robertson 2016; Landolt, Villegas, and Villegas 2012).

3. Twenty-eight percent of primary school students live in households where annual family income is under CAD30,000, and 21 percent are in households in the CAD30,000 to CAD49,000 family income bracket (TDSB 2012).

4. Direct quotes from interviews are coded using the designation "Int[#]" to correspond to individual respondent interview numbers.

5. The Canadian case stands in contrast to that of the United States, where people are likely to enter the country undetected and spend years with unauthorized status. In the United States, the work of legal status—and conditionality of presence—is different and centers on avoiding detection and deportation.

6. OSAP offers funding to citizens, permanent residents, and approved refugees.

References

Aberman, Tanya, Francisco Villegas, and Paloma E. Villegas, eds. 2016. *Seeds of Hope: Creating a Future in the Shadows*. Toronto: FCJ Refugee Centre.

Alpes, Maybritt Jill, and Alexis Spire. 2014. "Dealing with Law in Migration Control: The Powers of Street-level Bureaucrats at French Consulates." *Social and Legal Studies* 23 (2): 261–274.

Black, Richard, Michael Collyer, Ronald Skeldon, and Clare Waddington. 2006. "Routes to Illegal Residence: A Case Study of Immigration Detainees in the United Kingdom." *Geoforum* 37 (4): 552–564.

Bonilla Silva, Eduardo. 2006. *Racism without Racists: Color-Blind Racism and the Persistence of Social Inequality in America*. Lanham, MD: Rowman and Littlefield.

Crépaud, François, and Delphine Nakache. 2006. *Controlling Irregular Migration Canada. Choices* 12 (1). Montreal: Institute for Research on Public Policy.

De Genova, Nicholas. 2002. "Migrant 'Illegality' and Deportability in Everyday Life." *Annual Review of Anthropology* 31:419–447.

Elgersma, Sandra. 2014. "Temporary Foreign Workers." Background paper. Ottawa: Library of Parliament.

Foster, Jason. 2012. "Making Temporary Permanent: The Silent Transformation of the Temporary Foreign Worker Program." *Just Labour: A Canadian Journal of Work and Society* 19:22–46.

Gerstle, Gary, and John Mollenkopf, eds. 2001. *E Pluribus Unum? Contemporary and Historical Perspectives on Immigrant Political Incorporation*. New York: Russell Sage Foundation.

Gleeson, Shannon. 2012. *Conflicting Commitments: The Politics of Enforcing Immigrant Worker Rights in San Jose and Houston*. Ithaca, NY: Cornell University Press.

Goldring, Luin, and Patricia Landolt. 2013. "The Conditionality of Legal Status and Rights: Conceptualizing Precarious Non-citizenship in Canada." In *Producing and Negotiating Non-Citizenship: Precarious Legal Status in Canada*, edited by Luin Goldring and Patricia Landolt, 3–27. Toronto: University of Toronto Press.

Goldring, Luin, Carolina Berinstein, and Judith K. Bernhard. 2009. "Institutionalizing Precarious Migratory Status in Canada." *Citizenship Studies* 13 (3): 239–265.

Gonzáles, Roberto. 2015. *Lives in Limbo: Undocumented and Coming of Age in America*. Berkeley: University of California Press.

Hudson, Graham, Idil Atak, Michele Manocchi, and Charity-Ann Hannan. 2017. "(No) Access T.O.: A Pilot Study on Sanctuary City Policy in Toronto, Canada." RCIS Working Papers no. 2017/1. Toronto: Ryerson Centre for Immigration and Settlement.

Hulchanski, David. 2010. "Three Cities within Toronto: Income Polarization among Toronto's Neighbourhoods, 1970–2005." Toronto: Neighbourhood Change Community-University Research Alliance (CURA), St. Christopher House, and Cities Centre.

Hynie, Michaela, Chris I. Ardern, and Angela Robertson. 2016. "Emergency Room Visits by Uninsured Child and Adult Residents in Ontario, Canada: What Diagnoses, Severity, and Visit Disposition Reveal about the Impact of Being Uninsured." *Journal of Immigrant and Minority Health* 18:948–956.

Jimenez, Marina. 2006. "Ottawa Rules Out Amnesty For 200,000 Illegal Workers." *Globe and Mail*, October 27.

Johnson, Corey, Reece Jones, Anssi Paasi, Louise Amoore, Alison Mountz, Mark Salter, and Chris Rumford. 2011. "Interventions on Rethinking 'The Border' in Border Studies." *Political Geography* 30 (2): 61–69.

Landolt, Patricia, and Luin Goldring. 2016. "Assembling Noncitizenship through the Work of Conditionality." *Citizenship Studies* 19 (8): 853–869.

Landolt, Patricia, Paloma E. Villegas, and Francisco Villegas. 2012. "Patchworks of Access: Education and Healthcare for Immigrants with Precarious Legal Status." Research summary. Toronto: Centre of Excellence for Research on Immigration and Settlement (CERIS).

Marrow, Helen B. 2012. "Deserving to a Point: Unauthorized Immigrants in San Francisco's Universal Access Healthcare Model." *Social Science and Medicine* 74 (6): 846–854.

Menjívar, Cecilia. 2006. "Liminal Legality: Salvadoran and Guatemalan Immigrants' Lives in the United States." *American Journal of Sociology* 111 (4): 999–1037.

Morris, Lydia. 2003. "Managing Contradiction: Civic Stratification and Migrants' Rights." *International Migration Review* 37 (1): 74–100.

NOII (No One Is Illegal). 2006. "Access to Education without Fear of Deportation." Letter, May 24. Toronto: NOII. http://toronto.nooneisillegal.org/node/390.

———. 2015. *Often Asking, Always Telling: The Toronto Police Service and the Sanctuary City Policy*. Toronto: NOII. http://rabble.ca/sites/rabble/files/often_asking_always_telling_-_kedits_dec_1.pdf.

Nyers, Peter. 2006. "The Accidental Citizen: Acts of Sovereignty and (Un)making Citizenship." *Economy and Society* 35 (1): 22–41.

Ong, Aihwa, and Stephen J. Collier, eds. 2005. *Global Assemblages: Technology, Politics, and Ethics as Anthropological Problems*. Malden, MA: Blackwell.

Ontario Government. n.d. Ontario Education Act. RSO 1997, Chapter E2. Toronto: Ontario Ministry of Education. https://www.ontario.ca/laws/statute/90e02?_ga= 1.42353253.1320585842.1480385668#BK58. Accessed July 2, 2018.

Pratt, Anna. 2005. *Securing Borders: Detention and Deportation in Canada*. Vancouver: University of British Columbia Press.

Saad, Samia. 2011. "A Secret Life: The Psychosocial Impact of Falling Out of Status." Master's thesis, York University, Toronto.

Sassen, Saskia. 2006. *Territory, Authority, Rights: From Medieval to Global Assemblages*. Princeton, NJ: Princeton University Press.

Satzewich, Victor. 2013. "Visa Officers as Gatekeepers of a State's Borders: The Social Determinants of Discretion in Spousal Sponsorship Cases in Canada." *Journal of Ethnic and Migration Studies* 40 (9): 1450–1469.

Schweitzer Reinhard. 2014. "The Making and Unmaking of Irregular Migration: Migrant 'Illegality,' Regularisation, and Deportation in Spain and the UK." *Integration and International Migration: Pathways and Integration Policies*. Integrim Online Papers. http://www.integrim.eu/wp-content/uploads/2014/02/Schweitzer-the-m aking-and-unmaking-of-irregular-migration.pdf.

Spire, Alexis. 2008. *Accueillir ou reconduire: Enquête sur les guichets de l'immigration.* Paris: Raisons D'Agir.

Statistics Canada. 2016. Table 051–0020, Number of Non-Permanent Residents, Canada, Provinces, and Territories, Quarterly (Persons). Ottawa: Statistics Canada.

TCF (Toronto Community Foundation). 2016. *Toronto's Vital Signs, 2016 Report.* Toronto: TCF. https://torontofoundation.ca/wp-content/uploads/2018/02/TVS 16FullReport.pdf.

TDSB (Toronto District School Board). 1999. "Equity Foundation." Policy P.037 CUR. Toronto: TDSB. http://www.tdsb.on.ca/Portals/0/HighSchool/docs/200.pdf.

———. 2012. "2011–2012 Students and Families: Demographic Profile." Census Fact Sheets. Toronto: TDSB. http://www.tdsb.on.ca/Portals/research/docs/2011-12Cen susFactSheet1-Demographics-17June2013.pdf.

TRC (Truth and Reconciliation Commission of Canada). 2015. *Honouring the Truth, Reconciling for the Future: Summary of the Final Report of the Truth and Reconciliation Commission of Canada.* Winnipeg: TRC.

Tyack, David. 2001. "Schools for Citizens: The Politics of Civic Education from 1799 to 1990." In *E Pluribus Unum? Contemporary and Historical Perspectives on Immigration and Political Incorporation*, edited by Gary Gerstle and John Mollenkopf, 331–370. New York: Russell Sage Foundation.

Varsanyi, Monica, Paul G. Lewis, Doris Marie Provinem, and Scott H. Decker. 2012. "A Multilayered Jurisdictional Patchwork: Immigration Federalism in the United States." *Law and Policy* 34 (2): 138–158.

Vickstrom, Erik. 2014. "Pathways into Irregular Status among Senegalese Migrants in Europe." *International Migration Review* 48 (4): 1062–1099.

Villegas, Francisco. 2013. "Getting to 'Don't Ask Don't Tell' at the Toronto District School Board: Mapping the Competing Discourses of Rights and Membership." In *Producing and Negotiating Non-Citizenship: Precarious Status in Canada*, edited by Luin Goldring and Patricia Landolt, 258–273. Toronto: University of Toronto Press.

Villegas, Paloma E. 2012. "Assembling and Re(Making) Migrant Illegalization: Mexican Migrants with Precarious Status in Canada." PhD diss., University of Toronto.

———. 2013. "Negotiating the Boundaries of Membership: Health Care Providers, Access to Social Goods, and Immigration Status." In *Producing and Negotiating Non-Citizenship: Precarious Status in Canada*, edited by Luin Goldring and Patricia Landolt, 221–237. Toronto: University of Toronto Press.

———. 2014. "'I Can't Even Buy a Bed Because I Don't Know if I'll Have to Leave Tomorrow': Temporal Orientations Among Mexican Precarious Status Migrants in Toronto." *Citizenship Studies* 18 (3–4): 277–291.

Willen, Sarah S. 2012. "How Is Health-Related 'Deservingness' Reckoned? Perspectives from Unauthorized Im/migrants in Tel Aviv." *Social Science and Medicine* 74 (6): 812–821.

PART IV

UNITED STATES

CHAPTER 9

Indigenous Maya Families from Yucatán in San Francisco: Hemispheric Mobility and Pedagogies of Diaspora

PATRICIA BAQUEDANO-LÓPEZ

The first indigenous laborers from Yucatán traveled to the United States as part of the Bracero Program between 1942 and 1964 to work in California's agricultural fields (Loza 2016; Roman 2016). In the decades after the program ended, other immigrants followed this first group of laborers, working cyclically for approximately five years at a time in the United States before returning to Yucatán. Today, immigrants from Yucatán reside and work in US urban areas, mostly in service sector jobs. Many live in transnational family units with second-generation, US-born children (Baquedano-López and Borge Janetti 2017; Casanova 2011; Whiteside 2006). These transnational families have members and relatives in Mexico and the United States, and in their expanded social network they create and are part of transnational communities (Levitt 2001; Stephen 2007). Although California has long been a destination state, the greater San Francisco metropolitan area can be considered a new destination, as more and more immigrant indigenous Maya families have moved there in recent years (Baquedano-López and Borge Janetti 2017; Terrazas 2011). The growing presence of Mexican Maya indigenous students in K–12 schools also represents a noticeable demographic trend in the metropolitan areas of San Diego, Orange County, Los Angeles, and San Francisco, a trend that has not been addressed in educational research. We know very little about the ways these students enter the bureaucracies of education or about existing support structures they might find in schools and civil society. In this chapter, I draw from my ethnographic, linguistic, and anthropological study of a K–5 public elementary school I call Metropolitan Elementary School; it is in San Francisco and has a majority Latino,[1] Spanish-speaking student body representing various regions across Mexico and Central America. Indigenous students from Yucatán make up roughly 25 percent of the school's population. I advance a framework for rethinking the migration of indigenous groups (also known as members of original communities) as the deliberate movement across geopolitical borders to find and create a place for themselves in response to practices of continued settler colonialism in their communities of origin. These processes shed light on discussions of rights to land, education, and ultimately, to migrate. Furthermore, in this analysis I examine how these rights are understood, enforced, or curtailed by social institutions including the government, such as schools, and nonprofit organizations such as cultural, advocacy, or educational programs. I offer an in-depth analysis of parent-child interactions at a school-led workshop to illustrate how immigrant families develop pedagogies of migration that they consider beneficial for their children to witness and learn.

Indigenous Maya students are often labeled "Latino" and "Spanish-speaking" in school records even though many come from Yucatec Maya-speaking homes where Spanish is often a second language.[2] Such "Latinization" processes are also common in new destination sites (Salas and Portes 2017) as schools and other social institutions respond to a growing population of immigrants from Mexico and Central America by grouping them into a single immigrant category that homogenizes unique backgrounds and histories. Against this push to assimilate, families at Metropolitan Elementary find ways to recognize group differences while still expressing pan-ethnic solidarity in diaspora. The notion of "diaspora" as used here indicates the movement of people by force or choice from one nation-state to another. The movement both creates and advances ideological, social, and economic ties to the community of origin (Baquedano-López and Mangual Figueroa 2011). Here I follow James Clifford (1994:317), who has noted that groups in diaspora "work to maintain community, selectively preserving and recovering traditions, 'customizing,' and 'versioning' them in novel, hybrid, and often antagonistic situations." This repositioning of knowledge is what native scholar Sandy Grande (2004:175) considers an important decolonial act— an active recovery of knowledge that is historically and culturally reimagined and reinvested for current and future generations. Thus, parents at Metropolitan Elementary bring rich and complex understandings of their migratory experience and expect their children to acquire them as well.

Hemispheric Indigeneity and Migration: Land Rights and the Public Imaginary

The framework of hemispheric indigeneity advanced by Thomas Biolsi (2005) and Robin DeLugan (2010) is helpful for examining the relationship between indigenous self/selves and the politics of place. This framework considers indigenous peoples' migrations as actual disruptions to settler colonialism, given that many still live within the structure of a colonial formation based on settler land appropriation for profit (Veracini 2010; Wolfe 2006).[3] Neoliberal practices of binational agreements such as the North American Free Trade Agreement (NAFTA) and land tenure reforms are continued manifestations of the state of settler colonialism. Indigenous peoples' migration is both a response and resistance to the settler state (Castellanos, Gutiérrez Najera, and Aldama 2012). As with all social categories, the definition of "indigeneity" is fluid and context-based, but the 2004 example supplied by the UN Working Group for Indigenous Peoples most effectively reframes the settler colonial state and the ongoing demand for indigenous sovereignty.

> Indigenous communities, peoples and nations are those which, having a historical continuity with pre-invasion and pre-colonial societies that developed on their territories, consider themselves distinct from other sectors of the societies now prevailing on those territories, or parts of them. They form at present non-dominant sectors of society and are determined to preserve, develop and transmit to future generations their ancestral territories, and their ethnic identity, as the basis of their continued existence as peoples, in accordance with their own cultural patterns, social institutions and legal system. (UN Department of Economic and Social Affairs, 2004)

The reference to land rights is key, echoing the 1996 San Andrés Peace Accords between the Frente Zapatista de Liberación Nacional (FZLN) and the Mexican federal government, which also references territory as "the material basis for their reproduction as a people and the expression of the indissoluble unity between man, land, and nature" (UN Peacemaker 1996). It is thus possible to conceive of migration within the same hemisphere as extending the reach of those rights; that is, hemispheric migration of indigenous groups from Latin America represents an act of self-preservation from the neoliberal politics that continue to disperse and potentially compromise the life expectations of communities.

As an illustration, in the following excerpt from a translated interview conducted by my research team,[4] an indigenous immigrant mother at Metropolitan Elementary School wrestles with a new Latino identity politics in migration: "I think that I am like Maya. I am from the Maya culture, and I was born with my grandparents, who were pure Maya. . . . We always say that we are Latinas. A lot of people do not know [that we are Maya]. . . . Well, at first, when we say Maya, a lot of people used to tell me, 'No, you're Latinas.' Well, that's how it stayed. I am Latina then." This brief excerpt exemplifies the fluidity of categories, but not in a liberal or postmodern sense; rather, it demonstrates how the categories are deeply tied to systems of power. The notion of "purity" here is significant, for it signals this woman's understanding of and struggle with authenticity. It also reflects the ways she wrestles with "double consciousness" and the multiple perceptions she must try to reconcile (Du Bois 2003), including the external imposition of a new identity category in the statement "No, you're Latinas."

Public attention was first drawn to immigrants from Yucatán in San Francisco through stories in local newspapers such as "The Newest San Franciscans" (Burke 2002), "La nueva migración indígena: Los mayas de San Francisco" (Adelson 2002), and "From Southern Mexico to Northern California" (Hendricks 2003). These and other articles also discuss the economic precarities experienced by immigrants from Yucatán. The documentary film *El Recorrido/The Journey* (Bazúa Morales 2006) highlights migration from Oxkutzcab, Yucatán, a major sending city and a formerly rich agricultural area, to San Francisco; it features portraits of indigenous young men and adolescents crossing the US border and facing the dangers of HIV exposure, depression, and crime. While stories like these identified the growing indigenous immigrant population from Yucatán, many were couched in the language of a racialized and legendary Other, the immigrants as descendants of the great Maya civilization on the brink of an imagined second extinction in an unfriendly metropolis. The fact is that migration to San Francisco has been an ongoing phenomenon since the mid-twentieth-century conclusion of the Bracero Program. Moreover, there is great diversity within the population in terms of immigrant status (documented, undocumented, mixed-status), family situation (nuclear, extended, transnational), and economic level (business owners or managers, manual or service laborers, unemployed). More recent media reports have focused on the expanding influence of Yucatec cuisine in the Bay Area, some featuring restaurant owners, managers, and chefs from Yucatán (Fletcher 2009; Kauffman 2015) and thus providing a more complex view of a population that is making economic advances and participating visibly in civil society.

It is difficult to pinpoint the exact reasons behind the migration circuit between Yucatán and San Francisco. The economic integration efforts between Mexico and the United States, especially in the 1990s through NAFTA, have greatly affected migratory movements. Indigenous land tenure rights were compromised as economic need led to short-term-profit sale agreements between the government, developers, and indigenous communities. Changing the terms of subsidies allocated to small farmers led to an internal migration from rural to urban areas, a trend that began to support systems of labor outsourcing (Appendini 1996; Fox 2011; Fox and Rivera-Salgado 2004; Massey, Durand, and Malone 2003; Stephen 2007). While the Bracero Program was a significant precursor of outward migration from Yucatán to the United

States, it was not until the 1980s and early 1990s that the number of immigrants to the United States increased significantly (Barenboim 2013; Lewin Fischer 2007). Outmigration has also been attributed to the collapse of Yucatán's central industry, sisal rope (*henequén*), in the early 1990s, when manufacturers stopped receiving support from the Mexican government (Lewin Fischer 2007; Rodríguez, Wittlinger, and Manzanero Rodríguez 2007). The ensuing industrial crisis, advanced through unreasonable treaties and new agrarian laws—which offered purported choices for individuals to enter global markets through individual titling—led to massive migration from rural communities to cities like Mérida in Yucatán and Chetumal and Cancún in the state of Quintana Roo. With its tourist economy, Cancún is often described as an international "migration school" for indigenous peoples (Castellanos 2010; Lewin Fischer 2007). In less than a decade, the economic and political changes transformed landowning indigenous farmers into subsistence workers of the Global South, forcing a reterritorialization movement to the North that responds to and resists economic and land dispossession.

As for the US context, anti-immigrant sentiments and policies heightened as the trade agreements were being signed in the 1990s.[5] In 1994 California Governor Pete Wilson led an anti-Mexican immigration movement during his reelection campaign that culminated with the passage of Proposition 187, a ballot initiative that denied public services, primarily education and health care, to undocumented immigrants and their families. And while later deemed unconstitutional, the proposition contributed to the public perception of immigrants as draining public funds, thereby creating in the public imaginary an underclass of undesirable people. Such sentiments were revived through the 2016 presidential campaign of Donald Trump, his executive order banning immigration from certain countries,[6] and his hardened deportation policies to secure the US-Mexico border. Following California's Proposition 187, in 1996 Congress passed the Anti-Terrorism and Effective Death Penalty Act, which contained serious punitive provisions against immigrants, including the retroactive detention of any permanent resident or unauthorized immigrant convicted of a crime. In fact, that piece of national legislation effectively reframed undocumented migrants as terrorists, and with the provision restricting the number of appeals they could make to one, it limited their options for obtaining relief from unlawful imprisonment. Two years later, in 1998, California voters passed Proposition 227, dismantling bilingual education programs in favor of monolingual English instruction and leaving thousands of bilingual immigrant children and their families in educational limbo as new policies and programs were disestablished across the state's school districts. Eighteen years later, California voters amended the provisions of Proposition 227 and passed a new multilingual California act, Senate Bill 1174, which provided students and families with a choice to learn a language other than English in an increasingly globalized economy where multilingualism is considered an asset. The anti-immigration presidency of Donald Trump has laid out a path of intolerance and violence that is being felt across the social institutions that serve immigrants.

Settler Colonial States and Globalization: An Indigenous Cosmopolitanism?

Central to my argument is the proposition that indigenous migrants from Yucatán, already forced out of their lands as a result of Spanish colonial rule, continue to live within the structure of a colonial formation based on settler land appropriation (Veracini 2010; Wolfe 2006). Because of the United States' capitalist interests across much of Latin America, one can consider the entire area to constitute an enduring site of the colonial state. Under the 1992 agrarian law reform, communal Mexican lands known as *ejidos* could be divided into parcels for individual titling, which in turn could be traded, developed by third parties, or used for foreign investment. The prospects of entering the global market were enticing, to say the least, especially when such neoliberal maneuvers of the state complemented NAFTA regulations. However, the land sales led to increased privatization efforts and the loss of land rights as many indigenous families were forced to lease or sell their lands in a difficult economy (Cornelius and Myhre 1998). The practices once again rendered previously victimized indigenous peoples deterritorialized. Consistent with settler colonialism, new settlers—corporations—became emplaced on recently appropriated land through new investments. As amply discussed in the field of Native studies, such practices of settler emplacement create the conditions for indigenous erasure, in some instances through genocide, exploitation of land and resources, or relocation (Tuck and McKenzie 2015). A recent example in the United States of Native land exploitation is the water crisis created by the North Dakota Access Pipeline route, an oil pipeline running through North Dakota, South Dakota, Iowa, and parts of Illinois with potential damage to the quality of local water and to sacred burial sites. Even though Native communities in the area own the land through federal reservations and other reparations due to earlier politics of displacement, indigenous communities continue to be economically assailed by foreign investors (settlers) and their subsistence (water, land) threatened by capitalist projects. Hemispheric migration of indigenous groups is thus not just an effect of settler colonialism; it is also an act of self-preservation performed on behalf of future generations.[7]

Taking this understanding of settler emplacement and relocation as a starting point, I contend that the circuits of migration to global cities give rise to new subject formations among indigenous migrants. As transnational cosmopolitan subjects, indigenous immigrants can and often do claim rights as either rural or, in the case of immigrants in San Francisco, urban subjects. David Held (2010) has argued that at the core of cosmopolitan aspirations is people's desire to create communities unconstrained by space, that is, to create transnational or translocal communities. Writing more specifically on migration by indigenous groups in California, including some from Yucatán, DeLugan (2010:93) defines a new cosmopolitanism centered around an indigenous framework. She proposes the concept of an "indigenous cosmopolitanism," understood as the ways in which forms of difference (individual, ethnic, national) and unity (collective, indigenous, human) coexist. This framework troubles rather than neutralizes the experience of indigeneity in Latin America and the United States since there are multiple indigenous groups on the continent. It also shifts the dominant neoliberal paradigms of cosmopolitanism and globalization, which, Walter Mignolo (2000) has argued, erase significant historical differences and experiences that resulted from colonization. DeLugan's indigenous cosmopolitanism is a particularly valuable concept because it requires that we critically understand intersectionality in cosmopolitanism. Along with the impetus for urban relocation and its opportunities, long-standing inequalities are often being reproduced in new locations through continued racialization of gendered, immigrant bodies.

The receiving society and people in closer contact with recent immigrants have or develop notions about recent immigrants that often exemplify long-standing and new social and racial tensions. For example, a popular restaurant in the Mission District of San Francisco called Poc-Chuc has been well covered in the media with reviews and features on its owners, who are from Yucatán. At Poc-Chuc (the name of a citrus-marinated dish in Yucatán), the décor features designs inspired by Maya inscription and art, including a depiction resembling a deity from the *Chilam Balam*, a Maya text (figure 9.1).[8] For restaurant patrons, Maya significations and commodifications—food, images, and labor—socialize an episteme of the civilized in cosmopolitan culinary experience, a safe venturing into the Other (Said 1978). As for the owners, they must negotiate the politics of representation. Choosing a design that captures multiple readings of "indigenous" advertises both tradition and innovation as well as a link between the distal "there" and the proximal "here" of translocal cosmopolitanism, thus illustrating the difference and unity framework that DeLugan (2010) identifies as part of indigenous cosmopolitanism.

9.1. Maya representations

Strategies of Visibility in Migration

A 2010 survey from the Institute for the Development of Mayan Culture found that 24 percent of all migrants from Yucatán make the United States their destination, and 76 percent of those moved to California (Solis Lizama and Fortuny Loret de Mola 2010). Their population is still relatively small. According to the Instituto de los Mexicanos en el Exterior,[9] the Mexican consulate in San Francisco has been steadily granting 1,000 to 1,500 consular cards per year to immigrants from Yucatán that allow them to open bank accounts and perform other economic transactions.

Like other ethnic groups, immigrants from Yucatán necessarily build a structure of visibility and enact rights to the city through complex networks of family, friends, and associations based on communities of origin and migration (Adler 2004; Barenboim 2013; Burke 2004; Cornejo Portugal and Fortuny Loret de Mola 2011; Martell, Pineda, and Tapia 2007). Jonathan Fox and Gaspar Rivera-Salgado (2004) discuss the ways indigenous migrants from Oaxaca built what the authors call "translocal communities of citizenship" in becoming active members in the complex, multilocal, and multisited geographies they have constructed to survive in US cities. Hometown associations and community and cultural organizations based on translocal alliances are also institutions that crucially support immigrant integration into new societies while maintaining their ties to home communities, even when it involves overcoming legacies of regional conflict (Escala-Rabadán, Bada, and Rivera-Salgado 2006; Fox and Rivera-Salgado 2004).

Cultural preservation groups in northern California include grassroots organizations such as the Asociación Maya-Yucateca del Área de la Bahía (Mayab) in San Francisco and Chan Kahal in San Rafael. The latter has had more active relations with the government in Yucatán, occasionally participating in the Three-for-One program designed to spur infrastructure spending in migrant-sending areas.[10] It is important to note, however, that these institutionalized politics of recognition and enlistment seek to regenerate public funding previously taken from rural communities through neoliberal policies and treaties in Mexico that have benefited the few at the expense of the many (Appendini 1996; Ruiz 2010). And while these two organizations are not strictly hometown associations (Escala-Rabadán, Bada, and Rivera-Salgado 2006), their activities encompass efforts to provide education to children and youth, meet the needs of political organization and legal interpretation, and cultivate artistic and cultural traditions such as traditional dance and Maya language classes. The associations have also been working closely with other civic and binational organizations to arrange for medical and mental health services, family reunification, and repatriation at death, and they collaborate to secure the rights of this immigrant population. For example, concerning legal rights, Asociación Mayab has been supporting the inquiry into and legal efforts surrounding the death of Luis Góngora Pat, an immigrant from Yucatán killed in the Mission District by police in 2016. The circumstances of Góngora Pat's death have opened a window into the difficult lives of indigenous workers from Yucatán. He had been in San Francisco working janitorial and restaurant jobs for more than fourteen years, regularly sending remittances to his family in Yucatán. According to his relatives in San Francisco, it was only shortly before his death that he had become homeless and ill, and he was looking for a way to return home (Wong 2016). The murder case began unfolding in the midst of the Black Lives Matter movement and has drawn responses primarily from civil rights groups against police brutality toward racialized minorities and particularly toward the homeless in urban centers.

Grassroots fund-raising and legal and cultural actions, combined with the efforts of cross-border activism, create what Don Mitchell and Nik Heynen (2009) have called a "structure of visibility," which allows people to normalize a different way of being in the city.[11] For immigrants from Yucatán, cultural festivities in the public sphere include annual *vaquerías* and patron saint festivities in Southern California (Baquedano-López and Borge Janetti

2017; Solis Lizama and Fortuny Loret de Mola 2010).[12] In San Francisco, Asociación Mayab participates with other community organizations in the broader civic life by performing dances at county fairs, schools, restaurants, and museums. At the elaborate annual San Francisco Carnaval (Mardi Gras) parade, members of the Asociación Mayab and other groups from Yucatán who often come from as far north as Oregon, another new destination site, wear their traditional dress and dance along the parade route. Such instances demonstrate how multiple alliances between San Francisco's distinct Yucatecan groups, clubs, and organizations create opportunities for Maya immigrants to be visible and enact rights to the city (Lefebvre 1991; Mitchell and Heynen 2009).

Finally, within this community are a number of nonprofit organizations that in one way or another interface with the school I studied. An afterschool program I call the Star Program is an on-site resource that provides academic help, including language support, for immigrant families from Yucatán. The Asociación Mayab is another resource for indigenous Maya children that offers cultural revitalization programming such as traditional dancing and Maya lessons off-site. While it does not have an institutional agreement with Metropolitan Elementary, the Asociación Mayab affirms a sense of identity and belonging for the school's students. Having a nonprofit dedicated to issues affecting the immigrant community from Yucatán adds a layer of visibility to the community and the issues it faces.

Researcher Positionality and Approach

My inquiry into indigenous migration from Yucatán has its origins in my family's history. I am an immigrant to the United States, born in Yucatán and of a mixed racial heritage that includes a paternal grandmother who, I was told, spoke Maya and a little Spanish and a maternal grandfather born in Lebanon. My father's family moved from a smaller city, Conkal, to the capital city Mérida a generation before he was born. My grandmother died when my father was a child, and I imagine that her death curtailed any possibilities for cultural affiliation with the indigenous Maya side of my family. In the settler colonial state that operates in Yucatán, where there is a well-established racialized society with indigenous people at the bottom of the social hierarchy, her death simplified my family's categorization as mixed race and solidified our aspiring middle-class status. My maternal grandfather, originally from Zgharta, Lebanon, profited greatly from the sisal rope industry that would eventually collapse in the mid-1980s, several years after his death. I did not meet either grandparent, but their life itineraries influence my own in profound ways. My interest in knowing more about migration of indigenous Maya from Yucatán began after I moved to Berkeley, near San Francisco, from Los Angeles, where I had lived for a number of years. I clearly remember the morning I opened the *San Francisco Chronicle* to the headline I mentioned earlier, "The Newest San Franciscans." Although articulating different subject positions and economic means, I saw continuities and discontinuities in this "new" migration process that were parallel to my own. In my research projects over the years I have looked at the nexus of migration and education of Latino students in public schools, nonprofit day care centers, afterschool programs, and catechism classes in Catholic parishes. This study of indigenous students and families at Metropolitan Elementary School affords me the opportunity to further examine migration within hemispheric settler colonial practices and voice my own perspective on this process.

The research that informs this chapter was planned in two phases in order to understand the migratory circuit created and traversed by indigenous immigrants from Yucatán. The first phase was conducted in Yucatán during three short field stays in 2008–2009. With a team of researchers under my supervision, I carried out home visits with return migrant families, transnational families, and families who had not left Yucatán. We recorded several hours of video footage in some of the homes and conducted in-depth interviews with other people across different sectors of society, including journalists, government officials, high school teachers, and local university professors. The second phase of the study, 2013–2016, was primarily conducted at Metropolitan Elementary School and at its nonprofit afterschool Star Program, which espouses an academic and college-going curriculum. At the school, my research team examined the educational and linguistic experiences of indigenous students from Yucatán. We also studied the ways administrators, teachers, and other students responded to the growing number of indigenous Maya students; utilized strategies of inclusion (or exclusion); and articulated, took up, or rejected their own notions of indigeneity. We conducted weekly visits to classrooms and helped coordinate special school activities and events. We also followed community events outside the school that involved several government and nonprofit organizations serving this immigrant community.

Pedagogies of Diaspora at Metropolitan Elementary School

Metropolitan Elementary is one of seventy-two elementary schools in the San Francisco Unified School District. Despite the passing of Proposition 227, which eliminated bilingual education,[13] the district has waged a vigorous campaign to enlist students into its dual-language immersion program. Under this immersion model, children are instructed in Spanish for 80 percent of class time in kindergarten, moving toward 50 percent instructional time in Spanish by the fifth grade. While the school keeps records of languages spoken at home, primarily to determine how to place students in English-language learner programs, the exact number of students of indigenous background is not recorded. Many indigenous students are considered Latino if the language identified at home is Spanish; thus the school's Latino category includes indigenous students. For three consecutive years, we asked families to complete a language background questionnaire, and through interviews with students and families we estimated that 25 percent of the student population at the school was indigenous Maya. There were other indigenous students at the school whose home language was Mazahua (Central Mexico) or Ch'ol (Chiapas, Mexico).

During our weekly visits to the school, we began to observe a group of Latino parents advocating for academic programming that went beyond mere recognition of students' backgrounds through the popular educational and multiculturalist approach on display at ethnic festivities. The parents wanted to engage a critical perspective on issues that represented the complexity of immigrant families' lived experience, including family reunification, deportation, mixed legal residency status, and academic tracking of their children beginning at lower grade levels. I inquired about the possibility of working with these parents, and over time we established a *colaborativo* (collaborative) in the form of monthly workshops addressing the topics of interest generated by parents. Our first series of workshops, mostly held in Spanish, centered on art as a means to share family stories of migration from various Mexican and Guatemalan states. We requested space from the summer nonprofit Star Program to carry out the art projects over the course of four days, and we asked participants if we could videotape their interactions for further analysis. We began by having the families work on a monarch butterfly stencil template created by Bay Area artist and immigration activist Favianna Rodriguez (figure 9.2).[14] In this particular workshop, mothers and their children turned their art projects into opportunities to discuss citizenship, transnational and diaspora living, and cultural differences. The most significant pedagogical moment came during a "share-out" activity in which participating families took turns explaining their collaborative butterfly art to the rest of the group. The descriptions soon turned into migration *testimonio*, a familiar oral genre that produces and circulates discourses of solidarity (Beverley 2008); in turn, that can bring about social consciousness, transformation, and change (Delgado Bernal, Burciaga, and Flores Carmona 2012). The *testimonios* invoked a collectivity articulated among families through the recognition and validation of shared experience that connected a "desire for objectivity" with "the desire for solidarity" (Beverley 2008:571).

9.2. Butterfly stories

The families' *testimonios* served multiple functions. Discursively, they introduced to workshop participants, the director of the summer program, and the research team a powerful genre of recounting collective experiences that could perhaps be considered inappropriate pedagogical material—or even triggering—given its high emotional content. However, this genre has tremendous pedagogical value. During the activity, one of the mothers commented on the importance of knowing about immigrant families' histories and seeing oneself reflected in the curriculum. Additionally, the *testimonio* genre was being socialized to the children and scaffolded by the mothers with examples on how to present personal experiences of migration. In the following translated excerpt from a video recording of the event, a participant from Mexico, Ms. Almodóvar (pseudonym), was commenting on the art projects illustrating the common "here/there" polarity between home country and the United States as well as a view of migration as both liberatory and necessary for elevating humanity.

> I can talk about migration and all the anti-immigrant laws at the national level with them [the children], and they know, but it's not the same thing [as listening] to other versions from other people, right? We are living [in] a difficult moment about issues of migration that our children do not realize. Yes, they

know, but they do not hear it from us. That these deportations—all those children coming from Honduras! How they are throwing them out as if they were chickens! . . . In Honduras, El Salvador, they don't come because they want to come but because of the situation in our countries—the policies in our countries make us migrate to these countries.

At the workshops, Maya mothers and students were present but mostly silent; however, Ms. Almodóvar brought them into the general discussion. Turning to one of the mothers from Yucatán, she added, "We don't want to leave our culture. We don't want to leave our hot tortillas, the *panuchos*, right?"[15] The questions prompted a mother from Yucatán to say that her son loved *panuchos* very much. Ms. Almodóvar continued,

> Let's talk of all this culture of handmade tortillas, the mortar chili, of the little saucepan from the grandmother, because each thing has its own history. So this will make them wiser, and it will make them understand the needs of other people and that we are in the same situation, that we are human beings and as human beings we need respect. It does not matter [what] our gender, religion . . . political party [is]—what matters is human rights.

Ms. Almodóvar's words speak to the desire to render legible those things that make immigrants unique, here referencing cultural practices and even foods like *panuchos*. In doing so she invited an affiliative response from one of the mothers, who became a participant in the narrative. Moreover, the invocation of the grandmother figure universalizes and brings together disparate experiences to a single, core, maternal trope of family unification. The narrative socializes empathetic practices in general but also specifically toward immigrant families in the room.

We carried out the *colaborativo* workshops over the course of two years, varying their structure and content. In some instances, the pedagogical force of Maya indigenous parents addressing their own relocation experiences—like the mother who accepted the identity category of "Latina"—is reminiscent of the narrated experiences of other indigenous groups that US educational institutions have attempted to strip of their core indigenous identity (Lomawaima and McCarty 2006). But like them, Maya immigrants have fought back, advancing indigenous knowledge in many cases through community-based education and intervention. At Metropolitan Elementary School, indigenous and Latino parents' efforts to disrupt practices of assimilation broadcast an attentiveness and refusal of the dynamics of cultural and linguistic assimilation. In many ways, they too are actively advocating for their linguistic rights and for their rights as citizens of the district and city.

These advocacy efforts have received varying levels of support. In 2017, a three-week course on Maya culture and language for parents and students was held at the school in collaboration with researchers and teachers from the Instituto de Antropología e Historia site in Yucatán and the Centro de Educación, Capacitación y Difusión Humanística de Yucatán.[16] The course also covered linguistic rights in migration, a topic not always addressed in the context of indigenous Maya migration. It was a first-of-its-kind educational approach for parents and children that converted the school into what could be considered a semi-autonomous public space, to extend Fox and Rivera-Salgado's model of migrant civil society laid out in chapter 1 of this volume. In my experience working for more than eight years on indigenous Maya immigrant education issues, I have found that research-based and educational institutions are more receptive to aiding immigrant indigenous Maya families than are government immigration-based offices in Yucatán or nonprofit hometown associations in the United States.[17] It is not easy to pinpoint why that might be the case, but the lack of funding often prevents innovation and the sustainability of government-sponsored programs addressing immigrant issues. At the local community organization level, including hometown associations, membership and leadership structures are not always clear. Further, there are also long-standing issues of trust that need to be addressed and bridged with government officials, academic researchers, and community activists in order to support immigrant communities more fully.

Conclusion

Land privatization and other binational neoliberal policies affecting indigenous sovereignty, land, and cultural legacy have resulted in the forced migration of indigenous Maya to San Francisco's greater metropolitan area. Over the course of two decades, a mostly male labor population of immigrants has expanded to include transnational families with children born in the United States, establishing second- and third-generation Maya entering US public schools and other social institutions. I find the framework of hemispheric indigeneity (Biolsi 2005; DeLugan 2010) helpful for rethinking indigenous peoples' migration as disruptions to settler colonialism's fixed-place practices such as the reallocation and sale of *ejido* lands in Mexico and tribal reservations' land loss in the United States; it is a lens through which to examine mobilities and resistances at the hemispheric scale. Indeed, as the *testimonio* of Ms. Almodóvar indicates, immigrants understand that place is unfixed, and they recognize and identify with a range of experiences across different hemispheric locations — the unaccompanied children from Central America, the homemade meals where "home" is a multiple referent, and even the universal grandmother trope of family reunification. Her perspective illustrates how mothers' stories can carry an important pedagogical force for socializing children, other parents, and school staff to understand the disjunctures immigrants face and to mobilize resources toward linguistic preservation as cultural inheritance. The parental interventions at the workshops were also central in teaching the importance of respecting cultures, identities, and immigrant families' human rights.

In an era of restrictive migration practices under the Trump administration, already exemplified in executive orders against immigrants, it becomes vital to recognize the government's practices of surveillance and deportation. Through programming and other interventions, researchers and grassroots organizations can lend support to immigrant communities and bring attention to issues related to the education of their children. The threat of school choice and privatization as well as the loss of access to public services will continue to affect families in migration, given that they still depend on US economic and political decisions for crucial support. As the population grows and indeed as US-born Maya children become the "newest San Franciscans," as the *San Francisco Chronicle* story heralds, possibilities for engaging multiple subjectivities in the public imaginary will emerge. It is imperative that those working with immigrant communities continue to lend their resources and voices to advance a fair and just society in these unsettling times.

Notes

I am grateful to the teachers, parents, and students at Metropolitan Elementary School for their ideas and invaluable commentaries on immigration. I thank the members of my research team at the University of California, Berkeley: graduate students Gabriela Borge Janetti, Rosalinda Godinez, Susana Castro, and Omi Salas-Santa Cruz; and students from the Undergraduate Research Apprentice Program Rocio Aguilar, Marilu Aguilar Moreno, Diana Gama, Luz Bertadillo, Jessica del Castillo, Stefany Espana, Diana Gama, Ezequiel Gorrocino, Mirayda Guzman, Danitza Morante, Nerelyn Hernandez, Karla Garcia, Catalina Monteon, Maricruz Pool-Chan, Alejandra Ramirez, Sujey Reynoso, Jason Whang, and Consuelo Velazquez. Funding for this project was provided by a grant from the Spencer Foundation and a faculty grant from the University of California Institute for Mexico and the United Sates and the Consejo Nacional de Ciencia y Tecnología (UC MEXUS–CONACyT).

1. The term "Latino" here is used as a rubric for a much more complex set of identities and experiences that are not always gendered and male. Other uses include "Latin@" to avoid male gender marking in Spanish and "Latinx" as a gender-neutral notation that expands the female/male gender binary. Latinos also represent a multi-

plicity of race and ethnic groups, including people of Afro-descent, whites, mestizos, indigenous people, and members of other racial groups with distinct although shared histories (Aparicio and Chavéz Silverman 1997).

2. Yucatec Maya, Maaya t'aan, is the indigenous language spoken in the Yucatán Peninsula. It is one of sixty-eight indigenous languages spoken in Mexico.

3. See also Goeman (2014) for a discussion of the Native American (indigenous) spatial politics for reclaiming place through cultural, historical, and discursive practices.

4. Translations are mine unless otherwise indicated.

5. In 1986 the US Immigration Reform and Control Act provided the opportunity for 2.3 million Mexicans to obtain legal status, but most immigrants from Yucatán did not benefit from the amnesty law because they did not meet the continuous US residency requirement, indicating perhaps that the immigrant population at the time had shorter spans of stay in the United States (Adler 2004; Martell, Pineda, and Tapia 2007).

6. Executive Order Protecting the Nation from Foreign Terrorist Entry into the United States, January 27, 2017 (Washington, DC: White House), https://www.white house.gov/the-press-office/2017/01/27/executive-order-protecting-nation-foreign -terrorist-entry-united-states.

7. An example is the high number of unaccompanied minors arriving in the United States in the summer of 2014, many of them indigenous Guatemalans who left their rural communities in response to violence and death threats by either the government or transnational gangs.

8. The *Chilam Balam* is a series of texts of the seventeenth and eighteenth centuries that contain both history and prophecy, combining elements of precolonial and colonial life in Yucatán. In one of the texts the world is explained as being held up by four carriers or gods representing four cardinal points. The Poc-Chuc restaurant image resembles the god Chac-Pahuatun. See Maya Web, http://www.mayaweb.nl, and Ralph Roys's 1967 translation, *The Book of Chilam Balam of Chumayel*.

9. In 2003 the Instituto para Mexicanos en el Exterior was created under the presidency of Vicente Fox to support initiatives and social integration of Mexican communities outside of Mexico. http://www.ime.gob.mx/gob/estadisticas/usa/estadisticas_usa .html.

10. Typically the Three-for-One program for migrants provides three pesos in federal, state, and local funds for each peso contributed by hometown associations for projects vetted by the Mexican government. The program is described in greater detail in Fox and Rivera-Salgado's chapter 1 of this volume.

11. Don Mitchell and Nik Heynen (2009) were referring to the rights to the city of homeless people, but the process can apply to immigrant groups as well.

12. A *vaquería* is a festivity that originated in colonial times to celebrate the branding of cattle.

13. Under the regulations of Proposition 227, bilingual education is available if parents sign a waiver to place their children in a bilingual program at their school. The San Francisco Unified School District also sponsors the Seal of Biliteracy program to recognize the linguistic abilities of its students (Tucker 2014).

14. An earlier analysis of the data was presented at an American Anthropological Association meeting (Baquedano-López and Borge Janetti 2014).

15. A *panucho* is a fried corn tortilla stuffed with refried black beans and topped with shredded turkey and marinated red onion slices.

16. The center is part of Yucatán's Secretaría de Investigación, Innovación y Educación Superior.

17. The Instituto para el Desarrollo de la Cultura Maya del Estado de Yucatán (Indemaya) has launched several programs attending to immigrants' needs with varying degrees of sustainability and success. Cabecitas Blancas (Little white heads) is a short-term family reunification program that covers the expenses of parents over sixty years old to visit their immigrant children in the United States; it is supported by Mexico's Secretaría de Relaciones Exteriores and the Mexican consulates in the United States.

References

Adelson, Naomi. 2002. "La nueva migración indígena: Los mayas de San Francisco." *La Jornada*, November 10. http://www.jornada.unam.mx/2002/11/10/mas-naomi.html.

Adler, Rachel. 2004. *Yucatecans in Dallas, Texas*. Boston: Pearson/Allyn and Bacon.

Aparicio, Frances, and Susana Chávez Silverman. 1997. *Tropicalizations: Transcultural Representations of Latinidad*. Hanover, NH: University Press of New England.

Appendini, Kirsten. 1996. *Changing Agrarian Institutions: Interpreting the Contradictions*. CERLAC Working Paper Series. Toronto: Centre for Research on Latin America and the Caribbean, York University.

Baquedano-López, Patricia, and Ariana Mangual Figueroa. 2011. "Language Socialization and Immigration." In *Handbook of Language Socialization*, edited by Alessandro Duranti, Elinor Ochs, and Bambi Schieffelin, 536–563. Malden, MA: Wiley-Blackwell.

Baquedano-López, Patricia, and Gabriela Borge Janetti. 2014. "Latina/o Parents Re-Creating and Re-Socializing Parent Involvement in School: A Case Study of a School in Northern California." Paper presented at the American Anthropological Association meeting, Washington, DC, December 3.

———. 2017. "The Maya Diaspora Yucatán–San Francisco: New Latino Educational Practices and Possibilities." In *US Latinization: Education and the New Latino South*, edited by S. Salas and P. Portes, 161–183. Albany: SUNY Press.

Barenboim, Deanna. 2013. "Belonging out of Place: Navigating 'Illegality' and Indigeneity in Migrant Maya California." PhD diss., University of Chicago.

Bazúa Morales, Carlos, prod. and dir. 2006. *El Recorrido—The Journey: Oxkutzcab, Yucatán, to San Francisco, California*. Film. Xibalba Productions.

Beverley, John. 2008. "Testimonio, Subalternity, and Narrative Authority." In *A Companion to Latin American Literature and Culture*, edited by Sara Castro-Klarén, 571–583. Malden, MA: Blackwell.

Biolsi, Thomas. 2005. "Imagined Geographies: Sovereignty, Indigenous Space, and American Indian Struggle." *American Ethnologist* 32 (2): 239–259.

Burke, Garance. 2002. "The Newest San Franciscans/Recent Maya Immigration Is Changing the Face of the City and Forging a Link to the Yucatan." *San Francisco Chronicle*, April 28. https://www.sfgate.com/magazine/article/The-Newest-San-Franciscans-Recent-Mayan-2844276.php.

———. 2004. "Yucatecos and Chiapanecos in San Francisco: Mayan Immigrants from New Communities." In *Indigenous Mexican Migrants in the United States*, edited by Jonathan Fox and Gaspar Rivera-Salgado, 343–354. La Jolla, CA: distributed by Lynne Rienner for the Center for US-Mexican Studies, University of California, San Diego.

Casanova, Saskias. 2011. "Ethnic Identity, Acculturation, and Perceived Discrimination for Indigenous Mexican Youth: A Cross-Cultural Comparative Study of Yucatec Maya Adolescents in the US and Mexico." PhD diss., Stanford University.

Castellanos, M. Bianet. 2010. "Cancún and the Campo." In *Holiday in Mexico: Critical Reflections on Tourist Encounters*, edited by Dina Berger and Andrew Grant Wood, 241–264. Durham, NC: Duke University Press.

Castellanos, M. Bianet, Lourdes Gutiérrez Najera, and Arturo Aldama, eds. 2012. *Comparative Indigeneities of the Americas: Towards a Hemispheric Approach*. Tucson: University of Arizona Press.

Clifford, James. 1994. "Diasporas." *Cultural Anthropology* 9 (3): 302–338.

Cornejo Portugal, Inés, and Patricia Fortuny Loret de Mola. 2011. "'Corrías sin saber adónde ibas': Proceso migratorio de mayas yucatecos a San Francisco, California." *Cultura y Representaciones Sociales* 5 (10): 82–106.

Cornelius, Wayne A., and David Myhre. 1998. Introduction to *The Transformation of Rural Mexico: Reforming the Ejido Sector*, edited by Wayne. A. Cornelius and David. Myhre, 1–20. La Jolla, CA: Center for US-Mexican Studies, University of California, San Diego.

Delgado Bernal, Dolores, Rebeca Burciaga, and Judith Flores Carmona. 2012. "Chicana/ Latina Testimonios: Mapping the Methodological, Pedagogical, and Political." *Equity and Excellence in Education* 45 (3): 363–372.

DeLugan, Robin. 2010. "Indigeneity across Borders: Hemispheric Migrations and Cosmopolitan Encounters." *American Ethnologist* 37 (1): 83–97.

Du Bois, W. E. B. 2003. *The Souls of Black Folk*. New York: Barnes and Noble. Originally published 1903.

Escala-Rabadán, Luis, Xóchitl Bada, and Gaspar Rivera-Salgado. 2006. "Mexican Migrant Civic and Political Participation in the US: The Case of Hometown Associations in Los Angeles and Chicago." *Norteamérica* 1 (2): 127–172.

Fletcher, Janet. 2009. "Yucatecan Connection." *San Francisco Chronicle*, April 26.

Fox, Jonathan. 2011. "Indigenous Mexican Immigrants." In *Beyond la Frontera: The History of Mexico-US Migration*, edited by Mark Overmyer-Velázquez, 161–178. New York: Oxford University Press.

Fox, Jonathan, and Gaspar Rivera-Salgado 2004. "Building Civil Society among Indigenous Migrants." In *Indigenous Mexican Migrants in the United States*, edited by Jonathan Fox and Gaspar Rivera-Salgado, 1–65. La Jolla: distributed by Lynne Rienner for the Center for US-Mexican Studies, University of California, San Diego.

Goeman, Mishuana. 2014. "Disrupting a Settler Colonial Grammar of Place." In *Theorizing Native Studies*, edited by Audra Simpson and Andrea Smith, 235–265. Durham, NC: Duke University Press.

Grande, Sandy. 2004. *Red Pedagogy: Native American Social and Political Thought*. Lanham, MD: Rowman and Littlefield.

Held, David. 2010. *Cosmopolitanism: Ideals and Realities*. Cambridge, England: Polity.

Hendricks, Tyche. 2003. "From Southern Mexico to Northern California: As Numbers Grow, Immigrants from Yucatán Getting Higher Profile." *San Francisco Chronicle*, November 25. http://www.sfgate.com/bayarea/article/From-southern-Mexico-to -Northern-California-As-2526010.php.

Kauffman, Jonathan. 2015. "Why Are So Many Chefs Burning My Food—Deliberately?" *San Francisco Chronicle*, April 10. http://www.sfchronicle.com/restaurants /article/Why-are-so-many-chefs-burning-my-food-6192774.php.

Lefebvre, Henri. 1991. *The Production of Space*. Translation by Donald Nicholson-Smith. Cambridge, England: Blackwell.

Levitt, Peggy. 2001. *The Transnational Villagers*. Berkeley: University of California Press.

Lewin Fischer, Pedro. 2007. "Yucatán as an Emerging Migrant-sending Region." In *Mayan Journeys: US-bound Migration from a New Sending Community*, edited by Wayne A. Cornelius, David Fitzgerald, and Pedro Lewin Fischer, 1–26. La Jolla: Center for Comparative Immigration Studies, University of California, San Diego.

Lomawaima, K. Tsianina, and Teresa McCarty. 2006. *To Remain an Indian: Lessons in Democracy from a Century of Native American Education*. New York: Teachers College.

Loza, Mireya. 2016. *Defiant Braceros: How Migrant Workers Fought for Racial, Sexual, and Political Freedom*. Chapel Hill: University of North Carolina Press.

Martell, Alpha, Maribel Pineda, and Luis Tapia 2007. "The Contemporary Migration Process." In *Mayan Journeys: US-bound Migration from a New Sending Community*, edited by Wayne A. Cornelius, David Fitzgerald, and Pedro Lewin Fischer, 49–88. La Jolla: Center for Comparative Immigration Studies, University of California, San Diego.

Massey, Douglas S., Jorge Durand, and Nolan J. Malone. 2003. *Beyond Smoke and Mirrors: Mexican Immigration in an Era of Economic Integration*. New York: Russell Sage Foundation.

Mignolo, W. 2000. "The Many Faces of Cosmo-polis: Border Thinking and Critical Cosmopolitanism." *Public Culture* 12 (3): 721–748.

Mitchell, Don, and Nik Heynen. 2009. "The Geography of Survival and the Right to the City: Speculations on Surveillance, Legal Innovation, and the Criminalization of Intervention." *Urban Geography* 30 (6): 611–632.

Rodríguez, Andrea, Jennifer Wittlinger, and Luis Manzanero Rodríguez. 2007. "The Interface between Internal and International Migration." In *Mayan Journeys: US-bound Migration from a New Sending Community*, edited by Wayne A. Cornelius, David Fitzgerald, and Pedro Lewin Fischer, 73–88. La Jolla: Center for Comparative Immigration Studies, University of California, San Diego.

Roman, Raul. 2016. "The Side of Mexican Immigration You Need to See." *Huffington Post*, October 22. http://www.huffingtonpost.com/raul-roman/side-of-mexican-immigration-that-you-need-to-see_b_8361908.html.

Roys, Ralph, trans. 1967. *The Book of Chilam Balam of Chumayel*. Norman: University of Oklahoma Press. Originally published in 1933.

Ruiz, Ramón. 2010. *Mexico: Why a Few Are Rich and the People Poor*. Berkeley: University of California Press.

Said, Edward. 1978. *Orientalism*. New York: Pantheon.

Salas, Spencer, and Pedro Portes, eds. 2017. *US Latinization: Education and the New Latino South*. Albany: SUNY Press.

Solis Lizama, Mirian, and Patricia Fortuny Loret de Mola. 2010. "Otomíes hidalguenses y mayas yucatecos: Nuevas caras de la migración indígena y viejas formas de organización." *Migraciones Internacionales* 5 (4): 101–138.

Stephen, Lynn. 2007. *Transborder Lives: Indigenous Oaxacans in Mexico, California, and Oregon*. Durham, NC: Duke University Press.

Terrazas, Aaron. 2011. "Immigrants in New Destination States." Washington, DC: Migration Policy Institute. http://www.migrationpolicy.org/article/immigrants-new-destination-states#4.

Tuck, Eve, and Marcia McKenzie. 2015. *Place in Research: Theory, Methodology, and Methods*. New York: Routledge.

Tucker, Jill. 2014. "SF Seen as Model in Bilingual Education over English Only." *San Francisco Chronicle*, February 13. https://www.sfgate.com/education/article/S-F-seen-as-model-in-bilingual-education-over-5229826.php.

UN Department of Economic and Social Affairs, Division for Social Policy and Development. 2004. Workshop on Data Collection and Disaggregation for Indigenous People. Secretariat of the Permanent Forum on Indigenous Issues, January 19–21, United Nations, New York. PFII/2004/WS.1/3.

UN Peacemaker. 1996. Joint Proposals that the Federal Government and the EZLN Agree to Remit to the National Debating and Decision-Making Bodies in Accordance with Paragraph 1.4 of the Rules of Procedure. February 16. New York: United Nations. http://peacemaker.un.org/mexico-jointproposals96.

Veracini, Lorenzo. 2010. *Settler Colonialism: A Theoretical Overview*. New York: Palgrave.

Whiteside, Anne. 2006. "'We Are the Explorers': Transnational Yucatec Maya-speakers Negotiating Multilingual California." PhD diss., University of California, Berkeley.

Wolfe, Patrick. 2006. "Settler Colonialism and the Elimination of the Native." *Journal of Genocide Research* 8 (4): 387–409.

Wong, Julia Carrie. 2016. "The Life and Death of Luis Góngora: The Police Killing Nobody Noticed." *The Guardian*, August 12. https://www.theguardian.com/society/2016/aug/12/luis-gongora-san-francisco-police-shooting-homelessness.

CHAPTER 10

Binational Health Week: A Social Mobilization Program to Improve Latino Migrant Health

LILIANA OSORIO, HILDA DÁVILA,
AND XÓCHITL CASTAÑEDA

Latino or Hispanic migrants compose a significant portion of the US population, economy, and culture. Yet despite their unquestionable and valuable contribution to the country, many remain disenfranchised from the formal health care system. This population faces several barriers that limit access to health care including language, low socioeconomic status, geographic isolation, cultural practices, immigration status, and lack of health insurance. The development and implementation of public policies to address those barriers is imperative not only for the well-being of the migrants themselves but also for the good of the community at large. At the same time, grassroots actions and campaigns, in coordination with government and private sectors, could improve the health of Latino migrants in the short run and long run. When dealing with migrant populations' health and well-being, there must be a shared responsibility from governments and institutions in their countries of origin, transit, and destination.

Binational Health Week (BHW) is a multilevel, collaborative initiative created to respond to some of the barriers faced by Latino migrants when accessing health care and health information in the United States and Canada. It encompasses a series of health promotion and health education activities including workshops, insurance referrals, vaccinations, and medical screenings. Since its inception in 2001, BHW has delivered health education and promotion to more than five million underserved Latinos in North America. BHW facilitates the creation of networks to increase access to care for a marginalized population, provide a platform to discuss the importance of migrant health and pave the way for new health policies. Today, BHW is one of the largest mobilization efforts of government agencies, community-based organizations, and volunteers in the Americas to improve the health and well-being of the underserved Latino population living in the United States and Canada.

We look at the socioeconomic and health status of Latinos in the United States and their health insurance and health care situations. Thousands of local agencies are working to improve the quality of life of Latino immigrants, with the collaborative strategies and partnerships of Mexican and Latin American government institutions and the Health Initiative of the Americas. These are examples of how countries of origin create alliances with institutions and community groups in the countries of destination that can result in complex but fluid cooperative social networks and innovative outreach strategies to promote healthy habits and prevent diseases among migrant communities.

We analyze Binational Health Week using a collective impact framework that lays out conditions for success such as common agendas and ongoing communication (Kania and Kramer 2011). Beyond its direct work in migrant communities, BHW seeks to promote and create systematic changes in the health of migrants by advocating for public policies and empowering communities to embrace such changes. We reflect as well on the weaknesses and limitations of the BHW initiative and on challenges and opportunities under the new political administration in the United States.

Latinos in the United States

Latinos make up one of the fastest-growing groups in the United States. In 2015 Latinos were 17.6 percent of the total US population, up from just 3.5 percent in 1960. According to projections from the Pew Research Center, the Latino share of the US population, including US-born and foreign-born Latinos, is expected to reach 24 percent by 2065 (Flores 2017). Only 34.4 percent of all Latinos in the United States in 2015 were born in other countries, down from 40 percent in the early 2000s. While immigration from Mexico has decreased, Mexicans are still by far the largest immigrant origin group in the country (Zong and Batalova 2016). In 2016 the foreign-born population in the United States reached 43.7 million, with 26 percent originating from Mexico. Immigration from Central and South America combined was only 14.5 percent (Brown and Stepler 2016).

About 32 percent of the Latino population in the United States in 2016 was younger than eighteen years, compared to 19 percent of the white population, making Latinos the youngest major racial or ethnic group in the United States. About 28 percent of Latinos in 2016 were so-called millennials, defined as people born between 1981 and 1996, compared to 20 percent among whites. The median age for Latinos was twenty-eight years, way below the median age of forty-three for whites (Patten 2016).

Latinos have had a growing impact on the US economy. From 2009 to 2013, Latinos accounted for 43.4 percent of total growth in jobs held. Unemployment rates have dropped since the recession of 2007–2009 for all Americans. Among Latinos, the rate declined from a high of 12.8 percent in 2010 to 6.4 percent in 2015 but still was higher than the unemployment rate of 4.8 percent among non-Latinos. The median household income for Latinos stagnated after the recession; in 2014 it was $42,491, and their poverty rate was 23.6 percent (Lopez, Morin, and Krogstad 2016).

When looking at occupations, the majority of Latinos have low-paying jobs and work in physically demanding sectors, in what are often referred to as the "three D jobs" because the work is considered dirty, dangerous, and difficult (Schenker 2011). In 2014, 27.3 percent of workers in construction were of Latino origin. Other industries with high concentrations of Latinos in 2014 included agriculture, forestry, fishing, and hunting (23.1 percent) and leisure and hospitality (22.3 percent) (US BLS 2015). Immigrant workers are more likely than native-born workers to experience workplace accidents, injuries, and even death caused by repetitive movement and strain. Despite the health risks, Latino immigrants are drawn to those kinds of jobs because in general they do not require specialized skills and pay much more than the migrants would receive in their countries of origin (Schenker 2011). As for representation in other sectors, Latinos in 2014 had the lowest share of employment in public administration (11.4 percent), financial activities (11.3 percent), and information (10.5 percent) (US BLS 2015).

In terms of health, according to the US Centers for Disease Control and Prevention (CDC), Latinos had lower death rates from most of the ten leading causes of death in the United States when compared to non-Hispanic whites, with the exception of diabetes, liver, and kidney disease. Latinos were about 50 percent more likely than non-Hispanic whites to die from diabetes or liver disease (Dominguez et al. 2015). Mental health is a concern among Latinos. The National Survey on Drug Use and Health in 2016 reported that 15.7 percent of Latinos in the United States aged eighteen and older reported having mental illnesses in the past year (US SAMHSA 2016).

Among the barriers and social factors that affect the health of Latinos and their access to health services—such as limited English proficiency, low levels of education, low incomes, and immigration status—lack of health insurance plays a major role. After the establishment of the Affordable Care Act (ACA) in 2014, about 20 million people gained access to health insurance in the United States by 2016 and the uninsured population fell to historic lows (Chen et al. 2016). In 2016 the nonelderly uninsured rate was 10.3 percent, down substantially compared to 18.2 percent in 2010. Still, 27.6 million people remained without coverage in 2016 (KFF 2017). The ACA insurance reform and expansion explicitly targeted a population that at that moment was more likely to lack health insurance: adults with low and moderate incomes, young adults, owners of small businesses and their employees, and part-time workers. Minority groups, particularly Latinos, make up a large share of many of these groups. When looking into how the uninsured adult population ages nineteen to sixty-four has shrunk by race and ethnicity, we see that Latinos, who composed the largest share of the uninsured at 43.2 percent in 2010, made up 24.8 percent in 2016. The uninsured rate among African Americans declined from 27.2 percent to 14.8 percent and that of non-Hispanic whites from 16.4 percent to 8.7 percent in the same period (Collins et al. 2016). Yet despite the efforts to reach and enroll more people as the total number of uninsured adults has fallen, Latinos have become a larger share of the remaining uninsured population.

Several factors have prevented people, especially Latinos, from enrolling in health insurance. The ACA bars undocumented immigrants from receiving Medicaid coverage and purchasing health insurance through the ACA marketplaces or exchanges. Also, while many documented, eligible Latinos have gained health insurance in the Medicaid expansion that covers people with incomes up to 138 percent of the federal poverty level, by 2016 eighteen states had not yet expanded Medicaid, among them Florida and Texas, where a large percentage of Latinos live. Other limitations include difficulty in navigating the enrollment process, concerns about health insurance affordability and government subsidy eligibility, and unawareness of the marketplaces (Collins et al. 2016). Not having health insurance affects individual health because it limits access to preventive care and services for major health conditions. The cost of health care in the United States is so high that without health insurance it is almost impossible for many to access it. Uninsured adults are far more likely than those with insurance to postpone health care or forgo it altogether. The consequences can be severe, particularly when preventable conditions or chronic diseases go undetected or do not receive the proper care and/or treatment (KFF 2017).

Under Donald Trump's administration and a Republican majority in Congress, the future of health care, particularly for the immigrant population, is even more uncertain. President Trump has been very outspoken against immigrants in the United States and clear about his intentions to deport undocumented individuals, limit benefits to documented immigrants, and repeal the ACA, also known as Obamacare.

Shared Responsibility for Migrants' Health and Well-Being

When looking at renowned health programs developed for the Mexican migrant population living in the United States, we identify three key institutions behind those programs, the Instituto de los Mexicanos en el Exterior (IME, Institute for Mexicans Abroad), Mexico's Secretaría de Salud (Secretariat of Health), and the Health Initiative of the Americas.

The IME was established in 2003 under the Secretaría de Relaciones Exteriores (SRE, Secretariat of Foreign Affairs) with the objectives of promoting strategies, developing programs, and gathering recommendations of community members and organizations to improve the quality of life among Mexican citizens abroad (Délano 2011). Since then, the institute has established strong collaborations with civic organizations in the United States to facilitate the dissemination of information and the planning and implementation of community actions. Its programs fall under the categories of health, education, culture, community development, financial education, and sports promotion.

The Secretaría de Salud through its Dirección General de Relaciones Internacionales (General Directorate of International Affairs) is responsible for promoting international cooperation in health matters between Mexico and other countries as well as with multilateral agencies and global events, with the aim of achieving equity in health, combating disease, and prolonging and improving the quality of life. One of its objectives is to promote, develop, and coordinate institutional, national, and binational actions that improve the health conditions of the Mexican migrant population abroad (Mexico, Secretaría de Salud 2015). Its main programs related to migrant health are Binational Health Week, Ventanillas de Salud (Health Windows), a temporary agricultural workers program, repatriation of seriously ill nationals, comprehensive health care modules for returnees, and the Research Program on Migration and Health.

The Health Initiative of the Americas was established in 2001 as a program of the School of Public Health at the University of California, Berkeley. Its mission is to facilitate and optimize resources in the United States, Mexico, and other Latin American countries to improve the health and well-being of the Latino population living and working in the United States. The initiative draws upon the multidisciplinary scholarship and the moral calling of UC Berkeley faculty and students to produce new knowledge through action-oriented research; teaching and mentoring; and service and community engagement programs to reduce the health disparities of the less advantaged Latino population in the United States. Considered one of the leading programs on migration and health, the Health Initiative of the Americas works alongside various institutions of government, academia, and the private sector as well as with community-based organizations. Strong partnerships at local, national, and international levels facilitate and support the initiative's effective outreach campaigns, which connect health resources to Latino communities.

A shared endeavor of the three programs is Binational Health Week. The concept was modeled after Mexico's highly successful National Health Weeks, intensive community efforts to provide free vaccines to children, adolescents, and adults. Mexico's Secretaría de Salud has since 1980 implemented three nationwide health weeks per year, and today the events provide health services besides immunizations, such as the distribution of vitamins, iron, folic acid, and oral serum, and education in health topics including sexual and reproductive health and domestic violence (Flisser et al. 2008). Given the large population of Mexicans living in the United States who lack access to the health weeks in Mexico, the Mexican government and the Health Initiative of the Americas decided to hold at least one similar week each year in the United States to provide health information and services to the Mexican immigrant population. In October 2001 the first Binational Health Week was celebrated in seven California counties. Each county created a local task force formed by a diverse group of government, private, nonprofit, and community organizations and planned one or more health activities to provide linguistically and culturally appropriate health information and free health services to Mexican immigrants and other Spanish speakers in their geographic area. Under the slogan "Aunque estés lejos, no estás solo" (Even though you are far away, you are not alone), four Mexican consulates in California and local task forces celebrated the first BHW with ninety-eight events serving approximately 19,000 people. Over the years, BHW has proved a tremendous success and grown exponentially, providing health information and services to 320,000 Latinos on average annually in October throughout the United States and Canada. Today, governments from other Latin American countries are also participating in BHW.

The Role of Civic Engagement in BHW

High levels of positive and motivated civic engagement can lead to greater trust and improved quality of life (Nath 2012). Understanding the lived realities of populations is essential to creating and delivering appropriate public health interventions such as BHW. One of the major successes of BHW has been its volunteer networks organized through local task forces. The networks have been essential in strengthening connections among myriad organizations (public, private, and philanthropic), immigrant communities including those without regular sources of health care coverage, and the undocumented population. Many of the networks' members are trusted community leaders; they are natural partners for BHW campaigns who offer their resources and expertise. The collaboration not only builds trusting relations with the migrant communities and diverse stakeholders but also leverages human and financial resources so as to increase the program's impact. Through the task forces, BHW has developed strong social networks that now extend beyond BHW and are nestled deeply in the community. Research shows that immigrants need different kinds of social networks or ties to better adapt to their new life and benefit from community resources. Among these, strong ties or social bonds with their ethnic enclave help immigrants become integrated into the host economy, while weak ties or bridging ties facilitate access to the resources required to participate fully in community life (Bourdieu 2011; Brissette, Cohen, and Seeman 2000; Pfeffer and Parra 2009).

It is important that task force members see the benefit to being part of BHW; otherwise, their commitment will waver. Over the years, the membership of the task forces has changed for various reasons; sometimes there are policy changes or priority shifts within their organizations, some may not have had enough time to devote to BHW, and others may not have benefited from the collaboration as expected. Generally, though, over the years of BHW, the task forces have grown in number and strength as the impact of their collective work is demonstrated. Although the activities of BHW last only a week or in some locations a month, the relationships and collaborations that are created through the networks go beyond BHW itself and endure. The underlying assumption of all parties is that BHW has a noble and specific goal: to improve the health of underserved Latinos.

Community-based organizations are a vital component of BHW task forces. Their main contribution is linking marginalized and vulnerable populations to the health system. The organizations are more likely to employ culturally and linguistically competent staff that has earned the trust of and understands the populations they serve. Connecting and empowering community-based organizations has been one of BHW's key successes, enabling widespread social mobilization. One of the most valuable gains is that culturally appropriate messages are delivered in Spanish, as many of the volunteers are also of Latino origin. In this way, the people served and the volunteers are reaffirming their cultural nexus.

Besides offering workshops and trainings to community members, some BHW activities are targeted at *promotores*, also known as community health workers, and health care providers. For example, around 200 *promotores* attend the annual San Diego Promotores Conference every October as part of BHW. The conference offers plenary presentations and workshops on diverse health topics as well as opportunities for personal and professional development. Each year, agenda topics are selected based on a combination of current health issues and relevant events as well as on the evaluations and feedback provided by participants from the previous year's conference. Speakers from around the nation are selected for their expertise and invited to participate. The conference is also a way to recognize and celebrate the wonderful work that *promotores* do on a daily basis to improve the health of their communities.

Binational exchange programs for *promotores* are also scheduled during BHW. The one-week cultural immersion experiences are designed to expose *promotores* from Mexico and the United States to the specific needs and obstacles faced by mobile populations and their implications for health-seeking behavior, health status, and risk perception. Through site and home visits, participants experience firsthand the context in which the immigrant population lives and works and where their American peers operate.

Health professionals participate in some workshops scheduled during BHW as well, on issues related to health behavior, traditional medicine, and culture-bound syndromes. There is evidence that this learning process has enriched the services offered by medical personnel to underserved communities in a variety of ways. These kinds of learning experiences expand curricula beyond the traditional biomedical model, and the knowledge helps service providers to overcome the stigma and stereotyping associated with immigrant groups and at the same time promote patient-centeredness (Towle and Godolphin 2013). These meaningful encounters have been shown to foster positive attitudes and empathetic understanding as well as encourage an individualized approach to patients. Indeed, health care providers have stated that their interactions with Latino patients have improved after participating in BHW's cultural training workshops.

Growth of BHW

Over the years, BHW has experienced unprecedented growth as first Mexican and then other Latin American consulates joined the movement. In 2006 El Salvador and Guatemala formally participated in BHW through their consulates in the United States and Canada, and in the following years the governments of Colombia, Honduras, Ecuador, Bolivia, and Peru followed suit. The partnerships were officially established through memoranda of understanding between the Health Initiative of the Americas and the countries' foreign relations offices. At the local level, BHW continues to reach deeper into immigrant communities through the incorporation of new partners. In Chicago, for example, thirteen Latin American consulates participate in the program, which they have renamed Latin American Health Week. Other cities with a large Latino presence like Los Angeles, Miami, Houston, San Francisco, New York, and Toronto also count on the participation of consulates of several Latin American countries. The activities have grown to extend beyond a week, with most task forces organizing events throughout the whole month of October.

The BHW concept continues to reach more countries. In 2017 Colombia's Ministry of Foreign Affairs, through its program Colombia Nos Une, expanded BHW from its consulates in the United States and Canada to those in Mexico, Venezuela, Ecuador, Chile, Argentina, Uruguay, Costa Rica, Panama, Brazil, France, Spain, and Belgium. Officials in Honduras and Guatemala are considering similar efforts. With such momentum, BHW has evolved into one of the largest mobilization efforts in the Americas to improve the health and well-being of the Latino migrant population.

Access to Health Services

One of BHW's major goals is to facilitate access to preventive health services for underserved Latin American migrants, especially those lacking health insurance. For many beneficiaries, the services offered at BHW events are their only opportunity to access free health screenings in settings where they feel culturally and linguistically comfortable and, more important, where they feel secure. In surveys carried out at BHW events, approximately 30 percent of respondents stated that the health services provided were the first they had received in the United States. Health services usually include glucose, cholesterol, and HIV testing, body mass index calculations, blood pressure screenings, dental and vision checkups, mammograms, breast exams, Pap smears, and vaccinations, among others. In 2016 alone, approximately 60,000 health services were provided during BHW events. The wide range of services is made possible through the collaboration of all the organizations that are part of the existing 133 local task forces in the United States, which include approximately 5,000 agencies and 15,000 volunteers (HIA 2016). To ensure any necessary follow-ups the services are provided in collaboration with local medical providers, community clinics, hospitals, and medical schools.

Every year, BHW organizers spotlight specific health issues that have significant impacts on the Latino community. Some recur every year, such as access to health care, chronic diseases including obesity and diabetes, infectious diseases including HIV and tuberculosis, and occupational health and safety, while others are included as a response to the constantly changing needs of the Latino migrant population. As such, there have been specific campaigns for emergent issues including disaster preparedness, H1N1 influenza, and the Zika virus. BHW benefits from parallel campaigns that also occur in October such as National Breast Cancer Awareness Month, National Latino AIDS Awareness Day, and Lead Week, to name a few, and task force leaders are encouraged to join such national efforts. As October marks the beginning of the flu season, BHW events present a perfect venue to provide free flu shots, especially to those who do not have health insurance. The popularity of BHW speaks for itself, as thousands of Latinos receive flu shots and other recommended vaccines during the events.

Creative and Culturally Appropriate Outreach Strategies

Rallying the community to attend health events is not an easy task; it requires a lot of planning, outreach, and creativity. The promise of free vaccines, health insurance information, and health pamphlets would not be enough to draw the crowds necessary to make BHW successful. According to the cultural theory of risk perception, individuals worry most about the risks that directly affect their well-being and will address these needs first, often overlooking other issues (Carter-Pokras et al. 2007; Lindell and Perry 2004). To attract migrant families to health events, then, it is crucial to provide information and services on health issues that are relevant to them while at the same time framing the activities in a festive and culturally attractive manner. At health fairs one is likely to find other offerings including immigration consultations with lawyers, children's activities, music, traditional dance performances, healthy cooking demonstrations, ethnic food festivals, and much more. BHW task forces devote particular attention to promoting health in a multicultural, fun, and enjoyable environment.

Sports events and physical activities are also key components of BHW. In Los Angeles the local task force annually celebrates the soccer tournament Copa Binacional de Salud, in which hundreds of enthusiastic players of different ages and divisions participate. Soccer and basketball tournaments, walks, marathons, and Zumba and yoga classes are central attractions at the events organized by BHW task forces. All skill levels are targeted, from beginners to the most experienced participants. Regardless of the competitive level, what really matters is that through BHW the entire Latino community is encouraged to be physically active. Usually health fairs accompany the sporting and exercise events to offer participants information, referrals, and resources.

BHW events take place in diverse venues. The idea is to bring health information and service provision to where Latinos live, work, or congregate—to familiar places where they feel secure and comfortable. Event venues range from parks, churches, and schools to consulates, agricultural fields, supermarkets, community clinics, day labor centers, and libraries, among others. When health events are organized close to their homes or workplaces, people are more likely to attend, participate, and ultimately receive the information and services offered (Cassady et al. 2012).

One of the main partners and venues for BHW activities have been the Ventanillas de Salud in all fifty Mexican consulates in the United States. The Secretaría de Salud and the IME sponsor the Ventanillas de Salud to promote healthy habits, help prevent diseases, and refer individuals to health services. In a safe, friendly, and familiar environment, staff members refer visitors to health services available in their area of residency and provide them with information and education on a variety of health topics. Ventanillas de Salud operate year-round, and during BHW they expand their services. Their staff members play active roles in planning and implementing BHW activities. A significant number of Ventanillas de Salud partners are also members of BHW task forces.

A Collective Impact Initiative

BHW's success lies in the synergy of bringing together hundreds of organizations and thousands of individuals who are committed to improving the quality of life of migrant families. John Kania and Mark Kramer (2011) define such collective impact as "an innovative and structured approach to making collaboration work across government, business, philanthropy, nonprofit organizations, and citizens to achieve significant and lasting social change." The underlying assumption is that by working together people can accomplish more than by working individually. Kania and Kramer explain that successful collective-impact initiatives typically have five conditions: backbone support, a common agenda, shared measurements, mutually reinforced activities, and continuous communication.

Backbone Support

Collaboration cannot occur and be sustained without an infrastructure of backbone support organizations (Kania and Kramer 2011). For BHW, those organizations have been the Secretaría de Salud, the Instituto de los Mexicanos en el Exterior, and the Health Initiative of the Americas. Representatives of these organizations constitute the BHW steering committee. Each year they lay out the program's goals and objectives, as well as the methods and steps needed to achieve a successful Binational Health Week. The foreign relations offices of other participating Latin American countries also make decisions related to participation and communication with their respective consulates.

The steering committee structures the design of each year's program while relying on local task forces to organize their activities according to their own local needs and resources. Tasks of the steering committee include identifying potential sponsors, inviting allies at federal and state levels, seeking linguistically and culturally appropriate health educational materials to distribute during the events, guiding local task forces from planning through implementation and evaluation of their activities, collecting and analyzing results, and disseminating evaluation reports. The committee also decides the slogan and image to be used each year during BHW activities.

Common Agenda

The common agenda of BHW is to deliver actions for the immigrant community, health care providers, and all those interested in improving the health and well-being of the people of Latin American origin living in the United States and Canada. This goal can be achieved only by organizing targeted, multilevel activities. Besides providing health education and services to the underserved Latino population throughout the two destination countries, BHW aims to create awareness of the importance of migrants' health by involving health care providers, the media, and elected officials. Several activities of BHW have a public policy component to explain what Latino migrant populations need to thrive as individuals and members of society. These presentations are given not only in the countries of destination—the United States and Canada—but also in the countries of origin because the health of migrants is a shared responsibility.

Shared Measurement

Collecting data and measuring results has been one of the biggest challenges of BHW but one it has largely met. The importance of such measurements cannot be overstated, as they are the only way to determine and promote BHW's effectiveness. Basic quantitative information collected includes the total number of events and participants, number and type of health screenings provided, number of organizations involved in planning and implementing events, and number of volunteers helping at the events. Each task force submits a final report including qualitative descriptions of activities, participants, media, impact, mobilization of resources, and photos. To conclude BHW's activities, task force coordinators present the results to their local partners. They then hold debriefings to analyze lessons learned and develop strategies to improve the activities the following year. At the same time, the Health Initiative of the Americas collaborates with the countries' representatives to write a comprehensive report that includes results from all activities reported from the task forces. The report is then posted on the BHW website.

Mutually Reinforced Activities

BHW's success relies in part on the diversity of the stakeholders that participate in the program. Since the target audience is Latin American migrants, the participation of the governments of their countries of origin is very important. Governments bear certain responsibilities for public health and protection of their citizens, wherever they live. Through specific programs created by their foreign relations offices such as the Instituto de los Mexicanos en el Exterior or Colombia Nos Une, governments dedicate financial resources and consular personnel to plan and carry out activities aimed at meeting the needs of their nationals living and working abroad. Government agencies from BHW-participating countries allocate thousands of dollars through their respective consulates to support BHW activities. Meanwhile, local task forces raise more funds and seek in-kind contributions though local partners.

Another example of mutually reinforced activity is the community education that is presented at the local level during Binational Health Week through the vision and dedication of many individuals and institutions committed to improving immigrant health. Health education is delivered through interactive learning activities with culturally and linguistically appropriate materials. Educational events take place in tandem with free services such as immunizations and medical screenings. Evidence shows that BHW educational efforts have ripple effects that reach beyond the communities served in the United States and Canada. Through family and community ties and the active participation of institutions such as the consulates of Latin American countries, the outreach has had a beneficial social impact on immigrants' communities of origin.

In the United States, several health programs at state and local levels are dedicated to educating the population on diabetes, heart health, breast cancer, nutrition, addictions, and much more. When these programs deploy their resources to help the Latino community specifically and provide information in Spanish, they become natural partners for BHW. Programs with community health workers make excellent partners because they are familiar with the needs and assets of the community and are connected to and trusted by the target population. Other key partners have direct relations with the communities as well and are able to offer resources such as space for events, volunteers, and event promotion. Schools, churches, libraries, and community centers fall into this category.

Latin American hometown associations have been created by migrants in many parts of the United States to connect their communities of residence with their communities of origin, and collaborating with them makes it much easier to reach and mobilize community members. The associations help to promote the events and to invite dancers, singers, and various cultural groups to be part of BHW events, making them more fun and attractive.

BHW has gained widespread recognition and support at the community and grassroots levels and has been able to attract a population hard to reach through conventional efforts; its success in doing so is in part due to the cultural dimension it uses to promote health. Through the BHW model, immigrant communities come together around health issues in ways that are familiar to them and settings where cultural aspects such as music, dance, and art are incorporated. This is a complicated undertaking. Foundations and private companies offer the necessary economic support to carry out the activities. It is also important to engage the media with the task force and invite them to take part in the planning and development of the BHW events and to support their promotion. In addition, representatives of local governments are contacted to develop, to the greatest extent possible, public policies that help improve the health and well-being of Latinos on a permanent basis.

Continuous Communication

Binational Health Week could not take place without efficient communication channels. The planning of BHW events takes most of the year. Usually beginning in March, the steering committee schedules monthly calls to decide general issues such as the official dates of BHW; place and date of the inaugural event and the Binational Policy Forum on Migration and Global Health; slogan, image, and health themes for the year; and strategy for working with the consulates and task forces.

A bilingual website dedicated to BHW (binationalhealthweek.org, semanabinacionaldesalud.org) posts information for BHW coordinators and others interested in the program. The website provides details on how to establish local task forces, organize health fairs and workshops, and request proclamations and resolutions for BHW. It offers template letters for inviting elected officials and media representatives, steps to request funds, and directories of community clinics, foundations, and hometown associations as well as data collection forms and follow-up steps. Each task force can adapt the materials and recommendations to its local needs. The website also has a section where BHW coordinators can get educational materials in Spanish on topics including access to health care, infectious diseases, chronic diseases, women's health, mental health, adolescent health, and occupational health.

Most BHW coordinators are not health experts and therefore it is essential to provide them with some basic training on Latino health issues and where to find reliable information. With support from the US Centers for Disease Control and Prevention, the Centers for Medicare and Medicaid Services, National Institutes of Health, National Public Health Information Coalition, and UC Berkeley Labor and Occupational Health Program, among other entities, informative webinars are offered to BHW coordinators and members of their task forces. Webinar topics can range from the Affordable Care Act and health care access to HIV/AIDS, tuberculosis, diabetes, cardiovascular diseases, eye health, occupational health, influenza, Zika, and more. Webinar presentations are in Spanish, and besides clearly describing the main aspects of the topic and its relevance for the Latino population, speakers share educational materials available in Spanish. Electronic copies of the educational resources and PowerPoint presentations are posted on the BHW website and are available to the coordinators. The Health Initiative of the Americas has developed other materials for BHW coordinators such as media campaigns, fact sheets on specific health topics, bilingual dictionaries of health-related terms, manuals for *promotores*, and migration and health reports.

BHW Organization

BHW efforts are not centralized or micromanaged. Rather, the steering committee provides the global vision and coordination and relies on local task forces and partner agencies to own and carry out the work. This open structure is what has made BHW so effective, as stakeholders consider the BHW mission their own and translate the larger vision into local realities. The work styles of task forces can vary greatly. From the guidelines they are given, the task forces decide what kinds of events to organize, what topics to cover, what services to offer, which partners to include, and whom to target. They also decide the delegation of tasks and efforts within the group, the communication channels, the frequency of meetings, and the priorities. Flexibility at the local level is key to the success of the collective effort because it is based on the recognition that each region, each city, has its own needs, resources, and ways of doing business. What works in New York City may not work in Brownsville, Texas, but what really matters is that the stakeholders, in their own ways, achieve the collective goal of providing adequate information and health services to the Latino population.

Policy Advocacy for Systemic and Sustained Change

To raise awareness and propel political action to address the health care challenges confronting immigrants, it is imperative to involve policy makers in BHW. Although migration is a global phenomenon, it has local and regional impacts and requires the involvement of government officials and decision makers at local, state, national, and regional levels.

Communities can be empowered by developing the capacity to influence and support policy efforts that respond to community needs. In this regard, BHW's work at the local level is complemented by strong engagement from stakeholders and decision makers. BHW task forces invite local elected officials to be part of Binational Health Week, contribute to planning activities, attend inaugural and media events, and present resolutions recognizing BHW. More than four hundred resolutions and proclamations endorsed BHW in the United States by 2017.

BHW connects communities with state, national, and binational policy efforts through the Binational Policy Forum on Migration and Global Health. The forum kicks off BHW and is held alternately in the United States and Mexico. The goal of the forum is to convene key stakeholders from the United States, Mexico, Canada, and Latin America to discuss migrant health challenges and explore opportunities to work collaboratively to improve the health and well-being of Latino migrant populations. The forum spotlights immigrant health issues and receives significant media coverage. It usually counts on the participation of high-level government officials of the United States, Mexico, and other Latin American countries as well as directors of health programs, academic experts in migration and health issues, and community leaders and advocates. Three hundred to seven hundred people attend the forum each year.

Furthermore, BHW serves as a platform for the Latin American consular networks to reach and strengthen ties with the communities they serve. The policy impact of BHW is evidenced by the active participation of these networks. Members advocate for their immigrant populations in the United States, provide resources, and mobilize broader networks to support and implement BHW activities.

Challenges and Opportunities

BHW has not been immune to challenges and growing pains. From the perspective of government commitment, we have to consider the effect of political changes in the United States and in the Latin American countries that are part of the effort. New administrations bring new political agendas, and depending on how they prioritize the health and well-being of their diasporas, the attention and support for activities such as BHW will vary. Also, the fluctuating economies of the countries of origin have direct impacts on the resources dedicated to government programs dealing with migrant affairs. Over the years, some countries and organizations that used to be strong BHW partners have reduced or withdrawn their participation because of a shift in priorities or lack of funding under new administrations. At the same time, other countries and partners join or enhance their participation in BHW when it aligns with their political and strategic agendas. This is where the role of backbone organizations becomes critical in keeping up constant communication with established and new partners and monitoring political and economic changes to keep the program consistent and relevant.

Other challenges include the outreach to rural communities that have become the destination of new Latino migrant groups. From 2000 to 2010, the rural Latino population in the United States grew by 44.6 percent, especially in areas traditionally considered white (Burton et al. 2013), transforming many small rural communities racially and economically (Carr, Lichter, and Kefalas 2012). Poverty among Latinos living in rural America is high, especially among the children of immigrants, exceeding 50 percent in some towns (Burton et al. 2013; Lichter 2012). It is also well known that rural areas are far worse in terms of population health and health care than urban areas (McLaughlin, Stokes, and Nonoyama 2001). The rapid growth of the Latino population in rural communities has abruptly increased the demand for health and social services, where resources are already scarce and culturally and linguistically appropriate services are almost nonexistent.

To serve these isolated populations that often lack reliable transportation and cannot travel to the consular offices, the consulates organize periodic visits called "mobile consulates" to those areas to provide standard consular services of documentation and information. Personnel from the Ventanillas de Salud often accompany the consular representatives and supply health information and services. The Mexican government, through the US-Mexico Border Health Commission and financial support from the binational initiative Juntos Podemos (Together We Can), has implemented medical mobile units to visit remote areas with high concentrations of Mexican migrants. The mobile units operate in collaboration with local health organizations and providers in the United States. In 2017 eleven medical mobile units across the United States provided much-needed health information and services to underserved populations, mainly of Mexican origin. The Ventanillas de Salud and the mobile medical units organize special outreach activities in October to complement the efforts of BHW.

Conclusion

BHW is the largest mobilization effort addressing the health care needs of Latino migrants and their families living in North America. Since 2001 BHW has played a fundamental role in creating opportunities for discussion and collaboration among local, state, and federal programs as well as health care providers seeking to improve the quality of life of millions of Latinos. BHW events are a catalyst for continued, empowering collaboration and actions, from grassroots to policy-making levels, to increase health education and provide health services to a large population disenfranchised from the US health care system.

BHW has been successful in maintaining a focus on health education and health promotion. The work strategy has used a grassroots approach to mobilize networks, promote strong partnerships with public and private institutions and government agencies, generate awareness among the general public and government officials about the plight of migrant workers and their families, and prompt discussions of policies of inclusion in health and other social services.

The Mexican government has been fundamental in developing and expanding BHW and other health programs for Mexicans living abroad. Mexico has consistently provided resources and support to these programs, and their actions have become a model for many other Latin American countries looking to better serve their communities abroad. Meanwhile, the consistent effort and dedication of the Health Initiative of the Americas has been instrumental to the continuation and growth of the BHW program. Having the University of California, Berkeley, an academic institution of great recognition and reputation, as a partner in the United States has helped bring together diverse partners throughout the country and supplied resources to support the health activities.

After the 2016 presidential election in the United States, the position of the federal government toward immigrants living in the United States and people wanting to come to it changed dramatically. President Trump's anti-immigrant rhetoric and executive orders have created great alarm among different sectors nationally and internationally. The Latino immigrant population, which contributes so much to the social, economic, and cultural well-being of the country, is at high risk of being even more marginalized. At the same time, parallel to new immigration laws and regulations, the government is in the process of dismantling the Affordable Care Act. Many Democrats and Republicans are afraid of the repercussions that these changes could have in terms of access to health care, and it is quite likely that there could be devastating effects in the Latino community. Since the implementation of the ACA, the uninsured rate among Latinos was reduced by 20 percent (Doty and Collins 2017), mainly through the Medicaid expansion. For Americans who purchased health insurance through ACA marketplaces or exchanges, 84 percent received federal subsidies in 2017. It is easy to conclude that any reduction or elimination of federal subsidies could significantly reverse the gains in health insurance coverage that the country has witnessed.

But when there are challenges, opportunities arise. In this moment when the health and well-being of Latino immigrants are threatened, the role of civic society gains prominence, and collective efforts like BHW become more relevant. It is essential to continue and enhance programs like this one, not only to provide culturally and linguistically appropriate health information and services to a vulnerable Latino population, but also to continue the empowerment process in which the voices of the migrants can be heard and their contributions to the nation recognized. We must continue to reach out to and work together with strategic allies in all sectors, including the political one, because the only way to have healthy communities is by providing health care access to all, regardless of their country of origin or their immigration status. We are convinced that the health of a country is also the health of its immigrants and that change must be made through organized, collective, and focused actions.

References

Bourdieu, Pierre. 2011. "The Forms of Capital." In *Cultural Theory: An Anthology*, edited by Imre Szeman and Timothy Kaposy, 81–93. Malden, MA: Wiley-Blackwell.

Brissette, Ian, Sheldon Cohen, and Teresa E. Seeman. 2000. "Measuring Social Integration and Social Networks." In *Social Support Measurement and Intervention: A Guide for Health and Social Scientists*, edited by Sheldon Cohen, Lynn G. Underwood, and Benjamin H. Gottlieb, 53–85. New York: Oxford University Press.

Brown, Anna, and Renne Stepler. 2016. "Statistical Portrait of the Foreign-Born Population in the United States." Washington, DC: Pew Research Center. http://www.pew hispanic.org/2016/04/19/2014-statistical-information-on-immigrants-in-united -states/.

Burton, Linda M., Daniel T. Lichter, Regina S. Baker, and John M. Eason. 2013. "Inequality, Family Processes, and Health in the 'New' Rural America." *American Behavioral Scientist* 57 (8): 1128–1151. http://doi.org/10.1177/0002764213487348.

Carr, Patrick J., Daniel T. Lichter, and Maria J. Kefalas. 2012. "Can Immigration Save Small-Town America? Hispanic Boomtowns and the Uneasy Path to Renewal." *Annals of the American Academy of Political and Social Science* 641 (1): 38–57. http:// doi.org/10.1177/0002716211433445.

Carter-Pokras, Olivia, Ruth E. Zambrana, Sonia E. Mora, and Katherine A. Aaby. 2007.

"Emergency Preparedness: Knowledge and Perceptions of Latin American Immigrants." *Journal of Health Care for the Poor and Underserved* 18 (2): 465–481. http://doi.org/10.1353/hpu.2007.0026.

Cassady, Diana, Xóchitl Castañeda, Magdalena Ruiz Ruelas, Meredith Miller Vostrejs, Teresa Andrews, and Liliana Osorio. 2012. "Pandemics and Vaccines: Perceptions, Reactions, and Lessons Learned from Hard-to-Reach Latinos and the H1N1 Campaign." *Journal of Health Care for the Poor and Underserved* 23 (3): 1106–1122. http://doi.org/10.1353/hpu.2012.0086.

Chen, Jie, Arturo Vargas-Bustamante, Karoline Mortensen, and Alexander N. Ortega. 2016. "Racial and Ethnic Disparities in Health Care Access and Utilization under the Affordable Care Act." *Medical Care* 54 (2): 140–146. http://doi.org/10.1097/MLR.00 00000000000467.

Collins, Sara R., Munira Z. Gunja, Michelle M. Doty, and Sophie Beutel. 2016. "Who Are the Remaining Uninsured and Why Haven't They Signed Up for Coverage?" Issue brief, publication 1894, vol. 24. New York: Commonweath Fund. https://www.commonwealthfund.org/publications/issue-briefs/2016/aug/who-are-remaining-uninsured-and-why-havent-they-signed-coverage.

Délano, Alexandra. 2011. *Mexico and Its Diaspora in the United States: Policies of Emigration since 1848*. Cambridge, England: Cambridge University Press.

Dominguez, Kenneth, Ana Penman-Aguilar, Man-Huei Chang, Ramal Moonesinghe, Ted Castellanos, Alfonso Rodriguez-Lainz, and Richard Schieber. 2015. "Vital Signs: Leading Causes of Death, Prevalence of Diseases and Risk Factors, and Use of Health Services among Hispanics in the United States, 2009–2013." *Morbidity and Mortality Weekly Report*, May 8. Washington, DC: National Centers for Disease Control and Prevention. https://www.cdc.gov/mmwr/preview/mmwrhtml/mm6417a5.htm.

Doty, Michelle M., and Sara R. Collins. 2017. "Millions More Latino Adults Are Insured under the Affordable Care Act." *To the Point*, January 19. New York: Commonwealth Fund. http://www.commonwealthfund.org/publications/blog/2017/jan/more-latino-adults-insured.

Flisser, Ana, J. L. Valdespino, Lourdes García-García, Carmen Guzman, M. T. Aguirre, M. L. Manon, and Teresa W. Gyorkos. 2008. "Using National Health Weeks to Deliver Deworming to Children: Lessons from Mexico." *Journal of Epidemiology and Community Health* 62 (4): 314–317. http://doi.org/10.1136/jech.2007.066423.

Flores, Antonio. 2017. "Facts on U.S. Latinos, 2015: Statistical Portrait of the Hispanics in the United States." Hispanic Trends, September. Washington, DC: Pew Research Center. http://www.pewhispanic.org/2017/09/18/facts-on-u-s-latinos/.

HIA (Health Initiative of the Americas). 2016. *XVI Binational Health Week: Because the Right to Health Has No Borders*. Annual report. Berkeley: HIA, University of California. https://hiaucb.files.wordpress.com/2017/09/2016-bhw-report.pdf.

Kania, John, and Mark Kramer. 2011. "Collective Impact." *Stanford Social Innovation Review* (Winter). https://ssir.org/articles/entry/collective_impact.

KFF (Kaiser Family Foundation). 2017. "Key Facts about the Uninsured Population." San Francisco: KFF. http://kff.org/uninsured/fact-sheet/key-facts-about-the-uninsured-population/.

Lichter, Daniel T. 2012. "Immigration and the New Racial Diversity in Rural America." *Rural Sociology* 77 (1): 3–35. http://doi.org/10.1111/j.1549-0831.2012.00070.x.

Lindell, Michael K., and Ronald W. Perry. 2004. *Communicating Environmental Risk in Multiethnic Communities*. Vol. 7. Thousand Oaks, CA: Sage.

Lopez, Mark Hugo, Rich Morin, and Jens Manuel Krogstad. 2016. "Latinos Increasingly Confident in Personal Finances, See Better Economic Times Ahead." Washington, DC: Pew Research Center. http://www.pewhispanic.org/2016/06/08/latinos-increasingly-confident-in-personal-finances-see-better-economic-times-ahead/.

McLaughlin, Diane K., C. Shannon Stokes, and Atsuko Nonoyama. 2001. "Residence and Income Inequality: Effects on Mortality among U.S. Counties." *Rural Sociology Society* 66 (4): 579–598.

Mexico, Secretaría de Salud. 2015. Dirección General de Relaciones Internacionales: Objectives. Mexico City. https://www.gob.mx/salud/acciones-y-programas/direccion-general-de-relaciones-internacionales.

Nath, Saheli. 2012. "Civic Engagement in Low Income and Minority Neighborhoods, and the Role of Public Investment." *Undergraduate Economic Review* 9 (1): article 8. https://digitalcommons.iwu.edu/cgi/viewcontent.cgi?article=1204&context=uer.

Patten, Eileen. 2016. "The Nation's Latino Population Is Defined by Its Youth." Washington, DC: Pew Research Center. http://www.pewhispanic.org/2016/04/20/the-nations-latino-population-is-defined-by-its-youth/.

Pfeffer, Max J., and Pilar A. Parra. 2009. "Strong Ties, Weak Ties, and Human Capital: Latino Immigrant Employment outside the Enclave." *Rural Sociology* 74 (2): 241–269.

Schenker, Marc. 2011. "Migration and Occupational Health: Understanding the Risks." *Migration Information Source*, October. Washington, DC: Migration Policy Institute. https://www.migrationpolicy.org/article/migration-and-occupational-health-understanding-risks.

Towle, Angela, and William Godolphin. 2013. "Patients as Educators: Interprofessional Learning for Patient-Centered Care. *Medical Teacher* 35 (3): 219–225

US BLS (US Department of Labor, Bureau of Labor Statistics). 2015. *Hispanics and Latinos in Industries and Occupations*. Washington, DC: US BLS. https://www.bls.gov/opub/ted/2015/hispanics-and-latinos-in-industries-and-occupations.htm.

US SAMHSA (US Substance Abuse and Mental Health Services Administration). 2016. Hispanic or Latino 2016 NSDUH Summary Sheet. National Survey on Drug Use and Health. https://www.samhsa.gov/data/report/2016-nsduh-race-and-ethnicity-summary-sheets.

Zong, Jie, and Jeanne Batalova. 2016. "Mexican Immigrants in the United States." *Migration Information Source*, October. Washington, DC: Migration Policy Institute. https://www.migrationpolicy.org/article/mexican-immigrants-united-states.

CHAPTER 11

"American in Every Way, Except for Their Papers": How Mexico Supports Migrants' Access to Membership in the United States

ALEXANDRA DÉLANO ALONSO

At a speech at the Annual Conference of National Alliance for Latino Elected Officials on June 28, 2014, Eduardo Medina Mora, Mexican ambassador to the United States, described the Mexican government's policy agenda in the United States in the following way: "[Our] ultimate goal is that Mexicans and Latinos in the United States fully integrate, participate and thrive in their communities . . . [by offering consular support] in their path to gain full access to civic, social, economic, and political rights." The ambassador described how consulates have transcended their traditional role, transforming these offices into "integration centers where migrants have access to a wide array of services and programs, from *matrículas consulares* and passports, to health information and financial literacy programs." The objective, he explained, is to "empower our community while helping them to stay in touch with Mexico."[1]

This may seem surprising—and is even portrayed by some as a threat to the sovereignty of and citizenship in the United States (Gonzalez 2016)—from the traditional view of the integration process that regards such protections as solely the responsibility of the country of destination. Yet Mexico's discourse has been not only favorably received but also actively supported by many US government officials and institutions, as well as by civil society groups across national, state, and local levels.

Mexico and other Latin American countries are increasingly considering it necessary to help their populations gain "full access to civic, social, economic, and political rights" in another country—as Ambassador Medina Mora expressed it in his speech. This reflects a rapidly growing consensus among most countries in the world that it is beneficial to establish or extend policies to strengthen ties with their emigrant populations.

Most of the literature on diaspora and emigration policies has looked at the economic and political interests that drive state policies focused on attracting remittances or investments, extending rights such as dual citizenship or absentee voting, or supporting the formation of migrant organizations (Collyer 2013; Gamlen 2006; Goldring 2002; Levitt and de la Dehesa 2003; Smith 2008; Varadarajan 2010). Yet there is limited work on the origin country's role in actively supporting the integration of migrants in the country of destination or the impact of such policies (Desiderio and Weinar 2014). Similarly, there is scant research on state-led efforts to reach second- and third-generation migrant populations or on the success or limits of such strategies (Portes and Fernandez-Kelly 2015). Through an analysis of Mexican consulates' promotion of naturalization campaigns and their outreach to undocumented youth who qualify for DACA, I examine the interests that drive such policies in order to better understand their sustainability and implications for the populations they target.

That these policies focus specifically on supporting migrants' integration and empowerment through access to services, information, or a change in legal status to help them assert their rights in the United States demonstrates a shift toward an expanded interpretation of citizen rights from the perspective of origin countries. Compared to other diaspora policies, promoting migrants' integration in the country of destination shifts the focus from extending rights or opportunities in the origin country to how origin-country support can benefit migrants in the country of destination. Moreover, the policies I discuss concentrate on populations with precarious legal status—defined as either undocumented or permanent residents without US citizenship whose status limits their access to public benefits or puts them at risk of deportation (Goldring and Landolt 2013). An estimated 56 percent of the 11 million Mexican immigrants in the United States were undocumented in 2013 (Zong and Batalova 2016). In this case, beyond emphasizing the economic advantage these emigrants can offer Mexico in the long term through remittances or investments, the origin-country government concentrates on helping them access basic services in the country of destination, including low-cost health care options, education, and language programs that will help improve their well-being, give them a better chance at upward mobility, and possibly transform negative perceptions about Mexico and Mexicans in the eyes of the US general public.

The two initiatives I examine are focused on naturalization and access to DACA and are an outgrowth of programs developed by the Mexican government in the 1990s: the Programa de Atención a las Comunidades Mexicanas en el Exterior created in 1990, which in 2003 became the Instituto de los Mexicanos en el Exterior (IME, Institute for Mexicans Abroad). Originally centered on education and health initiatives—primarily targeting migrants with precarious legal status and limited access to social services—the

original program and later institute expanded significantly in terms of resources, partnerships, and range of issues. The institute's services have come
to include financial literacy, labor rights, leadership development, and civic
participation.

The public schools, hospitals, clinics, churches, banks, credit unions, universities, hometown associations, labor unions, and government offices in
the United States that establish partnerships and share resources with the
Mexican consulates to extend such services clearly see a great advantage in
doing so because it allows them to reach a population that has limited access to such programs due to language barriers, lack of information, or fear.
As Shannon Gleeson (2012) has noted, consulates have a certain legitimacy
among the migrant populations that fills a gap in service provision where
neither US public institutions nor civil society groups can reach the target
groups. Yet the objectives of the various actors in reaching these populations are not necessarily the same. For the Mexican government, immigrant
integration through access to basic services, education, empowerment, and
naturalization is framed as an economic and political strategy to legitimize
its migration and development policies in an uncertain US political climate.
Even if such policies address some of the core needs and demands of migrant communities and their organizations in the United States, they also
continue a legacy in which the root causes of migration and the need for opportunities for return and reintegration are left unaddressed.

Beyond Circularity: Promoting Integration
through Naturalization

Although present in the Mexican government's conception of these programs since the IME's creation in 2003, the language of integration has been
incorporated more explicitly into the Mexican government's discourse regarding its diaspora policy objectives over recent years. Although the government does not offer a clear definition of the term, the implementation of
a strategy to promote "integration" and empowerment in the country of destination has consistently focused on expanding access to social services for
migrants who are settled in the United States. This focus has three key implications for how Mexico has conceptualized and implemented its migration
and diaspora policies.

First, by acknowledging that migrants are integrating in the United States,
Mexico made a fundamental change in the discourse of circularity that had
long predominated in government accounts of the population's migration
there. The Mexican government recognized that migrants no longer travel

to the United States to work for a few months and then return to Mexico, as they did prior to the US Immigration Reform and Control Act regularization program of 1986 and the stricter enforcement of border controls starting in the mid-1990s. For a number of reasons—including economic conditions and safety concerns in Mexico that do not make it an attractive place to return to and border controls and organized crime that make it more difficult to cross back and forth without the required legal permissions—migrants stay longer or permanently in the United States, settling there with their families and thus becoming a more visible presence within US communities (Massey 2010). Under such circumstances, the Mexican government argues that what it can and should offer its citizens who will not return are services to support their well-being in the country where they have chosen or been forced to settle.

Second, the focus on integration implies a further step in a gradually expanded interpretation of the limits of Mexico's involvement in US affairs. For many years the Mexican government used the discourse of nonintervention as an excuse for its limited engagement in US immigration policy (Délano 2011). Now, by taking an explicit position promoting integration programs for Mexicans in the United States, the Mexican government is revealing an expanded conceptualization of its power and responsibility to protect the rights of migrants abroad. Despite ever-present concerns about backlash from US conservative groups in response to more extensive activities that promote migrants' access to services and support systems, the Institute of Mexicans Abroad, Mexican consuls in the United States, and the Mexican Embassy in Washington, DC, have increasingly referred to these programs more explicitly as part of Mexico's commitment to a *shared responsibility* in managing migration.

Third, supporting integration in the destination country is a response to a trend toward more permanent residence of migrants with legal status and lower rates of voluntary return. However, it is also an implicit (or explicit) recognition of the origin country's inability to provide these opportunities back home and the lack of political will to address the root causes of migration and develop comprehensive programs focusing on return and reintegration.

The emphasis on Mexicans' long-term settlement in the United States and the fact that approximately half of Mexican migrants in the United States do have legal status explain the recent addition of "support for naturalization in the United States" to the list of services that Mexican consulates provide. This program is more robust than the government's information campaigns, which were launched after Mexico passed its dual citizenship law in 1996. These campaigns encouraged naturalization as a way for Mexican migrants to defend their own interests in an environment of anti-immigrant sentiment.

Beyond allowing dual citizenship, as many other countries have done for similar reasons, Mexico has for many years supported education programs, including English-language and citizenship courses, to help migrants prepare for their naturalization tests through the Plazas Comunitarias adult education program sponsored by Mexico's education office in partnership with schools and community centers in the United States. The most recent naturalization program, officially launched in October 2015 to coincide with the US primary election cycle represents a significant step forward in these efforts as the consulates — rather than their partners in schools and community centers — directly offer seminars and information on naturalization processes. This, according to the Mexican minister for foreign affairs, "will allow Mexican migrants and the Mexican origin population in the United States to obtain important economic, social and political benefits, as well as strengthen their ties with both countries" (SRE 2015). Although not openly stated, it is clear that the Mexican government recognizes that citizenship will grant those who are eligible access to crucial rights and political power. The naturalization initiative is also propelled by the long-term goal of cultivating political leadership and participation among the Mexican American community that can influence US politics in a favorable way for Mexico and Mexicans in the United States.

Mexican officials explain the focus on citizenship acquisition in the United States as a natural evolution of Mexico's gradually expanding interpretation of consular protection activities and responsibilities. However, it is noteworthy that only a few years back, such origin-country support was considered impossible. The narrative has since shifted as Mexico, applying the same logic with which it aided its citizens abroad through assistance programs, began to promote US citizenship for them. This is a significant departure from the more guarded discourse vis-à-vis naturalization of the past and stems from the confidence that the Mexican government gained in successfully presenting these programs as compatible with the interests of some sectors within the US government and civil society.

Beyond reforming legislation to allow migrants to choose to become citizens in another country without compromising their citizenship in their country of origin, the country of origin here is actively promoting the acquisition of another citizenship and supporting its nationals in the process — through lawyers who offer personal assistance at the consulates, information about financial options to pay the application fee, and referrals to relevant nonprofit organizations. Such support, Mexican officials claim, is part of the government's responsibility to protect its citizens' rights, support that it justifies because settlement has become more permanent in the destination country. Meanwhile, the government does not acknowledge that significant obstacles remain for migrants' voluntary return to the origin country. Although they are critical of it, many community leaders and advocates see this consular involvement as positive, as it builds on the work they have been doing for decades and can help supply information and services to more people. The reach of the consulates' program is still limited, and few people know about it. None of the students in the citizenship course at the Hermandad Mexicana organization that I visited in the fall of 2016 were aware of the support they could have received at the Mexican Consulate in Los Angeles. When I explained the services to them and asked what they thought about their origin-country government supporting them in becoming US citizens, their reactions were enthusiastic. I recorded this student's response in my field notes of October 11, 2016: "I never heard that the consulate was promoting this issue. But it's good that they are doing it—it creates more opportunities for us. They should help us more here. This is our life; this is where we are focused. It's good for many people. We then have rights there [in Mexico] and here [in the United States]."

One of the challenges activists see is that the different actors working on the common cause of integration and citizenship for Latinos do not always work together. Raúl Murillo, president of the Los Angeles chapter of the Hermandad Mexicana Nacional, explained in a 2016 interview, "We have the service providers, the unions, the community organizations, the consulates, Mexican and Central American, the media. We could mobilize millions. But our actions are atomized. If, for example, the consulates really put their resources to work, the financial support, and the networks to get everyone on the same page, they could help us do so much more."[2] This statement demonstrates that while consulates are considered a significant resource for migrant communities, there are limitations to their efforts, in this case due to scarce resources and a lack of cohesion among migrant-serving organizations. The consulate cannot always resolve such divisions and in fact often exacerbates them.

Like many of the consular services focused on social assistance—including education, health care, labor rights, and financial literacy—promoting naturalization for Mexican legal permanent residents is presented primarily as an instrument to protect their rights as well as to integrate and empower the community. Julián Escutia Rodríguez (2016:139), head of Hispanic Affairs and Consular Issues at the Mexican Embassy, has explained, "Dual citizenship is not only an instrument for integration, but also a tool for preventive protection that closes the gap between rights for US citizens and foreigners." Although the discourse around this initiative does stress the importance of supporting a binational identity, most of the benefits are explained in relation to life in the United States. These benefits are stressed as ways to reduce the vulnerability of individuals and their families and expand opportunities for new citizens: avoiding deportation, traveling freely, being able to run for office and vote, accessing credit and financial aid, and securing jobs limited to US citizens (Sada Solana 2016:232–233). This is a clear example of how Mexico's diaspora policies have shifted from a framework based on the circularity of migration flows and the potential for return to the idea that as migrants are now firmly settled in the United States, it is better for them and for the Mexican government's goals to support their integration there. While the origin country's move toward promoting such policies can certainly be considered beneficial from the perspective of migrant rights, it also raises questions about how that responsibility manifests or fails to do so at different stages of the migration process, including the root causes of migration, the protection of rights throughout their transits, and their access to rights upon return.

Given the specific spatial and temporal context in which these policies have emerged, it is also necessary to evaluate the sustainability of such initiatives over time as well as their relevance for other cases in which elements such as precarious legal status and migrant organizations may be absent. Furthermore, how might these initiatives evolve as a result of changes to the institutional and political contexts — in the origin and destination countries — or to the characteristics of the migrant population?

Diaspora Engagement beyond the First Generation

The Obama administration's announcement of the Deferred Action for Childhood Arrivals (DACA) program in 2012 opened a possibility for hundreds of thousands of "Dreamers" — a term coined by undocumented migrant youth activists often used to refer to undocumented migrants brought at an early age to the United States by their parents[3] — to reconnect physically with a country of origin they had not been able to visit for many years and, in some cases, that they barely remembered. In addition to granting temporary protection from deportation and access to a Social Security number that allows undocumented youth to work in the United States, the DACA program includes the option to apply for advance parole to travel outside of the country with the possibility of re-entering the United States.[4] Re-entering with DACA also allows recipients of this advance parole permit to fulfill the requirement of "legal entry." This eliminates their record of "illegal entry" and, if they are eligible, lets them adjust their status without having to leave the country to apply for legal permanent residence. Initially, few DACA recipients ventured to leave on their own amid uncertainty about whether they would be denied entry upon return,[5] but gradually—and up until the beginning of the Trump administration—a growing number began to participate in university-sponsored study-abroad trips.

Drawing on a number of years of experience in providing legal support and assistance on topics ranging from health to tax preparation, the Mexican government responded to the wave of requests not only by efficiently processing identity documents but also by establishing workshops, seminars, and training programs at Mexican consulates in the United States to help DACA applicants, including migrants from other Latin American countries, submit their paperwork. The consulates also offered potential DACA recipients opportunities to obtain GEDs through the Plazas Comunitarias adult education programs so they could be eligible. By the end of 2014 the Mexican consular network had held almost 6,000 information seminars and legal clinics that served 468,579 youth. The events were organized in partnership with immigrant advocacy groups, law schools, churches, and specialized lawyers.[6]

According to the Migration Policy Institute, consular support is a key factor in the success of Mexican applicants in obtaining DACA permits compared to other nationalities (Hooker, McHugh, and Mathay 2015:42).[7] Mexican consulates throughout the United States offered clinics with lawyers and personalized support to fill out applications. In some cases, consulates provided financial support and connected applicants with institutions that could help defer the $465 application fee. Moreover, they opened their workshops and information sessions to all Spanish-speaking immigrants regardless of their countries of origin, and many Mexican consulates organized joint events with other Latin American consulates to inform their communities about the DACA program.

The interactions between Mexican consulates and Dreamers revealed the potential of working with the so-called 1.5 generation—a term coined to identify those who migrated as children or young adults but lived most of their formative years in the destination country (Portes and Rumbaut 2006). Reyna Torres Mendivil, director-general of the Office for the Protection of Mexicans Abroad, recognized in 2015 that as a result of DACA, the Mexican government "discovered a generation with which we had not had previous contact."[8] Efforts to engage Mexican and Mexican American youth in the United States had been made in the past through the Institute of Mexicans Abroad and the consulates, but as Torres Mendivil's remark makes clear, the government was missing the mark in terms of understanding their needs and offering them something of value. DACA workshops, by contrast, offered something tangible and urgent and provided an opportunity for consular officials to directly engage the younger generation.

Mexico's Secretariat of Foreign Affairs recognized the DACA program as an opportunity to reach out to a group of migrants with a high profile within the media and political spheres. For the Mexican government, long engaged in developing a wide range of programs to provide assistance to and protect the rights of its nationals in the United States, it has been a challenge to connect to younger generations, including the second generation and the 1.5 generation. Beyond cultural programs and celebrations of national holidays, engaging these groups in political and economic activities related to Mexico has had limited success. These generations have different needs than their parents in relation to consular services, the traditional gateway through which governments interact with their populations abroad. The 1.5 generation's connections to their origin country are distinct from other migrants and at times contradictory (Anderson and Solís 2014; Gil 2014:6). That they were born in Mexico but lived most of their lives in the United States, a country where many of them cannot exercise full membership due to their undocumented status, creates a unique identity, one that makes it hard to locate "home" (Anderson and Solís 2014; Gil 2014).

The overtures to Dreamers made by the Mexican government demonstrate how diaspora policies vary depending on the group being targeted, the location, and the political and institutional context in which they are embedded in the country of destination. Variations in diaspora policies have been identified in a number of cases and explained as the result of racial, ethnic, gender, or class differentiations (Ho 2011; Mullings 2011); age, sex, educational, legal, and occupation status; or by their perceived utility from a domestic or foreign policy perspective (Tsourapas 2015). In this case, a change in the Dreamers' precarious status through DACA was crucial in forging a connection between them and the Mexican government since applying for DACA required the support of the origin-country government in providing access to documents. Responding to a temporary change in the legal status of undocumented youth, the Mexican government was able to mobilize and adapt a consular infrastructure developed over many years to provide resources and support to help migrants access benefits available to them in the United States.

Beyond attending to the immediate needs of the Dreamers and helping them achieve a form of temporary protected status, the Mexican government also used the opportunity to further its broader economic and political interests. The Mexican government regards Dreamers as a particularly important asset from a political standpoint: they grew up in the United States, they understand how the system works, and they are "American in every way, except for their papers" (Obama 2012), as some US politicians and media outlets tend to portray them.[9] Forging a connection with this group, then, was considered vital for achieving the origin country's objective to improve the image of Mexicans in their country of destination and to secure Mexico's economic and political interests there.

Prior to DACA, the Mexican government's initial recognition of undocumented youth's needs and demands was translated into a relatively small scholarship program, IME Becas, started in 2005. The troubling dropout rates among first- and second-generation Mexicans in US high schools as well as the generally low levels of education among first-generation Mexican migrants had been a central focus of the government for many years. The problems had mainly been addressed through adult education programs in the Plazas Comunitarias. The shift from supporting solely adult education programs to including scholarships for college students was seen by the Mexican government as a way to make a greater impact through its diaspora programs. Between 2005 and 2016, an estimated 60,000 students benefited from the IME Becas program (IME 2015); 4,300 scholarships were granted to college students, and the rest went to adult education students at Plazas Comunitarias.[10] For many, being an IME scholarship recipient is a source of pride and motivation to go to school and work for the benefit of the community as a whole as well as an opportunity to rediscover one's roots, as expressed by some of the CUNY–IME Becas scholarship recipients.[11]

The scholarships were an initial step that allowed the Mexican government to reach a population of 1.5- and second-generation Mexicans and Mexican Americans that it couldn't previously access, as Carlos González Gutiérrez, former executive director of the IME, explained in a 2015 interview: "Through the Becas and the DACA process, little by little we have been able to create a relationship. They are very different from the previous generation; they don't have the resentment, the suspiciousness, the impatience or the deep mistrust that their parents may have."[12] For many Dreamers, the process of applying for the scholarships was the first contact they had had with the consulates. Reportedly, this was mostly a positive experience for them, though there is still significant mistrust between them and the government.

On one hand, the case of undocumented youth eligible for DACA highlights the importance of migration status in determining the focus and goals of diaspora policies as well as the origin country's ability to develop relations with emigrants. The Dreamers' change in status through DACA, even if temporary, enhanced their economic and political power,[13] making them a valuable asset for the Mexican government inasmuch as they have the ability to improve the image of the Mexican community in the United States and at the same time, Mexican migrant youths' perceptions of their origin country while also potentially contributing to it economically.

On the other hand, the rapprochement with Dreamers or the 1.5 generation through DACA workshops, IME Becas, and sponsored trips reveals the limitations of a government discourse that attempts to balance the tension that arises from promoting the integration of migrants in their country of destination while seeking to maintain their connection with and leverage their contributions to the origin country. The tensions were most evident when those participating in the sponsored trips met returned or deported Dreamers, referred to by some as "the other Dreamers,"[14] those who were now living in Mexico, continuing their activist efforts originally deployed in the United States, and beginning to organize new networks.

From 2005 to 2015, more than two million migrants returned to Mexico voluntarily or involuntarily (CONAPO 2015). By some estimates, 550,000 of them were eighteen to thirty-five years old (Anderson and Solís 2014:9). In contrast to the welcome received by the Dreamers sponsored by Mexico's Secretariat of Foreign Affairs, deported or voluntarily returned Dreamers face significant obstacles upon their return to Mexico. They receive little if any institutional support and carry social stigmas that create barriers and limit their access to basic services, educational and employment opportunities, and full participation in the country where they were born and are recognized as citizens.

The contrast between the two groups' experiences reveals the precarious status of undocumented youth in both their destination country and their country of origin. It also exposes some of the limits of the Mexican government's transnational approach to protecting its citizens' rights regardless of where they live. The Mexican government has developed a transnational network of social welfare services in the United States in areas such as health care, labor rights, financial literacy, and education to support the Mexican population abroad, particularly first-generation, undocumented migrants. It presents such diaspora programs as working toward two main goals: to support migrants' empowerment and integration into the society of the country where they reside and to foster the migrants' connections with Mexico and secure their contributions to their origin country's development. However, assisting migrant populations in the United States has not spurred government officials to support or develop relationships with them upon their return to Mexico, where they face similar forms of exclusion and unfulfilled needs despite being Mexican citizens. While there have been attempts by civil society groups in Mexico to adapt government programs that are used to help migrants in the United States, institutional support for returned migrants in Mexico is extremely limited.

The paradoxes inherent in the country of origin's attempt to engage and assist undocumented migrants in the United States is evident in the limited infrastructure and resources available to support the same migrants' reintegration in Mexico. Mexico's unidirectional diaspora policy is clearly focused primarily on improving the lives of migrants in their country of residence, a controversial but also expansive goal in its interpretation of sovereignty and citizenship; the government tries to temper criticism by stressing the migrants' potential contributions to the development of their origin country. Yet the limits of a policy that does not invest enough resources and infrastructure to protect the rights of this returning diaspora or support and leverage the skills and resources of returnees have become starkly apparent in the context of the massive influx of deported and returned migrants in recent years.[15]

The Spatial and Temporal Dimensions of Diaspora Policies

The increase in restrictionist legislation and xenophobic discourse, the record numbers of deportations, and the failure of comprehensive immigration reform efforts since the early 2000s have pushed Mexico and other Latin American countries to expand their reach to their migrant communities and join efforts to increase access to services and rights available to them in their destination countries, to combat anti-immigrant legislation, and to support policies focused on the migrants' social well-being. At that time, the Obama administration generally favored mechanisms to protect migrant rights and provided an environment in which origin-country governments could develop programs that otherwise might have been dismissed as interventionist or simply found no support within US institutions. A significant example is the labor rights collaboration of several Latin American countries, including Mexico, and the Philippines with the US Department of Labor to support and educate migrants making claims against their employers (Gleeson 2012). While such initiatives can be seen as examples of expanded collaboration between origin and destination countries, even within the Labor Department, those in charge of the programs were cautious about how and where they discussed the collaborations for fear of backlash from the public and within the federal government.[16] The shift taking place under the Trump administration will certainly exacerbate such concerns and probably lead to a significant retreat in what have been considered successful and expansive efforts to protect the rights of all workers.

At the state and local levels, there are wide variations among Mexican consulates—that is, whether they are more proactive or reactive and the partnerships that they are able to establish—according to the political and institutional context. Some cities actively support coalitions and work closely with the Mexican government to promote programs such as city identification cards, while others limit their collaboration to more basic diplomatic interactions. Asked at a lecture on October 16, 2017, at Columbia University about how to assess the results of this day-to-day work that is mostly conducted behind the scenes, former Mexican ambassador to the United States Arturo Sarukhan responded that the effects are hard to measure from a national perspective. The focus, he stated, should be on changes at the state and local levels, where the pressure exerted by coalitions of civil society, Mexican and other Latin American consulates, the media, and the private sector have helped shift attitudes and policies or strengthened existing support of migrant communities. While those efforts may have tangible results at the local level, the election of Donald Trump in November 2016 clearly demonstrates the difficulty of translating such visions of social inclusion and the prospects for cooperation across sectors, beyond borders, and into the national agenda. Given the discourse and proposals put forward by the Trump administration, it is evident that the gaps these diaspora policies attempt to fill will become even wider, with more individuals pushed into the shadows amid widespread fear about accessing public services that are available to them. However, it is not clear whether the Mexican government will maintain a relatively proactive stance, particularly with regard to controversial programs such as the promotion of naturalization, which can generate more backlash in a time when anti-immigrant discourse is emboldened. The consulates' relations with Dreamers will also be affected by legislative changes such as the end of DACA or an immigration reform that specifically benefits this group.

Diaspora policies, like other transnational political practices, are clearly shaped by the specific times and places in which they operate, in both the origin and destination countries. Natasha Iskander (2015:113) argues that the focus of migrant organizations on incorporation or development changes over time and is shaped by the "specific political opportunities and constraints of the moment." In the case of Mexico, diaspora policies have responded to a specific context shaped by several factors: the characteristics of migrants, specifically their precarious migration status and patterns of settlement; their organizational capacity (here the strength of the Dreamers' activist networks that has led to legislative changes and made them visible and politically valuable for the Mexican government and other actors); the political and institutional environment in the country of settlement; the absence of an integration policy and the lack of support systems for undocumented populations in the United States; and an anti-immigrant backlash, locally or nationally.

A shift in US immigration policies—whether in the form of comprehensive immigration reform including a path to citizenship or more mass deportations and termination of DACA during the Trump administration— will have a fundamental impact on origin countries' diaspora policies. In the DACA process, Mexican consulates were crucial in supporting regularization through providing documentation, information, and consultations with lawyers. But it is unclear what else the consulates have to offer beyond such services to a population that is fully integrated into the destination country in the sense that migrants understand the country's institutional framework, speak the language, and generally have access to the available opportunities regardless of legal status. Some migrants continue to need consular support because of language or cultural barriers, but over time, the role played by consulates as a bridge to membership in the destination country is diminished as migration patterns shift. Mexico has anticipated such changes in the needs of its migrant population by focusing on access to citizenship, engaging with 1.5- and second-generation youth through scholarship programs and sponsored trips to Mexico, and developing networks of professionals within the diaspora. Still, such policies are inevitably linked to US immigration policies that affect those most vulnerable due to their precarious legal status. It remains to be seen whether during the Trump administration origin countries are prepared to respond if there is an increased need for such services, especially since Mexico's focus and resources have already shifted toward emergency legal aid and support in cases of detention and deportation. At the same time, given the prospect of an increase in deportations and returns, there is growing pressure on Mexico to develop more comprehensive policies surrounding reintegration. However, these efforts misguidedly continue to be treated as separate from the vision of access to membership and integration that has guided Mexico's consular work in the United States.

Notes

This chapter is based on the author's book *From Here and There: Diaspora Policies, Integration, and Social Rights beyond Borders* (New York: Oxford University Press, 2018).

1. Eduardo Medina Mora, remarks at the 31st NALEO Annual Conference, San Diego, CA, June 28, 2014, http://embamex.sre.gob.mx/eua/index.php/en/comunica dos2013/784.

2. Raúl Murillo, interview by the author, Los Angeles, October 11, 2016.

3. The term is associated with the proposed Development, Relief, and Education for Alien Minors (DREAM) Act to grant undocumented migrant youth legal status and a path to citizenship under certain conditions.

4. DACA required applicants to have been under the age of thirty-one on June 15, 2012; to have continuously resided in the United States since June 15, 2007; to

have been physically present in the United States on June 15, 2012, and at the time of making the request for consideration of deferred action with US Customs and Immigration Services (USCIS); to have had no lawful status on June 15, 2012; to currently be in school, have graduated or obtained a certificate of completion from high school, have obtained a general education development (GED) certificate, or have been honorably discharged as a veteran of the US Coast Guard or Armed Forces; and to have no convictions for a felony, significant misdemeanor, or three or more other misdemeanors or pose a threat to national security or public safety (USCIS, http://www.uscis.gov/humanitarian/consideration-deferred-action-childhood-arrivals-daca; US Department of Homeland Security, http://www.dhs.gov/deferred-action-childhood-arrivals.

5. Republicans vowed to end DACA, and they blocked its expansion to eliminate the age limit and include parents of US citizens and residents through the Deferred Action for Parental Accountability (DAPA) program. The DAPA case (*United States v. Texas*) was heard by the US Supreme Court in June 2016; justices deadlocked in a 4-4 decision. The case was sent back to the lower court, and its decision was to maintain a nationwide injunction on DAPA. The Trump administration announced the termination of DACA in September 2017.

6. Data were provided by the Mexican Embassy in Washington, DC, by email on August 20, 2015.

7. See also Rusin 2015 and Semple 2013.

8. Reyna Torres Mendivil, interview by the author, Mexico City, January 16, 2015.

9. See also Vargas 2012.

10. Data were provided by email to the author from the IME, August 21, 2015. It must be noted that non-Mexican students also have received IME Becas, including for college. Most Plazas Comunitarias adult education programs offered by the Mexican consulates, partner community organizations, and public schools do not make a distinction regarding the students' nationalities. For college applications, institutions such as City University of New York that receive IME Becas funding require recipients to have shown leadership in their communities. Its 2015 Becas webpage states that recipients had to "demonstrate a record of service in the Mexican immigrant community as well as commitment to future service with the Mexican community" (CUNY BECAS Scholarships, http://www.lehman.cuny.edu/cuny-mexican-studies-institute/scholarships.php).

11. Examples of posts from 2013 Becas recipients are posted at CUNY's Jaime Lucero Mexican Studies Institute blog at http://www.lehman.cuny.edu/cuny-mexican-studies-institute/Blogs2013.php.

12. Carlos González Gutiérrez, phone interview by the author, August 10, 2015.

13. See, for example, the Migration Policy Institute's study about economic contributions of DACA recipients (MPI 2015).

14. The term "the other Dreamers" was coined by Jill Anderson and a small group of activists. It later informed the title of a book of testimonials by deported and returning youth (Anderson and Solís 2014). Adopted by some of the returned Dreamers to describe themselves, the term often serves as a shorthand to recognize the ongoing connections of returning youth to the United States. The group is relatively small— the activists included only about 100 returned Dreamers, but they estimated close to 500,000 in Mexico—and several became active upon returning to Mexico. As some have done in the United States, certain activists in Mexico have rejected the term "Dreamer" (Mundo Citizen 2016). I thank Jill Anderson for her suggestions on this point.

15. This phenomenon is also visible in other countries including Ecuador (Hiemstra 2019; Margheritis 2016) and El Salvador (Coutin 2016), and it has been present in other mass deportations from the United States to Mexico (Alanís Enciso 2015).

16. Labor Department official in charge of collaboration with consulates at the department's Bureau of International Labor Affairs, interview by the author, Washington, DC, October 14, 2014.

References

Alanís Enciso, Fernando Saúl. 2015. *Voces de la repatriación. La sociedade mexicana y la repatriación de mexicanos de Estados Unidos (1930–1933)*. San Luis Potosí, Mexico: Colegio de San Luis.

Anderson, Jill, and Nin Solís. 2014. *Los otros dreamers*. Mexico City: Offset Santiago.

Collyer, Michael, ed. 2013. *Emigration Nations: Policies and Ideologies of Emigrant Engagement*. New York: Palgrave Macmillan.

CONAPO (Consejo Nacional de Población). 2015. Numeralia migratoria. Mexico City: CONAPO. http://www.omi.gob.mx/es/OMI/Numeralia_Migratoria.

Coutin, Susan. 2016. *Exiled Home: Salvadoran Transnational Youth in the Aftermath of Violence*. Durham, NC: Duke University Press.

Desiderio, Maria Vincenza, and Agnieszka Weinar. 2014. *Supporting Immigrant Integration in Europe? Developing the Governance for Diaspora Engagement*. Washington, DC: Migration Policy Institute.

Délano, Alexandra. 2011. *Mexico and Its Diaspora in the United States: Policies of Emigration since 1848*. New York: Cambridge University Press.

Escutia Rodríguez, Julián. 2016. "La doble nacionalidad como instrumento de vinculacion e integracion." *Revista Mexicana de Política Exterior* 107:129–141.

Gamlen, Alan. 2006. "Diaspora Engagement Policies: Who Are They and What Kinds of States Use Them?" Working Paper no. 32, Oxford: Centre on Migration, Policy and Society, University of Oxford.

Gil, Isabel. 2014. *Documenting Undocumented Strategies*. New York: Center for Mexican Studies, Columbia University. https://centerformexicanstudies.wordpress.com/2014/03/17/documenting-undocumented-strategies/.

Gleeson, Shannon. 2012. *Conflicting Commitments: The Politics of Enforcing Immigrant Worker Rights in San Jose and Houston*. Ithaca, NY: Cornell University Press.

Goldring, Luin. 2002. "The Mexican State and Transmigrant Organizations: Negotiating the Boundaries of Membership and Participation in the Mexican Nation." *Latin American Research Review* 37 (3): 55–99.

Goldring, Luin, and Patricia Landolt, eds. 2013. *Producing and Negotiating Non-Citizenship: Precarious Legal Status in Canada*. Toronto: University of Toronto Press.

Gonzalez, Mike. 2016. "Mexico's American Diaspora." *National Affairs* 28 (Summer).

Hiemstra, Nancy. 2019. *Detain and Deport: The Chaotic US Immigration Enforcement Regime*. Athens: University of Georgia Press. In press.

Ho, Elaine L. E. 2011. "Claiming the 'Diaspora': Sending State Strategies, Elite Mobility, and the Spatialities of Citizenship." *Progress in Human Geography* 35 (6): 757–772.

Hooker, Sarah, Margie McHugh, and Angelo Mathay. 2015. "Lessons from the Local Level: DACA's Implementation and Impact on Education and Training Success."

Washington, DC: Migration Policy Institute. https://www.migrationpolicy.org/research/lessons-local-level-dacas-implementation-and-impact-education-and-training-success.

IME (Mexico, Instituto de los Mexicanos en el Exterior). 2015. "IME Becas 2015–2016." *Boletín Especial Lazos*, no. 1613, December 5. Mexico City: IME.

Iskander, Natasha. 2015. "Partners in Organizing: Engagement between Migrants and the State in the Production of Mexican Hometown Associations." In *The State and the Grassroots: Immigrant Transnational Organizations in Four Continents*, edited by Alejandro Portes and Patricia Fernandez-Kelly, 111–138. London: Berghahn.

Levitt, Peggy, and Rafael de la Dehesa. 2003. "Transnational Migration and the Redefinition of the State: Variations and Explanations." *Ethnic and Racial Studies* 26 (4): 587–611.

Margheritis, Ana. 2016. *Migration Governance across Regions: State-Diaspora Relations in the Latin America-Southern Europe Context*. London: Routledge.

Massey, Douglas, ed. 2010. *New Faces in New Places: The Changing Geography of American Immigration*. New York: Russell Sage.

MPI (Migration Policy Institute). 2015. Lessons from DACA's Implementation and Its Impact on Education and Training. Webinar, January 7. Washington, DC: MPI. http://www.migrationpolicy.org/events/lessons-daca%E2%80%99s-implementation-and-its-impact-education-and-training.

Mullings, Beverley. 2011. "Diaspora Strategies, Skilled Migrants, and Human Capital Enhancement in Jamaica." *Global Networks* 11 (1): 24–42.

Mundo Citizen. 2016. "Separating from a Movement That Never Was: Los Otros Dreamers and the 'Dreams in Mexico' out of Reach for Most." Blog post, May 12. https://mundocitizen.com/2016/05/12/separating-from-a-movement-that-never-was-los-otros-dreamers-and-the-dreams-in-mexico-out-of-reach-for-most/?utm_content=bufferc2aa2&utm_medium=social&utm_source=twitter.com&utm_campaign=buffer.

Obama, Barack. 2012. "Remarks by the President on Immigration." June 15. Washington, DC: White House. https://www.whitehouse.gov/the-press-office/2012/06/15/remarks-president-immigration.

Portes, Alejandro, and Patricia Fernandez-Kelly, eds. 2015. *The State and the Grassroots: Immigrant Transnational Organizations in Four Continents*. London: Berghahn.

Portes, Alejandro, and Ruben Rumbaut. 2006. *Immigrant America: A Portrait*. Berkeley: University of California Press.

Rusin, Sylvia. 2015. "Origin and Community: Asian and Latin American Unauthorized Youth and U.S. Deportation Relief." Washington, DC: Migration Policy Institute. http://www.migrationpolicy.org/article/origin-and-community-asian-and-latin-american-unauthorized-youth-and-us-deportation-relief.

Sada Solana, Carlos Manuel. 2016. "Si eres mexicano, siempre serás mexicano": La importancia de la identidad binacional. Interview. *Revista Mexicana de Política Exterior* 107 (May–August): 231–237.

Semple, Kirk. 2013. "Advocates Struggle to Reach Immigrants Eligible for Deferred Action." *New York Times*, December 8. http://www.nytimes.com.

Smith, Robert C. 2008. "Contradictions of Diasporic Institutionalization in Mexican Politics: The 2006 Migrant Vote and Other Forms of Inclusion and Control." *Journal of Ethnic and Racial Studies* 31 (4): 708–741.

SRE (Mexico, Secretaría de Relaciones Exteriores). 2015. "La Canciller Ruiz Massieu promueve empoderamento de comunidad mexicana en Nueva York." Comunicado no. 568, October 10. Mexico City: SRE. https://embamex.sre.gob.mx/eua/index .php/es/comunicados/comunicados-2015/1001-la-canciller-ruiz-massieu-pro mueve-empoderamiento-de-comunidad-mexicana-en-nueva-york.

Tsourapas, Gerasimos. 2015. "Why Do States Develop Multi-Tier Emigrant Policies? Evidence from Egypt." *Journal of Ethnic and Migration Studies* 41 (13): 2192–2214.

Varadarajan, Latha. 2010. *The Domestic Abroad.* Cambridge, England: Cambridge University Press.

Vargas, Jose Antonio. 2012. "We Are Americans, Just Not Legally." *Time,* June 25. http://time.com/2987974/jose-vargas-detained-time-cover-story/.

Zong, Jie, and Jeanne Batalova. 2016. "College-Educated Immigrants in the United States." Washington, DC: Migration Policy Institute. http://www.migrationpolicy .org/article/college-educated-immigrants-united-states. Accessed February 12, 2016.

Epilogue: Theorizing State-Society Relations in a Multiscalar Context

SHANNON GLEESON AND XÓCHITL BADA

In this edited volume, we have brought together a series of multidisciplinary perspectives to illuminate the dynamics of state-society relations as they pertain to immigration policies. We developed a cross-sectoral, multisited, and multiscalar lens to highlight the importance of destination countries and, increasingly, countries of origin. By focusing on North America we were able to contrast three receiving countries: Canada, the United States, and Mexico, which sends the largest flow of migrants north while also being a major transit country for Central American migrants.

A primary contribution of these institutional analyses and case studies has been the chronicling of migrant integration efforts in host societies such as migrant worker rights in Canada, health services in the United States, and educational access in Toronto and San Francisco. We documented how countries of origin are increasingly advocating for the rights of their conationals living abroad and those who return, through bilateral agreements, federal partnerships, and relations with subnational government actors.

As revealed in this ambitious compilation, civil society's capacity to advocate at each scale—federal, state, and local—in origin and destination countries is constrained by the institutionalization of civil society in each country, the structural limitations of the policies at hand, and the asymmetric power between origin and destination actors. We profiled efforts by well-funded transnational coalitions such as those working on issues of migrant worker rights at the level of global governance as well as severely underfunded, localized battles such as those being waged by informal migrant groups lobbying local schools or by the families of murdered Central American migrants.

In this conclusion we synthesize the findings from these case studies using the analytical framework of state-society relations. We consider the factors that determine success in these collaborations and contestations and argue for the importance of a cross-sectoral, multisited and multiscalar approach to studying migrant advocacy moving forward.

When and How Do State-Society Relations Matter?

As outlined in the appendix, tables E.1 and E.2, each of the case studies in this volume describes a process in which civil society actors were actively involved in the federal, state, and/or local arenas. Their engagement is especially significant given the devolution of immigration enforcement to subnational and private actors. These case studies reveal that—as opposed to what the dominant narratives might suggest—civil society is almost always at the root of formal partnership programs. The importance of this advocacy is clearly evidenced in the case of migrant worker rights in North America, where NGOs pushed for accountability under NAFTA side agreements, and in efforts to limit immigration enforcement in schools in Canada, where advocacy groups demanded compliance from school officials. Beyond helping to generate these policies, sustained interventions by migrant civil society actors remain crucial to their initial and continued implementation. Sustainable coalitions and alliances are key ingredients for policy implementation and social accountability. These policy battles also become a means of building civil society capacity, as alliances demonstrate the potential to mature, expand to extraregional countries, and gain more visibility in future campaigns.

Where, then, does the sending state fit into the triad of origin state, destination state, and civil society? Mexico provides an instructive example given its well-developed consular corps and federated structure of governance. That Mexico also inhabits a contradictory position, as both a major sending and transit country, amplifies the implications of its demands vis-à-vis the rights of its own migrants living abroad. Because of the massive deportations experienced by Mexican nationals since the mid-2000s, the Mexican government has also been reluctantly forced to turn its gaze to the domestic organizations advocating on behalf of transit and returned migrants, especially for young deportees claiming their right to education and those who have been murdered and disappeared while trying to cross into the United States.

Collaboration: Successes and Challenges

In this volume we have extended conversations around migrant civil society by focusing on efforts to lobby and collaborate with government actors in sending and receiving regions. The key question thus becomes this: Under what conditions do these partnerships emerge and obtain success? Our results have identified the positive instances of collaboration and, equally significantly, where such collaboration was absent. Additionally, looking beyond the proliferation of formal policies and partnerships, our findings illuminate a number of challenges in actually materializing real changes on the ground.

The case studies here have focused on well-organized campaigns that managed to attract the public's attention, and each effort met with varying levels of success. In our introduction to the volume we highlight the promising creation of the North American Agreement on Labor Cooperation but reveal that the practical ability to enforce these trilateral accords was ultimately hampered by the power asymmetries between the countries involved and the lack of a mechanism to hold each country accountable. However, we also point out that while global governance has fallen short in regulating labor, the symbolic power of this soft law has been more effective at pushing reforms in regulating migrant labor recruiting practices.

In other cases, we saw surprisingly strong investment from both sending and receiving countries, as with the Binational Health Week initiative described by Liliana Osorio, Hilda Dávila, and Xóchitl Castañeda in chapter 10. Here, a robust network of health care providers created a prototype of a safety net for impoverished migrants. One factor determining the program's success was the strong investment of political will, financial resources, and coordination capacity by the Mexican government, paired with an already robust network of nonprofit health providers. That migrant health is intricately tied to public health concerns in the destination country likely helped this model succeed. However, as the authors hint, a closer look into the network reveals important rural versus urban variations in terms of the effectiveness and accessibility of Binational Health Week and its yearlong services across localities.

Other chapters delve into local variations in migrant organizing. In chapter 9, Patricia Baquedano-López illuminates a circumscribed though important case study for understanding how a local indigenous migrant community can advocate for a culturally appropriate public education curriculum. She reveals the importance of several civil society groups that would perhaps be ignored in any formal assessments of civic engagement based on officially registered organizations. These groups, some formal, some less formal, nonetheless play an important role in communicating the interests of this relatively new indigenous migrant group. Baquedano-López stresses the need to recognize diversity within national-origin flows. This requires continued advocacy with policy makers, who may have gained the support of previous

flows of mestizo migrants but are now being held accountable by new indigenous communities with distinct linguistic and cultural needs. Notably missing from such accounting is the role of the Mexican federal government or
the state of Yucatán. The author hypothesizes that their absence could perhaps be attributed to a historical lack of trust toward government authorities
as well as to the inability of the subnational and federal levels of government
to procure reliable funds to guarantee the sustainability of indigenous educational programs for migrant communities in the United States.

Other important factors determining the success of the various campaigns discussed in this volume include the maturity and density of civil society groups on both sides of the border (as newer coalitions may take time
finding effective strategies), the political context of migrant rights (with
some issues being more politically charged than others), and the capacity to
leverage influence across different levels of government to achieve results.

Toward a Broader Agenda: The Importance of a Cross-Sectoral Transnational Lens

A multidisciplinary institutional analysis of migrant rights, this volume reflects a cross-sectoral, multisited, and multiscalar lens. We chose to focus on
relations between government actors and civil society, including variations
across policy realms including global labor regulation, public education, public health, and criminal justice. Given our limited regional focus, we have
knowingly overlooked several sectors and binational relations, such as sustainable trade and rural development, environmental justice, and suffrage
rights coalitions. To fill this gap, future research should pay more attention
to variations across specific policy arenas at local, state or provincial, federal,
and transnational scales.

To be sure, there are important scope conditions for our findings. The
experiences of traditional reception countries like the United States and
Canada are not likely to mirror those of other destinations that lack the same
bureaucratic capacity for immigration enforcement and migrant integration.
To wit: the Mexican government's failure to offer immediate public education access (as a result of bizarre bureaucratic obstacles) to thousands of
Mexican American children caught in the US deportation regime illustrates
the urgent need to interrogate the processes of integration of returned migrants to labor markets and educational opportunities. We know very little
about the educational outcomes of US-born Mexican American children who
return to Mexico and continue their education in public schools that have no
programs dedicated to integrating students whose first language is English

or other nonindigenous languages. It is also unclear whether states closer to the border have fared any better than those in the so-called cradle of Mexican migration. Studying these outcomes will become increasingly important under Trump-era immigration enforcement policies in the United States that are likely to strand large numbers of deportees along Mexican border states—deportees who may decide to linger in these regions in the hope of easier reentry. While Trump's famous campaign promise of a border wall remained unfunded well into his presidency, it has represented an effectively menacing rhetorical construction to fuel anxiety and amplify uncertainty among migrants and would-be migrants alike.

Our research here has admittedly focused on primarily positive examples of collaboration. Further work should continue to examine efforts to enforce rights across borders, especially in varied federalist contexts such as that of Canada, where provinces have control over policies in a way that they do not in other countries; for example, collective bargaining is a provincial matter in Canada. We acknowledge, however, that these comparisons are very challenging to carry out, given the many factors at play and the multiplicity of social and institutional actors involved. Moving forward, we will continue to examine consular advocacy on behalf of migrant worker rights across traditional and new migrant destinations in the United States. Beyond the immigration arena, our findings pave the way for future research in other areas of policy making that implicate state-society collaboration and contestation.

Appendix: Topics and Locations Covered in the Chapters

Table E.1. Topics covered, by place, administrative level, and focus on origin versus destination

	Focus on origin		
Nation	*Federal level*	*State/provincial level*	*Local level*
Canada	**Governance** (Serna de la Garza)	—	—
United States	**Governance** (Serna de la Garza) **Labor** (Bada and Gleeson) **Health** (Osorio et al.)	**Education** (Jacobo-Suárez)	**Membership** (Fox and Rivera-Salgado)
Mexico	**Governance** (Serna de la Garza) **Labor** (Bada and Gleeson) **Health** (Osorio et al.) **Membership** (Délano Alonso)	**Governance** (Ortega Ramírez)	**Membership** (Fox and Rivera-Salgado)

	Focus on destination		
Nation	*Federal level*	*State/provincial level*	*Local level*
Canada	**Membership** (Délano Alonso) **Labor** (Galvez et al.)	**Labor** (Galvez et al.)	**Education** (Landolt and Goldring)
United States	**Membership** (Délano Alonso)	**Membership** (Fox and Rivera-Salgado)	**Education** (Baquedano-López)
Mexico	**Human rights** (Delgadillo et al.) **Education** (Jacobo-Suárez)	**Membership** (Fox and Rivera-Salgado)	—

Table E.2. Chapters by rights arena and geographic location

		Geographic location			
Rights arena	Author	Canada	United States	Mexico	Central America
Governance	Serna de la Garza	—	—	—	—
	Ortega Ramírez	—	Hometown associations	—	—
Human rights	Delgadillo et al.	—	—	Trans-national NGOs	Trans-national NGOs
Labor	Bada and Gleeson	—	Trans-national NGOs	Trans-national NGOs	—
Inter-national unions	Galvez et al.	–	–	–	
Education	Landolt and Goldring	Domestic NGOs	—	—	—
	Baquedano-López	–	Informal migrant cultural groups	–	–
	Jacobo-Suárez	—	—	Domestic NGOs	—
Health	Osorio et al.	–	Formal health service providers	—	—
Membership	Délano Alonso	—	Legal aid and educational support groups	—	—
	Fox and Rivera-Salgado	—	Migrant-led civil society	Migrant-led civil society	—

Editors and Contributors

Editors

XÓCHITL BADA is an associate professor in the Latin American and Latino Studies Program of the University of Illinois at Chicago. Her articles have appeared in *Forced Migration Review*, *Population, Space, and Place*, *Latino Studies*, and *Labor Studies Journal*. She is the author of *Mexican Hometown Associations in Chicagoacán: From Local to Transnational Civic Engagement* (Rutgers University Press, 2014). Her areas of specialization include migrant access to political and social rights, migrant organizing strategies, violence and displacement, and transnational labor advocacy mobilization in Mexico and the United States. She is the coeditor of the forthcoming *Oxford Handbook of Sociology of Latin America*.

SHANNON GLEESON is an associate professor in the Department of Labor Relations, Law, and History at Cornell University's ILR School. She is the author of *Conflicting Commitments: The Politics of Enforcing Immigrant Worker Rights in San Jose and Houston* (Cornell University Press, 2012) and *Precarious Claims: The Promise and Failure of Workplace Protections in the United States* (University of California Press, 2016). Her research includes the role of Mexican consulates in protecting the rights of immigrant workers (with Xóchitl Bada), the local implementation of the 2012 Deferred Action for Childhood Arrivals (DACA) program (with Els de Graauw), and the impacts of temporary legal status on immigrant workers (with Kati Griffith).

Contributors

PATRICIA BAQUEDANO-LÓPEZ works in the Critical Studies of Race, Class, and Gender cluster of the Graduate School of Education, University of California, Berkeley. She was the director of the UC Berkeley Center for Latino Policy Research from 2007 to 2009 and from 2014 to 2017. She studies the intersection of language, race, and migration and its effects on education. A strand of her work focuses on constructions of indigeneity and Latinidad in schools. She is principal investigator on a project funded by the Spencer Foundation to examine the educational experiences of indigenous students of the Maya diaspora (Yucatán-California). She is a co-editor, with Pedro Portes and Spencer Salas, of *U.S. Latinos and Education Policy: Research-based Directions for Change* (Routledge, 2014).

XÓCHITL CASTAÑEDA is a medical anthropologist and the director of the Health Initiative of the Americas (HIA) in the School of Public Health, University of California, Berkeley. She has published more than 150 manuscripts and served as consultant to more than thirty national and international institutions. Her vision and commitment led to the creation of binational health programs. Under her direction, the HIA has coordinated Binational Health Week since 2001. She has served twice as adviser to Mexico's Instituto de los Mexicanos en el Exterior (IME, Institute for Mexicans Abroad) and national coordinator of its Health Commission in the United States.

RODOLFO CÓRDOVA ALCARAZ is a vice president of Impacto Social Metropolitan Group in Mexico City. He was the deputy director of the Fundación para la Justicia y el Estado Democrático de Derecho. He has conducted studies on European integration and professionalization of civil society organizations and worked for international institutions and civil and academic organizations in North America, Europe, and Africa on projects related to migration, development, and human rights. He was the first president (2013–2015) of the Citizens Council of the Instituto Nacional de Migración in Mexico.

HILDA DÁVILA is the general director of the Office of International Relations, Mexican Secretariat of Health. One of her responsibilities is overseeing Ventanillas de Salud, a program in conjunction with the Institute for Mexicans Abroad and Mexican consulates in the United States. Her areas of specialization are public health and obesity preventive care programs.

ALEXANDRA DÉLANO ALONSO is an associate professor and the chair of the Global Studies Department at the New School, as well as holding the Eugene M. Lang Professorship for Excellence in Teaching and Mentoring. Her work focuses on diaspora policies, transnational relations between states and migrants, immigrant integration, and the politics of memory in relation to undocumented migration. She is the author of *From Here and There: Diaspora Policies, Integration and Social Rights Beyond Borders* (Oxford University Press, 2018) and *Mexico and Its Diaspora in the United States: Policies of Emigration since 1848* (Cambridge University Press, 2011; Colegio de México, 2014).

ANA LORENA DELGADILLO is the executive director of the Fundación para la Justicia y el Estado Democrático de Derecho. She is a human rights lawyer and has collaborated in the design of several laws and commissions to prevent violence against women, including Mexico City's Women's Law to Access a Life Free of Violence and the Commission to Prevent and Eliminate All Forms of Violence against Women in Ciudad Juárez and the state of Chihuahua. She has worked with NGOs including the Argentine Forensic Anthropology Team and collaborated in the Interamerican Commission on Human Rights hearing on institutional violence against women.

JONATHAN FOX is a professor at the School of International Service at American University and the director of its Accountability Research Center, an action-research incubator. His research addresses relations between citizen participation, transparency, and accountability.

ANDREA GALVEZ is a liaison for Mexico and Central America for United Food and Commercial Workers (UFCW), developing human and labor rights programs to improve migrant workers' conditions and focusing on the regulatory framework of labor mobility. She was a coordinator in the Agricultural Workers Alliance center in Quebec supporting temporary foreign workers in collaboration with UFCW Canada.

ALMA GARCÍA is a human rights defender and the former coordinator of family support services, analysis, and documentation for the Fundación para la Justicia y el Estado Democrático de Derecho. She has worked on issues of migration and forced and involuntary disappearances with the Casa del Migrante de Saltillo Coahuila (Frontera con Justicia) and Foro Nacional para las Migraciones en Honduras (FONAMIH). With the Centro Diocesano para los Derechos Humanos Fray Juan de Larios she has accompanied the families of migrants, families of disappeared people, and migrants in transit. She has conducted national and international advocacy, documentation, and analysis of human rights violations and social support for victims.

PABLO GODOY is a special assistant to the national president of UFCW Canada and is the Ontario Federation of Labor vice president representing workers of color. He coordinates Students against Migrant Exploitation, a nationwide student movement advocating support and mobilizing action to address the plight of migrant workers. He chairs the Ontario Federation of Labor Human Rights Committee.

LUIN GOLDRING is a professor of sociology at York University. Her research interests include noncitizenship, citizenship, and belonging; social inequality; immigrants and precarious work; and critical and transnational migration studies. Her research examines the multilevel production and negotiations of precarious legal status, the "chutes and ladders" of legal status trajectories, and the long-term implications of precarious legal status for im/migrant incorporation and social inequality. She is a co-editor, with Patricia Landolt, of *Producing and Negotiating Non-Citizen Precarious Legal Status in Canada* (University of Toronto Press, 2014).

MÓNICA JACOBO-SUÁREZ is a professor in the Interdisciplinary Program on Policy and Educational Practices at the Centro de Investigación y Docencia Económica in Mexico City. Her areas of specialization include educational reintegration of migrant students in Mexico, bilingual education, research design and policy evaluation, and the Latin American diaspora in the United States. Her published works include "Back Home without Apostille: Mexican-American Students in Mexico" in *Sinéctica* 46. She combines her research agenda with active collaboration with pro-immigrant organizations in the United States and Mexico. She is a member of the Identity and Education Working Group for Return Migrants convened by Mexico's Secretariat of the Interior.

PATRICIA LANDOLT is an associate professor of sociology at the University of Toronto. Her work examines processes of differential inclusion associated with global migration. She has conducted research on Salvadoran transnational migration, Latin American refugee political incorporation, racialized workers' experiences of precarious work and income security, and the ways these intersect with precarious legal status. Her research focuses on patchwork access to schooling for students with precarious legal status in two Toronto neighborhoods; it is part of her broader conceptual interest in probation and the conditionality of noncitizenship.

PAUL MEINEMA is the national president of UFCW Canada, the country's leading private-sector union, with more than 250,000 members. He is also an executive vice president of UFCW International and a member of the UFCW International Executive Committee.

LILIANA OSORIO is a deputy director of the Health Initiative of the Americas (HIA) in the School of Public Health, University of California, Berkeley. Since joining HIA in 2002, she has been involved in projects including coordination of Binational Health Week, the Binational Policy Forum on Migration and Public Health, the Summer Institute on Migration and Global Health, and the Binational Promotores Program. She is the editor of four editions of *The English-Spanish Dictionary of Health-Related Terms* and has coproduced educational manuals for community health workers and fact sheets on migrant health issues.

GASPAR RIVERA-SALGADO is the project director and a faculty member at the Center for Labor Research and Education, University of California, Los Angeles, teaching courses on immigration issues and on work, labor, and social justice in the United States. He also directs the Institute for Transnational Social Change based at the UCLA Labor Center. He has extensive experience as an independent consultant on transnational migration, race and ethnic relations and diversity trainings for large organizations. He is a co-editor, with Jonathan Fox, of *Indigenous Mexican Migrants in the United States* (Center for US-Mexican Studies, University of California, San Diego, 2004) and, with Edward Telles and Mark Sawyer, of *Just Neighbors? Research on African American and Latino Relations in the United States* (Russell Sage, 2011).

JOSÉ MA. SERNA DE LA GARZA is a researcher at the Instituto de Investigaciones Jurídicas of the Universidad Nacional Autónoma de México, a member of the Academia Mexicana de Ciencias, the president of the Mexican section of the Iberoamerican Institute of Constitutional Law, and an associate member of the International Academy of Comparative Law. He has been a visiting professor at the School of Law at the University of Texas, Austin, and a summer visiting scholar at the Max Planck Institut für Ausländisches Öffentliches Rechts und Völkerrecht in Heidelberg, Germany.

ADRIANA SLETZA ORTEGA RAMÍREZ is a professor of international relations at Benemérita Universidad Autónoma de Puebla, Mexico. Her research interests include migration policies, US-Mexico relations, and international relations of local governments. She is the editor of *Teorías de relaciones internacionales en el siglo XXI. Aproximaciones críticas desde México* (Centro de Investigación y Docencia Económicas, 2016) and *Puebla y sus migrantes: Tendencias y retos de la agenda pública* (Gernika, 2014). She is the author of *Políticas migratorias sub-nacionales en México. Evaluación de las oficinas estatales de atención a migrantes* (Plaza y Valdés, 2012).

Index

Page numbers in *italics* refer to tables and figures.